iPhone® 5

ALL-IN-ONE

FOR

DUMMIES®

2ND EDITION

by Joe Hutsko and Barbara Boyd

WILEY

John Wiley & Sons, Inc.

iPhone® 5 All-in-One For Dummies®, 2nd Edition

Published by
John Wiley & Sons, Inc.
111 River Street
Hoboken, NJ 07030-5774

www.wiley.com

Copyright © 2013 by John Wiley & Sons, Inc., Hoboken, New Jersey

Published by John Wiley & Sons, Inc., Hoboken, New Jersey

Published simultaneously in Canada

For general information on our other products and services, please contact our Customer Care Department within the U.S. at 877-762-2974, outside the U.S. at 317-572-3993, or fax 317-572-4002.

For technical support, please visit www.wiley.com/techsupport.

Wiley publishes in a variety of print and electronic formats and by print-on-demand. Some material included with standard print versions of this book may not be included in e-books or in print-on-demand. If this book refers to media such as a CD or DVD that is not included in the version you purchased, you may download this material at http://booksupport.wiley.com. For more information about Wiley products, visit www.wiley.com.

Library of Congress Control Number: 2012954760

ISBN 978-1-118-40794-3 (pbk); ISBN 978-1-118-49052-5 (ebk); ISBN 978-1-118-58860-4 (ebk); ISBN 978-1-118-58877-2 (ebk)

Manufactured in the United States of America

10 9 8 7 6 5 4 3 2 1

WILEY

About the Authors

Joe Hutsko is the author of *Green Gadgets For Dummies, Flip Video For Dummies* (with Drew Davidson), and *Mac All-in-One For Dummies* (with Barbara Boyd). For more than two decades, he has written about computers, gadgets, video games, trends, and high-tech movers and shakers for numerous publications and websites, including the *New York Times, Macworld, PC World, Fortune, Newsweek, Popular Science, TV Guide,* the *Washington Post, Wired, Gamespot, MSNBC, Engadget, TechCrunch,* and *Salon.* You can find links to Joe's stories on his blog, JOEyGADGET.com.

As a kid, Joe built a shortwave radio, played with electronic project kits, and learned the basics of the BASIC programming language on his first computer, the Commodore Vic 20. In his teens, he picked strawberries to buy his first Apple II computer. Four years after that purchase (in 1984), he wound up working for Apple, where he became the personal technology guru for the company's chairman and CEO. Joe left Apple in 1988 to become a writer and worked on and off for other high-tech companies, including Steve Jobs' one-time NeXT. He authored a number of video game strategy guides, including the bestsellers Donkey Kong Country Game Secrets: The Unauthorized Edition, and Rebel Assault: The Official Insiders Guide.

Joe's first novel, The Deal, was published in 1999, and he recently rereleased a trade paperback edition of it with a new foreword by the author (bit.ly/thedealjoehutsko).

Barbara Boyd is the co-author with Joe of the third edition of *Macs All-in-One For Dummies* and the first edition of *iPhone 4S All-in-One For Dummies.* She is also the author of *AARP Tech To Connect: iPad and iCloud For Dummies In A Day.* When not writing about technology, Barbara writes about food, gardens, and travel. She's written for *ChilePepper Magazine, Islands,* and *BeeCulture.*

Barbara worked at Apple from 1985 to 1990, beginning as Joe's assistant and the first network administrator for the executive staff. She then took a position as an administrator in the Technical Product Support group. Barbara recalls working with people who went on to become top names in technology — it was an exciting time to be in Silicon Valley and at Apple in particular. That experience instilled a lifelong fascination with technology and Apple products. Her interest and experience led to subsequent jobs in marketing and publishing at IDG (International Data Group) and later for a small San Francisco design firm. In 1998, she left the corporate world to study Italian, write, and teach.

Presently, Barbara stays busy writing, keeping up with technology, growing olives, and beekeeping. (She's a certified honey taster.) Barbara divides her time between city life in Rome and country life on an olive farm in Calabria, which she blogs about (intermittently) at honeybeesandolivetrees.blogspot.com/.

Dedication

Joe Hutsko: I dedicate this book to my fabulously thoughtful, kind, caring, smart, creative, beautiful, and amazing co-author — and lifelong friend (and karmic life preserver) — Barbara Boyd.

Barbara Boyd: I dedicate this book to my wonderful husband, Ugo de Paula. This book had an extremely tight turnaround, and it wouldn't have been possible without his loving support.

Authors' Acknowledgments

You see the author's names on the cover, but these books (like any book) are really a collaboration, an effort of a many-membered team. Thanks go to Bob Woerner at Wiley for renewing this title. We were thrilled to once again work with our superb project editor, Linda Morris, who pulled everything together with a calm demeanor. It's also a pleasure to again work with our favorite technical editor, Dennis R. Cohen; his intelligence, editing skill, and wit do not go unappreciated. Thanks, too, to the anonymous people at Wiley who contributed to this book — not just editorial, but tech support, legal, accounting, and even the person who delivers the mail. We don't know you but we appreciate the job you do; it takes a lot of worker bees to keep the hive healthy, and each task is important to the whole.

We want to thank our agent, Carole Jelen, for her astute representation and moral support.

Thanks to the folks at Apple who developed such a cool product, and specifically to Keri Walker for her ongoing editorial product support.

Also, a special thanks to the app developers who shared their products and their time — their names are too many to list here, but please take our word for it when we say this book wouldn't have been complete without their support.

Thanks as well to you, dear reader, for buying our book — we had you in mind at every turn of a page.

Joe adds: Special thanks to the awesome team at Philadelphia's Walnut Street Apple Store, especially Max, Latifa, Ron, Mario, Andrew, Larry, Heidi, and Mikal.

Barbara adds: At the risk of repeating myself, not a day goes by that I'm not grateful to my dear, friend of more than 30 years, my co-author, Joe. His honesty and transparent work style make every co-authoring project a joy, but mostly I'm thankful for his kind, always-present friendship.

Publisher's Acknowledgments

We're proud of this book; please send us your comments at http://dummies.custhelp.com. For other comments, please contact our Customer Care Department within the U.S. at 877-762-2974, outside the U.S. at 317-572-3993, or fax 317-572-4002.

Some of the people who helped bring this book to market include the following:

Acquisitions and Editorial

Project Editor: Linda Morris

Executive Editor: Bob Woerner

Copy Editor: Linda Morris

Technical Editor: Dennis Cohen

Editorial Manager: Jodi Jensen

Editorial Assistant: Anne Sullivan

Sr. Editorial Assistant: Cherie Case

Cover Photo: © Darren Utt/iStockphoto. Image of iPhone: John Wiley & Sons, Inc.

Cartoons: Rich Tennant (www.the5thwave.com)

Composition Services

Project Coordinator: Patrick Redmond

Layout and Graphics: Jennifer Creasey

Proofreaders: Lindsay Amones, Melissa Cossell, John Greenough

Indexer: Steve Rath

Publishing and Editorial for Technology Dummies

    Richard Swadley, Vice President and Executive Group Publisher

    Andy Cummings, Vice President and Publisher

    Mary Bednarek, Executive Acquisitions Director

    Mary C. Corder, Editorial Director

Publishing for Consumer Dummies

    Kathleen Nebenhaus, Vice President and Executive Publisher

Composition Services

    Debbie Stailey, Director of Composition Services

Table of Contents

Introduction

Apple has built its reputation on creating intuitive, user-friendly products. Just tapping through the buttons and apps on the screen, you get a rough idea of how your iPhone works and can probably manage to do a few things. We think that's kind of like using 10 percent of your brain: You get by, but you're not living up to your maximum potential.

We wrote this book to take your iPhone use to a higher level. This book probably covers some apps or functions that don't interest you or are unnecessary for the way you use your iPhone, so it's unlikely that you'll reach 100 percent, but we'll be really and truly happy if you up your percentage a bit, say, to 75 or 80 percent. It'd be plain wasteful to use your iPhone as a simple phone when it's so much more.

About This Book

To write this book, we looked into every nook and cranny of iPhone. Short of telling you how to take it apart, which would void your warranty, we believe we get pretty darn close to telling you all there is to know. That said, Apple releases iOS updates frequently — this book is based on iOS 6.0 — and we encourage you to keep your iPhone and app software up to date and stay informed as to how to use features that may be added with updates.

If you only want a broad overview of what your iPhone does and how to work with it, you can read Book I, which explains iPhone basics (what your iPhone can do, how your iPhone is organized, and how to use the multitouch screen and voice-recognition interface) and then just skim the other minibooks, which are divided by task, and explain each app in depth.

We're not perfect, so we undoubtedly missed something. Let us know. Your comments, questions, and compliments help us to improve future editions. Drop a note to us at babsboyd@me.com.

Conventions Used in This Book

To help you navigate this book efficiently, we use a few style conventions:

- Website addresses, or URLs, are shown in a special monofont typeface, like this.

- Numbered steps that you need to follow are set in **bold**.

- Sequential commands are shown as Settings➪General➪Network, which means tap Settings, tap General, and then tap Network on your iPhone. Store➪View My Account means to click the Store menu and drag to click the View My Account option on your computer.

- The first time we mention a button or icon, we show you what it looks like in the margin so you can find it more easily on your iPhone. The same button may be used in different apps and tapping it elicits the same function regardless of the app it's in.

- Sidebars present technical information that you don't have to know but that might interest those of you who want to understand the technology behind the function.

What You're Not to Read

This book doesn't have to be read cover to cover — you can pick and choose the chapters that pertain to how you use your iPhone. However, even if you are familiar with iPhone, we recommend you skim the beginning chapters. That way, you'll understand the commands we use in later chapters.

You don't have to read sidebars. Reading the sidebars can increase your iPhone knowledge, but skipping them won't inhibit your iPhone use. Same goes for Technical Stuff blips: They contain fun information, but they're not life-threateningly necessary.

Foolish Assumptions

We made a few assumptions about you when writing this book. To make sure we're on the same page, we assume that

- You know something, but not necessarily a lot, about cellular phones and you want to learn the basics and more about iPhone.

- You have at least a general concept of how to use the web and e-mail.

- You'll read through the introductory chapters if you find yourself scratching your head when you see terms like *tap, swipe,* and *flick,* or anything else that we think you should know but you don't.

- You acknowledge that it's up to you to go on the web to find updated information about the products described throughout this book.

- You'll check with your cellular service provider to know how many minutes or megabytes are included in your monthly allotment and under what circumstances you might incur additional charges, although we do give you some warnings throughout the book when additional charges are more likely.

✏ You know that technology is changing faster than we can keep up and even geeks like us can't stay on top of everything. You will, therefore, let us know about cool stuff you find along the way in your iPhone journey so we can consider it for future editions of this book.

✏ You're not all work and no play. You want to have some fun with your iPhone and maybe even be entertained while you're learning how to use it.

How This Book Is Organized

This book is divided into minibooks, which are further divided into chapters. You can read it cover to cover, but we recommend you familiarize yourself with iPhone basics in Book I, and then skip to the book or chapters that talk about the functions or apps that you use most or are most interested in using. We think you should also take a look at functions you doubt you'll use because you might find you like those functions.

The more you use your iPhone, the more you begin to understand the basic commands and techniques used across the iOS platform. We take you beyond the basics in the books and chapters that follow, giving you tips and showing you advanced settings throughout.

Book I: Meet iPhone

This minibook explains the functions you need to know to use your iPhone: basics like turning it on and off, adjusting the volume, charging the battery, and how to use the multitouch and voice-recognition (also known as Siri) interfaces. Buttons, icons, notifications, and badges that you might encounter are introduced. We give you an overview of the built-in apps and explain iPhone's settings in detail so you can customize them to your liking. This is also where you can find a troubleshooting question-and-answer guide and tips for avoiding problems.

Book II: Stocking iPhone with iTunes Apps and Add-ons

This minibook explains the concept of syncing (that is, having the same information in two or more devices and having changes made on one device appear automatically on the other device). Your iPhone uses iCloud to sync with your computers and any other iOS devices you have. Also in this minibook, you learn about the App Store and how to shop for other Apple and third-party apps, and Newsstand and how to subscribe to and read newspapers and magazines on your iPhone. The last chapter discusses hardware accessories that enhance your iPhone, such as speakers and protective cases.

Book III: Communications Central: Calls, Messages, and the Web

This minibook gets to the core communications functions of your iPhone. It explains everything about making phone calls, checking voicemail, using iPhone's video chat app FaceTime, sending text and e-mail messages, exchanging messages with Macs and other iOS devices with iMessage, and surfing the Internet with Safari, iPhone's web browser. For those of you who use social networks, we show you how Facebook and Twitter are integrated into various apps on your iPhone.

Book IV: Making iPhone Your Personal Assistant

Contact management, time management, getting directions, storing boarding passes and store cards, taking notes, and reminding you when to be somewhere to meet someone to do something — your iPhone can do it all and we explain it in this minibook. This minibook covers the unexpected iPhone apps like Maps and Compass, Weather, Stocks, and Calculator as well as the basic PDA apps: Contacts, Calendar, Notes, Voice Memos, Reminders, and the new addition, Passbook.

Book V: Let iPhone Entertain You: Photos, Video, Music, and More

This minibook is about having fun with your iPhone. Amateur photographers and videographers like using iPhone as a still and video camera and for sharing images via Photo Stream as well as messages and e-mail. For those who never want to stop learning, there's an introductory course to iTunes U. This minibook also gives all the details for finding new media in the iTunes Store or Podcast catalog and then having the best experience when listening to music, watching movies and TV shows, reading books, and streaming podcasts.

Bonus Content on the Web: Apps for Every Type of Task

In this online content, you learn how to expand your iPhone beyond the standard Apple apps. Each chapter presents a selection of apps that add a feature or function to your iPhone, or enhance something it already does. For the business user or busy household manager, there are budgeting, task management, and faxing apps. For the social butterfly, there are communications and networking apps. Quiet types might enjoy e-reader and radio apps. There's something for everyone in the leisure, fitness, health, home, and travel apps. Access the online content at `www.dummies.com/go/iphoneaio2efd`.

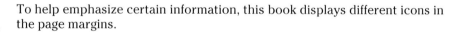

Icons Used in This Book

To help emphasize certain information, this book displays different icons in the page margins.

The Tip icon points out bits of information that can help you do things better and more efficiently or tells you something useful that you might not know.

This icon highlights interesting information that isn't necessary to know but can help explain why certain things work the way they do on your iPhone. Like sidebars, you can skip this information if you're in a hurry. On the other hand, you might find something helpful.

This icon gives you a heads-up about something that can go wrong if you're not careful. Be sure to read the warning fully before following related instructions.

This icon points out information that's been mentioned somewhere else in the book but is related to the topic nearby. If you ignore it, you won't cause problems, but you could miss something useful.

Where to Go from Here

As Julie Andrews sang in *The Sound of Music*, "Let's start at the very beginning, it's a very good place to start."

If you're new to iPhone, closely read the first few chapters to get an understanding of how your iPhone works, the command conventions it uses, and how to perform the basic functions. Then move on to chapters that interest you, perhaps starting with the phone and messaging functions before moving up to Internet access, and lastly looking at the multimedia apps like Music, Podcasts, and Camera.

If you're familiar with your iPhone already, skim through the opening chapters to learn about the recent iOS 6 changes, and then go where you wish: to a chapter on a function you haven't used before, which might be the video camera or Passbook, or to a function you use a lot but would like to know better, such as Messages.

No matter where you begin, our goal is to give you the tools to get the most out of your iPhone and encourage you to expand your knowledge and explore the many ways of iPhone.

Occasionally, we have updates to our technology books. If this book does have technical updates, they will be posted at `www.dummies.com/go/iphoneaio2efdupdates`.

Book I
Meet iPhone

*i*Phone is so much more than a phone. The first chapter of this minibook presents an overview of the hardware features and preloaded apps on your iPhone. Each of these is explained in depth in dedicated chapters throughout the book. In Chapter 2, we explain the icons and messages you see on your iPhone's screen, how to turn your iPhone on and keep the battery charged, and the different ways you can connect to the Internet. In Chapter 3, we explore the multitouch interface. This chapter is crucial to understanding how to use your iPhone, and here we define manual and spoken commands that will be used throughout the other chapters of this book. We introduce the apps that came with your iPhone in Chapter 4 and show you how to adjust the basic settings. We think of the last chapter of this minibook as the preventive maintenance chapter. Chapter 5 gives you a heads-up for some common problems you might encounter. We think if you read about these potential snags before they happen, you'll be calmer and better prepared to fix them — if they happen.

If you're on your second, third, or even fifth iPhone, you can probably skim this Part — take a look at the Table of Contents to find the sections that explain what you don't already know. If you're an iPhone newbie, this minibook is for you.

Chapter 1: Exploring the Many Faces of iPhone

In This Chapter

↳ **Considering iPhone carriers**

↳ **Making phone calls**

↳ **Sending messages**

↳ **Surfing the web and playing games**

↳ **Taking photos and video**

↳ **Being entertained**

Y ou bought this book, so you probably already have an iPhone — maybe this is your second or third. More than likely, you've taken it out of the box already and made a few phone calls or sent a text message. We're here to tell you there's a lot more.

This is the "whet your appetite" chapter. We look at the hardware, software, and a few unseen secrets of your iPhone. We just want to start you thinking about how you can get the most out of your iPhone. We introduce you to all your iPhone can do, and then you can pick and choose the topics and tasks where you want to dive deeper and go to those chapters for the details. Sticking with our appetite metaphor — or is it a simile? — if this chapter is the hors d'oeuvres, the following mini-books and chapters are the main courses, side dishes, and dessert. *Bon appétit*!

Looking at Your iPhone from Every Angle

With the release of iPhone 5, Apple took the recognizable, sleek design of iPhone one step further. iPhone 5 is the supermodel version of its predecessors — taller, slimmer, and lighter. On the surface, iPhone 5 might not seem all that different, but it has new things inside, and some functions and features on the outside have been moved and improved. Here we take a look at the hardware and a closer look at what's inside.

Front, back, top, bottom

The iPhone 4 and 4S models have a glass body, front, and back. iPhone 5 keeps the glass front (on the screen side), but replaces the back with an aluminum sheath bordered by inlaid glass at the top and bottom. Barbara's iPhone 5 literally flew out of her hand and landed facedown on a concrete sidewalk, soliciting an audible gasp from surrounding bystanders. She picked it up and couldn't find a scratch on it. We don't recommend you throw your iPhone around, but accidents do happen and the iPhone is tougher than it looks.

Around the edges of your iPhone is a metal band. It's a beautiful design element, but it also functions as an antenna (or as two antennae on the 4S and 5).

Notice the buttons and holes around the edges and on the front and back. You'll find them in different positions depending on the model you have, but the functions are the same:

- On/off sleep/wake switch
- Microphones — three altogether (up from two on the iPhone 4 and 4S)
- Lightning port
- Volume buttons
- Silent/ring button
- Two video/still objective lenses
- LED light
- SIM tray
- Speaker
- Headset jack
- Home button

We explain all of them in Book I, Chapter 2.

What you don't see can help you

Your iPhone has antennae and sensors to support the functions of the apps you use. One visible antenna is the metal band around the outside that connects to the cellular network. iPhone 4S and 5 actually switch between two antennae to receive and transmit, which increases data transfer speeds and call quality. Here's what those visible and not-so-visible parts do:

- **GPS and GLONASS:** Finds your location, gives you directions in Maps, and geotags your photos. In Book V, Chapter 1, we explain how geotagging identifies your location when you take a photo.

✔ **Wi-Fi:** Connects to available Wi-Fi networks.

✔ **Cellular antenna:** Connects you to a selection of the following networks: LTE, GSM/EDGE, CDMA EV-DO, UMTS/HSPA +/DC_HSDPA, or 3G networks. We explain the different types of cellular networks, and what all these nerdy terms and acronyms mean, in Book I, Chapter 2.

✔ **Gyroscope:** Used to find your location when GPS or GLONASS aren't accessible.

✔ **Magnetic-field sensor:** Positions the Compass.

✔ **Proximity sensor:** Turns the touchscreen off when you hold the phone close to your ear, so you don't accidentally tap the mute button while you're in the middle of a conversation. As soon as you move iPhone a few 16ths of an inch from your head, the screen is activated.

✔ **Tilt sensor:** Senses motion, which is particularly useful when playing games that involve driving or flying.

✔ **Accelerometer:** Allows for landscape display.

✔ **Bluetooth:** Connects to other Bluetooth 4.0–enabled devices.

✔ **Ambient light sensor:** Adjusts the screen when you're using your iPhone in low- or bright-light situations.

✔ **Moisture sensor:** Lets Apple know if your iPhone has gone for a swim. If you purchased AppleCare+, Apple may replace or repair your phone for up to two accidents after you pay a deductible. Learn about AppleCare in Book I, Chapter 5.

Other stuff in the box

Your iPhone comes with a few nice accessories, too. Here's what you'll find when you open the box:

✔ **EarPods:** Stereo earphones with a built-in microphone and volume control buttons. The newly released design comes with iPhone 5 or can be purchased separately if you have an iPhone 4S or earlier.

✔ **USB cable connector:** Connects your iPhone to a USB port on your computer, in your car, and on the USB power adapter. iPhone 5 has the new 9-pin reversible Lightning connector, whereas iPhone 4S and earlier has a 30-pin, one-way connector.

✔ **USB power adapter:** Connects to the USB cable connector and plugs into an outlet to charge your iPhone's battery.

✔ **Finger Tips guide:** Apple's quick guide to iPhone functions and features.

✔ **Product info:** Legal and technical information.

Considering iPhone Carriers and Configurations

When iPhone was first released, only one cellular service provider was available in the U.S.: AT&T. The situation was similar in other countries — only one cellular service provider supported iPhone. With subsequent releases, many carriers now support iPhone and that's made the situation both more convenient and more confusing for the consumer. Verizon, Sprint, and regional providers joined AT&T in offering cellular service contracts that include iPhones. In Europe, Vodafone is popular, although many countries also have country-specific carriers with competitive pricing.

Unlocked iPhones, which are iPhones you purchase outright without a service contract, work with carriers who use the GSM standard (see the following paragraph). In the U.S., AT&T, T-Mobile, and 30 or so regional carriers use GSM, as do most of the carriers outside the U.S. A customer in good standing can request that his CDMA carrier unlock his iPhone so it can access the GSM networks overseas, but nonetheless remains tied to the national and roaming costs associated with the cellular service contract.

GSM (Global System for Mobile) and CDMA (Code Division Multiple Access) are the telecommunications standards used for cellular networks. GSM, as its name implies, is the worldwide standard, whereas CDMA is limited to America and parts of Asia. CDMA offers slightly better data transfer, although GSM is steadily improving. The GSM standard stores your phone number and account information on a SIM card, whereas in the CDMA standard, the phone number and account information is programmed in the phone itself. Some CDMA networks require a SIM in order to connect to a GSM network outside the U.S. Sprint offers one so you can access the GSM network used by Sprint's partners in Europe. iPhones come with either GSM (with an AT&T contract or unlocked) or CDMA (Verizon or Sprint contracts).

You've probably heard a lot about LTE and have perhaps come to two conclusions: It's faster than other data transfer protocols and it's not available everywhere. You'd be right on both counts. LTE, which stands for Long Term Evolution, and is sometimes referred to as 4G (for fourth-generation) is designed to use different radio frequencies at higher speeds. Without getting into a bunch of technical gobbledygook, LTE means your web page, e-mail, video streaming, and any other stuff you do online works faster. In Philadelphia, Joe found LTE to be up to two times faster than his Wi-Fi connection and depending on your location, you could find similar results. In North America as well as Japan, Russia, India, Australia, and Brazil, you find broad commercial coverage, whereas in Europe, China, Mexico, and some emerging African and South American countries, 4G LTE support is in the works.

With so many different plans available from multiple national and regional carriers, we can't take responsibility for advising you on which to choose.

We can, however, give you some things to think about — and questions to ask prospective providers — when choosing. Here are a few things to consider so you can compare plans from different carriers and make an informed decision:

- **How much time do you spend on the phone?** Do you make many calls or just check in now and then? Three hundred and sixty minutes for a month is 12 minutes a day, whereas 1,000 minutes is just over a half hour a day. If you're thinking about replacing your landline with a cell phone, 1,000 minutes may not be enough.

- **When do you use your phone?** Some plans offer lower nighttime and weekend rates. If you spend your weekdays at your office and make most of your calls on the company phone, this type of contract may work for you.

- **Who do you call?** Some plans offer a you-and-me or family discount for one number, or a group of numbers, that you call more than any other or some even offer all mobile-to-mobile calls for free.

- **Where do you use your phone?** If you travel around the country, you probably want a call plan with nationwide coverage. If you're a homebody, a regional plan is probably just fine.

- **Do you travel overseas?** If you do, shop around for the best roaming rate or, if you frequently go to the same country, consider getting a local, rechargeable SIM card and using that in your iPhone when you're out of the U.S.

- **Do you send text messages?** Text messages may be billed at a per-message rate or your plan may include a limited (or unlimited) number of messages or KBs and you pay a per-message or per KB rate if you exceed the limited number. iMessage lets you send text messages for free to other iPhone, iPad, and iPod touch users (as well as users of Macs running OS X 10.8 or later).

- **How much cellular data usage do you need?** Wi-Fi is widespread in the U.S. Even the smallest one-café town seems to offer free Wi-Fi if you buy a cup of coffee, which makes cellular data less necessary. Most plans these days offer unlimited Internet access, although 50MB is the file size limit for downloading over a 3G or LTE cellular network.

When contracting with a cellular service provider, make sure to ask what charges you'll incur if you go over the minutes or data transfer limits — even going slightly over can cost a lot. Some carriers send an alert when you reach your limit or offer an app that tracks your usage, or a Usage category, in the provider section of Phone Settings.

The Big Picture: It's All That and More!

Your iPhone is more than just a phone. It's your online communications tool, personal digital assistant, entertainment source, camera, and — in a pinch — even a flashlight. With each new generation, iPhone has added more functions and features. iPhone itself is the hardware and the iOS and apps are the software that let you do so many things. In the next few sections, we give you the proverbial taste of what you can do.

Phone

Clearly, iPhone is a cellular telephone (see Figure 1-1) that makes voice calls and offers text messaging. Nothing extraordinary there. The standout functions include multimedia messaging with active links in messages you send and receive. Consider visual voicemail that displays a list of messages so you can listen to the most important ones first rather than go through them in chronological order. Add to that not one but two ways to communicate cost-free with other iOS device owners: FaceTime lets you communicate via video chat and iMessage, which is part of Messages, gives you multimedia message exchanges. We explain the ins and outs of phoning and messaging in Book III, Chapters 1 and 2. For those times you don't feel like talking to anyone, iOS 6 offers a Do Not Disturb function that blocks incoming calls and alerts.

Figure 1-1: IPhone as phone.

Music and videos

This is not your standard MP3 player. With the iPhone 5's four-inch Retina display and excellent stereophonic output, your iPhone plays music, movies, podcasts, and more with crisp, clear sound and images. From the iTunes Store, you can download music, movies, TV shows, and audiobooks. Podcasts and iTunes U now have their very own apps to download and enjoy podcasts and courseware. Connect your iPhone to a monitor or television with a cable or via AirPlay or Apple TV and watch everything on a big screen. All you have to do is pop the popcorn. Check out Book V, Chapters 2, 3, and 4 to learn all about the iPod, iTunes, and audio and video functions.

Camera and video camcorder

The eight megapixel iSight camera places the digital still camera on iPhone 4S and iPhone 5 in the same class as many digital cameras. And iPhone 4S and 5 rear-facing cameras capture 240-degree panoramic photos and high-definition video in 1080 rows of pixels. The LED flash next to the objective lens on the back of your iPhone illuminates both still photos and videos. The Photos app, which you use to organize and view your photos and videos after you capture them, also gives you a few editing options. Go to Book V, Chapter 1 for detailed information.

Personal digital assistant

With Siri, the voice-recognition interface, at your side or in your hand, iPhone is your very personal personal digital assistant (PDA for short). Just speak your commands to Siri and it (she?) does what you ask, such as typing and sending a dictated e-mail, finding a florist, or changing your dentist appointment. We explain how to use the Siri interface in Book I, Chapter 3.

Don't let Siri steal the limelight from iPhone's other PDA features. The resident apps complete iPhone's PDA role. Contacts eliminates the need for a paper address book. Calendar replaces your time management system, and Notes makes all those scraps of ideas and grocery lists obsolete, while Reminders makes sure no task or appointment is forgotten. We show you how to use your iPhone's PDA apps along with Voice Memos, Clock, and Calculator in Book IV.

Internet communicator

You start to see the real power of your iPhone when you go online. Able to access the Internet via either your cellular network, 3G, LTE, or Wi-Fi, you never have to miss another time-sensitive e-mail or tweet. You can search the Internet with Safari as you would on any computer. For example, you can search for movie times, book airline tickets, settle bets with Wikipedia, and read the news from your favorite news outlets. Safari's Reading List function lets you store an article to read later, even when you're offline — you can catch up on your reading while flying. Book III, Chapter 3 explains Safari.

You access your e-mail accounts through Mail. If you have multiple accounts, you can sync them all with Mail and see them individually or all together. Learn all about Mail in Book III, Chapter 4.

Facebook and Twitter are integrated throughout the apps in iOS 6. For example, you can share or tweet photos, links, and locations directly from the Photos, Safari, or Maps app. See Book I, Chapter 4 to learn more.

Your iPhone comes with some specific apps that gather information from the Internet, as shown in Figure 1-2. Passbook manages your store cards, coupons, and boarding passes so you can (almost) leave your wallet at home. Stocks lets you follow international investment markets as well as your personal investments. Weather leans on Yahoo! to bring you the weather forecast for cities you want to know about. We take you through these apps in Book IV, Chapter 3.

Figure 1-2: iPhone's great graphics make reading websites easy on the eyes.

Personal GPS navigator

Between the Compass and Maps apps and the GPS, Wi-Fi, and cellular sensors, 99 percent of the time, your iPhone can tell you where you are and tell you how to get where you want to go. What's more, in coordination with Yelp!, Maps and Siri can give you suggestions for vendors and services, like bookstores, museums, and restaurants, based on your location. The links in Maps are active — as they are in most iPhone apps — so you just click on the suggested vendor and the website for that vendor opens in Safari. We explain how to use Maps and Compass in Book IV, Chapter 3.

E-book and document reader

E-readers and tablets are all the rage and the iPhone 5's larger screen and document-reading capabilities makes reading easier than ever on your iPhone. We talk about iBooks, the Apple app for electronic books, and

Newsstand, the folder that organizes and updates your magazine and news-paper app subscriptions, in Book I, Chapter 4. You can download books directly from iTunes to your iPhone.

You can also read many types of documents on your iPhone. If a colleague sends you a PowerPoint presentation or a PDF document as an e-mail attach-ment, just tap on the attachment and your iPhone opens it so you can review it. You can't edit the document (without an additional app), but you can print the document from your iPhone with AirPrint, if there's an AirPrint-enabled printer on your wireless network.

Personal fitness trainer

In Book I, Chapter 4, we talk about the Nike+ iPod app, which tracks the dis-tances and times of your runs or walks by receiving information from a sen-sor in certain models of Nike running shoes. That's not the only app that helps you stay fit. The App Store boasts dozens of apps that create workout routines or track your progress toward fitness goals.

Pocket video game console

With all the ruckus, you might think Angry Birds is the only game in town. Actually, the App Store boasts more than 100,000 games, and many are free. Take that, Nintendo DS! With iPhone, you have a video game console with you at all times, the popular game Temple Run is shown in Figure 1-3, and with Game Center, you can play against friends online and see who has the highest score.

Systemwide functions

The keyboard, used in any app where typing is involved, supports 50 languages. Voice Control can ini-tiate phone calls, control Music, and tell you what time it is. Siri (iPhone 4S or later) can do those tasks and

Figure 1-3: Your iPhone is also a tiny game console.

more. Accessibility settings make iPhone easier to use with features like enlarged font sizes, custom vibration signals for incoming calls, and spoken text. Guided Access helps those with learning disabilities stay focused on one task.

Notifications, such as text messages, calendar requests, reminders, and voicemails come in while you're doing other things and you get a small indication at the top of the screen. When it's convenient, you can see them all together in the Notifications Center, as shown in Figure 1-4, and choose to which and when you want to respond.

iCloud syncs your contacts, calendars, notes, browser tabs, photos, documents, and more across Apple and third-party apps on all your devices, including Mac and Windows computers.

If you want to find something, Spotlight searches from within many of the apps on your iPhone, and you can search Wikipedia and the web directly from Spotlight.

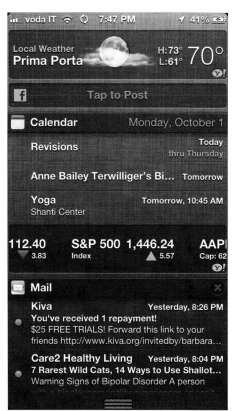

Figure 1-4: Quickly view upcoming appointments, weather, and stocks in the Notification Center.

And a thousand other things!

Even if you never add another app to your iPhone, it can do a lot, but adding third-party apps ups the potential even higher. In the bonus content on this book's companion website, we try to knock your socks off by introducing some of the newest and most innovative, problem-solving apps available. The minibook is divided into six chapters ranging from practical business solutions and creativity tools to apps for sports, cooking, and travel. (For more on how to access the companion website, see this book's Introduction.) We certainly found apps we never imagined existed when we were researching them for this book, and we hope this nudges you to do some research on your own. Figure 1-5 shows one of Barbara's favorites, StarWalk.

With that, dear reader, you should have some idea of where you want to go.

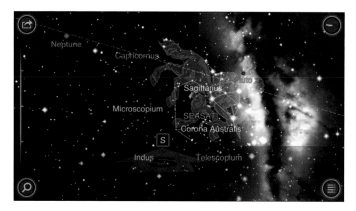

Figure 1-5: StarWalk is a location-based astronomy guide.

Chapter 2: Activating and Understanding Your iPhone

*I*n Chapter 1 of Book I, we gave you the "big picture" view about everything iPhone can do. In this chapter, we tell you how to use your iPhone's hardware and understand the interface. We begin with the most obvious tasks: turning your iPhone on and off, activating your iPhone, and adjusting the volume level. Then we review the basic layout and features of iPhone's screen: things like the Home screen, status bar icons, notifications, and badges. We explain different types of connections you make with your iPhone — Internet and network connections, GPS connections, and printer connections. At the end of the chapter, we take a look at some of the ways you can modify your iPhone to make it easier to use if you have vision, hearing, or tactile challenges or if a young person who uses your iPhone has learning disabilities.

Turning iPhone On and Off

The first thing you have to do to use your iPhone is . . . turn it on. Although your iPhone has few external buttons, if you're new to iPhone, knowing which button is the power switch may not be so obvious. Take a look at Figure 2-1, which details the external parts of iPhone. The On/Off Sleep/Wake button and the Home button are found in the same place on all iPhone models. Here's how they work:

Volume Up and Down

Mute

On/Off Sleep/Wake button

SIM card slot

Home button

Figure 2-1: External switches turn iPhone on and off, and wake it from a restful sleep.

✔ **On/Off Sleep/Wake Button:** This button is on the top of iPhone, to the right, and it does two things. When you press and hold it, it turns iPhone on or off, and when you tap it, it wakes iPhone from sleep or puts iPhone to sleep.

- To turn iPhone on, press and hold the On/Off Sleep/Wake button. The Apple logo appears in the center of the screen. After 30 seconds or so, the lock screen appears with a bar at the bottom of the screen and the helpful words *Slide to Unlock*. Drag your finger from left to right across this bar and the home screen opens. If you have a Subscriber Identity Module, better known as a SIM card, with a PIN or Personal Identification Number, or have set up a security passcode, a message comes up with two buttons: OK and Unlock. Tap the right button to open a keypad where you enter the PIN code of your SIM card to unlock it. Tap the left OK button, and you can use iPhone apps but not any of the phone, message, or Internet features. (We explain security passcodes in Book I, Chapter 4.)

- To turn iPhone off, press and hold the On/Off Sleep/Wake button until the red bar appears with the message *Slide to Power Off*. Drag your finger from left to right across this bar to turn iPhone off. Tap the Cancel button at the bottom of the screen if you change your mind.

- To put iPhone to sleep, press the On/Off Sleep/Wake button once. To wake or unlock iPhone, press either the On/Off Sleep/Wake button or the Home button, which is the round button below the screen that we explain in a couple of paragraphs. A slider appears at the bottom that reads *Slide to Unlock*. Slide your finger across this slider, and the Home screen opens.

- iPhone goes to sleep or locks (not to be confused with the SIM lock) automatically when you don't touch the screen for one minute. You can change this setting to up to five minutes or never in Settings⇨General⇨Auto-Lock. (That means tap Settings, tap General, tap Auto-Lock.) This saves battery power and keeps you from unintentionally opening an app or making a call by accidentally touching the Home screen. When iPhone is asleep or locked, you still receive phone calls, messages, and alerts — unless you have the Do Not Disturb function activated — and can listen to music. You can also adjust the volume of a call or music with the volume buttons on the side of the phone.

Tap the On/Off Sleep/Wake button once to silence an incoming call. The caller hears four rings before the call goes to voicemail. Tap twice and the call is sent directly to voicemail. You also have incoming call response options, which we explain in Book III, Chapter 1.

✔ **Home Button:** This is the round, central button on the front of iPhone, below the screen.

- Press this button once to return to the Home screen at any time from any app. Pressing this button once when iPhone is locked wakes iPhone the same way as the On/Off Sleep/Wake button does.

- Press once from the first Home screen to open Spotlight Search (which we explain in Book I, Chapter 3).

- Press once from any Home screen other than the first one to return to the first Home screen.

- Quickly press the Home button twice, also known as a double-click, to open the multitasking bar and switch from one app to another. More about that in Book I, Chapter 3.

- If iPhone is sleeping, double-click the Home button to open both an on-screen Camera button and on-screen iPod commands to pause, play, fast-forward, or rewind. We explain everything about the Camera in Book V, Chapter 1, and about the iPod on iPhone in Book V, Chapter 3.

Activating Your iPhone

Even though your iPhone has lots of other applications besides calling, you can't use any of them until your iPhone is connected to a cellular network through your cellular service provider, and if it's a GSM phone, has a SIM card installed. You can purchase an iPhone with a cellular network contract or without a contract, which is called an *unlocked* iPhone. Here's the difference:

- **Contract:** iPhone is activated when you sign up for a service plan with an iPhone service. In the U.S., your cellular network carrier choices are AT&T, which uses the GSM (Global System for Mobile Communications) cellular communications protocol; Verizon; and Sprint, which use the CDMA (Code Division Multiple Access) cellular communications proto- col. We explain both GSM and CDMA in the "Making Connections" sec- tion of this chapter. You register your phone with the network and pick a plan for the number of calling minutes, SMS messages, and Internet service usage you want.

- **Unlocked:** iPhone 5 arrives without a nano-SIM (that's the little chip inside that gives you access to the cellular network), while iPhone 4 and 4S have a micro-SIM, which is a bit smaller than a normal SIM and a bit bigger than the nano-SIM. You purchase a nano-SIM from a service pro- vider and then purchase prepaid calling minutes in a pay-as-you-go option. Cellular broadband Internet access is sold separately. You can use an unlocked iPhone with a contract; in that case, you bought your iPhone outright so the monthly contract should be less than iPhone plus a cellular service fee. T-Mobile provides national pay-as-you-go service and about 30 regional carriers offer pay-as-you-go service. Unlocked iPhones work only with carriers who use the GSM cellular communica- tions standard (AT&T and T-Mobile in the U.S.). If you spend a lot of time overseas, say in France, you can purchase a prepaid SIM in France, which you put in your iPhone when you're there. (Check with your U.S. service provider to see any unlocking has to be performed stateside first.) When you're in the U.S., you put the U.S.-based SIM in your iPhone.

If you bought your iPhone with a cellular service contract, it's already activated when you bought it; if, for example, you bought it at an Apple Store, an AT&T store, or other retail outlet such as Wal-Mart or Best Buy. If you bought your iPhone through the online Apple Store and selected a carrier, you only need to turn your iPhone on and follow the onscreen instructions.

If you bought an unlocked iPhone, you must purchase and insert a GSM nano-SIM. To insert the nano-SIM, do the following:

1. **Insert the end of a paper clip into the hole on the SIM card tray on the right side of your iPhone.**

   The SIM card tray pops open.

2. **Place the SIM card in the tray, matching the cut corner of the SIM card to the cut corner in the tray.**

3. **Push the SIM card tray closed.**

When you turn on your iPhone for the first time, the Setup Assistant takes you through a series of screens where you type in the requested information or choose from a list and tap Next or Done. You have to have a Wi-Fi or cellular network data connection to complete activation; otherwise, you must connect your iPhone to your computer with the USB connector cable. The Setup Assistant asks for the following information:

- **Language:** Tap your selection in the list.

- **Country:** Tap your selection in the list.

- **Wi-Fi network:** A list of available Wi-Fi networks appears. Click the one you use and type in the password. If Wi-Fi is unavailable, you can connect your iPhone to your computer with the USB to Dock connector cable and choose Connect to iTunes.

- **Location Services:** We recommend that you choose Enable Location Services, which lets various iPhone apps such as Maps and Reminders to use your location to better perform operations.

- **Set Up iPhone:** If this is your first iPhone, you can choose Set Up as New iPhone or you can restore from a backup of your iPad or iPod touch, which puts your apps, data, and media on your iPhone. If you are moving from an older iPhone to a newer model, first backup your old phone and then choose Restore from iCloud Backup or Restore from iTunes Backup (whichever you use). Learn all the details of syncing, restoring, and using iCloud in Book II, Chapter 1.

✔ **Sign in or create an Apple ID:** Although you can choose to skip this step, your Apple ID lets you

- Store your iPhone backup on iCloud, Apple's remote storage site.
- Make purchases from the iTunes Store and the App Store.
- Sign in to FaceTime.

If you have separate Apple IDs for iTunes and iCloud, follow the onscreen instructions to sign in to both. iCloud requires ID with an e-mail format, such as babsboyd@icloud.com, so you may have to create a new account to activate iCloud. The Setup Assistant asks you to create an ID and password and set up a security question — a question only you know the answer to that Apple asks if you forget your password or if you call for customer service and the technician wants to verify your identity.

✔ **iTunes Sign in:** Type your Apple ID and password and Agree to the Terms and Conditions when asked.

✔ **iCloud Set up:** You can choose to use iCloud or decline and then set up iCloud later, as explained in Book II, Chapter 1.

✔ **Messaging:** Choose which phone number and e-mail address other people can use to reach you on iMessage and FaceTime.

✔ **Diagnostics:** We recommend you choose Automatically Send. Tap Start Using iPhone after you complete the setup procedure.

Turning Up the Volume

When you're in a noisy place and don't want to miss a call, you might want to have the ringer at full volume. On the other hand, if you're in a meeting but waiting for an important call, you may want to keep your iPhone silent and choose to respond only to that one not-to-be-missed call. Here we explain how the three buttons on the left of your iPhone control volume:

✔ **Volume Buttons:** You find the volume buttons — two round, slightly raised buttons — on the left side of iPhone. The button on top with the plus sign increases volume; the lower button with the minus sign lowers volume. When you are engaged in a call or using an app that has volume, be it music, a video, or a game, these buttons control the volume of the thing you are listening to, watching, or playing. When iPhone is awake, but not otherwise engaged in a noisy activity, these buttons control the volume of both the ringer and alerts, unless you've turned that feature off within the sound settings, as we explain in Book I, Chapter 4.

The button used for increasing volume doubles as a shutter button for the Camera. (Refer to Book V, Chapter 1 to learn about using your iPhone's camera and video recorder.)

✔ **Silent/Ring Switch:** The switch above the volume buttons is a mute button. Push it to the back and you see a red bar. This is the Off or silent position. Pushed to the front is the On or ring position. When iPhone is in silent mode, it vibrates when calls or alerts come in. If your iPhone rings and you prefer not to answer, you can turn the Silent/Ring switch off. Your caller continues to hear the phone ring until he decides to hang up or leave a voicemail message, but your iPhone will be silent. See Book III, Chapter 1 for information about using the Do Not Disturb feature, which blocks incoming calls, messages, and alerts.

When iPhone is in silent mode, alarms are still audible. The audio for Music and some games will be heard through the speaker or earphones, if you happen to have those plugged into your iPhone (and into your ears, of course).

Interpreting the (Visual) Signs

You spend a lot of time looking at your iPhone and understanding what you see helps you use your iPhone more efficiently. In this section, we explain what you see on the Home screen, how to interpret the Status Bar icons, and how to respond to notifications iPhone sends you when it has something important to communicate.

Home screen

The point of departure for everything iPhone is the Home screen, which features three basic parts (or zones), as you can see in Figure 2-2. At the very top is the *status bar*, which we get to in just a few paragraphs. The bulk of the iPhone 5 screen holds up to 20 app buttons and folders (16 on earlier iPhone models), which can hold up to 16 apps (we talk about folders in the next chapter). Four of the Home screen's apps stay tacked at the bottom of the screen in what's called the *dock*, which makes it easy to get to your four most-favorite apps no matter which Home screen you're viewing.

Between the last row of apps and the dock is a tiny magnifying glass and a line of dots (one of which is white, the others are gray). These represent the Spotlight Search screen (the magnifying glass) and the number of Home screens you have. You may have up to 11 Home screens plus the Spotlight Search screen. (Refer to Book I, Chapter 3 for a full explanation of

Spotlight Search.) The white dot tells you which of the Home screens you're on. In Figure 2-2, you see the first dot is white followed by seven gray dots, which means this is Home screen one of eight. Flick the current Home screen to the left, and the screen moves one screen to the left; flick the Home screen to the right, and the screen moves one screen to the right. Touch the dots toward the left, and the screen moves one screen to the left; touch the dots to the right, and the screen moves one screen to the right.

Tap any of the app icons on the Home screen, and the associated app opens. If you tap a folder, it opens. Then you tap the app inside the folder that you want to launch. Double-click the Home button and the apps that are open appear in the multitasking bar.

Staying informed with status bar icons

The status bar runs across the very top of your iPhone in either portrait or landscape view. Its icons give you information about your cellular

Figure 2-2: The Home screen is the point of departure for iPhone.

and/or wireless network connection, battery life, and auxiliary functions you may have turned on, such as Do Not Disturb and the alarm clock. Here is an explanation of each one. Remember, you won't see them all at once on your iPhone, and some you may never see:

✔ **Airplane Mode:** You see this icon if you've turned Airplane mode on in Settings. Airplane mode turns off all connections to your cellular network, Wi-Fi, and Bluetooth. You can still listen to music, watch videos, and play games. You can also reread e-mail or SMS messages that have been downloaded. In some countries, you may turn on Wi-Fi while your iPhone is in Airplane mode. See Book I, Chapter 4 for more details on Airplane Mode.

✔ **Alarm:** Appears if you set an alarm using the Clock app, we explore the Clock app in Book IV, Chapter 2.

✓ **Battery:** Indicates how much charge remains on the battery. It's green if the battery is between 100 and 20 percent charged. It changes to red and shows just a tiny portion on the left when less than 20 percent charge remains. It has a lightning bolt on it when the battery is being charged. You can read more about charging the battery later in this chapter.

✓ **Bluetooth:** Shows that Bluetooth is turned on. When it's blue or white, you are connected to another Bluetooth device such as a headset. When it's gray, Bluetooth is on but no device is connected. If you think Bluetooth is Bluebeard's brother, read more about this connection protocol in the "Making Connections" section of this chapter.

✓ **Call Forwarding:** On GSM models (an unlocked Apple iPhone or an AT&T iPhone, refer to the "Considering iPhone Carriers and Configurations" section in Book I, Chapter 1), appears when you've forwarded your calls to another phone number. The call forwarding settings are explained in Book III, Chapter 1.

✓ **Cell Signal:** Indicates the strength of the cellular signal your iPhone is connected to. If you have no bars or just one, the signal is weak — more bars, stronger signal. *No Service* appears when iPhone is unable to pick-up a signal from your cellular provider. If Airplane Mode is turned on, you see the airplane icon instead of the cell signal bars.

✓ **Do Not Disturb:** Reminds you that you have activated the Do Not Disturb feature.

✓ **EDGE (E):** Appears when iPhone is connected to your cellular provider's EDGE data network for accessing the Internet. GSM models support EDGE networks. Read more about Internet access later in this chapter.

✓ **GPRS/1xRTT:** GSM models use the GPRS (General Packet Radio Service) network and CDMA models use the 1xRTT (1x Radio Transmission Technology) network to access the Internet when those networks are available. Read more about Internet access in the "Making Connections" section later in this chapter.

✓ **Location Services:** When you see this icon, an app, such as Maps, is tracking your current location coordinates in order to provide you with nearby information or other services, such as the closest cafe or directions to the pet supply store across town.

✓ **Lock:** This icon indicates iPhone is locked. Tap the On/Off Sleep/Wake button to unlock. Of course, you won't see this often because if your phone is locked, the Home screen and status bar aren't visible.

✓ **LTE:** Lets you know you have an LTE cellular connection.

✓ **Network Activity:** Spins when iPhone is accessing a cellular or Wi-Fi network for any app that uses the Internet, such as Safari or the App Store. It also appears when iPhone is syncing iCloud information over-the-air, or sometimes when an app is performing other data-related activities.

 ✓ **Personal Hotspot:** This icon is active when you've connected to another iPhone or a 3G/4G iPad that is providing a Personal Hotspot.

 ✓ **Play:** Appears when you're listening to music or audio using iPod, or when you're listening to other audio, such as a streaming radio program.

 ✓ **Orientation Lock:** This reminds you that you've turned off the landscape view feature. You can turn your iPhone every which way, but the screen remains in portrait position — unless you open an app that only works in landscape position, such as some games or videos.

 ✓ **Syncing:** Indicates that your iPhone is syncing with iTunes or iCloud.

 ✓ **TTY:** Indicates your iPhone is configured to work with a Teletype (TTY) machine.

 ✓ **UMTS/EV-DO (3G or 4G):** Indicates when GSM models are connected to the UMTS (Universal Mobile Telecommunications System) network, or CDMA models are connected to the EV-DO (Evolution-Data Optimized) network to access the Internet when those networks are available. Read more about Internet access in the "Making Connections" section later in this chapter.

 ✓ **VPN:** Indicates iPhone is connected to a VPN (Virtual Private Network).

 ✓ **Wi-Fi:** Indicates iPhone is connected to a Wi-Fi network. The more bars, the merrier — er, we mean, the more stable — the connection. Read more about wireless connections in the "Making Connections" section of this chapter.

Understanding status bar colors

In iOS 6, the status bar changes color depending on the app you're using — black in Weather and Stocks, blue in Calendar and Clock, gray in Photos. Third-party apps use other colors of their liking.

A second colored line of the status bar appears when you are engaged in one activity, such as a phone call, and begin another activity, such as opening Notes to jot down something your caller is telling you. These are what the different colors mean:

✓ **Green:** A phone or FaceTime call is active but you are doing something else. You can continue to converse while you do the other activity; it's helpful to put the call on speakerphone before opening another app.

✓ **Red:** Voice Memos is recording while you're doing other things. Tap the red bar to return to the Voice Memos app and stop recording.

Noticing notification messages and badges

When iPhone wants to get your attention and tell you something, it communicates via badges and messages. These are different than alerts, alarms, and reminders that you set on your iPhone in that they contain information iPhone wants to give you. You see two types of badges as shown on the App Store, Facebook, Mail, and CNN buttons in Figure 2-2:

🠦 White numbers inside a red circle that appear in the corner of certain app icons, such as Mail and Facebook. The number indicates how many unread messages await you in those apps.

🠦 Blue and white sashes that read New, such as on the CNN icon, letting you know the app has recently been added to your iPhone. The New sash also appears on unread books in iBooks and unread periodicals in Newsstand.

There are also two kinds of notification messages. The first kind requires a response and appears when you want to do something but iPhone needs something else to happen before it can complete the task. These messages appear in rectangular boxes in the middle of the screen and typically display buttons you can tap to respond to with a certain action. In the example in Figure 2-3, for instance, you have the choice of acknowledging the notification message by tapping Cancel, or by tapping Disable to turn off Airplane mode.

The second kind of notification is when you're doing one thing, say having a phone conversation, and another thing happens, say, you get an incoming e-mail. You see a notification banner across the top of your iPhone's screen. You can choose to respond or ignore it. If you ignore the banner, it disappears in a few seconds. iPhone saves all your notifications in the Notification Center, as shown in Figure 2-4, which you can see by swiping down from the top of the screen. You choose which apps you want to see in the

Figure 2-3: Notification messages often have buttons that give you a choice of actions to take.

Notification Center in Settings, which we cover in Book I, Chapter 4. You also choose whether alert-generating apps display alerts, banners, badges, or none of the three.

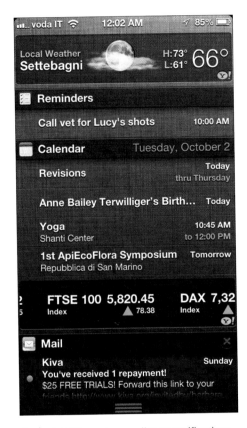

Figure 2-4: iPhone keeps all your notifications in one place, the Notification Center.

Charging Your iPhone Battery

Your iPhone is useless with an uncharged battery. How long the battery charge lasts is something engineers and developers are constantly trying to improve. Our experience is that our iPhone battery charge lasts about a day. We frequently check e-mail and surf the web. We frequently connect via Wi-Fi. Games, Music, Video, and Wi-Fi or LTE connections consume juice. A few levels of Angry Birds and the battery power notification message comes up. The good news is that iPhone recharges in less than an hour, and you can charge the battery in several ways, which we describe here. We outline tips for obtaining a longer battery charge in Book I, Chapter 5.

The battery icon in the status bar indicates how much battery power you have. If you want a specific percentage to show, tap Settings➪General➪Usage and turn on the Battery Percentage switch toward the bottom of the screen.

Plugging into the USB charger

Your iPhone comes with a USB connection cable and a USB power adapter. To charge the battery, plug the dock connector into the dock port at the base of your iPhone — with iPhone 5's Lightning connector you don't have to worry about which way is up as it can be plugged in either way. Plug the USB end into the USB power adapter and plug the power adapter into an electrical outlet. iPhone beeps, which lets you know it's actively charging.

The power adapter automatically adjusts to 110 or 220 voltage, based on the voltage for the location you're plugging into. If you are using your iPhone outside the U.S., you have to purchase an adapter that changes the plug conformation to meet the outlet style of the country you're visiting. You can find a kit at the Apple Store (store.apple.com/us) or single adapters at TravelProducts.com (www.travelproducts.com/). Or you can charge your iPhone with your computer's USB port as we explain next.

Charging with your Mac or PC's USB port

You can also charge your iPhone battery by connecting it directly to a USB port on your computer. Again, iPhone beeps, which lets you know it's being charged. If your computer is turned off or is sleeping, your iPhone battery may drain instead of charge, so make sure your computer is on if you want to charge your iPhone with it.

Although plugging your iPhone into any recent or new Mac can charge your iPhone, the same isn't necessarily true for recent or new Windows desktop and notebook computers or older Macs. Apple claims that's because the USB ports on certain of those models don't pass through enough wattage to charge your iPhone. If connecting your iPhone to your USB port doesn't yield a charge, try plugging into a powered USB port dock. If that doesn't work, you'll have to plug into a charger to charge your iPhone.

Don't pull the cable to detach your iPhone from your computer. Always grasp the hard, square part of either end of the USB cable to remove it.

Either way you charge, if your iPhone is locked or sleeping and you tap the Home key, a big battery symbol displays your iPhone's current charge level, as shown in Figure 2-5. When it's completely charged, the battery is entirely green.

If iPhone's battery charge drops very low or runs down completely, your iPhone automatically shuts itself off. To bring your iPhone back to life, you must attach the USB cable to a power source (your computer or an electrical outlet). When your iPhone shuts itself off because the battery charge is too low or nearly empty, you won't be able to use your iPhone until the battery reaches a minimal charge level. Usually you only have to wait a few minutes before your iPhone turns itself on again.

Apple and other third-party vendors make charging accessories. For models prior to iPhone 5, you can use an iPhone dock, which is a type of base that you set your iPhone in to charge the battery and it's convenient to have on your desk to keep your iPhone close at hand. For iPhone 5, you have to use a Lightning adapter and then plug the iPhone with the adapter into the dock but it isn't very stable. You can also purchase battery packs that you attach to your iPhone to get a longer charge. If you spend a lot of time in your car, another option is a USB adapter that plugs into the cigarette lighter or built-in USB port to charge your iPhone.

Figure 2-5: When the battery is charging, you see this screen when you wake or unlock your iPhone.

Making Connections

One of the biggest advantages of iPhone is the ability to connect to a variety of signal sources: to the Internet via your cellular carrier's data network or via a Wi-Fi network, or to other devices like printers, keyboards, and hands-free headsets using Bluetooth. To help you understand all of your iPhone's many connection options, we've organized those options into three sections: cellular and wireless connections, Personal Hotspot and tethering, and lastly, Bluetooth and GPS connections.

Cellular

When you activate your iPhone with a carrier, you gain access to that carrier's cellular voice and data network. iPhone uses two types of cellular connection protocols: the CDMA type used by Sprint and Verizon in the U.S., and the GSM type used by AT&T in the U.S. and in most countries outside the U.S. Without boring you with too many technical details, your iPhone typically connects using one or more of the following protocols:

✔ **LTE:** Long Term Evolution is the most recent cellular communications protocol. Both GSM and CDMA model iPhones can access the LTE network where it's available.

✔ **GSM (Global System for Mobile Communications) models**

✔ **3G/UMTS:** 3G is the third generation protocol standard that uses the UMTS (Universal Mobile Telecommunications System) cellular frequency. This protocol is faster than EDGE, but consumes more battery power. Try using Safari or Mail with 3G on and off to note any connection speed differences (tap Settings⟹General⟹Cellular⟹Enable 3G). If 3G is on but unavailable, iPhone defaults to EDGE.

  • **EDGE:** Enhanced Data for GSM Evolution is the first-generation protocol standard for connecting to the Internet over the cellular carrier network. EDGE often offers a more stable, albeit slower, connection than 3G because it offers wider network coverage.

  • **GPRS:** General Packet Radio Service supports both second- (2G) and third-generation (3G) cellular telephony. Usage is based on volume rather than time. If neither EDGE nor 3G is available, iPhone defaults to GPRS.

✔ **CDMA (Code Division Multiple Access) models**

  • **EV-DO:** The Evolution-Data Optimized is a 3G or third generation protocol, similar to UMTS for access speed.

  • **1xRTT:** 1x Radio Transmission Technology is an alternative 3G protocol.

Unlike GSM-model iPhones, if you have a CDMA iPhone and are actively transferring data over your carrier's cellular network — to check your e-mail or browse a web page, for instance — you cannot also engage in an active phone call while those data-related activities are underway. Any calls you may receive while using your cellular carrier's data connection are sent directly to your voicemail. You can make and receive calls while doing those data-related things on your CDMA iPhone if you are connected to a Wi-Fi network.

When your iPhone is connected to the Internet with one of these protocols, the associated icon appears in the status bar, as mentioned earlier in this chapter.

If you happen to be outside your carrier's network, you can try to access the Internet through another carrier. This is called Data Roaming and is enabled by tapping Settings⟳General⟳Cellular and flipping the Data Roaming switch to On.

Data Roaming, especially if you're out of the country, can rack up sizeable surcharges. Check with your carrier for Data Roaming fees before being surprised with a whopping bill at the end of the month.

If your cellular carrier contract has a data transfer limit, you can monitor your cellular data usage by opening Settings⟳General⟳Usage⟳Cellular Usage. You should tap Reset Statistics at the end of the month or on the day when your period renews. Using Wi-Fi for data access is an alternative if you have free or low-cost Wi-Fi service in places where you use your iPhone.

Wi-Fi

You may want to say that cellular is wireless, and you'd be right. But Wi-Fi is wireless, only better. Connecting to the Internet using iPhone's Wi-Fi feature is almost always the fastest — and cheapest — way to connect to the Internet although some iPhone 5 users are reporting transfer speeds up to two times faster than Wi-Fi on the LTE network. Wi-Fi networks blast their typically close-range signals from a device known as a wireless router, which is connected to a broadband modem, which in turn is typically connected to your cable or phone company's broadband Internet service (or whatever the Wi-Fi router you tap into is connected to, be it at your favorite cafe, on a train, or a public library, for example). Other people can connect their Wi-Fi enabled devices as well, making the group of you a network, as opposed to a single connection. You may need a password to access a Wi-Fi network, and some Wi-Fi services charge an hourly or daily fee to access their networks.

To join a Wi-Fi network, follow these steps:

1. **Tap Settings on your Home screen, and then tap Wi-Fi.**

   The Wi-Fi Networks screen opens.

2. **Tap the toggle switch to turn Wi-Fi on.**

   The screen expands to give you the option to Choose a Network, as seen in Figure 2-6. iPhone detects servers in the area and the Wi-Fi symbol indicates how strong the signal is: The more waves, the stronger the signal. Servers that require a password have a closed lock icon next to them.

Some Wi-Fi networks may require you to agree to the provider's terms before you can use the network. In those cases, a prompt appears, asking for your permission to launch Safari to view the provider's web page, where you typically tap a checkbox indicating you agree to the legal mumbo jumbo listed on the web page. In other cases, you have to type in a user name and password in order to agree to the provider's terms.

iPhone remembers Wi-Fi networks you previously connected to and automatically reconnects whenever you're in range of those Wi-Fi networks. Tap the disclosure triangle next to a network name and then tap the Forget this Network button to immediately disconnect from a Wi-Fi network you're connected to. Tapping this option also erases any password or other information you may have typed in to connect to the Wi-Fi network.

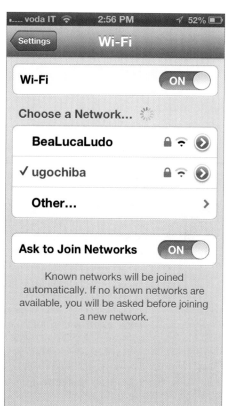

Figure 2-6: Choose a wireless network from the list of visible servers.

If you know the name of the network you want to join and it's not in the list, do this:

1. **Tap Other.**

    The Other Network pane opens.

2. **Type in the name of the network in the Name field.**

3. **If the network has a password, tap Security.**

    The Security screen opens.

4. **Choose the type of password this network uses and tap the back button that reads Other Network.**

    The Other Network screen reopens, and the cursor is blinking in the Password field.

5. **Type in the password.**

6. **Tap the Join button.**

   You return to the Wi-Fi Networks screen. A checkmark appears next to the highlighted name of the network you've joined. iPhone automatically remembers any Wi-Fi network you've joined and connects to it whenever you're in its range.

Information about and configuration options for the Wi-Fi network you're connected to appear beneath the Forget this Network button. Scroll down the list to see the Wi-Fi network's information and configuration options. Chances are you'll probably only view or change these additional Wi-Fi network settings if the tech folks at the company or organization that operates the network tell you that you need to and provide you with the necessary details you must type in to make the connection.

The Wi-Fi icon in the status bar shows iPhone's connection status and the strength of the signal.

Personal Hotspot and tethering

When another device uses your iPhone's Internet connection to connect to the Internet, that's called *tethering*. Tethering essentially turns your iPhone into a miniature Wi-Fi router that broadcasts a signal that you or a few others can tap into with your notebook computer, your iPad, or most any other Wi-Fi enabled gadget. A Wi-Fi network you can connect to is typically referred to as a *hotspot* and on your iPhone, this feature is called Personal Hotspot. You can also connect your computer to iPhone's Personal Hotspot feature using a USB cable, rather than connect using Wi-Fi.

To use iPhone's Personal Hotspot feature, you must pay your cellular service provider a separate fee in addition to your existing cellular service plan. Contact your provider for details. Personal Hotspot also quickly consumes the battery charge.

To share an Internet connection using your iPhone's Personal Hotspot feature, follow these steps:

1. **Tap Settings on the Home screen.**

2. **Choose Personal Hotspot or if Personal Hotspot isn't in the top level of Settings, tap General⇨Cellular⇨Personal Hotspot.**

3. **Tap On.**

   Take note of the Wi-Fi Password given on the Personal Hotspot screen.

If Bluetooth is turned off, a notification appears asking if you want to turn Bluetooth on or use Personal Hotspot only with Wi-Fi and USB. Although you can use Bluetooth, we recommend either Wi-Fi or USB because a Bluetooth connection is painfully slow.

4. **Choose one of the options below to connect:**

   • **To connect a computer using the Personal Hotspot feature's direct cable option, connect iPhone to your computer with the USB cable.**

     In Network preferences, choose iPhone. Follow the onscreen instructions to configure the connection if this is the first time.

   • **To connect a computer or other device (such as an iPad, another iPhone, or an iPod touch) using that device's built-in Wi-Fi feature, choose your iPhone from the list of Wi-Fi networks that appears on the device.**

     Type the Wi-Fi password shown in the Personal Hotspot settings.

5. **A blue band appears at the top of your iPhone screen whenever a device is connected.**

The Personal Hotspot icon appears in the status bar when your iPhone is connected to another iPhone's Personal Hotspot, not when your iPhone is the Personal Hotspot.

Bluetooth

The iPhone 4S and 5 use the Bluetooth 4.0 protocol. Bluetooth is a short-range (up to 300 feet) wireless protocol used to attach, or pair, devices to your iPhone. Unlike Wi-Fi, which broadcasts its availability continuously, Bluetooth has to be turned on to make your iPhone or other device discoverable so that they can see each other. A passkey or PIN (Personal Identification Number) is used to make that connection private.

One of the most common devices paired with iPhone is a wireless headset. This small device is either inserted in your ear or wrapped around it and has both a speaker to hear the person you're talking to and a microphone so they can hear you. You can have phone conversations without risking strangulation by earphone cord or, worse yet, catching the cord on something, resulting in your iPhone flying through the air and smashing on the floor. (Yeesh, just writing that makes us shudder.)

Other devices that you might want to pair with your iPhone are earphones for listening to music, a physical keyboard, or your car so you can answer calls by tapping a button on the steering wheel or radio. If you pair two iPhones, you can share photos, files, and even an Internet connection between them. To connect devices to your iPhone via Bluetooth,

1. **On your iPhone, go to Settings⇨Bluetooth and tap the Bluetooth button on.**

   The Bluetooth screen opens, as shown in Figure 2-7. Tapping On makes your iPhone discoverable, which means other devices with Bluetooth turned on can see your iPhone. The Bluetooth icon appears in the status bar.

2. **Turn on Bluetooth on the device you want to connect so it too is discoverable.**

   If the device is another iPhone or computer, you have to turn on Bluetooth on that iPhone or computer too. Active devices show up in a list on the Bluetooth screen on your iPhone.

   A Bluetooth headset only needs to be turned on. Obviously a headset doesn't have a keypad to enter a passkey, but it comes with an assigned passkey, which you need to pair it with your iPhone. Check the instructions that came with the headset for the passkey code or try **0000**. (It's usually the default passcode.)

Figure 2-7: Bluetooth lets you connect devices to your iPhone.

3. **In the list, tap the device you want to pair with your iPhone.**

4. **Enter the passkey on the keypad that appears on your iPhone, if requested.**

   The two devices can now communicate across the Bluetooth connection.

5. **To turn Bluetooth off and make your iPhone undiscoverable, tap Settings⇨ Bluetooth⇨Off.**

Carrier

This setting appears on GSM models (such as the AT&T iPhone or an unlocked iPhone) when you are outside your service provider's network. Tap Carrier and choose the network you want to use. You may incur Roaming Charges when you use a different network.

Choose which apps use cellular data in Settings➪General➪Cellular.

GPS

iPhone's built-in GPS or Global Positioning System sensor determines your location. Apps like Compass use GPS to find true north, and Maps pinpoints where you are in relation to where you want to go, or where you came from. The Camera uses GPS to do geotagging, which is adding the location to a photo when it's taken. Reminders uses GPS to provide location-based alerts. The GPS is accessed when you check-in to some third-party apps or social networks. To learn more about using the Compass and Maps apps, go to Book IV, Chapter 3. We explain everything about the Camera in Book V, Chapter 1.

To turn the GPS sensor on

1. **Tap Settings on the Home screen.**

2. **Tap Privacy➪Location Services.**

3. **Tap the toggle switch to turn Location Services on.**

   The screen displays a list of the apps that find Location Services useful. You can select which apps you want to give that option to, as shown in Figure 2-8. We explain other features and functions of Location Services in Book I, Chapter 4.

Figure 2-8: The Location Services list displays apps that use the GPS sensor.

The Location Services icon appears in the status bar when you are using an app that uses it.

Printing from your iPhone

The utopian idea of a paperless society may be near, but it hasn't arrived yet. Words and images on a piece of paper are sometimes necessary. AirPrint enables your iPhone to print directly to an AirPrint-enabled printer. Many types of files can be printed: e-mail messages and any readable attachments, photos, web pages, even PDFs. Apps you download from the App Store may also support AirPrint. AirPrint couldn't be easier. Here are the steps to take to print from your phone:

1. **Make sure the printer you want to use is on the same Wi-Fi network that your iPhone is connected to.**

2. **On your iPhone, open the document you want to print.**

3. **Tap the forward or action button, depending on which app you want to print from.**

4. **Tap the Print button.**

   The Printer Options screen opens, as you can see in Figure 2-9.

5. **Tap the Printer button to select the printer you want to use.**

   Another screen opens, showing the printers that are available in the Wi-Fi vicinity.

6. **Tap the printer you want to use and then tap the Printer Options button at the top left of the screen.**

7. **Select the number of copies you want to print by tapping the plus and minus buttons.**

   Depending on the app and the printer, you may also have the option to choose double-sided printing and/or a range of pages.

8. **Tap Print, and walk over to the printer to pick up your page.**

Figure 2-9: Choose your printer and the number of copies from the Printer Options screen.

Adjusting Accessibility Options for Easier Operation

With the Accessibility settings, Apple addresses the physical challenges that some users might have with iPhone's interface. They've created optional features that customize the interface to make iPhone more accessible. From the Home screen, tap Settings⇨General and then scroll down to Accessibility. You see the screen in Figure 2-10. We recommend that you consult Chapter 32 of iPhone's User Guide (`manuals.info.apple.com/en_US/iphone_ user_guide.pdf`) for complete instructions on how to get the most out of the Accessibility features. The features are divided into four categories: Vision, Hearing, Learning, and Physical & Motor. Here we briefly explain each feature:

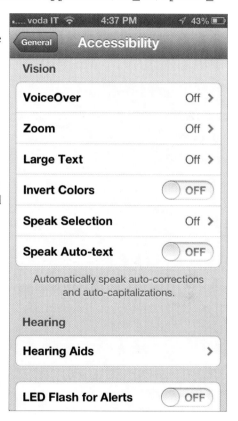

✓ **VoiceOver:** Turn this setting on to hear an audible description of the buttons on the screen. With some practice, vision-impaired iPhone users can learn the tapping, double-clicking, and flicking movements necessary to use apps. Within VoiceOver, you can adjust the speaking rate, attach a Braille device, select which parts of a web screen you wish to have read, and which language you want VoiceOver to speak.

✓ **Zoom:** The Zoom feature enlarges the entire iPhone screen when you double-tap with three fingers. Use three fingers to move from left to right on the screen and one finger to move the screen up and down. Double-tap again with three fingers to return to normal size.

Figure 2-10: Customize Accessibility functions to make the most of your iPhone user experience.

You can't use VoiceOver and Zoom simultaneously.

✓ **Large Text:** Tap the Large Text switch and a list of text sizes from 20 point to 56 point text appears. Tap the size you wish to use. Your choice is reflected in Calendar, Contacts, Mail, Messages, and Notes.

- **Invert Colors:** Turn this feature on and all color on the display is inverted, like a photo negative.

- **Speak Selection:** Turn this feature on to have iPhone read selected text out loud, even if VoiceOver is turned off.

- **Speak Auto-text:** Corrections iPhone makes automatically while you're typing are spoken out loud if this function is turned on.

- **Hearing Aids:** For those who use a hearing aid, turning this feature on may reduce interference.

- **LED Flash for Alerts:** When this feature is turned on, the LED next to the camera lens on the back of your iPhone flashes when iPhone is locked or asleep. It works whether the ring volume is on or not.

- **Mono Audio:** This feature changes the left and right sound channels into a mono channel that comes through both sides so those who can hear with only one ear hear both parts.

- **Guided Access:** Lets you limit iPhone use to one app and even limit features within that app so someone with attention or learning disabilities can stay focused on one task.

- **AssistiveTouch:** Lets you use an adaptive accessory, such as a joystick, to control your iPhone. You can also adjust tracking speed or create custom gestures to make them easier.

- **Home-Click Speed:** Adjust the double- and triple-click speed of the Home button.

- **Incoming Calls:** Lets you designate the headset or speaker as the default device for incoming calls.

- **Triple-click Home:** You can choose to associate a triple-click of the Home button with one of three Accessibility functions: VoiceOver, Zoom, or White on Black.

Other Accessibility Features

While the functions controlled by the Accessibility settings are reflected across iPhone, some apps contain accessibility features that are specific to those apps. Here are some:

- **Custom Ringtones and Vibrations:** Create and assign unique ringtones and vibration patterns for individual contacts in Contacts. Refer to Book IV, Chapter 1 to learn about the Contacts app.

- **Closed Captioning:** Go to Settings⚐Video and turn on Closed Captioning.

 ✔ **Voice Control:** Press and hold the Home button on your iPhone, the center button on iPhone's headset, or the button on a Bluetooth headset to open Voice Control. You can ask iPhone to call a person, tell you what time it is, or play a song in Music. On iPhone 4S or later, Siri, if enabled, performs the Voice Control functions.

 ✔ **Visual Voicemail:** This feature is explained more in Book III, Chapter 1. In a nutshell, iPhone adds pause and playback functions to voicemail messages and allows you to check your messages in any order you wish.

 ✔ **Minimum Font Size for Mail Messages:** With the settings for Mail, you can establish a minimum font size to make Mail messages easier to read.

 ✔ **Widescreen Keyboard:** Many apps that use the keyboard let you turn your iPhone to landscape position to use a wider keyboard.

 ✔ **TTY Support:** You can add a TTY adapter to attach a Teletype machine to your iPhone.

Adjust the Accessibility settings from iTunes by connecting your iPhone to your computer with the USB cable. Open iTunes, and click the Configure Universal Access button under Options.

Chapter 3: Controlling the Multitouch and Voice Recognition Interfaces

In This Chapter

✓ Learning the moves: tapping, flicking, and zooming

✓ Leaving Home and going Home again

✓ Organizing apps and folders every which way you can

✓ Talking to your iPhone

✓ Commandeering the keyboard

✓ Searching here, there, and everywhere

*I*f you activated your iPhone and explored some of the options as we discussed in the first two chapters of this book, you've already intuitively used a couple of the multitouch gestures — tap and possibly scroll. You also used the keyboard to type your Apple ID and maybe you tried talking to Siri.

In this chapter, we formally introduce you to all of iPhone's gestures, and show you how they work. We give you examples of when and where to use them. We explain how the Home screen is organized and what the Home button does, and show you how to organize apps and folders on the Home screen. We then introduce you to Siri, your iPhone's voice-commanded virtual assistant. We tell you how to tell Siri to make a phone call, give you directions, settle a sports bet, and a dozen or so other tasks. For the times when you don't have Wi-Fi or if you're using an iPhone 4 or earlier, we explain the Voice Control option. We give you a guided tour of the keyboard, and we give you some tricks that can make typing and editing easier. At the end of the chapter, we show you how to use Spotlight Search so you can find apps, phone numbers, music, and more on your iPhone and beyond.

Learning the Moves

You've probably been using touchscreens for a decade or more and not really noticed. Many ATMs are touch screen, when you pay with a credit card at a large store you sign on the screen and then tap OK with the stylus. Your iPhone's touchscreen is similar. You need just a few good moves to make iPhone do all the things you're used to doing with a phone and more. These are the finger gestures that control everything on your iPhone:

- **Tapping:** A tap is lighter than pressing a button. It's a quick touch without any holding. Tap an app button on the Home screen to open the app. Tap an item in a list to select it. Variations on tapping are

    - **Double-tap:** Two quick taps zoom in and zoom out of a web page, e-mail message, or photos. A double-tap also changes the Shift key to a Caps Lock key if you enable that function in Settings⟳General⟳ Keyboard. A single tap zooms in on a map, but to zoom out on a map, you need to do the . . .

    - **Two-finger tap:** On a map in the Maps app, a two-finger tap zooms out of the map; tap twice with a single finger to zoom in again.

- **Scrolling:** Scrolling is a dragging motion done with one finger, or more if that's more comfortable for you. You can even rest one finger on the screen and scroll with another one. Touch the screen and drag up or down. In some apps and websites, you can scroll left or right, too. Scrolling is most often used to go through a list, such as Contacts, or to rotate a rotor like the one used to set the alarm clock, which we explain in Book IV, Chapter 2. Scrolling doesn't select or open anything, it only moves the list. You must tap to select.

- **Pulling:** Pulling is a scroll with a specific starting point. Place your fingertip on the status bar and pull down to open the Notification Center or pull your list of messages down as far as they go. They refresh.

- **Flicking:** Touch your finger to the screen and quickly flick it up, or left, or right, and down. Flicking left and right on the Home screen moves to the next or previous screen. Flicking in a list, instead of scrolling, moves the list up and down more quickly. You can wait for it to stop or tap when you see what you're looking for, and then tap the item you want to select.

Your iPhone has many options to make gestures easier for people with visual, auditory, or manual dexterity challenges. You adjust those settings by going to Settings⟳General⟳Accessibility. Read about them in Book I, Chapter 2.

- **Zooming in and out:** Pinch and spread (unpinch) two fingers together or apart to zoom out and in on photos, web pages, and other elements.

✔ **Sliding:** Slider bars show up when you want to turn your iPhone on or off or wake it from sleep. They also appear on the lock screen when your iPhone rings, as shown in Figure 3-1. Touch and hold the slider bar on the arrow on the left and slide your finger across the bar to the right. The action listed on the slider bar happens.

✔ **Pressing:** Press the physical buttons on your iPhone: the Home, the On/Off Sleep/Wake, or the volume buttons. You switch the Silent/Ring button on and off. We explain these buttons in Book I, Chapter 2.

✔ **Double-clicking:** Double-clicking the Home button reveals the multitasking bar at the bottom of the screen, which shows apps that are running. You can then tap the app you want to switch to.

✔ **Triple-click Home:** Press the Home button three times to activate functions that are selected in Accessibility Settings: VoiceOver, Invert Colors, Zoom, and/or AssistiveTouch.

Figure 3-1: Use the sliding move on slider bars, mostly to unlock your iPhone.

Home, Away from Home, and Home Again

The Home screen is what you see when your iPhone is awake and you aren't using an app. The Home screen is actually more than one screen. You move between one Home screen and the next by flicking left to go to the next screen to the right and flicking right to go back. You can have up to eleven Home screens.

The round, slightly depressed button centered beneath the screen is the Home button. When you press this button, four things may happen, depending on your point of departure:

✓ From an open app, you return to the Home screen you most recently viewed, so if you tap an app on the fifth Home screen and then press the Home button, you return to the fifth Home screen.

✓ From the second to the eleventh Home screen (if you have multiple Home screens), you return to the first Home screen.

✓ From the first Home screen, you go to the Spotlight Search screen.

✓ From the Spotlight Search screen, you return to the Home screen.

If your iPhone is sleeping or locked when you press the Home button, a slider bar appears that reads Slide to Unlock. Refer to Figure 3-1. Touch the arrow and slide your finger across this slider in the direction the arrow is pointing, and the last screen you were viewing appears. It could be a Home screen or a running app.

Going from top to bottom, the Home screen has a status bar that tells you about the various connections your iPhone is tapped into at the moment, as well as the current time of day. We explain the status bar icons in Book I, Chapter 2. Below the status bar are 20 spaces for apps or app folders (16 on iPhone 4S or earlier). We go over folders in the "Organizing Apps and Folders" section later in this chapter. At the bottom of the screen, you see up to four more app buttons. This area is known as the *Dock*. Place four app buttons you use frequently there, and they appear in a fixed position at the bottom of every Home screen. Figure 3-2 shows the first and second Home screen on Barbara's iPhone. Notice that both screens have Phone, Mail, Safari, and Music in the Dock, which are the four preset Dock apps.

You can also create a widget, which is an icon that links to a specific web page in Safari. The widget appears on your Home screen and when tapped, automatically opens the web page it's linked to. Refer to Book III, Chapter 3.

There's one other part to the Home screen. Those tiny gray and white dots floating just above the Dock indicate how many Home screens you have. The white dot tells you which screen you're on. See how it moves from the first to the second position in Figure 3-2. If you look closely, you see a teensy magnifying glass to the very left of the dots. This represents the Spotlight search screen. Flick to the right from the first Home screen and a search screen opens. We explain searching in the section "Shining a light on Spotlight searches" later in this chapter.

Dots indicate Home screens   Dock apps

Figure 3-2: The four apps in the Dock remain in the same position when you move from one Home screen to another.

Launching and Managing Apps

Apps, short for applications, are the programs on your iPhone. Book I, Chapter 4 summarizes the apps that come with your iPhone, and other chapters throughout the book cover each app in depth. The online bonus content for this book presents some third-party apps we think you'll like. (See this book's Introduction for more about the bonus content.) Here, we tell you how to launch and close apps, and how to organize the app buttons on your Home screen.

Launching apps

To launch or open an app on the Home screen, tap the app icon. You can also ask Siri to open an app for you. You may see icons that have a white outline border; these are folders, which can contain up to sixteen apps (12 on iPhone 4S and earlier). To launch an app that resides in a folder, tap the folder. It opens. Tap the app button you want to launch. To close the folder, tap it or the Home screen.

Switching between apps

Instead of opening an app, closing it, returning to the Home screen, and then opening another app, you can have multiple apps open at the same time — although you just see one app at a time on your screen. When you double-click the Home button, the screen shifts up, as in Figure 3-3. Four app buttons appear beneath the active screen in the multitasking bar. These are the apps that you most recently used that haven't been shut down. This is especially helpful when you want to cut and paste from one app to another, which we explain in the section about using the keyboard.

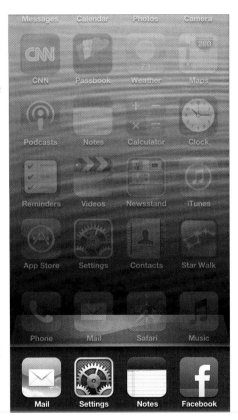

Although you see four at a time, up to 50 can be open. Flick left and right to move through the app buttons. Tap the button for the app you want to switch to or tap the screen to return to the active app. Flick left to right from the first screen to reveal the orientation lock button and music and video playback controls.

Figure 3-3: The multitasking bar lets you switch between open apps without returning to the Home screen.

Closing apps

To quit apps and remove them from the multitasking bar, press and hold one of the app buttons in the multitasking bar. All of them start to wiggle and shake, and a minus sign in a red circle appears on the left shoulder of each app icon. Tap the minus sign and the app closes. The remaining app buttons shift to fill in the space. Press the Home button when you've finished closing apps and they stop wiggling.

TIP

Although Apple insists you don't need to quit apps you're no longer using, some apps — like the National Public Radio (NPR) app, for instance — do continue using some of iPhone's available memory, processing brainpower, and battery when it's in the multitasking bar, even when you aren't using it. Call us obsessively compulsive, but both of us authors regularly double-click the Home button and close apps we aren't using.

Organizing Apps and Folders

Your iPhone comes with the included apps displayed on the first two Home screens. You may want to rearrange the apps so that the ones you use most frequently are at the top of the Home screen, you may want to group similar apps in a folder, or you may want to change the apps that are in the Dock. As you add new apps, you'll want to arrange them in a way that makes sense to you. You can move apps around on your iPhone and from iTunes.

Organizing apps on your iPhone

To organize apps from your iPhone, follow these steps:

1. **Press and hold any app button on your Home screen.**

   This part is fun, especially if you're new to iPhone. Try it — we'll wait.

2. **Any of the apps that have circled Xs on the upper left corner can be deleted. To delete an app, just tap the circled X.**

   A message opens asking if you really want to delete that app, as shown in Figure 3-4. Tap the appropriate button: Delete, if you want to delete that app, or Cancel, if you tapped the circled X by mistake.

   Don't worry — if you delete an app by mistake, iTunes maintains a copy of all your apps, free or purchased, so you can reinstall it but you could lose

Figure 3-4: A notification message asks for confirmation before deleting an app.

data or documents created with the app if they aren't backed up to your computer or iCloud.

 The Apple apps that came with your iPhone can't be deleted although you can place ones you don't use in a folder so they're out of sight and some of them may be hidden by turning on Restrictions as explained later in this chapter.

3. **Touch and drag the app buttons around to arrange them in a way you like, even from one Home screen to another.**

   The Photos app button is being moved in Figure 3-5.

4. **To change the four apps that are in the Dock, you first have to drag one out, and then you can replace it with another app.**

   You don't have to have four apps in the Dock. If you prefer three or two or none, you can move the buttons out of the Dock onto a Home screen. Or you can place up to four folders on the Dock instead of single apps.

 Even if you choose to delete an app from your iPhone, it remains in iTunes on your computer and even if you delete it from your computer, iTunes keeps a record of which apps you download and install so you can re-install later, as long as the app is still available. You never know if you might want to use removed apps at a later date.

Figure 3-5: Drag the app icon to the position you want.

Folders

Folders give you the option of putting like-minded apps together in one place so you can find them quickly and easily.

Adding folders

To add a folder, press and hold your finger on an app on the Home screen until they start a-wigglin' and a-jigglin'. Then, follow these steps:

1. **Lift your finger.**

2. **Touch and drag one app button over another app button.**

   A square is formed around both apps and their icons are greatly reduced. The folder opens beneath the square, as shown in Figure 3-6.

3. **If you want to add another app to the folder, tap the folder.**

   The folder closes.

4. **Touch and drag another app into the folder.**

5. **Tap the Home button to save the new folder.**

If a folder has already been created but you want to add apps to it, press and hold an app to make them wiggle and then drag the app you want into the folder. To remove apps, while the apps are wiggling, tap the folder you want to change to open it. Drag apps out of the folder onto the Home screen. A folder is automatically deleted when all apps are moved out and it's empty.

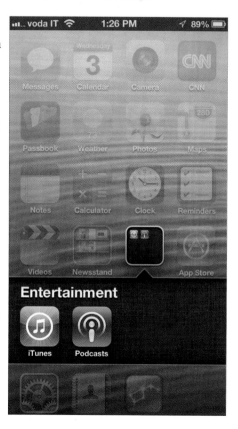

Figure 3-6: Drag one app over another to create a folder that holds up to 16 apps.

Renaming folders

iPhone assigns a name it thinks is appropriate by default, such as Utilities, Productivity, Lifestyle, or Entertainment, based on the kinds of apps you put in the folder, but you can change the name with these steps:

1. **Press and hold an app on the Home screen.**

2. **Tap the wiggling folder whose name you want to edit.**

3. **Tap the circled X on the right of the field where the name is written.**

   The field is erased. A cursor appears at the beginning of the field and the keyboard opens.

4. Tap out the name you wish to give this folder.

5. Tap the Done key on the bottom right of the keyboard.

6. Tap outside the folder to close it.

The buttons are still wiggling.

7. Tap the Home button to save the renamed folder.

Each Home screen on an iPhone 5 can hold 20 apps or app folders. Each app folder can hold up to 16 apps. Add four app folders containing 16 apps each on the Dock, and some quick multiplication and addition results in the possibility of 3,584 apps on your iPhone! Actually, that's how many app *icons* you can have on your iPhone. You can have as many *apps* as your iPhone's memory will hold. You can find them with Spotlight even if you don't see them on the Home screen.

If your apps folder has a badge on the upper right corner, the number on the badge is a cumulative number of items that need attending to, such as unread messages, app updates, or information updates.

When you have a lot of apps and folders, moving them around from screen to screen can be tedious. Luckily, you can also organize your Home screens, apps, and folders in iTunes. (See Figure 3-7.) Connect your iPhone to your computer with the USB connector cable, select your iPhone and then Apps. Move things around as you would on your iPhone but with the ease of the trackpad or mouse. After you make your changes and the Home screens are organized, click the Sync button to sync your changes with your iPhone.

Figure 3-7: Organize your apps and folders via iTunes.

Switching Between Portrait and Landscape Views

You might have noticed that if you rotate your iPhone 90 degrees to the left or right, the screen rotates too. This is considered switching between a portrait, or vertical, view and a landscape, or horizontal, view. Many games, as well as movies viewed in Videos, work only in landscape view. Some apps and the Home screen work only in portrait view. The supplied apps that can be viewed in both portrait and landscape are Safari, Mail, Messages, Maps, Notes, Contacts, Stocks, Photos, Camera, Calculator (changes to a scientific calculator in landscape view), Calendar (changes to a multiday calendar in landscape view), and Music in playback mode.

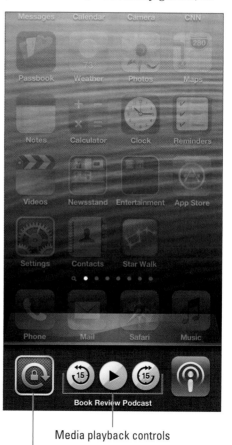

You can lock your iPhone so it stays in portrait view by doing the following:

1. **Double-click the Home button to open the multitasking bar.**

2. **Flick to the right to go beyond the first set of four app buttons.**

   Two controls open: the Portrait Orientation Lock button and the media playback controls.

3. **Tap the Portrait Orientation Lock button.**

   A lock appears to show that Portrait Orientation Lock is on and the same icon appears in the status bar to remind you it's on. See Figure 3-8.

4. **Repeat the steps to turn Portrait Orientation Lock off.**

Media playback controls

Portrait Orientation lock

Figure 3-8: The Portrait Lock and media playback controls are to the left of the first multitasking bar.

Commandeering the Keyboard

For many iPhone users, the keyboard is the hardest thing to get used to. You may think the keys are too small for your fingers. However, with a little practice, the keyboard becomes second nature in no time. Any time you tap in a blank field, the keyboard opens and a blinking cursor appears in that empty field. This occurs in apps like Mail, Messages, Notes, or when you're filling out a form on a web page in Safari, and when you're adding contacts and calendar entries when using those respective apps.

The keyboard functions we describe here work in any app that uses the keyboard so, like most things iPhone, after you hone your skills in one app, they apply across the board in all your iPhone apps.

Keyboard settings

The default keyboard has the classic QWERTY format that you may have learned in high school typing class — that's where we learned how to touch type. If you write in a language other than English, however, you'll want to add a keyboard that reflects the language you want to type in — and recognizes words in that preferred language. You'll get crazy suggestions if you type in Swedish with an English keyboard and dictionary. You also have some other optional keyboard functions that you activate, or deactivate, in Settings. Read below to learn about your options and follow these steps to change them:

1. **Tap Settings on the Home screen.**

2. **Tap General⟳Keyboard.**

   The screen shown in Figure 3-9 opens.

3. **Tap the toggle switch to turn the function on or off.**

   - **Auto-Capitalization:** Automatically capitalizes the letter "I" when it stands alone and capitalizes the first letter after any punctuation that iPhone recognizes as a new sentence. If you use Emoji, this function also capitalizes the first letter after you insert a smiley face, heart, or one of the other myriad icons.

   - **Auto-Correction:** Automatically corrects words as you are typing using iPhone's built-in dictionary. For example, as in Figure 3-10, if you type **nyprs**, "notes" appears in a box beneath the word. If you tap the space bar, the return key, or a punctuation key, the suggestion is accepted; tap the X on the box, or just keep typing to complete your word, and your typed word remains. The dictionary automatically adds names from Contacts so it recognizes many names you type. Your iPhone learns your idiosyncrasies, adding words you type frequently, that it doesn't know, to the dictionary.

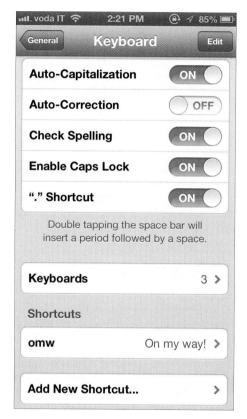

Figure 3-9: The Keyboard settings let you control automatic keyboard functions.

Figure 3-10: Turn Auto-Correction on to get suggestions for presumed typing errors.

- **Check Spelling:** iPhone underlines words it thinks are spelled wrong. Tap the underlined word and iPhone shows you possible replacement words. Tap the one you want or tap elsewhere on the screen to decline. If iPhone thinks the word is spelled wrong but doesn't have a suggestion, a flag reads No Replacement Found and you have to correct the word, if necessary, on your own.

- **Enable Caps Lock:** When this is on, you can quickly tap twice on the shift key and it changes to a caps lock key.

- **"." Shortcut:** Double-tapping the space bar inserts a period and then one space. This feature is very handy as you tap the same key — the space bar— twice rather than changing the keyboard layout, tapping the period, changing the keyboard back again, and then tapping the space bar.

4. **To change the keyboard layout, tap Keyboards.**

5. **Tap English or whichever language's keyboard you wish to edit.**

   Most languages have optional keyboard layouts. The screen opens (refer to Figure 3-11) and displays options for the Software Keyboard Layout, that is the keyboard on your iPhone, and for a Hardware Keyboard Layout, which is a peripheral keyboard that you use with your iPhone. You can choose the Software Keyboard Layout you're used to using. Choose the Hardware Keyboard Layout that corresponds to the type of peripheral keyboard you use with your iPhone.

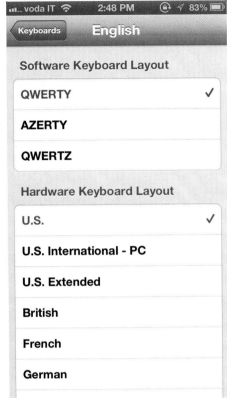

6. **Tap Keyboards in the upper left to return to the Keyboards settings.**

7. **Tap Add New Keyboard to add another language-specific keyboard.**

   A list of languages opens. Many languages have multiple options, such as the Chinese handwriting option or the Swiss or Canadian French option.

8. **Tap the language you want to add.**

   It automatically appears in the list of keyboards.

Figure 3-11: Choose the Software Keyboard Layout that suits you; the Hardware Keyboard Layout should match that of the peripheral keyboard you use.

9. **Repeat steps 7 and 8 to add other languages or tap Keyboard in the upper left to return to the Keyboard settings.**

   To delete a language, tap Edit, and then tap the red and white minus sign to the left of the language. Tap the Delete button that appears. To rearrange the order of the languages, touch and drag the rearrange button (it looks like three stacked horizontal lines) to move the languages to the order you want.

10. **Tap Add New Shortcut.**

Shortcuts let you type a few letters that your iPhone interprets and expands into a longer phrase. For example, type **omw** in a message and it becomes "On my way!" Type your text in the Phrase and Shortcut text fields and then tap Save.

If you add a word or phrase to Shortcuts without typing in the shortcut, the word or phrase is added to your Personal Dictionary and iPhone won't make suggestions for correcting it.

When you turn Documents and Data on in iCloud, your shortcuts sync between iOS devices. PDC! (That's short for "pretty darn cool.")

11. **Tap Keyboard in the upper left, General in the upper left, and then Settings in the upper left to return to the main Settings screen.**

**Book I
Chapter 3**

Controlling the
Multitouch and Voice
Recognition Interfaces

If you have more than one language activated, the keyboard includes a globe button appearing at the bottom of the keyboard. Tap the globe button to switch between languages. Tap and hold the globe button to see a pop-up list of languages you added and then slide to select the language, as shown in Figure 3-12.

Typing tips

Apple suggests, and we concur, that you begin typing with one index finger, probably that of your dominant hand, and gradually move up to two-finger or two-thumb typing. When you tap a key, the letter appears enlarged on the screen so you know which key you actually hit. If it's the letter you want, just lift your finger and that letter appears on the message, note, or field you're typing in. If it's not the letter you want, without lifting your finger, slide your finger to the key of the letter you want. As you slide, the enlarged letter changes to show which key your finger is on.

Figure 3-12: Tap and hold the globe button to choose from languages you activate on your iPhone.

As you become familiar with the tap typing technique with your index finger, you may want to try putting iPhone on a flat surface and typing with two index fingers. In the landscape position, you can hold your iPhone with both hands, placing your thumbs at the bottom and your middle fingers at the top. Use both index fingers to type.

For thumb-typing in either portrait or landscape position, cradle your iPhone in both hands, keeping them slightly relaxed, and use your thumbs to type. Say you're standing on a moving bus and have to hold on, leaving only one hand free to type an urgent message. With practice, you can cradle your iPhone in one hand and type with the cradling hand's thumb.

Turning your iPhone to landscape orientation makes the keyboard wider and the keys slightly bigger; however, the field where you are typing is smaller.

After you get going, iPhone uses an algorithm to predict the word you are typing so zones of letters imperceptibly increase in size to increase the probability that you hit the letter you want.

Keyboard layouts

Looking at the keyboard in Figure 3-13, moving top to bottom, left to right, you see the letters of the alphabet, the shift key, the delete key, the ABC/123 key, the globe key (if you've added a language), the microphone key (if you have an iPhone 4S or later), the space bar, and a return key. The keyboard changes slightly depending on what function you want to perform. When you are in a To field in Mail or in the URL field in Safari, the space bar shrinks to allow two more buttons next to it: an at (@) button and a dot (.) button. This makes typing an e-mail or website address easier. The Return key becomes the Search button in Spotlight and a Go button in Safari. In addition to these visible changes that make typing easier, there are some invisible shortcuts:

Figure 3-13: Familiarizing yourself with the keyboard layouts makes typing faster and more efficient.

✔ Double-tap the shift key to turn it into a caps-lock key so you can type in ALL CAPS. You have to turn this option on in the Keyboard settings.

✔ Tap the delete key once to delete one character to the left. Tap and hold the delete key and it begins deleting one letter after another. If you continue holding, it deletes whole words at once.

✔ Hold the ABC key and slide your finger to the symbol or number you wish to type. The character is typed but the keyboard reverts to letters.

✔ When the cursor is in the To field and you have the space, at, and dot buttons, touch and hold the dot key and a small window opens offering an assortment of the most common web suffixes: .com, .net, .edu, .org, and so on. If you've added an international keyboard, the local suffixes are included, for example .it for Italy and .eu for European Union.

✔ Tap the 123 key to change the keyboard to show numbers, as seen in Figure 3-14. The shift key changes to a symbols key; the 123 key changes to an ABC key. Tap the symbols key and the top row of the keyboard where the numbers were changes to show more symbols, as shown in Figure 3-14. Tap the ABC/123 key to return to the alphabet keyboard; tap the symbols key to switch between numbers and symbols.

Figure 3-14: The letters change to numbers when you tap the ABC/123 key and the numbers change to symbols when you tap the symbols key.

Some of the letters, when held, give non-English options, and some of the numbers and symbols give multiple options as well, as shown in Table 3-1. These options are from the U.S. English keyboard and may change when you change the keyboard language.

Table 3-1	Special Characters
Key Pressed	*Special Character*
A or a	à á â ä æ ã å ā
C or c	ç ć č
E or e	è é ê ë ē ẽ ę
I or i	Ì ¡ ī í ï î
L or l	ł
O or o	ō ō ø œ ó ò ö ô
N or n	ń ñ
S or s	ß ś š
U or u	ū ú ù ü û
Y or y	ÿ
Z or z	ž ź ż
Period	Ellipsis (…)
Question mark (?)	Upside-down question mark
Exclamation point (!)	Upside-down exclamation point
Apostrophe (')	Smart single quote and simple single quote
Hyphen/minus sign (–)	Em dash (—)
Dollar sign ($)	¥, €, ¢, £, ₩
Ampersand (&)	§
Quote (")	Left bracket, right bracket, lower quote, left and right smart quotes, simple quote
Percentage (found when you tap the symbols button after tapping the numbers button) %	‰

Editing Your Text

iPhone lets you type on a full keyboard in multiple languages. Messages and Mail offer character-limit-free SMS and e-mail functions, while Notes, Reminders, Contacts, and Calendar, not to mention document creation apps like iA Writer and Pages, give you plenty of opportunites to write and edit text. All this text means more chances of making mistakes, changing your mind, and wanting to move sentences around — in other words, you want to edit your text. iPhone has the basic editing capabilities of copy, cut, and paste, select or select all, even undoing and redoing. In Mail, you can stylize your text by making it bold, italic, or underlined and indent selections of text. We show you how to do each of these tasks in the following sections.

Selecting

You can tap once to insert the cursor somewhere in the middle of your text, and then make changes letter by letter or you can select a word, phrase, paragraph, or the entire text and make changes with this procedure:

1. **Tap the text you want to edit.**

   The keyboard appears and the cursor blinks more or less where you tapped.

2. **Press and hold your finger in the general area where you want to insert the cursor.**

   A magnifying loupe appears over the text with the cursor in the center.

3. **Drag your finger over the text until the cursor is at the point where you want it.**

4. **Lift your finger.**

   Two buttons appear: Select and Select All.

5. **Tap once to edit with the delete key and keyboard.**

   Select and Select All disappear and the cursor is where you put it.

6. **Tap Select to select the word or portion of the text; tap Select All to select the entire text.**

   The word is highlighted in blue and there are blue grab points on the upper left and lower right corner. (Refer to Figure 3-15.)

   If you select just one word, you can *cut* or *copy* that word, or iPhone can *suggest* synonyms or *define* the selected word — just tap the appropriate button.

7. **To select a portion of the text, touch and drag the blue grab points to select the text you want to cut or copy.**

8. **If you want to delete, press the cut button. If you want to copy or cut, and paste in another location, read on.**

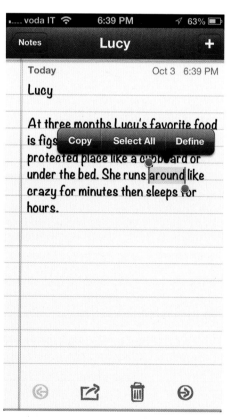

Figure 3-15: Use blue grab points to select the text you want to copy, cut, or replace with a suggested synonym.

Cutting, copying, and pasting

What if you want to copy something from an e-mail message you received and paste it onto an existing list in Notes for future reference? Here's how to copy and paste into an existing document:

1. **Following the previous steps to select the text you want to copy.**

   After you've tapped Select or Select All, a Copy button appears above the highlighted text.

2. **Open the document in the app where you want to place the copied text.**

   If, from our example, Notes is already open, double-click the Home button to open the multitasking bar, and then tap the Notes button. Otherwise, press the Home button to open the Home screen and tap Notes from there.

3. **Tap and hold on the screen where you want to insert the copied text.**

   The magnifying loupe appears, allowing you to move the cursor precisely where you want it.

4. **Lift your finger.**

   A Paste button appears.

5. **Tap the Paste button.**

   Your copied text is now in a new spot.

Copying and pasting isn't only for text within apps like Notes and Mail. You can copy a portion of a web page and paste it into an e-mail. Press and hold the part of the page you want to copy and the blue grabbers come up, along with a Copy button. Drag the grab points to select everything you want to copy, and then tap the Copy button. Open the app where you want to paste the selection. Press and hold until you see the Paste button. Tap Paste.

Undoing and redoing

To undo your edit, shake your iPhone. A message opens with the option to undo the last action or cancel. Tap the Undo button and you're home free. And if you want to redo what you thought you wanted to undo? Just shake your iPhone again and the buttons ask if you want to redo or undo or cancel, as shown in Figure 3-16.

Figure 3-16: Shake your iPhone to undo and redo the last edit you did.

Telling Siri What to Do

Having a personal assistant is no longer just an indispensable luxury for a few busy executives or celebrities. Siri on your iPhone is a close second to her human counterpart. With the latest iOS 6 version of Siri, there are even more tasks you can direct Siri to do. Following is a partial list of things Siri can help you with:

- Make phone calls
- Schedule meetings
- Open apps on your iPhone
- Write messages
- Give turn-by-turn driving directions
- Relay the weather forecast
- Find a restaurant and request reservations
- Use Find My Friends to see where the people you know are hanging out
- Tell you the score for last night's game and statistics for your favorite player
- Find the nearest movie theater, tell you what's playing, and buy tickets
- Play requested music
- Write your grocery list
- Set up reminders
- Make coffee and take out the trash — just checking if you were paying attention!

Siri requires an Internet connection. When you ask Siri to do something for you, the request is sent to the remote Siri server, which interprets your request and sends the answer back. Siri's response speed depends on the speed of your Internet connection. If you have a 3G or EDGE connection, the action will take longer (sometimes up to 10 seconds) than when you have a Wi-Fi or LTE connection.

To use Siri, first you have to turn it on by following these steps. While you're in Settings, you can adjust some of the Siri settings:

1. **Tap Settings⇨General⇨Siri.**

2. **Tap On to turn Siri on.**

3. **Adjust the following optional settings:**

   - Tap Language and then tap the language you want to use to speak to Siri.

- Tap Voice Feedback to choose if you want Siri to always repeat what you say. The default is only when you are in Handsfree mode, which is when you speak to Siri while using the headset, a Bluetooth device, or holding your iPhone to your ear.

- My Info tells Siri who you are. Tap it and Contacts opens; select your Info card. Siri also uses people you indicate as related to better understand your commands. See Book IV, Chapter 1 to learn how to use Contacts.

- Raise to Speak is a great way to use Siri in public. Tap On. When your iPhone is awake, even if the screen is locked, hold your iPhone upright in your hand and then bring it to your ear, you hear two rapid beeps to let you know Siri is ready to listen. Speak your request.

4. **Tap General and then Settings to return to the main Settings screen or press the Home button to return to the Home screen.**

To talk to Siri, do the following:

1. **Press and hold the Home button, the center button on the earphones, or the button on your Bluetooth headset, until the Siri screen opens.**

   You can do this from the Home screen or from within an app. Siri knows what you're doing and responds appropriately.

   Or, if you turned Raise to Speak On, press the Home button or the Sleep/Wake button to wake your iPhone and then bring your iPhone to your ear.

2. **Two rapid beeps let you know Siri is ready to listen. Following are examples of how Siri uses the apps on your iPhone. You don't have to open the app — just speak when Siri's ready:**

   - *All apps:* Say "Open StarWalk" or "Launch Mail."

   - *Calendar:* View and create events. Ask "Where is my 9 o'clock meeting?" or "Make appointment with Bill Jones for 10 am."

   - *Clock:* Set alarms, start the timer, find out the time in another city. Say "Set timer for 25 minutes." You can also simply ask what time it is.

   - *Contacts:* Ask for information about your contacts. Ask "What's Jim Rose's address?" If you refer to someone by first name only, Siri looks for matches in Favorites in Contacts and in Conversations in Messages, and then repeats the first and last name asking if it's the correct contact. It's quicker and easier to use both first and last names. Enter names of related people on your info card so Siri knows who "Mom" or "sister" are. Book IV, Chapter 1 is about Contacts.

- *Find My Friends:* Ask Siri where your friends are or who's near your current location.

- *Facebook/Twitter:* Ask Siri to post your status update to Facebook or Twitter, just make sure both are activated in Settings.

- *Mail:* Search and send e-mail. Say "E-mail Joe Hutsko about deadline."

- *Maps:* Get directions, find addresses. Ask "Where is the nearest Apple Store?" or "Give me directions from here to Paula's house."

- *Messages:* Read and send SMS and iMessages text messages. Say "Tell Darrin Smith I'm on my way."

- *Movies:* Ask "What movies are playing in Philadelphia?" or "What action films were released this week?"

- *Music:* Play artists, albums, playlists, or songs. Say "Play Blue."

- *Notes:* Create, search, and edit notes. Say "Note tablecloth is 104 by 84."

- *Phone:* Make a phone or FaceTime call. Say "Call Joe Hutsko" or "FaceTime Barbara Boyd."

- *Reminders:* Create, search, and change reminders. Say "Remind me to take book to Jen when I get home."

- *Restaurants:* Say "Make a reservation at Zuni Café for 8 pm Saturday."

- *Safari:* Search the web. Say "Search the web for cold remedies."

- *Sports Information:* Ask "Tell me Pete Rose's best batting average" or "Who won the Pac-10 game last night?"

- *Stocks:* Obtain stock info. Ask "What is the stock price for Apple?"

- *Weather:* Ask for forecasts. Ask "What is today's weather?" or "What's the forecast for Boston next week?"

- *WolframAlpha:* Answer factual, statistical, and mathematical questions. Ask "How fast is the speed of light?"

These are just a few suggestions to demonstrate Siri's vast capabilities, but we encourage you to experiment. Speak as you would to a person and see how resourceful Siri is when it comes to finding answers and assisting you in your day to day tasks.

3. **Siri makes an audible response and displays what was done on your screen, as shown in Figure 3-17 and 3-18.**

   Siri understands different ways of saying the same thing; however, if it's unsure of a command, Siri asks for clarification.

Figure 3-17: Siri reads and displays the response to your request.

Figure 3-18: Siri finds movies and restaurants.

4. **If Siri doesn't understand what you say, you can make corrections by doing the following:**

   - Type corrections in the bubble onscreen that shows what Siri understood or tap the microphone and dictate the correction. Tap Done when you finish.
   - If a word is underlined in blue, tap the word and then choose an alternative from the choices, or tap the microphone to dictate the correction.
   - Tap the microphone to speak to Siri and clarify your request.
   - To correct a message or e-mail before sending, dictate the changes or say "Send it" when it's correct.

5. **To cancel a request, say "Cancel," tap the microphone button, or press the Home button.**

WARNING!

In Settings⇨General⇨Passcode Lock, you can allow access to Siri even when your iPhone is locked. Doing this, however, compromises some of the Passcode Lock's security features.

Siri, take a memo

Any time you want to dictate instead of type, tap the microphone key on the keyboard, dictate, and then tap Done when you finish. Siri understands your dictation best when you dictate punctuation. Pretend you're speaking to a recorder that someone will transcribe. For example, to have Siri type:

Dear John, thank you for the new iPhone 5.

Say: "dear john comma thank you for the new iPhone 5 period"

Likewise to insert paragraphs, quotation marks, and any other punctuation that might be applicable to your dictated missive.

Using Voice Control

If you have an iPhone 4 or earlier or are in an area without Internet service, you can still instruct your iPhone to do simple tasks with Voice Control. Voice Control doesn't work if Siri is turned on; to turn Siri off, tap Settings⇨General⇨Siri⇨Off. Here's how to use Voice Control:

1. **Press and hold the Home button, the center button on the earphones, or the button on your Bluetooth headset, until the Voice Control screen opens, as shown in Figure 3-19.**

   The words that float across the Voice Control screen are suggestions for commands you can give.

   Two quick beeps let you know that Voice Control is ready to listen to your command.

Figure 3-19: You can command your iPhone to call someone, play a song, or tell the time with Voice Control.

2. **Speak the name of the person you want to call (or the artist you want to hear).**

   Voice Control replies with the name it understood. If it found more than one match, it reads off a list of the options. Repeat the option you want.

   If you asked for music, iPhone responds with "Playing songs by *artist's or album name*," and begins playing.

3. **Repeat the option that you want.**

4. **iPhone dials that person.**

   If Voice Control offers an option you don't want, say "No" or "Cancel." Voice Control closes and you have to start over.

Voice Control also tells time. Press and hold the Home button. When Voice Control opens, ask "What time is it?" Voice Control tells you.

Shining a Light on Spotlight Searches

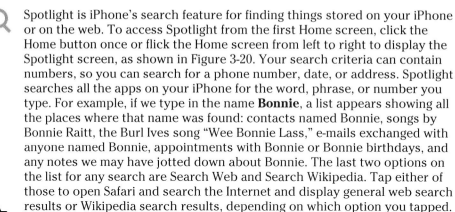

Spotlight is iPhone's search feature for finding things stored on your iPhone or on the web. To access Spotlight from the first Home screen, click the Home button once or flick the Home screen from left to right to display the Spotlight screen, as shown in Figure 3-20. Your search criteria can contain numbers, so you can search for a phone number, date, or address. Spotlight searches all the apps on your iPhone for the word, phrase, or number you type. For example, if we type in the name **Bonnie**, a list appears showing all the places where that name was found: contacts named Bonnie, songs by Bonnie Raitt, the Burl Ives song "Wee Bonnie Lass," e-mails exchanged with anyone named Bonnie, appointments with Bonnie or Bonnie birthdays, and any notes we may have jotted down about Bonnie. The last two options on the list for any search are Search Web and Search Wikipedia. Tap either of those to open Safari and search the Internet and display general web search results or Wikipedia search results, depending on which option you tapped.

If Spotlight finds an app with the word you're searching and it's in a folder, the name of the folder is displayed to the right of the result.

You also have access to Spotlight within many apps using the Spotlight search field at the top of an app's screen. In the Mail, Messages, or Contacts apps, tap the status bar to open Spotlight. In other apps, any time you see the magnifying glass icon, you can tap it to open Spotlight. To search for something within an app, do the following:

1. **Tap in the Spotlight field.**

   If you don't see the Spotlight search field — on app screens that support Spotlight — tap the status bar at the top of iPhone's screen to make the Spotlight search field appear or pull the app screen down to unhide the

Spotlight search field when you don't see it.

The blinking cursor appears and the keyboard opens.

2. Type in your word or phrase and then tap Search.

Spotlight searches within the app you're using and displays any items that match your search criteria.

3. Tap an item in the list to view that item's contents.

When you search from within an app, iPhone searches only in that app — in Mail that means the sender, recipient, and subject line only, not within the messages, and first, last, and company names in Contacts.

You can alter the Spotlight settings to limit your searches to certain apps or priority order in which the apps are searched. To change Spotlight settings,

1. Open Settings⇨General⇨ Spotlight Search.

The Spotlight Search list opens, as seen in Figure 3-21.

Figure 3-20: The Spotlight screen, to the left of the Home screen, searches all the apps on iPhone for occurrences of a word or phrase.

2. Tap the name of the app in the list to make the checkmark on the left appear or disappear.

A checkmark means Spotlight will search that app when looking for something from the Spotlight search screen or within that app.

3. To change the order of the apps, press and hold the re-order icon to the right of the app, and then drag up and down to move it.

Spotlight searches in the apps at the top of the list first when doing a search.

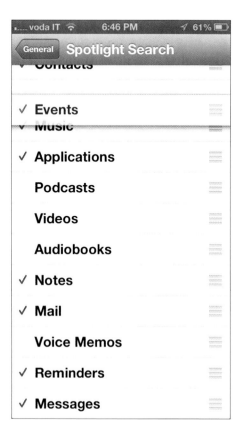

Figure 3-21: Change the priority of your searches in the Spotlight Search settings.

Chapter 4: Touring iPhone's Preloaded Apps and Settings

In This Chapter

✏ **Getting to know preloaded apps**

✏ **Adjusting basic settings to suit your style**

✏ **Invoking iPhone's security and privacy features**

✏ **Averting panic in case your iPhone is lost or stolen**

A s the name implies, your iPhone is first and foremost a cellular phone. Given its Internet capabilities of browsing the web and juggling e-mail, it's also a first-class smartphone. But you're probably starting to realize — if you didn't already know — that it's so much more. The apps that come with your iPhone make it a time and task manager, an address book, a photo album, an e-reader, and GPS navigator. This chapter introduces you to those apps, as well as every other preloaded app. We also show you how to download a few free iPhone apps that don't come preloaded on your iPhone: iBooks, Podcasts, and Find My iPhone.

In this chapter, we also show you how to adjust your iPhone's basic settings to suit your personal style, explain how to activate security features for protecting your iPhone from prying eyes, and introduce you to steps you can take to track down your iPhone (and even remotely erase your personal information) if your beloved gadget is ever lost or stolen.

Tapping into iPhone's Built-in Apps

Right out of the box, your iPhone is preloaded with a gaggle of great apps that can do just about everything except fold your laundry or take your dog for a walk. After you're familiar with your iPhone's user interface and multi-touch gestures, getting acquainted with the basic purpose and features of iPhone's apps can help you choose which apps you want to use right away.

When you turn on your iPhone for the first time, you see iPhone's apps arranged on the first Home screen page in a way Apple's iPhone designers figured probably makes sense for most people, as shown in Figure 4-1. We write about how to organize the Home screen in a way that makes sense to you, in Book I, Chapter 3.

Here's a roll-call rundown of your iPhone's apps, with bite-size descriptions of what each app can do, and pointers to the chapters you can read to learn more about each app:

Figure 4-1: iPhone's main Home screens display built-in apps and app folders.

- **Messages:** Use this app to send, receive, and manage SMS (Short Message Service) text messages, MMS (Multimedia Message Service) messages, and iMessages that can include photos, videos, contact information, web links, and map locations. (See Book III, Chapter 2.)

- **Calendar:** Create, manage, and search events that you can keep in sync with calendars you maintain on your Mac or Windows PC, your other iOS devices, and with any online calendars you access using iCloud, Microsoft Exchange, and Google Calendar accounts. (See Book II, Chapter 1, and Book IV, Chapter 2.)

- **Photos:** View, share, manage, and edit photos and videos captured with your iPhone, copied from your computer, saved from other apps, or downloaded from Photo Stream. Printing photos, viewing photos as a slideshow, assigning a photo to a contact card, or choosing a photo as your iPhone's wallpaper are just a few things you can do with Photos. (See Book V, Chapter 2.)

- **Camera:** Take photos and record videos, share them with others via iMessage and Mail, assign a snapshot to a contact card, and trim and upload videos directly to Twitter and FaceBook. (See Book III, Chapters 2 and 4, and Book V, Chapter 1.)

- **Videos:** Watch and listen to music videos, movies, and TV shows; stream video content to your AppleTV or connect your iPhone to a monitor or HDTV with the Lightning Digital AV adapter. (See Book V, Chapters 2 and 4.)

✔ **Maps:** Locate and view your current location on a map, search for world-wide locations, show traffic conditions, view information about a location, bookmark it or save it as a contact, call a location's phone number (if it's listed), get turn-by-turn directions, and share a location in an e-mail or SMS text message, iMessage, or tweet. (See Book IV, Chapter 3.)

✔ **Weather:** View current weather conditions, a 12-hour hourly forecast, plus a six-day forecast for one or more locations around the world. (See Book IV, Chapter 3.)

✔ **Passbook:** Manage your store cards, coupons, and boarding passes. Present the bar code in Passbook at the cashier or check-in counter to earn points, pay for purchases, and take advantage of discounts. (See Book IV, Chapter 3.)

✔ **Notes:** Create, view, and manage text notes you can sync with your computer using iTunes, or over the air using your iCloud, Gmail, Yahoo!, or Microsoft Exchange account. Copy and paste text to and from notes with other apps and share and print Notes. (See Book II, Chapter 1 and Book IV, Chapter 4.)

✔ **Reminders:** Create and manage an interactive to-do list. Add deadlines and locations, and set up alerts so you know when you have to be somewhere. (See Book IV, Chapter 2.)

✔ **Clock:** View the current time in your present location and other locations with World Clock; use Alarm to wake you up; tap Stopwatch to track a timed event, and use Timer to count down the hours, minutes, and seconds remaining 'til the cows come home. (See Book IV, Chapter 2.)

✔ **Stocks:** Stay on top of stock prices, track trading summaries, and view detailed market data and news. (See Book IV, Chapter 3.)

✔ **Newsstand:** Keep your magazine, newspaper, and journal subscriptions in one place. Connect to the Newsstand store to download the periodical's app and then subscribe in-app.

✔ **iTunes:** Browse, search, preview, and purchase music, movies, TV shows, ringtones, and audio books; rent movies; Genius makes recommendations for music, movies, and TV shows. (See Book V, Chapter 3.)

✔ **App Store:** Search, browse, and read reviews of thousands of apps that you can download for free or a fee. Review and download updates to installed apps you already own. (See Book II, Chapter 2.)

✔ **Game Center:** View and compare your game score rankings and achievements with friends and leaderboard top scores; invite friends and new opponents from around the world to compete in multiplayer games; and find Game Center-savvy games to play. (See Book V, Chapter 4.)

✓ **Utilities (folder):** Not an app, the Utilities icon is actually a folder containing other apps, as shown in Figure 4-2. The following apps may be in the Utilities folder or on the Home screen:

- **Contacts:** Contacts helps you create, view, and manage contact information to keep track of people and company names, addresses, phone numbers, e-mail addresses and instant messaging account names, birthday and anniversary dates, and other contact-related bits of information. (See Book II, Chapter 1 and Book IV, Chapter 1.)

- **Calculator:** Add, subtract, multiply, and divide with the basic keypad, or turn iPhone sideways to reveal a wider-ranging scientific calculator keyboard; copy and paste numbers to and from the calculator display. (See Book IV, Chapter 3.)

- **Compass:** Find out which direction you're facing, view your longitude and latitude coordinates, and switch between True North and Magnetic North bearings. (See Book IV, Chapter 3.)

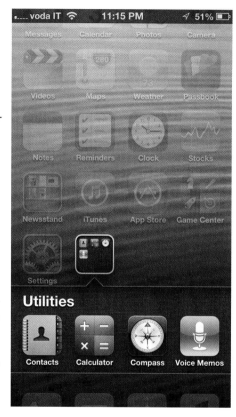

Figure 4-2: Tapping the Utilities folder reveals more apps stored inside the folder.

- **Voice Memos:** Record, replay, and manage spoken or other in-the-moment sounds you want to capture and listen to again (like a friend's live band performance); share your recorded ramblings as e-mail or text messages, and copy them to your computer with iTunes. (See Book II, Chapter 1 and Book IV, Chapter 4.)

✓ **Phone:** Use this app to place and answer calls; create, search, and edit Contacts, record your voicemail personal greeting and listen to, reply to, and manage voicemail messages; make and manage conference calls and FaceTime video chat calls. (See Book III, Chapter 1.)

✓ **Mail:** Send, receive, and manage e-mail messages for multiple e-mail account types, including Gmail, Yahoo!, AOL, and Hotmail. Access and stay in sync with iCloud and Microsoft Exchange e-mail, calendar, and contacts accounts; view, save, and print photo and document attachments; view and save video file attachments. (See Book III, Chapter 2.)

✔ **Safari:** Access and view websites; share links you like; create a reading list that you can return to when you have more time; read without distraction in Reader; switch between web page windows; create and manage bookmarks, and sync your bookmarks between iPhone and Safari or Internet Explorer on your computer; view, save and print web pages, photo files, PDF and other document files. (See Book III, Chapter 3.)

✔ **Music:** Listen to your music and audio books through your iPhone speaker, earphones, Bluetooth speakers, or external speakers connected to your iPhone. (See Book V, Chapters 2 and 3.)

✔ **Nike + iPod:** This app icon won't appear until you turn on the Nike + iPod feature in Settings (tap Settings ➪ Nike + iPod, and then tap the On/Off button). Use this app to record and monitor your walking and running workouts when linked to the Nike + iPod sensor tucked into the foot bed of your Nike+ running shoes (sensor and shoes sold separately); upload your workout data to the Nike+ website to view past workouts and track progress toward your running goals. (See Bonus Chapter 6 on this book's companion website.)

Want the same Nike + iPod workout goodness, minus having to spend big bucks to buy the sensor and sneakers? Head over to iPhone's App Store and install the "Nike+ Running" app (free), which uses your iPhone's built-in GPS feature to track your location, pace, and distance instead of relying on the Nike+ sensor and shoe combo. Although math was always Joe's worst subject, the way he sees it, if $E = MC^2$, then Nike+ = Nike + iPod – \$100 = :-).

Downloading Extra Apple iPhone Apps

The first time you use the App Store app, a notification asks "Would you like to download free Apple apps?" so you may already have some of these apps. If not, you can download them from the App Store.

We write about finding, browsing, installing, and updating apps with the App Store in Book II, Chapter 2.

The following is a rundown of extra Apple apps you can find and download using your iPhone's App Store app:

✔ **iBooks:** iBooks acts as your virtual doorway to Apple's iBookstore, where you can download free classics in e-book form, like *Great Expectations* and *War and Peace*, as well as purchase the latest bestsellers and other e-books. You can also read PDF and other e-pub documents downloaded from other sources such as Project Gutenberg (www.gutenberg.org/). (See Bonus Chapter 5 on this book's companion website.)

✔ **Podcasts:** In previous iOS versions, you listened to podcasts in the Music app. Now, podcasts have their own app with a beautiful interface. Browse the podcast catalog to find audio and video podcasts that interest you and stream, download, and subscribe. (See Book V, Chapter 3.)

✔ **iTunes U:** Like Newsstand, iTunes U manages all your coursework materials, such as videos, podcasts, e-books, and presentations. iTunes U links to the iTunes Store so you can find, subscribe to, and download iTunes U lectures you want to learn from. (See Book V, Chapter 2.)

✔ **Find My iPhone:** In the unhappy event your iPhone is lost or stolen, all may not truly be lost if you have the Find My iPhone feature turned on. The Find My iPhone app is not required to use the Find My iPhone feature, but lets you manage and track other iPhones or iPads. It's just so handy to have on hand to see those other gadgets, or to help a friend who may have misplaced or lost his iPhone. We tell you how to use the Find My iPhone feature and app at the end of this chapter.

✔ **Apple Store:** Browse and order Apple products online and have them shipped to your doorstep — or reserve them at your nearest Apple Store and then drop in to fetch your new goods in person, with directions to the store brought to you by your iPhone's own Map app. The Apple Store app also lets you make a date for One on One training, or reserve a seat at the genius bar or at upcoming events and training workshops.

✔ **Remote:** Taps into your home Wi-Fi network to turn your iPhone into a remote control for browsing and playing content stored in your computer's iTunes library or controlling AppleTV.

✔ **Find My Friends:** Apple's own social network app lets you know where your friends are. Add friends to Find My Friends and a map shows you where they are based on the location of their iOS devices.

Apple also offers several paid apps that are pared down versions of their Mac counterparts: iMovie, GarageBand, iPhoto, and the iWork apps, Pages, Keynote, and Numbers, are sold separately.

Adjusting iPhone's Settings

In browsing through the apps that came with your iPhone, you probably noticed a button called Settings. In Settings, you adjust iPhone's numerous settings to suit your style, including date and time, screen brightness, ringtone, and background wallpaper image options (to name a few). Turn Wi-Fi, cellular, and Bluetooth networking features on and off; tweak individual app settings and choose which ones can access your location or send you notification messages; create and manage e-mail, contacts, calendar, and notes accounts and settings; manage iCloud syncing and backup; and view information about your iPhone's system software, usage, and capacity. Settings is command central for just about everything your iPhone does.

On your journey through this book's many minibooks and chapters, we show you how to access and adjust iPhone's individual app settings on a need-to-know basis. For instance, in Book III, Chapter 1, we show how to adjust iPhone's Phone settings to turn on (or off) features like call forwarding and whether your Caller ID is displayed when you place calls to others.

Some settings, such as the image that appears behind the buttons on the Home screen — referred to as *wallpaper* — can be changed in more than one way. For instance, when you capture a photo with Camera, you can then choose that snapshot as your Home screen or Lock screen (or both) wallpaper image. Using the Photos app to browse images you copied from your computer is another way to change iPhone's wallpaper setting.

In the rest of this chapter, we show you how to change the basic settings you may want to change now or later, straight up, no stumbling-upon necessary.

Tap Settings to display iPhone's list of settings, as shown in Figure 4-3, and then scroll up and down the list and tap on one you want to change. We go through each setting here in order of appearance, and where we don't go into detail, we direct you to the chapter in which it's discussed.

Figure 4-3: Tapping into iPhone's list of Settings.

Airplane Mode

Airplane Mode is one of two top-level settings that feature a single On/Off button rather than the > symbol that, when tapped, displays the selected setting's individual options (and, in some cases, additional sub-settings options for that selected top-level setting).

Think of the Airplane Mode setting as your one-stop, instant-cut-off switch for immediately disconnecting every one of your iPhone's wireless connection "cords" in one fell swoop.

When turned on, the airplane icon appears in the status bar, indicating Airplane Mode's "no fly" zone is in effect.

This setting is called Airplane Mode because nearly every airline requires that you turn off all wireless devices while your journey is underway. In the case of your iPhone, hitting the Airplane Mode switch turns off the following wireless connection features:

- ✓ **Cellular voice and data**
- ✓ **Wi-Fi**
- ✓ **Bluetooth**

When Airplane Mode is on, you can't make or receive phone calls or messages, or browse the web or check your e-mail. Nor can you use wireless Bluetooth accessories like Apple's Bluetooth Wireless Keyboard, headsets, and headphones.

But that doesn't mean you can't use your iPhone to do things like listen to music or watch a movie (with wired earphones so as not to disturb fellow passengers, of course), read an e-book in iBooks, or play a favorite game.

Although most airlines require you to turn off wireless features on devices like notebook computers and smartphones like your iPhone, some airlines that offer in-flight Wi-Fi networks do let you turn on your gadget's Wi-Fi option to connect to the network while you're high in the sky. In those instances, you can turn on Airplane Mode to turn off your iPhone's wireless features, and then turn the Wi-Fi setting back on.

Wi-Fi, Bluetooth, Personal Hotspot, Carrier

These settings are presented in the "Making Connections" section of Book I, Chapter 2.

Do Not Disturb

Barbara uses Do Not Disturb on a daily, er, nightly, basis. Living in one time zone and working in another means messages and calls sometimes come in at 3 in the morning; she sets Do Not Disturb to enjoy an interruption-free night's sleep. Incoming calls are forwarded to voicemail and alerts for incoming Messages or other apps that audibly vie for your attention are silenced. You can adjust Do Not Disturb settings to allow calls to come through while blocking other alerts.

You can also manually turn on Do Not Disturb when you need some time without any intrusions or disruptions from your iPhone. Simply tap Settings↪Do Not Disturb ON. To automatically activate Do Not Disturb at a scheduled time every day, follow these steps:

1. **Tap Settings⟹Notifications⟹ Do Not Disturb to reach the screen as shown in Figure 4-4.**

2. **Tap Scheduled to the On position and then tap the From/To field to open a rotor where you choose the starting and ending time for Do Not Disturb to automatically activate.**

3. **Tap Do Not Disturb in the upper left to return to the previous screen.**

4. **Tap Allow Calls From.**

   A list of options appears that include

   - *Everyone:* This lets calls come through but blocks other alerts, such as incoming messages.

   - *No One:* We don't quite understand this option. If you want calls from No One, just don't turn the Allow Calls From option on.

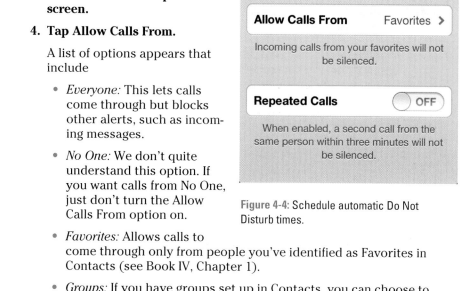

Figure 4-4: Schedule automatic Do Not Disturb times.

   - *Favorites:* Allows calls to come through only from people you've identified as Favorites in Contacts (see Book IV, Chapter 1).

   - *Groups:* If you have groups set up in Contacts, you can choose to receive calls from people in one or more group.

5. **Tap Do Not Disturb in the upper left to return to the previous screen.**

6. **Tap Repeated Calls On if you want to let a second call from the same number within three minutes to come through.**

7. **Tap Notifications in the upper left to return to the Notifications settings screen.**

 A quarter moon icon rises in the Status Bar to indicate Do Not Disturb is on.

Do Not Disturb blocks would-be disturbances as long as your iPhone is locked. If you unlock your iPhone, say to send a message to someone and a call comes in while you're typing the message, you'll receive the call (in Book III, Chapter 1 we explain how to decline incoming calls).

Notifications

Notifications offer a combination of sounds, alert messages, and badges that can appear on particular app icons to indicate you've received new messages or other kinds of updated information. You choose which apps alert you with notifications, and what kind of notification each uses: badges, banners, alerts, and, for some, sounds. The great thing about notifications is they grab your attention even if the app that's doing the attention-grabbing isn't running, as illustrated by Figure 4-5.

The Notification Center as shown in Figure 4-6 is a central location where all notifications are saved until you remove them. Hidden from view but always available, it appears when you pull or swipe down from the very top of the screen from any Home screen or app. If the app is in landscape view, swipe down from the top of that view. We explain responding to notification messages in Book I, Chapter 2; here, we explain

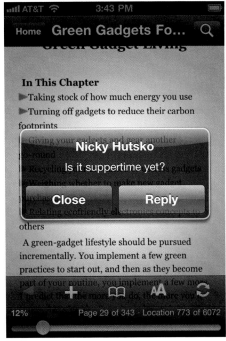

Figure 4-5: Notifications update you about apps even when you're using other apps.

how to designate the type of notifications you want to receive for each app that offers notification options.

1. Tap Settings⇨Notifications.

2. Tap either Manually or By Time in the Sort Apps section to choose how notifications are sorted in the Notification Center.

3. Refer to Figure 4-7, and notice how apps on your iPhone are divided into two sections: In Notification Center and Not in Notification Center.

4. Tap the name of each app in the list to choose if and how you want that app to send you notifications. Widgets, such as Weather and Stocks, only have an On/Off option.

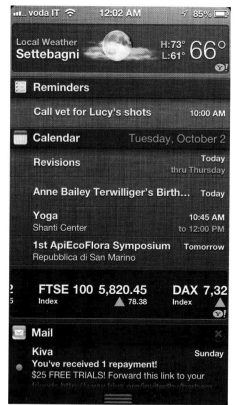

Figure 4-6: The Notifications Center keeps all your notifications in one place.

Figure 4-7: Notification settings on a per-app basis.

A screen similar to the one in Figure 4-8 opens. Do the following:

1. Tap Notification Center On if you want to see alerts from this app in the Notification Center.

   The app then appears in the In Notification Center list.

   Tap Show, which appears only if Notification Center is On, to choose how many items from this app you want listed in the Notification Center. For example, if you choose 5 for Mail, you see the five most recent messages you received in Mail listed in the Notification Center.

2. Choose the Alert Style you wish the app to use:

   • *None* means you don't want any alerts from this app.

   • *Banners* appear across the top of the Home screen or app you are using, and then automatically disappear after a few seconds.

   • *Alerts* appear in the center of the screen and require an action before they disappear.

Figure 4-8: Set notifications for each app that has a notifications option.

3. Tap the Badge App Icon On if you want to see the numbered badge on the right shoulder of the app's icon on the Home screen. Those numbers tell you, for example, how many unread e-mail messages you have in Mail or how many missed calls and unprocessed voice-mails you have in Phone.

   You can't turn the badge off for the App Store, which indicates how many app updates are waiting for you. Book II, Chapter 2 is about the App Store.

4. Tap Sounds (Ringtone in Phone, Text Tone in Messages, Alerts in Reminders and Calendar) to choose what you want to hear when something new happens in that app. Choosing different sounds for different apps helps you identify which app wants your attention. Some things to know:

- Apps like Phone, Messages, Reminders, and Calendar offer more options. We review these in the "Sounds" section later in this chapter.

- If both vibration and tone is available you can have one, both, or none.

- Apps that have just a Sound option play the pre-established sound that came with the app. You can only turn it On or Off.

5. Tap View in Lock Screen On or Off. When this option is turned on, you see notifications on the screen even when your iPhone is locked.

6. You may see other Notifications options, which vary from app to app. For example, Messages and Mail have a Show Preview option, which, when turned On, displays a few lines of the message in the notification. Photos includes Photo Stream Alert options.

7. Tap the Notifications button in the upper left corner to return to the previous screen, and then scroll through and tap the apps in both the In Notification Center and Not in Notification Center lists, repeating steps 1 through 6.

Some apps offer additional notification settings options that you find by tapping the app in the first level of Settings and then tapping Notifications.

5. **Tap the Edit button.**

6. **Tap and hold the rearrange button to the right of the app name, and then drag the app up or down to reorder the list as it will appear in the Notification Center.**

7. **Tap Done.**

8. **Tap Settings in the upper left to return to the Settings screen.**

Some apps and widgets behave in a particular way in the Notification Center:

- ✔ **Weather:** Shows the local weather based on your location (as long as Location Services are turned on).

- ✔ **Stocks:** Displays a ticker tape of the stocks that you follow.

- ✔ **Share Widget:** When turned on, you see a Facebook and/or Twitter button in the Notification Center that lets you post to your Facebook and/or Twitter account (you must be signed in to the account). This is different than turning on Facebook or Twitter in the Notification Center, which displays status updates and tweets from people you follow.

- ✔ **Show Government Alerts:** Some carriers offer this option in selected areas. In the US, on an iPhone 4S or later you can choose to receive presidential alerts, AMBER alerts, and/or Emergency Alerts.

General

The General setting screen shown in Figure 4-9 is actually a catch-all for more than a dozen individual settings — most of which we write about in greater detail in the chapters where those settings are called into play. Instead of giving you tap-by-tap instructions, the following list provides details for settings you won't find explained elsewhere in this book and points you in the right direction for the settings that are fully explained in other chapters:

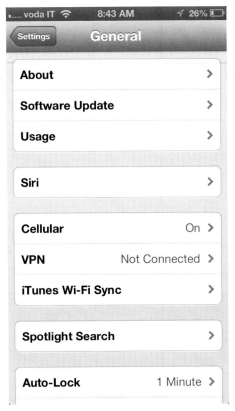

Figure 4-9: Speaking of General settings.

Many settings in Settings have multiple levels. Tap the arrow to the right of the item to go to a deeper level and see more options; tap the button in the upper left of the screen to return to the previous screen.

✔ **About:** Tap Name to change your iPhone's name. Beneath that, view detailed information about your iPhone that includes serial number, phone carrier, hardware model and software versions, the number of songs, photos, videos, and applications, the total amount of memory space storing all of those things are gobbling up (and how much memory space remains), a bunch of interesting-looking regulatory logos and glyph-like symbols that are sort of like virtual passport stamps, and page after page of tiny legal gobblygook describing a panic-inducing laundry list of permissions, rules, regulations, warnings, disclaimers, and outright threats that, were you to actually read all of it, would probably scare you so badly you'd wind up ditching your phone contract, selling or giving away your iPhone, and switching to tribal bongos or tin cans connected by a single length of string as your preferred mode of communicating with the rest of the world.

That said, two important items are buried at the bottom of the About list. Scroll down to the bottom and tap Advertising, and then tap Limit Ad Tracking to the On position to block apps from seeing what you do with your iPhone so they can then send you targeted ads.

The second item is Diagnostics & Usage. If you want to "help" Apple improve products by letting them know how you use your iPhone, tap Automatically Send. If you'd rather keep your business to yourself, tap Don't Send.

✔ **Software Update:** If a new version of the operating system, also known as iOS, is available, tapping this button downloads and installs it to your iPhone. Make sure your iPhone is connected to a power source while installing.

✔ **Usage:** Lists how much storage each app on your iPhone uses and how much overall storage remains. Tap an app to delete the app (if it isn't a preloaded app) or delete the contents of an app, such as courses in iTunes U or media in the Music app. If you activated iCloud, you see the total and available iCloud storage amounts (refer to Book II, Chapter 1 to learn about iCloud). Discloses how long you've used your iPhone since its last full charge.

Tapping the Cellular Usage button at the bottom of the screen opens another screen (refer to Figure 4-10). That screen shows the number of days and hours you spent on your iPhone during that period and during the total span of your relationship with your iPhone, the amount of data you've shuttled back and forth over your cellular carrier's network, and a button to reset the aforementioned stats so you can start tracking those figures. This can be important for you if you have limits on your calling and data plan.

The most useful button is, perhaps, the Battery Percentage setting. When you turn this setting on, it pins an estimated-percentage-remaining figure alongside your iPhone's pretty vague battery charge level indicator.

✔ **Siri (Only on iPhone 4S and later):** Turn Siri On or Off and choose how you interact with Siri. See Book I, Chapter 3.

Figure 4-10: Track your call and data usage.

✔ **Cellular:** Your one-stop wireless and networking control central for activating, deactivating and configuring your cellular data connections and choosing which apps use that cellular data connection. The Personal Hotspot settings here are the same as on the first Settings screen. See Book I, Chapter 2.

✔ **iTunes Wi-Fi Sync:** To sync your iPhone with iTunes without using the USB connector cable, tap Wi-Fi Sync and then tap Sync Now. See Book II, Chapter 1.

✔ **Spotlight Search:** For choosing which apps (and app contents) Spotlight searches, and the order in which they will be searched. See Book I, Chapter 3.

✔ **Auto Lock, Passcode Lock, and Restrictions:** We cover these in the next section, but in a nutshell, you use this trio of settings for choosing the length of time your iPhone waits before automatically locking the screen, for creating a secret passcode that must be keyed in to unlock your iPhone, and for activating and managing a slew of options for blocking (we mean, ahem, restricting) functions with a password.

✔ **Date & Time:** See Book IV, Chapter 2.

✔ **Keyboard:** See Book I, Chapter 3.

✔ **International:** Choose the written and spoken language you wish to use with your iPhone. Tap Region Format to set how dates, times, and phone numbers are displayed in apps that use that information.

✔ **Accessibility:** See Book I, Chapter 2.

✔ **Reset:** See Book 1, Chapter 5.

Sounds

By default, your iPhone is set to vibrate whenever a call comes in. You can choose whether you want that good vibration when your phone rings, when it's in silent mode, both, or none, as shown in Figure 4-11.

In the Ringer and Alerts section, dragging the volume slider left or right to decrease or increase ringtone and alert message sounds has the same effect as pressing your iPhone's actual volume buttons up or down. Turn off Change with Buttons if you don't want your iPhone's physical buttons (or, if plugged in, headset volume buttons) to change ringtone and alert volume levels. The volume buttons still let you increase or decrease the volume level of other sound-related output, such as music you're listening to, videos you're watching, and games you're playing as well as the voice of anyone you're speaking with on the phone.

In Sounds and Vibrations Patterns, tap the alert in the list, such as Ringtone or Calendar Alerts, and then choose the vibration and sound you want to associate with that type of alert. You can also choose None for either or both vibration and sound; see Figure 4-12. Scroll to the bottom of the Sounds screen to turn Lock Sounds (what you hear when you lock or unlock your iPhone) and Keyboard Clicks (what you hear when you type) Off or On.

Brightness and Wallpaper

Drag the slider left or right to decrease or increase your iPhone's screen brightness. Turn Auto-Brightness on if you want your iPhone to automatically (and only slightly) increase or decrease your iPhone's brightness level based on your environment. *Wallpaper* is the term used to describe the screen you see when your iPhone is locked, and the background image displayed behind app icons on the Home screen. You can choose the same image for both wallpaper choices, or you can choose a unique image for each choice.

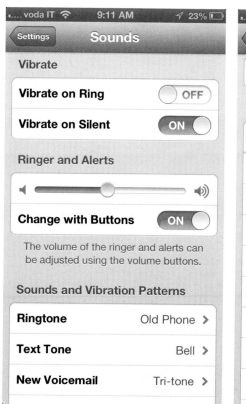

Figure 4-11: Checking out your Sounds settings options.

Figure 4-12: Each alert can have a different vibration pattern and sound.

Tap the double-thumbnails button showing your current wallpaper choice to display the locations you can choose to pick your new wallpaper. Tap one of the categories to see the images stored in that category. Wallpaper contains pretty pictures that came preloaded on your iPhone. Camera Roll is where you find any snapshots you captured using Camera, or any images you may have saved from web pages, e-mail, or text messages. Photo Library holds photos and images you may have copied from your computer using iTunes. My Photo Stream accesses your photos in Photo Stream. (See Book V, Chapter 1.)

Tap an image to preview what your choice will look like as a wallpaper image. If you choose an image from Cameral Roll, Photo Library, or Photo Stream, you can move or zoom the image in or out to adjust the image to your liking. Tap Cancel if you don't want to use the image and return to your choices. Or tap Set to choose the image, and then tap Set Lock Screen, Set Home Screen, or Set Both to set the image as your wallpaper of choice for either or both screens. You'll see a preview of how your wallpaper will appear in the thumbnails, as shown in Figure 4-13.

Privacy

This new addition to iOS 6 lets you control Location Services and shows you applications that have accessed information from other apps that are share-able such as Contacts, Calendar, and Photos, as well as Twitter and Facebook.

Many apps, like Weather, Maps, and Reminders tap into your iPhone's Location Services feature to pinpoint your current location to provide current weather conditions, or give you step-by-step directions to the nearest taco joint. In addition, there are system services that use your location to perform certain functions and to send information about your iPhone use to Apple.

Figure 4-13: Wallpaper choices you can live with.

To adjust your privacy settings, tap Privacy ⇨ Location Services to display the main Location Services setting switch and a list of all the apps that tap into your iPhone's Location Services features, as shown in Figure 4-14. Tap the On/Off button to turn your iPhone's Location Services feature on or off. The app list disappears when you turn the main Location Services feature off, and reappears when you turn Locations On again.

Scroll down the list of apps and tap the switch to turn an app's Location Services setting on or off. If you spot the Location Services icon beside an app in the list, that means the app tapped into your iPhone's Location Services sometime over the last 24 hours (refer to Figure 4-14).

Scroll to the bottom of the Location Services screen and tap the System Services button. These system-wide services use your location to perform functions such as calibrating the compass or providing traffic conditions in Maps. If you don't want any of these services to access your location or information about your iPhone use, tap the toggle switch to the Off position.

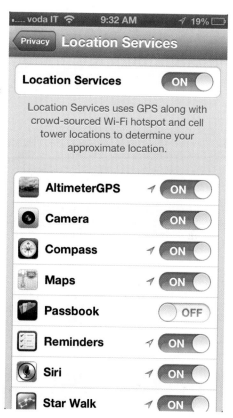

Book I
Chapter 4

Touring iPhone's
Preloaded Apps and
Settings

Figure 4-14: Location Services helps your iPhone find its way — and yours.

Scroll further down the System Services screen to turn the Location Services Status Bar Icon On or Off. When On, the arrow appears in the Status Bar whenever a System Services accesses your location.

Tap the back button in the upper left corner twice to return to the Privacy settings screen. Tap any of the apps in the Privacy list to see a list of other applications that have accessed information from that app. You can turn access to those apps on and off from this second-level screen.

Other Apple and third-party app settings

After the Privacy button, you see four sections that list other apps. We explain the settings for each app in the first three sections in other chapters of this book. The fourth section contains Apple and third-party apps that you installed. Tapping the app in the list opens a settings or information screen. There's no set rule for the type of settings options an app offers, so you have to poke around when you download a new app — or read the app's instructions either on your iPhone or on the app's website.

Activating iPhone's Security Features

This section is all about taking advantage of your iPhone's security and privacy options to ensure your personal data stays that way — personal, for your eyes only, or for others you may choose to share your iPhone with. To access the settings that follow, tap Settings, and then tap General.

Auto Lock

Locking your iPhone's screen helps conserve power and guards against unintentional screen taps, like when you're toting your iPhone in your pocket.

Tap Auto Lock and then choose the amount of time you want your iPhone to wait before it automatically locks the screen. Your choices range from one to five minutes, or you can choose Never, which means it's up to you to remember to press the Sleep/Wake button to lock your iPhone.

Even when locked, your iPhone can still receive calls, text messages, and inbound communications — unless you activated Do Not Disturb — and you can still listen to music or other audio.

Passcode Lock

Requiring a passcode to unlock your iPhone can help prevent others from viewing your personal data or making calls on your dime. To set it up, do the following:

1. **Tap Settings⬧General⬧Passcode Lock⬧Turn Passcode On.**

2. **Type in a four-digit passcode, and then type in the code a second time to verify your code.**

You can change your secret code anytime by tapping Change Passcode, entering your old passcode, and then entering a new passcode.

3. **Tap Require Passcode and then tap Immediately if you want your iPhone to require your passcode whenever you unlock it. Or choose one of the time-out options if you want your iPhone to require your code after the chosen amount of time has passed.**

4. **Tap Simple Passcode Off to use a more complicated passcode, such as an alpha-numeric combination.**

5. **Tap Siri, Passbook, and/or Reply with Message to the On position if you want these functions to work from the Lock screen.**

When Siri is accessible from the Lock Screen, security features such as the Passcode Lock are overridden and, therefore, compromised — even though your iPhone is locked, you (or someone else) can make a phone call via Siri.

6. **Tap Erase Data On to protect your personal information in the event your iPhone falls into the wrong hands.**

Erase Data erases everything stored on your iPhone if the correct passcode isn't entered after ten tries.

On GSM model iPhones, you can activate and change a PIN (personal identification number) to lock your iPhone's SIM card (some SIM cards come with a preset PIN). When activated, you must type in the PIN code whenever you turn iPhone off then on again. But unlike the Passcode Lock feature, which generously offers up to ten tries in the game of Guess Your Secret Code, the SIM Pin lock feature is less forgiving — after three failed attempts to crack the SIM code, unlocking the SIM pin may then require a unique Personal Unlocking Key (PUK) code to unlock your iPhone (which rightful owners may obtain by contacting their cellular carrier's customer service department).

Restrictions

If you share your iPhone with another person (or you're a parent or guardian who holds the keys to iPhone's kingdom), you can allow or restrict access to apps and features, or block access to content, such as songs containing explicit lyrics, or movies or TV shows based on their MPA rating.

To activate and adjust iPhone's restriction settings, tap Settings⟩General⟩ Restrictions. Tap the Enable Restrictions button and then type in a secret four-digit code, and then type in the code a second time to verify your code. Tap the apps and features you want to turn off or on as shown in Figure 4-15. App icons for any apps you restrict disappear from iPhone's Home screen.

Although you'd think turning off access to a certain app such as Safari, for instance, totally blocks your iPhone from accessing web pages, that isn't one-hundred percent true. Although the app icon disappears from the Home screen and browsing the web with Safari is therefore disabled, certain apps you may have installed on your iPhone may *still* access the web using their own web browser features. For instance, tapping a web page link that appears in the Facebook, Twitter, or Google apps opens those apps' built-in web browsers to display the content of a web page link.

If you want to "hide" some of the pre-loaded apps that can't be deleted from your iPhone, you may be able to restrict them, which removes the app button from the Home screen. The app is still on your iPhone but you don't see it.

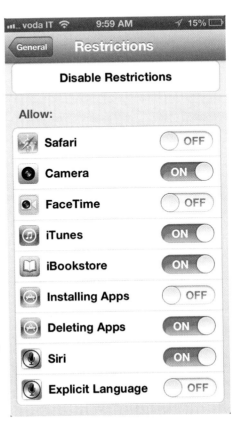

Figure 4-15: Pick and choose apps and features you want to block access to.

Taking Steps if Your iPhone Is Lost or Stolen

Your worst iPhone nightmare: Your beloved iPhone is lost or stolen. Don't panic — even though your iPhone may be gone for good (er, bad), all may not be totally lost. We're speaking of course of the personal data stored on your iPhone, which may be more valuable than your iPhone itself.

On this very personal matter, we have potentially good news, possibly great news, and maybe even fabulous news. First the potentially good news: If you turned on the Passcode Lock feature described in the previous section, whoever found or "borrowed" your iPhone must type in your secret passcode before they can even unlock your iPhone and start snooping around. Second, the possibly great news: If, in addition to turning on the Passcode Lock feature, you also turned on the Erase Data option, your iPhone develops a sudden case of permanent amnesia and erases everything stored on it if, after the tenth try, the interloper fails to guess your secret code.

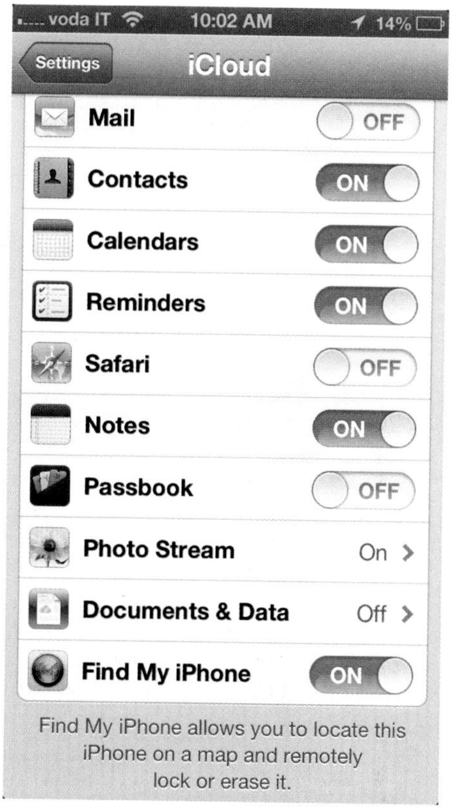

And finally, what may be the best-case-scenario news of all: Before unexpectedly parting ways, hopefully you configured the Find My iPhone feature we explain here.

To use Find My iPhone, you must have an iCloud account, and then turn on the Find My iPhone option in Settings⊐iCloud, as seen in Figure 4-16.

Figure 4-16: The Find My iPhone setting.

With Find My iPhone activated, you may be able to track down your iPhone's general location on a map using a web browser on your computer or other web-savvy gadget, or by using the Find My iPhone app installed on another person's iPhone, iPad, or iPod touch, which in turn may jog your memory as to where you may have lost or misplaced your iPhone (like between the sofa cushions in the den, or your gym locker).

What's more, you can command your iPhone to play a loud bleating sound to help guide you (or anyone nearby) to wherever it's hiding. You can lock your iPhone with a secret passcode you create on the fly in the event your iPhone wasn't already protected using the Passcode Lock feature before it vanished.

And finally, if you still can't find your iPhone, you can issue a "self-destruct" command that instructs your iPhone to erase everything stored on it. That way, you lose only your iPhone — which you can replace — but not your personal data and identity information.

To track down a missing iPhone, tap the Find My iPhone app on a friend's iPhone (or iPad or iPod touch), or visit www.icloud.com with your computer's web browser, and then log in using your iCloud user name and password. A map appears and shows your iPhone's current location, give or take a few — or a few hundred — feet, depending on the service's ability to accurately home in on your missing iPhone. Click the disclosure triangle or Devices list button to display more information and options, shown in Figure 4-17.

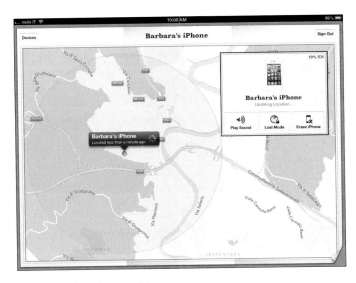

Figure 4-17: Locating your iPhone.

Choose one or more of the following actions, which take place immediately if your device is online. Otherwise, the action(s) occurs as soon as the device comes online:

- **Play Sound:** Click the button to play a sound on your device. The sound plays at full volume even if your device is muted.

- **Lost Mode:** When you click this button, you're asked to create a four-digit passcode. Type the digits two times, as asked, and then enter a phone number where you can be reached, which will be displayed on the screen. Click Next and then type in a message that will appear on the screen of your lost iPhone. Click Done. The phone number and message appear on your iPhone's screen and the passcode must be entered to unlock the device. You receive an e-mail confirming that your lost device has been locked and another e-mail with the device's location.

✔ **Erase:** If repeated attempts to reach out and touch someone who may be in possession of your iPhone go unanswered, this may be your last gasp option, especially if you have sensitive personal information on your iPhone and you have no luck retrieving it. Click Erase, and then enter your Apple ID password. Confirm by clicking Erase.

Chapter 5: Anticipating and Tackling iPhone Troubles

In This Chapter

✔ Keeping the battery charged

✔ Avoiding common iPhone problems

✔ Troubleshooting Q&A

You might think that near the beginning of a book is a strange place for the troubleshooting chapter. We decided to do things a little differently.

Often, when something goes awry, you panic — it's human nature. No one likes a glitch, or feeling unprepared or stupid. That's why we put this chapter up front. You can skim through the topics so if one of the problems we mention occurs, you won't be surprised or panicked. You'll know where to look to resolve the problem calmly and quickly.

We include some information here to help you avoid problems, along with the traditional troubleshooting question-and-answer format. In each chapter, we include some warnings of things that could happen and tips for how to resolve problems specific to the chapter at hand.

Keeping the Battery Charged

When you connect your iPhone to a power source, it charges in record time. Even if you have zero charge, in about an hour, you're up and running at 100 percent. Technically, you should get about 8 hours of talk time on an iPhone 5 on the 3G network. Realistically, if you play games and go on the Internet, you probably get less. Here are some tips for keeping the battery charged longer and for maintaining long battery life.

Usage	
iCloud	
Total Storage	25.
Available	23.
Manage Storage	
Usage	

> To preserve the overall life, you should cycle the battery on a monthly basis. *Cycling* is letting the battery completely discharge and then charging it fully.

Big battery consumers

The biggest battery consumer on your iPhone depends on how you use your phone. Ongoing actions quickly drain the battery, even ones you may not be aware of. For example, the System Services that use Location Services may be checking in to update your location. Another action that quickly drains the battery is when your iPhone searches for something it can't find, such as a Wi-Fi or cellular network, or when information is being continually pushed from the cloud. Keep these tips in mind for a longer battery charge:

- **Turn Off Location Services:** Go to Settings⇨Privacy⇨Location Services. Tap System Services to view the "invisible" apps that use Location Services, as shown in Figure 5-1. The gray Location Services icon lets you know which ones have been used in the last 24 hours. As far as we're concerned, you can switch most of them off. You can also turn off Location Services altogether, although the apps that use it, do so only when you're using them.

- **Turn Off Wi-Fi:** If you have Wi-Fi turned on and there's no Wi-Fi network, your iPhone keeps searching and searching and consuming battery power. To turn off Wi-Fi, tap Settings⇨Wi-Fi⇨Off.

- **Turn Off 3G/4G:** If 3G or 4G isn't available where you are or you don't need to access the 3G or 4G network, turn it off. Sometimes this actually improves access to your cellular calling network. It doubles your battery charge. Tap Settings⇨General⇨Cellular⇨Enable 3G/4G Off.

- **Turn Off Siri:** If you don't need Siri's assistance, may as well send her out to lunch since she's a power hog. Tap Settings⇨General⇨Siri Off.

| voda IT 🔋 | 4:59 PM | 90% 🔋 |

Location Services / System Services

Cell Network Search	⏻	ON
Compass Calibration	⏻	OFF
Diagnostics & Usage	⏻	OFF
Genius for Apps	⏻	OFF
Location-Based iAds		OFF
Setting Time Zone	⏻	ON
Traffic		OFF

⏻ A purple location services icon will appear next to an item that has recently used your location.

⏻ A gray location services icon will appear next to an item that has used your location within the last 24 hours.

⏻ An outlined location services icon will appear next to an item that is using a

Figure 5-1: System Services access Location Services without you knowing it, and drain your battery.

✔ **Turn On Airplane Mode:** If you happen to be out of your network range, say hiking in a remote area, your iPhone consumes a lot of battery power as it continually searches for the cellular network. Eventually the words *No Service* appear instead of the carrier name and your iPhone settles down and stops searching. Consider putting your iPhone in Airplane mode: Tap Settings➪Airplane Mode On.

✔ **Use Fetch Instead of Push:** Rather than having your iPhone constantly check for new information with Push, you can set your iPhone to sync with whichever cloud service you use, such as iCloud, Yahoo! Mail, or MS-Exchange, at set time intervals, or sync manually. Tap Settings➪Mail, Contacts, Calendars➪Fetch New Data➪Push Off.

✔ **Use Auto-Brightness:** Dimming your screen also improves the length of a charge. The ambient light sensor dims or brightens your screen based on the light it senses. You can turn the automatic adjustment on by going to Settings➪Brightness➪Turn Auto-Brightness On.

Gaming, watching videos, and surfing the web use big chunks of battery power. Playing a game helps pass the time on a long trip, but make sure you leave enough battery power to call your ride when you arrive at your destination, or that there's a power source into which to plug your iPhone.

Lesser battery consumers

You can turn off some apps to improve the length of time your battery stays charged. These features consume the battery only when they're being used, but sometimes a little extra charge makes all the difference. These are like leaving a nightlight on during the day. It consumes a little bit, perhaps unnecessarily:

✔ **Bluetooth:** Tap Settings➪General➪Bluetooth➪Off if you don't have any Bluetooth devices connected and don't plan to use any for a while. For example, leave Bluetooth on if you use it with the hands-free headset in your car, and you've just stopped to get groceries.

✔ **Cellular Data:** Tap Settings➪General➪Network➪Cellular Data Off. You can still use the phone and Wi-Fi connection.

✔ **GPS:** Tap Settings➪Privacy➪Location Services Off. As long as your iPhone doesn't need to track your location, this can be turned off. Many apps want to know where you are and, when opened, will you to turn on Location Services in Settings. You have to choose at that point to go to Settings and turn Location Services back on or tap Cancel and use the app without providing your location.

✔ **Phone:** Yes, your phone. Tap Settings➪Airplane Mode On. Both cellular and Wi-Fi are turned off, saving a heap of battery juice.

When charging your iPhone with the USB cable connected to a computer, make sure it's really charging — you see a lightning bolt in the battery icon on the status bar — if your computer is turned off or sleeping, it could drain your iPhone battery instead of charging it.

If you have a new iPhone or if suddenly your iPhone battery drains faster than usual, especially after an iOS update, try one of the following:

- Tap General➪Reset and then choose Reset All Settings. This "clears out" some of the cobwebs in your iPhone's circuitry and may fix battery charge problems.
- Double-click the Home button to see the apps in the multitasking bar. Press and hold one until they begin to wiggle, and then tap the X on each until you've closed all of them.

Tracking battery usage

Tap Settings➪General➪Usage to see how much time has passed since your last charge, as shown in Figure 5-2. Usage is how much you've used it. Standby is how much time your iPhone spent sleeping.

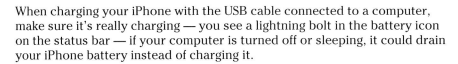

Figure 5-2: Usage shows how much you've used your iPhone since the last charge.

Changing the battery

If you keep your iPhone for many years, sooner or later, you'll need to replace the battery. Despite our DIY (do-it-yourself) world, you can't replace the battery yourself. You have to send it in to the Battery Replacement Program. For $85 (at the time of publication), you send your iPhone to Apple or take it to an Apple store, the battery is replaced, and Apple takes care of disposing of the old one. This service is covered if your iPhone is still under the one year warranty or you extended the warranty to two years with the AppleCare protection plan, which we explain in the last section of this chapter, "Getting Repairs If You Need Them."

Avoiding Common iPhone Problems

With iCloud syncing, your version of iOS should always be current. If you're having problems, tap Settings⟹General⟹Update just to be sure your iOS is current. Your apps need to be kept current, too. Keep your eye out for a badge on the App Store icon on the Home screen, which lets you know that one or more of your apps have updates available.

Make sure the SIM card is properly installed (if your iPhone uses one). If you dropped your iPhone, the SIM card may be slightly dislodged. Carefully insert the end of a paper clip in the hole of the SIM tray to open the tray. Take out the SIM card and re-insert it and then gently push the tray closed.

Here are a few other things to consider if you have a problem:

✒ **The headset is plugged in but you can't hear anything.**

Make sure the headset is plugged in all the way — it makes a little "click" when it is. It may not be compatible with the cover or bumper (those colored frames that go around iPhone's outer edge) you use; that is, the cover keeps the plug from going all the way into the hole. Although 1/8-inch plugs work most of the time, the specifications call for a 3.5 mm plug.

Make sure the jack is clean. If you use your iPhone in a dusty workshop or in the yard, or eat toast while texting, crumbs and particles can build up and block the audio jack. Use the end of a paper clip to gently clean the jack and try inserting the headset again.

✒ **The words *No Service* appear where your carrier's name usually appears.**

First, make sure you aren't in Airplane Mode. Then, try turning 3G/4G on or off. Try turning Airplane Mode On and then Off. Lastly, try turning your iPhone off and on again. Try moving closer to a window or going outside. If you have a weak signal, turning 3G/4G on can bring a stronger signal. If you're in a crowded area with lots of other cell phone users, turning 3G/4G off gives you access to a larger network.

✒ **You don't have Internet access.**

Assuming you have data service as part of your cellular contract, make sure you have a cellular data signal or are in a Wi-Fi zone. You see the icons in the status bar (see Book I, Chapter 2). Without one of these options, you can't get online. Try these tactics to solve the problem:

 • Disconnect and reconnect to the network. Tap Settings⟹Wi-Fi Off. Wait a minute, and then tap Wi-Fi On.

 • Try renewing the Dynamic Host Control Protocol (DHCP) lease, which is the access point that allows your iPhone to access a Wi-Fi network. Tap Settings⟹Wi-Fi. Tap the blue and white arrow to the right of the connected Wi-Fi network, and then tap the DHCP tab. Scroll down the screen and tap the Renew Lease button, as shown in Figure 5-3.

- Reset network settings by tapping Settings⇨General, and then scroll down to Reset, which is the last button on the screen. Tap Reset Network Settings.

- Look for interference from devices like walkie-talkies or baby monitors.

- If you know Wi-Fi should be available because, say, you're home, and none of these procedures work, the problem could be with the Wi-Fi router, modem, or incoming DSL line. Try turning your router off and on again or call your service provider.

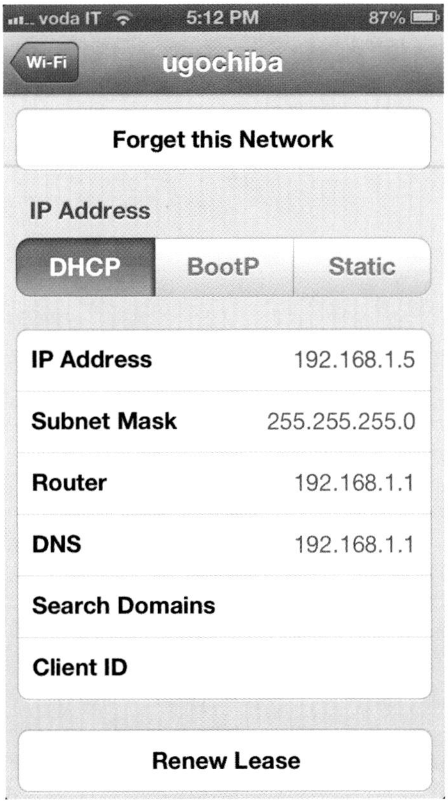

✓ **You can't send text messages.**

For SMS and MMS messages, make sure you have cellular service. iMessages require a Wi-Fi or cellular data connection, and iMessage has to be turned on in Settings⇨ Messages⇨iMessage⇨On. Check that the recipient's phone number has an area code and that you typed your message in the message field and not the subject line. Refer to Book III, Chapter 2 to find out more about text messaging.

Figure 5-3: Sometimes your lease is up and you have to renew to get Wi-Fi.

✓ **You can't receive or send e-mail or you see messages but you can't open them.**

Make sure you have an Internet connection, either through your cellular data network or Wi-Fi.

Try re-entering your password. Tap Settings⇨Mail, Contacts, Calendars⇨Account Name⇨Account. Delete and retype the password. See Book III, Chapter 4 for information about the Mail app.

Turn your phone off and back on.

🖙 **Syncing doesn't seem to work.**

If you use iCloud, make sure you are signed in to the correct account: Tap Settings⇨iCloud⇨Account and enter the Apple ID and password you use with iCloud — remember it must be in the form of an e-mail address.

If you use iTunes, make sure the USB connector cable is properly inserted in both your computer and your iPhone. If you sync wirelessly with iTunes, make sure your iPhone and computer are on the same wireless network. Refer to Book II, Chapter 1 for full details on syncing.

Troubleshooting Q&A

Here are some of the most common difficulties you may encounter with your iPhone and how to handle them:

Q: My iPhone won't turn on.

A: Probably the battery needs to be charged. Connect your iPhone to the USB connector cable and power adapter and begin charging. It takes about ten minutes for a completely dead battery to have enough charge to show signs of life. A lightning bolt appears on the screen, followed by the Apple logo, and you can turn your iPhone on at that point.

If you take your iPhone to the beach and leave it in your bag hanging on the back of your lounge chair (as Barbara's friend's teenage daughter did and then called in tears because her beloved iPhone wouldn't work), you risk overheating your iPhone. Likewise, leaving it out in the cold can send your iPhone into hypothermia. Signs of iPhone heat stroke, or frostbite, are a dimmed screen, weak cellular signal, and in the case of heat stroke, a temperature warning screen as your iPhone tries to cool itself, as shown in Figure 5-4. You cannot use your iPhone — except for an emergency call — when the temperature warning screen is visible. If

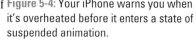

Figure 5-4: Your iPhone warns you when it's overheated before it enters a state of suspended animation.

your iPhone can't cool or warm itself, it goes into a deep sleep, a sort of iPhone coma, until it cools or warms. Put your iPhone in a cooler or warmer location. It will wake up once its internal temperature returns to normal.

Q: An app is frozen on my screen. Nothing closes it, the Home button doesn't work — it just sits there.

A: Force-quit the app. Hold down the Sleep/Wake switch until the Slide to Power Off message appears, and then hold the Home button until the frozen program quits and you return to the Home screen. The app should be fine the next time you open it.

Q: Um, force-quitting the app didn't work.

A: Force-restart your iPhone. Hold down the Home button and the Sleep/Wake switch simultaneously for about 10 seconds. Release when you see the Apple logo, which means your iPhone is restarting.

Q: The same app or apps keep giving me trouble.

A: Check if there's an update for the app or apps. If you haven't updated apps for a while and a badge on the App Store indicates you have apps to update, tap App Store and then tap the Updates button. Scroll through the list to see if the offending app is there, and if so, tap Update and then Open.

Try removing and reinstalling the troublesome app or apps. Press and hold any app on the Home screen until they begin to wiggle, and then tap the X on the app you want to remove. Even after you remove an app, you can install it again because the iTunes Store keeps a record of all the apps you installed.

Q: Nope, didn't work.

A: Try resetting your iPhone settings. Tap Settings↪General↪Reset↪Reset All Settings. This takes your settings back to how they were when you took your iPhone out of the box, or if upgrades have been released since you bought your iPhone, to the default settings for the most recent upgrade you performed. It doesn't remove any data, but you do have to redo any settings you had altered.

Q: I'm still having problems.

A: Tap Erase All Content and Settings. This does just what it says. This resets all settings and erases all your information and media by removing the encryption key to the data (which is encrypted using 256-bit AES encryption).

Make sure you back up your iPhone with iCloud or iTunes before tapping Erase All Content and Settings so you can sync after.

Q: Nothing seems to work.

A: Restore your phone. Restore erases your iPhone and returns it to the state it was in out of the box, but better than new because the the most recent operating system (the software that makes your iPhone work) will be installed. All contacts, photos, music, television shows, calendars, e-mails, notes, bookmarks, and third-party apps are deleted. This sounds like a drastic measure, and in a way it is, but it's not as bad as it seems. If you use iCloud to back up, you can restore from your iCloud account. If you use iTunes, try to sync with iTunes before restoring your iPhone. Even if you can't sync, your most recent backup is stored on iTunes on your computer. See Book II, Chapter 1 to learn about backing up with iCloud and iTunes.

Q: iTunes doesn't recognize my iPhone.

A: Do a Device Firmware Upgrade (DFU). DFU wipes out the old OS (but not your content) and installs a new one. You can then sync and restore as explained previously. The DFU procedure is

1. Turn off your iPhone.

2. Connect your iPhone to your computer.

3. Open iTunes.

4. Press and hold the Sleep/Wake and Home buttons for exactly ten seconds.

5. After ten seconds, release the Sleep/Wake button, but continue to hold the Home button for another ten seconds.

6. After ten seconds, release the Home button. iTunes now recognizes your iPhone.

7. Click OK. iTunes asks you to confirm.

8. Click Restore and Update.

Getting More Help

If you have a problem we didn't talk about or none of the previously discussed tactics work, you can still find more help on the Internet. Chances are someone else has encountered the same problem. Your first stop should be Apple's iPhone Support page at `www.apple.com/support/iphone`. You can contact Apple's technical support group for personalized attention. If your iPhone is your sole connection to the Internet, ask to use a friend or relative's computer or return to the store where you purchased your iPhone.

You can also search the discussion forums, as shown in Figure 5-5, where questions and answers are submitted by other iPhone users. Type in a few words that describe your problem and peruse the discussions. If you don't find a discussion pertinent to your problem, you can submit your question and usually an answer from another user is available within a day.

Figure 5-5: iPhone users exchange questions and answers on the discussion forums at the Apple website.

If you still don't find a satisfying answer, type a few key words about your problem in to one of the Internet search engines like Google (www.google.com) or Yahoo! (www.yahoo.com).

Wherever you search, you may be surprised to find that you aren't the first person to have the problem you're having.

Getting Repairs if You Need Them

We are always impressed with the seriousness and efficiency of Apple's warranty and repair service. Your iPhone includes a one-year limited warranty and 90 days of complimentary support. You can get two years of coverage and support if you buy AppleCare+, which now includes no-fault insurance so if you accidently drop your iPhone in the fish pond at the park, as long as you can scoop it out and take it to your local Apple Store, it will be repaired, or replaced, for a $49 deductible. You have to purchase AppleCare+ within 30 days of your iPhone purchase date. If anything goes wrong with your iPhone, call Apple or take it to an Apple Store.

If you can, back everything up before you leave your iPhone with Apple so you can re-sync on the repaired, or new, iPhone.

If you can't be without a cellular phone for two or three days, the Apple Store offers what's called the Express Replacement Service (ERS). If your iPhone is covered under AppleCare or AppleCare+, ERS is included. If your iPhone is not covered, you have to pay a fee that's somewhere between the value of your broken phone and the value of a replacement phone. Apple gives you a replacement iPhone, or sends one if you call instead of going to the Apple Store. You just have to insert your SIM card and sync what was on your broken iPhone to the replacement iPhone.

Book II
Stocking iPhone with iTunes Apps and Add-ons

The 5th Wave   By Rich Tennant

"Other than this little glitch with the landscape view, I really love my iPhone."

You could think of this minibook as the iPhone accessory book. The first chapter in this minibook explains how to move your data from your computer to your iPhone. If you're curious about iCloud, Apple's wireless syncing, document sharing, and storage service, read Chapter 1. The second chapter introduces you to apps — short for applications — and the App Store. Here we show you how to find and install third-party apps on your iPhone, including those for periodical subscriptions that are kept in Newsstand. The last chapter presents some pretty nifty hardware accessories — things like bumpers, cases, and speakers.

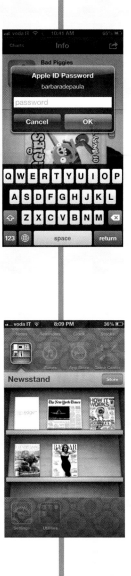

Chapter 1: Syncing and Backing Up Your iPhone

In This Chapter

✓ Creating an Apple ID

✓ Understanding the syncing relationship

✓ Syncing and backing up with iCloud

✓ Keeping documents in the cloud

✓ Syncing and backing up with iTunes

✓ Buying more iCloud storage

The information in this chapter is essential to using your iPhone, especially if you manage a lot of data like phone numbers and appointments that you don't want to lose and that you like to access from other devices, such as a computer or iPad. We explain the theory behind syncing, and then go through, step-by-step, how to sync the data between your iPhone, your computer, and other iOS devices using iCloud or iTunes. We outline how to back up everything on your iPhone and then use the backup should you lose everything on your iPhone. Lastly, we give you the steps you need to keep your iPhone and apps up-to-date with the latest versions.

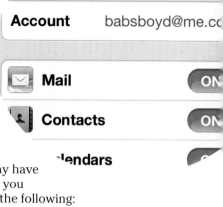

Creating an Apple ID

You need an Apple ID to do many tasks with your iPhone. Specifically, to download media and apps from iTunes and the App Store, and to use iCloud, you must have an Apple ID. You are asked for your Apple ID when you download software updates. You probably set one up when your phone was activated at the Apple Store or the retailer where you bought your iPhone or if you activated your iPhone yourself, you may have created one as part of the Setup Assistant procedure. If you skipped that step, you can create an Apple ID by doing the following:

1. **On the Home screen, tap Settings⇨Mail, Contacts, Calendars.**

2. **Tap the Add Account button.**

3. **Tap iCloud.**

4. **Tap Get a Free Apple ID.**

   The Create an Apple ID screen opens.

5. **Tap the Location field to select your location from the rotor that appears.**

   If Location Services is on, you won't see this and can go to Step 6.

6. **Tap the Month, Day, and Year fields to enter your birth date.**

   This information is used in conjunction with your secret security question in the event you forget your password and ask for help.

7. **Tap the Next button in the upper right corner.**

   The Name screen appears.

8. **Type your first and last name in the fields, and then tap Next in the upper right corner.**

   A second Create an Apple ID screen opens, as shown in Figure 1-1.

9. **Tap Use Your Current Email Address if you want to use an e-mail address you already have.**

   Or

   Tap Get a Free iCloud Email Address to create an e-mail address that will be your Apple ID and create an iCloud account that has e-mail, contact, and calendar services associated with it. (See Book III, Chapter 4, and Book IV, Chapters 1 and 2, respectively.)

10. **Tap in the E-mail field to type in the e-mail address you would like to use, either an existing e-mail or one you create with @icloud.com.**

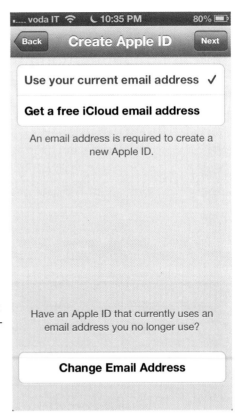

Figure 1-1: Use an existing e-mail address or create an icloud.com e-mail.

Think about it before choosing — you can't change your address after you create it.

The Apple ID Password screen opens.

11. **Type in your Password, and type it again in the Verify field to verify and register it.**

    Your password must be at least eight characters, containing at least one uppercase letter, one lowercase letter, and one number.

    This is your Apple ID password and must meet these requirements. Even if you use an existing e-mail address, the Apple ID password may be different than the password you use with the existing e-mail address to access your e-mail account.

    If your chosen e-mail is already in use by another person, a suggestion appears in the E-mail field. Likewise, if your password doesn't meet the password requirements, you are asked to create a different one.

12. **Tap the Next button.**

    The Security Info screen opens.

13. **Choose a security question from the list of suggestions or tap Create a Customer Question to use something that's easier for you to remember, but difficult for others to guess.**

    Tap in the Answer field and type the answer.

14. **The Email Updates screen opens. Choose On or Off to receive, or block, e-mail from Apple at this e-mail address.**

15. **Tap Next.**

16. **The iCloud screen appears.**

    Scroll to the bottom and tap the Agree button. (You can choose to have the document e-mailed to you so you can more easily read the terms you are agreeing to.) A dialog appears asking if you agree to the terms and conditions. Tap Agree.

17. **Your account is created and the iCloud screen opens.**

18. **Tap the features you want to use with iCloud.**

    We explain more about that later in this chapter.

19. **Tap Save.**

    The new iCloud e-mail account is added to your Mail accounts. (See Book III, Chapter 4 to learn about using Mail.)

20. **Make note of your @me.com e-mail address and keep your password in a safe place.**

21. **Press the Home button to return to the Home screen.**

Understanding the Syncing Relationship

Syncing, or synchronizing, is keeping your data on two or more devices — your iPhone and your computer and other iOS devices such as an iPad or iPod touch — up-to-date and mirrored on either device. Backing up is creating a copy of the data that's on your device and storing it somewhere else, be it your computer or a remote server. You begin using your iPhone by activating iCloud's backup and syncing functions or connecting your iPhone to your computer and opening iTunes.

iCloud is simple: Just a few taps and backup and syncing begins. Your data is stored in a remote Apple location, somewhere in North Carolina (at the time of writing), which is a good thing because if disaster or thieves strike your home and your computer breaks or disappears, your data is safe and sound. If you just don't like the idea of remote storage, you may prefer using iTunes to backup and sync your data. We find the process a bit tedious but, like iCloud, after it's set up, it's automatic. Although Apple seems to be going in the direction of all iCloud, all the time, we give you the details for both so you can choose between iCloud and iTunes or use a combination of the two for all your backing up and syncing needs.

Syncing and backing up with iCloud

In a nutshell — we prefer almonds — iCloud is Apple's over-the-air syncing, sharing, and storage service. You sign in to the iCloud service with your Apple ID, and then choose which types of data you want iCloud to sync and backup. iCloud offers an e-mail account and 5GB of free storage for the following:

- **Mail settings and messages**
- **Contacts settings and content, including Phone Favorites**
- **Calendars settings and content**
- **Reminders**
- **Notes**
- **Documents and data from iCloud-enabled apps**
- **Passbook**
- **Messages, iMessage, SMS, and MMS**
- **Photos and videos in your Camera Roll**
- **App data and documents**
- **Ringtones**
- **Device data such as wallpaper, Home screen, and app organization**
- **Safari bookmarks and tabs**

Purchased apps and media including music, iTunes Match content, TV shows, and books, and photos stored in Photo Stream don't count toward the 5 GB. If you need more storage space, you can purchase an additional amount on a yearly basis directly from the iCloud settings on your iPhone, which we explain later in this chapter.

iCloud does *not* back up the following:

- ✔ **Media that wasn't purchased in iTunes**
- ✔ **Audiobooks**
- ✔ **Podcasts**
- ✔ **Photos that you transferred from your computer to your iPhone**

When data, such as your contacts, calendars, or notes, is stored on iCloud, that data is optionally pushed to any device associated with your iCloud account such as your iPhone, iPad, iPod touch, and computer.

You can choose which types of data you want to store and sync with iCloud and which you want to sync with iTunes. However, you use iTunes for syncing music and other media, such as movies and podcasts.

iCloud comes with Mac OS X 10.7.2 Lion or later, and the iCloud Control Panel for Windows (Vista SP2 or later or Windows 7) is available for download at support.apple.com/ kb/DL1455.

Follow these steps to use iCloud to sync documents and data between your devices:

1. **Tap Settings⇨iCloud.**

   If you see the e-mail you used to set up your Apple ID, go to Step 5.

2. **Type in your Apple ID and password, as shown in Figure 1-2, and then tap Sign In. Your account is verified.**

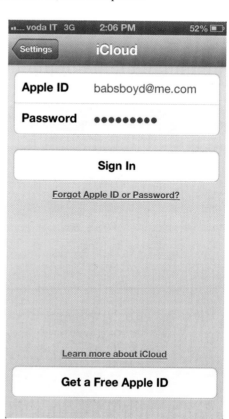

Figure 1-2: Use your Apple ID to sign in to iCloud.

iCloud only works with e-mail style Apple IDs. If your Apple ID is something like *johnsmith*, you must create a new one as explained at the beginning of this chapter.

3. **iCloud asks if you want to merge calendars, contacts, reminders, and bookmarks on your iPhone with iCloud. Tap Merge.**

4. **iCloud asks to use the location of your iPhone, which enables the Find My iPhone feature. Click OK.**

5. **The iCloud screen appears, as shown in Figure 1-3.**

   The switches you tap On indicate which data you want to sync with iCloud. Any changes you make on your iPhone are pulled into iCloud and pushed to the other devices, and vice versa when your devices are signed in to iCloud and connected to the Internet. iCloud keeps all your devices in sync.

   The exception is Photo Stream, which automatically uploads as many as 1,000 photos taken in

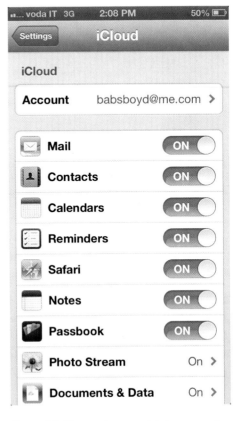

Figure 1-3: Choose the type of data you want to share with other devices using iCloud.

the last 30 days from your iOS devices — your iPhone, iPad, or iPod touch — or imported into iPhoto or Aperture on your Mac, and pushes them to the other devices and your computer.

Continue from above to use iCloud to back up your iPhone (instead of using iTunes).

6. **Scroll towards the bottom of the screen and tap Storage & Backup.**

   The Storage & Backup screen opens, as shown in Figure 1-4.

7. **Tap iCloud Backup On.**

   A message lets you know your iPhone will no longer back up to your computer when you sync with iTunes. Tap OK.

8. **Tap Manage Storage.**

   The Manage Storage screen opens, which shows you what is stored on iCloud, as in Figure 1-5. You can see that Barbara's iPad and old iPhone are backed up to iCloud.

   Notice the Documents & Data section, as shown in Figure 1-5. The iCloud-enabled apps installed on your iPhone are listed. You may have their counterparts on your computer. See the next section, "Keeping documents in the cloud," for more information about this feature.

Figure 1-4: Turn on iCloud back up on the Storage & Backup screen.

Figure 1-5: See what you have stored in iCloud from your iPhone.

9. **Tap your iPhone.**

The Info screen opens, as shown in Figure 1-6.

10. **The apps on your iPhone appear listed in the Backup Options section. Tap the switches On or Off to select which kind of data you want to back up. For example, tap a drawing app On to back up sketches you make.**

If, at some time in the future, you want to delete your backup, scroll to the bottom of this screen and tap Delete Backup, which both deletes your iCloud backup and turns it off.

11. **Tap Manage Storage in the upper left corner, and then tap Storage & Backup in the upper left corner of the next screen to reach the Storage & Backup screen.**

12. **Scroll to the bottom of the screen and tap the Back Up Now button.**

The button is grayed if you aren't connected to a Wi-Fi network. Back out of the iCloud settings screens to reach the main Settings screen. Turn Wi-Fi on, and then tap back into the iCloud settings screen. Tap Back Up Now.

The first backup may take a few minutes, depending on how much data you have on your iPhone. Your iPhone is backed up to iCloud. Subsequent backups take place once a day when your iPhone is attached to a power source, connected to Wi-Fi, and locked.

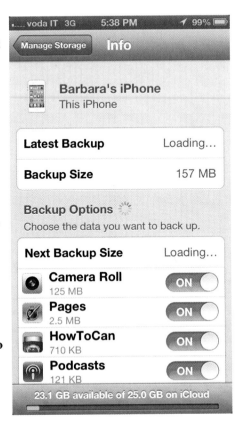

Figure 1-6: Choose the data you want to back up to iCloud.

Keeping documents in the cloud

With iOS 6, iCloud added the Documents in the Cloud feature, which lets you save documents directly in iCloud and then access them from all your devices that have the same app installed, and from your computer either in the app or from the www.icloud.com website. Documents in the Cloud works with iCloud-enabled apps, such as Pages, Numbers, and Keynote, as well as iA Writer, Autodesk Sketchbook Pro, Preview, and Day One. We use Pages as our example of how Documents in the Cloud works, but you could use another iCloud-enabled app in the same way. Follow these steps:

1. **Tap the iCloud-enabled app on your iPhone.**

   The first time you open the app, a message asks if you want to use iCloud to store documents from this app rather than storing them on your iPhone. Tap Use iCloud.

2. **Create a new document or open an existing one from those shown, as in Figure 1-7.**

3. **Type, draw, edit, whatever you want with the document.**

4. **Close the document.**

   You may see the words "Updating 1 Document" or something similar at the top of the screen.

5. **Press the Home button to exit the app.**

On other iOS devices such as an iPad or iPod touch, follow the same steps as for your iPhone. On your computer, do the following:

1. **Open the iCloud-enabled app that you used to create or edit your document.**

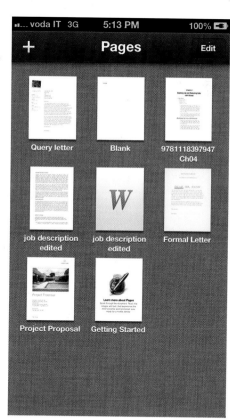

**Book II
Chapter 1**

**Syncing and
Backing Up Your
iPhone**

Figure 1-7: Share documents on all your devices with iCloud.

2. Click the iCloud tab.

The documents stored in iCloud for that app are listed in a window similar to that in Figure 1-8.

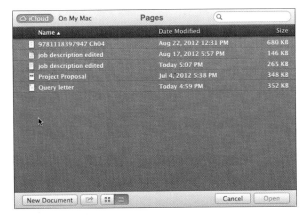

Figure 1-8: Open Documents in the Cloud on your computer directly from the app.

3. Double-click the document you want to open.

4. Edit the document.

5. Save the document as you normally would, but save it to iCloud.

You have the option to replace the existing document with the same name or save the edited document as a new document.

Syncing with iTunes

You can use iTunes to copy data from your computer to your iPhone. This data may include contacts, calendars, and e-mail accounts, and media such as songs, videos, and photos. After that initial connection and exchange of information, you use iTunes to keep the data on both devices in sync. You can set up a daily wireless sync, which is called iTunes Wi-Fi Sync, or you can physically connect your iPhone to your computer with the USB connector cable and run the iTunes Sync feature. Although Wi-Fi Sync is more convenient, it is slower than syncing with the USB connector cable.

When you sync your iPhone with iTunes, iTunes evaluates and compares the data on both devices. If two pieces of data are different — for example, say iTunes discovers two different home phone numbers for the same contact — iTunes replaces the older data (the phone number, in our example) with the more recent one.

You can also choose to sync only *some* kinds of your data and media, instead of syncing everything. What's more, any music, videos, podcasts, or apps that you download or purchase (rentals follow slightly different rules; see the following bullet on media from your iTunes library) on iTunes via your computer or iPhone is transferred to the other device when you perform a sync. iTunes syncs the following types of data:

- **Apps**
- **Calendars**
- **Contacts**
- **E-mail:** The account settings, but not the messages. This data only goes from your computer to your iPhone. Accounts set up on your iPhone will not be synced with your computer. If you find your e-mail account settings don't sync, you can set up the account directly on your iPhone as explained in Book III, Chapter 4.
- **Media from your iTunes library:** You can sync with one iTunes library at a time. Music and music videos, podcasts, ringtones, iTunes U lectures, books and audio books, movies, TV shows, photos, and videos. Movies rented on your computer can sync to your iPhone, but movies rented on your iPhone cannot sync to your computer. If you use iTunes Match you can't sync music but you can sync other media and data.
- **Reminders**
- **Web page bookmarks**

If you don't have iTunes installed on your computer, you have to download and install it before connecting your iPhone. Go to www.apple.com/itunes/ and click the blue Download iTunes button on the upper right side of the window. iTunes comes in both Mac and Windows versions. Scroll down to the bottom of the page under the hardware and software requirements if the version you need doesn't open automatically. Click either the Get iTunes for Windows or Get iTunes for Macintosh link (although it's highly unlikely you would have a Mac without iTunes). When the version you need is active, click Download Now. The download begins automatically. Follow the on-screen instructions to install iTunes on your computer.

The first sync with iTunes

Now, you're ready to connect your iPhone to your computer and iTunes. Even if you plan to use iTunes Wi-Fi Sync, you must connect your iPhone to your computer one time. The first time you connect your iPhone to your computer, iTunes opens and gives you a chance to name your iPhone and perform your first automatic sync. In this section, we go through those initial operations and then explain how to manually sync by going through the syncing options one by one. We then look at establishing the criteria for future syncing operations. These instructions are for iTunes 11, which you can download for free from the Apple website.

To begin, follow these steps:

1. **Connect your iPhone to your computer with the USB connector cable, using a port that is on your computer rather than one on the keyboard or hub (unless you have a powered hub).**

   iTunes opens. If iTunes doesn't open, open it manually.

2. **If this is the first time you connect an iPhone to iTunes, choose Set Up As New iPhone, and then click Get Started on the next screen. The iPhone Summary window appears; select your iPhone from the pop-up device menu at the top right of the window, as shown in Figure 1-9.**

   If iTunes doesn't recognize your iPhone, make sure the USB connector cable is firmly seated in both your iPhone and computer ports and that your iPhone is turned on.

   If iTunes still doesn't see your iPhone, choose iTunes⇨Preferences on a Mac or Edit⇨Preferences in Windows. Click the Devices icon at the top of the window that opens. Deselect the box next to Prevent iPods, iPhones, and iPads from Syncing Automatically. Click OK to activate the new setting.

Figure 1-9: Select syncing and backup options on the Summary window.

3. **Click on "iPhone" and type in the name you want to give your iPhone. (Refer to Figure 1-9.)**

   Don't worry: You can change the name of your iPhone later by tapping Settings⇨General⇨About on your iPhone and tapping the Name field.

4. **Choose one of the following in the Backups section:**

   - **iCloud:** Select this choice to use iCloud as your backup destination.

   - **This Computer:** Select this choice if you want to keep your

   - **iPhone backup on your computer:** You have a subchoice of Encrypt iPhone Backup. Type a password in the dialog that appears. When you restore a backup to your iPhone, you'll be asked to enter the password.

   Data from those types of programs on your computer are copied onto your iPhone into the corresponding apps, Contacts, Calendar, or Reminders (Tasks in Windows). Bookmarks from your web browser are copied to Safari on your iPhone and the account information for any e-mail accounts on your computer is copied into Mail on your iPhone. The messages themselves aren't copied.

   If you don't want to automatically sync even one of these apps, uncheck the box and proceed with a manual sync, as explained next.

5. **Select from the following in the Options section:**

   - **Automatically sync when this iPhone is connected:** Automatically launches iTunes and begins syncing when you connect your iPhone to your computer with the USB connector cable. When this box is not checked, you sync manually by clicking the Sync button in the bottom right corner.

     If the Prevent iPods, iPhones, and iPads from Syncing Automatically option in the Devices pane of iTunes Preferences (iTunes⟳ Preferences on a Mac; Edit⟳Preferences on a PC) is checked, this option appears dimmed and unavailable.

   - **Sync with this iPhone over Wi-Fi:** Your iPhone syncs with iTunes once a day when both your computer and iPhone are connected to the same Wi-Fi network, and iTunes is open on your computer. Apple recommends that your iPhone is connected to a power source and we concur. Although you can sync without power, it significantly drains the battery.

   - **Sync only checked songs and videos:** Only songs and videos that you manually check are synced. If you sync a playlist that contains unchecked songs and sync the playlist, the unchecked songs are not included in the sync. This means going through your iTunes library and manually selecting or deselecting all the songs and videos you have stored on your computer.

     If this item is unavailable, go to iTunes⟳Preferences⟳General and select Show List Checkboxes under Views, and click OK.

   - **Prefer standard definition videos:** Standard definition videos occupy less memory than high definition videos so you may prefer to sync SD videos to your iPhone.

TIP

- **Convert higher bit rate songs to 128/192/256 kbps:** iTunes automatically creates smaller audio files so you can squeeze more music onto your iPhone.

- **Manually manage music and videos:** Select this if you want to click and drag music and videos from iTunes to your iPhone. If you want to limit the music or videos stored on your iPhone, this may be a good option to choose. Everything else syncs automatically, such as contacts, calendars, mail, and bookmarks, which cannot be manually managed anyway.

- **Reset Warnings:** Click this button if, in the past, you've asked iTunes to stop showing you purchase and download warnings but you would like to see those warnings again.

- **The Configure Universal Access button:** Click this button to turn on the various Universal Access functions, such as VoiceOver and Speak Auto-Text. We explain Universal Access in Book I, Chapter 2 and also recommend you refer to Chapter 31 of iPhone's User Guide (`manuals.info.apple.com/en_US/iphone_user_guide.pdf`) for complete instructions on how to get the most out of the Accessibility features.

6. **Click Apply and proceed with the next sections to make choices for which data will sync.**

   The next time you connect your iPhone to your computer and open iTunes, choose your iPhone from the devices list on the upper-right of the iTunes window to manage your syncing options.

 You can override the automatic syncing on an as-needed basis by launching iTunes before you connect your iPhone to your computer. Press and hold ⌘+Option (Mac) or Shift+Ctrl (PC) and connect your iPhone. Hold the keys until your iPhone appears in the iTunes source list. Your iPhone won't sync automatically, but the settings you previously established remain unchanged.

Your syncing options in iTunes

Across the top of the iTunes window are eleven tabs: Summary, Info, Apps, Tones, Music, Movies, TV Shows, Podcasts, iTunes U, Books, Photos, and On This iPhone. We take a look at each of these in the following sections. When you have set up the options as you wish, you can click the Sync button and your iPhone will have all the data and media you want it to.

Summary

The Summary pane is divided into three sections. The first section, iPhone, tells you about your iPhone, the name and total storage capacity, the version of the operation system you're using, iPhone's serial number, and your iPhone's phone number.

You can see if your iPhone is up-to-date and when iTunes will automatically check again for an update. The Check for Update button gives you the option of checking for software updates before the date shown. If you know Apple has released an iPhone operating system software update, you can manually check and download that update by clicking this button.

The Restore iPhone button is used when you have problems with your iPhone or if you want to reset it to its original factory settings — say when you're giving or selling it to someone. All the contents are erased, and your iPhone wakes up restored as if it were fresh from the factory with the latest iOS.

Info

From the Info pane, you configure the sync settings for your data; that is, contacts, calendars, e-mail accounts, and your web browser. If you use iCloud, you'll see these options and can even select them, but you will also see a warning that you are syncing your iPhone with iCloud and syncing with iTunes as well may result in duplicates. You still use iTunes for media syncing, so you can skip down to the Music section. If you use Microsoft Outlook on a Mac, you must first turn on Sync Services in Outlook by clicking Tools⇨Sync Services and then selecting the items you want to sync, such as Calendar, Contacts, Tasks, and Notes. This syncs anything in Outlook with iCal/Calendar and Address Book/Contacts on your Mac, which you then sync with your iPhone with iTunes. Refer to Figure 1-10 for the following settings. You have to scroll down to see the last few:

- **Contacts:** If your contacts are divided into groups, you can choose to sync all your contacts or only subsets or groups of contacts. This is useful if you use your work computer to sync but don't want the company directory on your iPhone. Refer to Book IV, Chapter 1 to learn about the Contacts app.

  There is also an option to instruct iTunes what to do if, when syncing, it finds a new contact that's been created on your iPhone but hasn't been assigned to a group. Next to Add Contacts Created Outside of Groups on This iPhone to, choose a location from the pop-up menu.

- **Calendars:** You can sync calendars from more than one application including iCal, Calendar, and Microsoft Outlook 2011 (on a Mac), Microsoft Outlook, 2003, 2007, or 2010 (on a Windows computer), and Google Calendar. If you have more than one calendar created, you can pick and choose which to sync with your iPhone. You can also establish a cut-off date for old syncs, such as not syncing events older than 15 days. No sense clogging up your iPhone with the past. Refer to Book IV, Chapter 2 to learn about the Calendar app.

  Sync Calendars also syncs Reminders. If you want to pick and choose which calendars to sync, you can choose Reminders from the Selected Calendars list.

✔ **E-mail:** Only your account settings are synced, not the actual messages. You can choose which accounts you want on your iPhone.

On Mac, when you check the Sync Mail Accounts box, iTunes automatically checks the box next to the first account on the list. You can deselect that one and choose one or more other accounts. Say, for example, that you have an e-mail account for your golf league. You may not want to receive those messages on your iPhone, but just on your computer. Don't check the box next to that e-mail account name in the accounts list.

On Windows, check Sync Selected Mail Accounts From and then choose Outlook or Outlook Express from the pop-up menu.

Your password may or may not be synced with the account information. If you find iPhone asks for your password, you can add it permanently by tapping Settings➪Mail, Contacts, Calendar. Tap the account name and then type your password in the appropriate field.

Account settings move in one direction only: from your computer to your iPhone. If you set up e-mail accounts on your iPhone (as explained in Book III, Chapter 4), they must be set up manually on your computer, if you want them to be on your computer.

Figure 1-10: Choose your data sync settings from the Info pane.

✔ **Other:** Choose to sync bookmarks that you have in Safari on a Mac, or Safari or Microsoft Internet Explorer on Windows — the check boxes reflect the possible choices. You may want to delete old bookmarks you don't want any more before syncing.

✔ **Advanced:** Checking any or all of these boxes will replace, instead of sync, information on your iPhone with the information that's on your computer. Why would you do this? Say you tried to organize your contacts on your iPhone and made a mess. You could rework everything — with a full-size keyboard — on your computer and then over-write everything on your iPhone. Obviously, if you mainly use your iPhone to add or make changes to any of these apps, don't check this box.

Apps

You use the Apps pane, shown in Figure 1-11, to sync apps you buy in the Apps Store. If you set up automatic downloads for apps, you'll use this section only for rearranging apps and folders. In this pane, you can also copy documents between your iPhone and your computer with the Share Files feature.

Figure 1-11: Manage your apps and share files in the Apps pane.

Select the Automatically Sync New Apps box to sync to your iPhone new apps that you either downloaded to your computer or synced from another device, like an iPad.

On the left side, you see a list of all the apps you have on your computer. Scrolling through the list, notice that it's sorted by kind: iPhone, iPod touch, iPad Apps, and iPhone and iPod touch Apps. With the pop-up menu, you can also sort by name, category, date, or size. Click Install next to the apps you want on your iPhone or click and drag the icon from the list to the Home screen (on the right) where you want the app to reside.

On the right side is an image of your iPhone's Home screen. You can move the buttons around from screen to screen here, which is a lot easier than doing so on your iPhone when you have a lot of apps and folders. Follow these three steps:

1. **Click and drag the app icons around from Home screen to Home screen until they are in positions that you like and find useful.**

2. **Create folders by dragging one app icon over another.**

   The button is replaced by a highlighted square in which you see two or more tiny representations of the apps inside. A rectangle (the folder) opens beneath showing the apps that are in the folder. iPhone names the folder based on the kind of apps that are in it, but you can rename it by typing in the field.

3. **To delete an app, click on the X in the corner that appears when you hover the pointer over the app icon or click Remove in the apps list so it will be deleted from your iPhone during the next sync.**

   If you drag the pointer over the app and an X doesn't appear in the corner, that app cannot be deleted from your iPhone.

4. **After you've made the changes you want and your Home screens are neatly organized, click the Apply button to sync your changes with your iPhone.**

In the lower half of the Apps pane, as seen in Figure 1-12, you see File Sharing, which lets you share documents, created with apps that support file sharing, to and from your computer and iPhone. On the left are the apps you have that support file sharing; on the right are the files on your iPhone. To transfer files from your iPhone to your computer:

1. **Connect your iPhone to your computer and open iTunes, and then click the Apps tab.**

2. **From the list on the left, select the app that supports the document you want to share.**

   A list of available documents appears on the right.

3. **Click on the document or documents you want to transfer from your iPhone to your computer.**

4. **Click the Save to button at the bottom of the list.**

   Select the destination where you want to save the documents.

5. **Click Open (Mac) or OK (Windows).**

   The file is transferred to your computer.

Figure 1-12: Manage file transfers from the Apps pane.

To transfer files from your computer to your iPhone:

1. **Repeat Steps 1 and 2 of the previous list.**

2. **Click the Add button at the bottom of the list.**

   Select the file from your computer that you want to transfer from your computer to your iPhone.

3. **Click Open (Mac) or OK (Windows).**

   The file is transferred to your iPhone and can be opened with an app that supports that type of document. Select additional files to transfer more than one.

To delete a file from your iPhone, select the file in the list and then tap the Delete key (Backspace in Windows) on the keyboard.

Tones

If you download ringtones from the iTunes Store or create them with GarageBand, they are saved to iTunes and you see the Tones section. To sync those ringtones with your iPhone, click the Tones tab and then choose your syncing options, as shown in Figure 1-13. Select the box next to Sync Tones, and then choose All Tones or Selected Tones. If you choose Selected Tones, another box appears that lists all the ringtones you have in iTunes. Select the ones you want to sync to your iPhone.

Figure 1-13: Add custom ringtones to your iPhone.

Music

You have three choices for syncing music from iTunes to your iPhone. The first two are selected from the Music pane:

- ✔ You can sync the Entire music library, which is a great and easy choice if you have enough storage on your iPhone to hold your entire music library.

- ✔ You can sync selected playlists, artists, albums, and genres. Make the selections you want in the boxes, as seen in Figure 1-14. This is a good solution if you don't have enough iPhone memory or if you have a lot of music on your computer that you don't want on your iPhone.

Figure 1-14: Manage your music from the Music pane.

You have three other considerations on the Music pane:

- **Include Music Videos:** Any music videos you have will be synced to your iPhone from iTunes.

- **Include Voice Memos:** Voice memos from your iPhone are synced to iTunes. Automatically Fill Free Space with Songs: iTunes will sync as many songs as space on your iPhone allows. If you choose Selected Playlists, etc., and also choose Automatically Fill Free Space with Songs and there's enough room for your entire song library, all your songs will be copied to your iPhone.

The third choice made on the Summary pane is to sync only checked songs and videos. If you have a lot of music, this can be a long and tedious operation. The upside is that you have exactly the music you want on your iPhone. Here's how to do it:

1. **In the Summary pane, select Sync Only Checked Songs and Videos.**

2. **Click Apply and then click Done.**

   If iTunes begins syncing, drag the Slide to Cancel slider on your iPhone to interrupt the sync.

3. **Click Music in the pop-up menu on the left of the window.**

4. **Check all the songs and videos you want to sync to your iPhone. Uncheck any you don't want to sync, if they are checked.**

   You can also select a playlist from the Source list and check the songs in the playlist.

5. **When you finish your selection, click on your iPhone in the pop-up device menu on the upper right.**

6. **Click the Sync button on the bottom right corner.**

   Only songs and videos you checked are synced to your iPhone. The selection of checked music completely replaces the music on your iPhone, meaning that if a song is on your iPhone but remains unchecked on iTunes, it is deleted during the sync.

If you have selected Manually Manage Music and Videos on the Summary pane, you can click and drag media — songs, videos, podcasts, or playlists — from your iTunes library to your iPhone. Click the On This iPhone tab, and then click the media type you want to add to your iPhone from the list on the left. Click the Add To button in the upper right corner; the window splits into two panes. The pane on the left is iTunes on your computer and the pane on the right is your iPhone. Click and drag the items you want to move to your iPhone. You can navigate through different media types as well as change the views with the tabs at the top of the page. Click Done when you finish your selection.

When you choose to Manually Manage Music and Videos, you also have access to Autofill settings, as shown in Figure 1-15. Click Music from the list on the left. At the bottom of the window, you see a pop-up menu next to Autofill From; choose where you want iTunes to choose songs to automatically fill empty space on your iPhone, such as your entire Music library or a specific playlist. Click the Settings button and choose the criteria you want iTunes to use for autofill as well as how much space you want left for other things. Click OK, and then click Autofill.

The content will sync immediately. However, if/when someday you deselect Manually Manage Music and Videos, the content you added manually will be removed when you automatically sync. This won't make a difference if the media you manually transferred is included in the automatic sync; however, it is a hassle if you have a lot of music on your iPhone that you copied from other sources.

Figure 1-15: The Autofill Settings dialog.

You can choose to convert songs to 128 Kpbs AAC by selecting that option on the Summary pane.

Movies

With iPhone's increased storage space and fabulous display, watching movies on your iPhone has become a realistic choice. Syncing gives you the option of downloading and beginning to watch a movie on one device and then syncing and watching through to the end on the other device. If you fall asleep watching a movie on your computer in the evening, you can sync it to your iPhone and watch the end during your train commute the next morning. If you sign in to your iCloud account on both your iPhone and your computer, you can begin watching on one device, pause or stop the video, and then pick up where you left off on another device. If you click the Movies tab at the top of iTunes, you have a couple of options:

- **Click the Sync Movies check box only:** Movies you have on iTunes appear in the Movies box. Manually select the movies you want to sync by selecting the box next to the name of the movie to select.

- **Click the Sync Movies and the Automatically Include check boxes:** The pop-up menu is activated as shown in Figure 1-16, which lets you choose

  - All or all unwatched movies
  - A quantity of 1, 3, 5, or 10 watched movies
  - A quantity of 1, 3, 5, or 10 unwatched movies, either the most or least recently released.

  An unwatched movie is one that hasn't been seen on either iTunes or your iPhone. After you watch a movie on your iPhone, this information is sent to iTunes during the next sync.

- **Rented Movies:** Click the Move button next to any rented movie you want to sync to your iPhone. Remember, movies rented from iTunes expire in 24 hours from the time you begin watching or in 30 days, even if you haven't watched it, whichever comes first.

If you have begun watching the rented movie, it picks up where you left off when you open it on your iPhone.

Book II
Chapter 1

Syncing and Backing Up Your iPhone

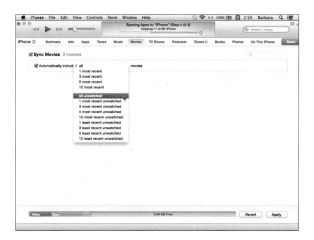

Figure 1-16: The pop-up menu in the Movies pane lets you choose which movies to sync.

Music videos are downloaded and imported into the Movies library of iTunes. If you want the music video in the Music library, click the video, and then click Get Info. Under the Kind list, choose Music Video, and then click OK. iTunes moves it from Movies to Music, although it will be in Videos on your iPhone.

TV Shows

Who watches TV shows on TV anymore? With iTunes, you can download free or purchased episodes and watch them when you want — on your computer or your iPhone. Watch out, though: A single half-hour episode takes about 250MB of storage, so your iPhone fills up fast if you don't manage the sync process. Alternatively, if you're connected to your Wi-Fi network, you can use Home Sharing to stream the show from your computer to your iPhone. Here's what you need to know:

1. **Click the box next to Sync TV Shows at the top of the pane to activate the other options.**

2. **Click the box next to Automatically Include and the criteria you choose in the two adjacent pop-up menus will be applied to all the shows you have on iTunes.**

3. **Choose one selection from each of the two pop-up menus:**

   Left menu:

   • All, which includes watched and unwatched

   • All unwatched

   • 1, 3, 5, or 10 of the newest episodes, watched and unwatched

   • 1, 3, 5, or 10 of the most recent unwatched episodes

   • 1, 3, 5, or 10 of the oldest unwatched episodes

   Right menu:

   • Apply your choice to either all shows in your iTunes library or selected shows, in which case the Shows section appears, as in Figure 1-17. Click the box next to the shows you want to apply your choices to.

   Or

4. **To pick and choose manually among the shows you have in your library, deselect the box next to Automatically Include.**

5. **Click Show in the Show box.**

   The episodes appear in the Episodes box on the right.

6. **Select the check box next to the episodes you want to sync to your iPhone.**

Figure 1-17: Choose to sync single episodes of whole series from the TV Shows pane.

You can check the options under Include Episodes in Playlists to sync those found in your Purchased or Recently Added playlists.

TIP

If you want to include or exclude a watched or unwatched episode without changing your syncing options, click TV Shows in the Library section of iTunes' Source list. Control+click or right-click the episode and choose Mark as Unwatched or Mark as Watched (whichever you have already done and want to change).

Podcasts

As with movies and television shows, you can pick and choose the podcasts you want to sync based on whether you've listened to it, the number of podcasts you want to sync, and the newest or oldest of those in your iTunes library. And, like movies and televisions shows, if you begin listening to a podcast on either device and then sync the devices, the podcast picks up where it was stopped, regardless of which device you listen on.

1. **Click the box next to Sync Podcasts at the top of the pane to activate the other options.**

2. **Click the box next to Automatically Include and the criteria you choose in the two adjacent pop-up menus will be applied to all the shows you have on iTunes.**

3. **Choose one selection from each of the two pop-up menus:**

   Left menu:

   • All, which includes played and unplayed podcasts

   • 1, 3, 5, or 10 of the most recent played and unplayed episodes

- All unplayed podcasts
- 1, 3, 5, or 10 of the most recent unplayed
- 1, 3, 5, or 10 of the least recent unplayed
- All new podcasts
- 1, 3, 5, or 10 of the most recent new podcasts
- 1, 3, 5, or 10 of the least recent new podcasts

Right menu:

- Apply your choice to either all podcasts in your iTunes library or selected podcasts, in which case a check box appears next to each podcast in the list. Click the box next to the shows you want to apply your played, unplayed, new, 1, 3, 5, or 10 choices to.

Or

4. **To pick and choose manually among the podcasts you have in your library, uncheck the box next to Automatically Include.**

5. **Click on Podcast in the podcast box.**

    The episodes appear in the Episodes box on the right.

6. **Click the check box next to the episodes you want to sync to your iPhone (see Figure 1-18).**

Figure 1-18: Manually select the episodes of a podcast you want to sync.

iTunes U

iTunes U has opened up a universe of knowledge, giving you access to grammar and high school lessons and lectures from universities and colleges around the world. You find videos and audio books, post-graduate seminars, and presentations from museums like the Metropolitan Museum of Art and organizations like the American Society of Clinical Oncology that give lifelong learning a whole new definition. Printed material associated with iTunes U courses is found in the Books section of iTunes. The steps to sync episodes from iTunes to your iPhone are as follows:

1. **Select the check box next to Sync iTunes U at the top of the pane to activate the other options.**

2. **Select the check box next to Automatically Include and the criteria you choose in the two adjacent pop-up menus is applied to all the shows you have on iTunes.**

3. **Choose one selection from each of the two pop-up menus:**

   Left menu:

   - All, which includes played and unplayed lectures or episodes

   - 1, 3, 5, or 10 of the most recent played and unplayed episodes

   - All unplayed episodes

   - 1, 3, 5, or 10 of the most recent unplayed

   - 1, 3, 5, or 10 of the least recent unplayed

   - All new episodes

   - 1, 3, 5, or 10 of the most recent new episodes

   - 1, 3, 5, or 10 of the least recent new episodes

   Right menu:

   - Apply your choice to either all collections in your iTunes library or selected collections, in which case a check box appears next to each item in the list. Select the check boxes next to the shows you want to apply your choices to.

   Or

4. **To pick and choose manually among the lectures you have in your library, deselect the box next to Automatically Include.**

Book II
Chapter 1

Syncing and Backing Up Your iPhone

 5. **Click Episode in the Collections box.**

 The episodes appear in the Items box on the right.

 6. **Select the check box next to the episodes you want to sync to your iPhone.**

In Movies, TV Shows, Podcasts, and iTunes U, when you set your sync options using one of the numbered selections (5 most recent unplayed, or 10 least recent unwatched), the selection changes as you download new media to iTunes. If you choose a specific episode or movie, it remains selected for subsequent syncs until you deselect it (or it expires, if it was rented).

Books

Books manages e-books, PDFs, and audio books. Audio books, which became popular as books-on-tape, have been around for a while. Commuters used to pop a cassette into their car stereos and listen to their favorite author's latest novel while driving to work. Today, the Internet holds myriad titles of every genre, which you can download to your computer.

E-books, or electronic books, have been on the scene for a couple decades now, too. Your iPhone can function as both an audio book listening device and an e-book reader — cool! You do have to download the iBooks app from Apple or one of the other reader apps to view e-books in the ePub or PDF format on your iPhone; we talk about those other apps in the bonus content on this book's companion website. (For more on the website, see the Introduction to this book.) Syncing media from iTunes to your iPhone to read in iBooks works pretty much the same as for other media, but we show you what to do anyway:

 1. **Select the check box next to Sync Books at the top of the pane to activate the other options.**

 2. **If you click All Books, all the e-books that you see in the Books box are synced to your iPhone.**

 Or

 3. **Click Selected Books, and then set your criteria by choosing from the pop-up menus in the Books section:**

 • **Books and PDF files, Only Books, or Only PDF files**

 • **Sort by Authors or Sort by Title:** This doesn't change your syncing option, but can make finding the books you want to sync easier.

 4. **Click the boxes next to the books you want to sync, as shown in Figure 1-19.**

Figure 1-19: Make syncing selections for e-books and audio books from the Books pane.

To sync e-books or documents that are neither ePub nor PDF files, you have to use the File Sharing section of the Apps sync panel.

The Audio Books section works the same way:

1. **Click the box next to Sync Audio Books at the top of the pane to activate the other options.**

2. **If you click All Audio Books, all the audio books that you have on iTunes are synced to your iPhone.**

   Or

3. **Click Selected books, which opens the Audio Books and Parts boxes.**

4. **Select the check boxes next to the items you want to sync in the Audio Books and Parts lists.**

Photos

The Photos pane lets you move photos from your computer to your iPhone. (From one computer only; if you try to move photos from a second computer, the originals are erased from your iPhone.)

To do the reverse (that is, move photos from your iPhone to your computer), you use your photo management program such as iPhoto or Photoshop Elements, which considers your iPhone a digital camera or external drive with images. Photos are synced with photo management software. Another option is the Photo Stream feature of iCloud, where your photos are stored in Photo Stream on iCloud and then pushed to your devices, such as your iPhone or your computer.

We talk about Photos and Photo Stream in Book V, Chapters 1. To move copies of photos from your computer to your iPhone, follow these steps (refer to Figure 1-20):

1. **Select the check box next to Sync Photos From and choose the photo management application or folder where your photos reside.**

2. **Click Include Videos at the top if you want videos included in your selection.**

3. **Click All Photos, Albums, (Events, or Faces are visible if you use iPhoto or Aperture on a Mac) to copy every photo in that application. However, photos that are in a format that is incompatible with your iPhone won't be copied.**

   Or

4. **Click Selected Albums, (or Events or Faces on a Mac), and Automatically Include.**

   Boxes appear for Albums and Events. Mac users who work with iPhoto or Aperture have the Faces option too.

   If you choose a single folder in Step 1, a selected button appears which reads All Folders. You can't deselect this button.

   If you choose a folder that holds other folders, your options are All Folders or Selected Folders, and you can choose from the subfolders from the list that appears.

Figure 1-20: Move photos from your computer to your iPhone in the Photos pane.

5. **Define what you want to automatically include by choosing one of the following from the pop-up menu:**

- **No events:** Only photos you choose from the boxes below will be included. Nothing is synced automatically.

- **All events:** Selects and syncs all the events in the events box.

- **The most recent 1, 3, 5, or 10 events:** Selects and syncs from one to 10 of the most recent events, which you see at the very bottom of the Events list. You may have to scroll down to see them.

- **Events from the last 1, 2, 3, 6, or 12 months:** Selects all events that took place in the time period you select.

6. **In addition to defined events, you can choose albums and faces to sync by selecting them in the corresponding boxes.**

The number of photos included in the selection appears in gray next to the selection.

Responding to a dialog to copy your photos or videos

If you've taken any photos with your iPhone since the last sync, your photo management software may automatically open and ask if you want to import the photos from your iPhone. To turn this function on, or off, do the following:

On a Mac:

1. Choose Finder⇨Applications or click Launchpad on the Dock.

2. Open Image Capture.

3. Click your iPhone in the Devices list.

4. In the pop-up menu entitled Connecting this iPhone Opens, choose No Application if you want no application to open when you connect your iPhone to your computer. Alternatively, you can choose from one of the applications shown to open that application when you connect your iPhone.

5. Choose Image Capture⇨Quit Image Capture to exit Image Capture. The new setting is saved and occurs the next time you connect your iPhone.

On Windows Vista or later:

1. Choose Start⇨Control Panel.

2. Choose Hardware and Sound.

3. Choose AutoPlay.

4. Open the Apple iPhone list in the Devices section.

5. Choose Take No Action if you want no application to open when you connect your iPhone to your computer. Alternatively, you can choose from one of the applications shown to open that application when you connect your iPhone.

We talk more about photo management in Book V, Chapter 1.

iPhone supports many common image file types including GIF, PNG, JPG, although iTunes doesn't sync exact copies of your photos but files that have been converted to fit iPhone's screen size. This conversion gives you better viewing quality and uses less storage space on your iPhone.

iTunes works with the latest versions of the iPhoto and Aperture photo management apps on the Mac and Photoshop Elements on Windows. Consult the Apple iTunes website to determine if older versions are compatible.

The iTunes sync

Now that you've set the criteria for your sync, all that remains is to click the Sync or Apply button in the bottom right corner. Sync changes to Apply when you make changes to your Sync options.

When you connect your iPhone to your computer in the future, choose your iPhone from the devices list at the top of the iTunes window, and then click Sync to perform a sync that uses the criteria you established. If you select Automatically Sync When This iPhone is Connected on the Summary pane, the sync happens without clicking the Sync button. If you also select Sync With This iPhone Over Wi-Fi, your iPhone will sync with iTunes once a day when both your computer and your iPhone are connected to the same Wi-Fi network and to a power source.

When you click Sync (or Apply), iTunes syncs the categories where you have selected the Sync check box at the top of the pane. If you deselect the Sync check box at the top of the Music pane, for example, when you sync, all the music on your iPhone will be deleted, although it remains on iTunes.

Disconnecting iPhone

To disconnect your iPhone from your computer, click the eject button next to your iPhone's name in the upper part of the iTunes window, and then disconnect the cable. If the sync is taking longer than you thought, and you have to go somewhere and take your iPhone with you, you can disconnect your iPhone and go where you need to go. When you're ready, reconnect your iPhone to your computer, and iTunes and iPhone take up syncing where they left off. If you get a call while you're syncing, your iPhone is so smart that it pauses the syncing session when the phone rings and picks up when the call is finished.

Gauging Your Storage Needs

There are two considerations you have to think about with regards to storage. One is how much space is on your iPhone for syncing your apps, media, documents, and data. The second is whether your backup location offers enough storage. If you use iTunes and back up to your computer, this probably isn't a concern; if you use iCloud, you may need to purchase storage beyond the complimentary 5 GB. We talk about both here.

Checking your iPhone's storage capacity

When you're ready to sync, make sure you have enough room on your iPhone before actually hitting the Sync button. Your iPhone's storage capacity depends on which version of iPhone you have.

Considering that the operating system itself takes up about one gigabyte of memory and another half a gigabyte is kept as a reserve for apps running in the background, that leaves you with 15 gigabytes on a 16GB phone, 31 on a 32GB phone, or 63 on a 64GB phone. That sounds like a warehouse of storage, until you start loading apps, movies, TV shows, podcasts, and games on your iPhone, when you find out it fills up fast. There are two ways to know how much space you have on your iPhone:

- **On iPhone:** From the Home screen, tap Settings ⇨General⇨About. The list tells you how much memory is occupied by Songs, Videos, Photos, and Apps and tells you how much memory is Available.

- **On iTunes:** When your iPhone is connected to iTunes and selected in the source list, you see a colored bar near the bottom of the iTunes window (as you see in the preceding figures) that illustrates how much space each type of data will occupy on your iPhone when you perform the sync you've set up. If you are in the Music pane and you deselect the Sync Music box, the blue section of the bar that represents audio files shrinks. If your iPhone is nearly full, you can play with your syncing options and see how they affect the storage capacity. Click once on one of the titles under the chart and the number of items in each category is displayed. Click a second time and it displays how long it will take to listen to all the audio and video in your library. Click a third time to return to the gigabyte numbers.

If you have more media than memory, you have a couple of choices for managing and choosing which data to sync:

- Manually select which music, videos, and podcasts you want on your iPhone and sync only those.

- Subscribe to iTunes Match to listen to music in streaming, which we explain in Book V, Chapter 3.

Book II Chapter 1

Syncing and Backing Up Your iPhone

Adding storage capacity to iCloud

iCloud gives you 5 GB storage for mail, contacts, calendars, documents, and backup. Media purchased from iTunes and photos stored in Photo Stream don't count toward that limit. If you find the 5 GB isn't enough, you can delete some of the things you store in iCloud or purchase more storage. Here's how to do both:

1. **Tap Settings⟳iCloud.**

2. **Tap Storage & Backup at the bottom of the screen.**

3. **Tap Manage Storage.**

4. **Look at the apps in the Documents & Data list.**

   If you see an app that's taking up a lot of memory, tap that app to see a list of documents stored on iCloud, as shown in Figure 1-21.

5. **If there are documents you can delete, tap Edit in the upper right corner, and then tap the minus sign next to the document you want to delete or tap Delete All to eliminate all the documents from that app in iCloud.**

   If the documents you delete are only stored in iCloud, you lose them completely. Open and save the documents on your computer before deleting them from iCloud if you want to keep a copy.

6. **If you want to keep the documents and prefer to increase your iCloud storage, tap Storage & Backup to return to the Storage and Backup screen, and then tap Change Storage Plan.**

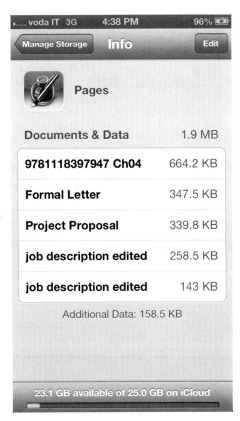

..... voda IT 3G	4:38 PM	96%
Manage Storage	**Info**	Edit

Pages

Documents & Data	1.9 MB
9781118397947 Ch04	664.2 KB
Formal Letter	347.5 KB
Project Proposal	339.8 KB
job description edited	258.5 KB
job description edited	143 KB

Additional Data: 158.5 KB

23.1 GB available of 25.0 GB on iCloud

Figure 1-21: See the documents stored in iCloud for each app.

The Buy More Storage screen opens, as shown in Figure 1-22. You see your current plan and both upgrade and downgrade options.

7. **Tap the plan you wish to purchase, and then tap the Buy button.**

8. **Enter the password for your Apple ID, if requested, and then enter your payment information.**

9. **Tap Done.**

Your credit card is charged for the amount indicated immediately and on an annual basis until you downgrade, as we explain next.

 You can also purchase iCloud storage through the System Preferences↪iCloud on your Mac or by clicking Start↪Control Panel↪iCloud in Windows.

If you purchase more storage and then find you don't need it, you can downgrade at any time so your credit card will be charged less or not at all when the renewal date arrives. Do the following:

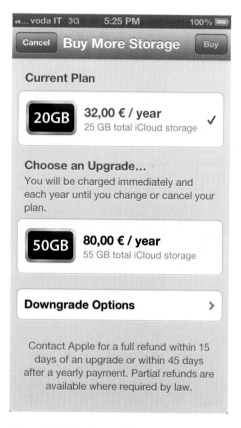

Figure 1-22: Purchase additional storage on iCloud.

**Book II
Chapter 1**

Syncing and
Backing Up Your
iPhone

1. **Tap Settings↪iCloud↪Storage & Backup↪Buy More Storage.**

2. **Tap Downgrade Options.**

3. **Tap the storage plan you want when your current plan expires.**

4. **Tap Done.**

5. **Tap the back button to return to the main Settings screen, and then press the Home button to close Settings.**

Syncing with More Than One iPhone or iTunes Computer

Used to be that you had one computer every two and a half households and the only music you heard through the phone was your father singing "Happy Birthday" to you. Today, you probably have a computer at home and one at work, and maybe a notebook computer, too. Perhaps you share your home computer with your significant other or children and each of them has an iPhone. Apple has lightened up on its one iPhone-one computer monogamy policy. Here we give you a way to use multiple computers with one iPhone as well as multiple iPhones with one computer, too.

One iPhone, multiple computers

The fact is, different pieces of our lives often overlap. You want the contacts on your notebook and desktop computers and your iPhone and iPad to be the same and you want the option of making changes in either of those places and syncing with the other two. The simplest solution is an over-the-air, or OTA, syncing and storage service, like iCloud as explained at the beginning of this chapter. Just sign in to the same iCloud account on all your devices and everything is kept in sync.

However, if you're an iTunes diehard, iTunes does let you merge contacts, calendars, e-mail accounts, bookmarks, and notes from two or more computers on your iPhone. It works like this:

1. Follow the instructions outlined previously in this chapter, sync your iPhone and one of your computers, for example, a notebook.

2. Connect and sync your iPhone with the other computer, say, a desktop. Set the same preferences in the Info pane as you did on your notebook. iTunes give you two options:

    • **Merge Info:** iPhone keeps the information from your notebook and merges it with the information on your desktop.

    • **Replace Info:** The information that was synced from the first computer is replaced by the information on the second computer.

One computer, multiple iPhones

Your family members share one computer and each of you has an iPhone. You can sync more than one iPhone with the same computer. Each device is recognized by its unique name.

On a Mac, each iPhone can use different sync settings; on Windows, each phone has to use the same settings. Each person has a separate Apple account because each iPhone has an Apple account associated with it. You probably each have different media that you'd like to sync with your respective iPhones.

The ideal solution — the one we highly recommend — is to set up separate user accounts on the Mac or Windows computer for each user, who in turn would have his own iTunes library to sync to his iPhone.

If for some reason the idea of separate user accounts doesn't work for you, you can sync different sets of media by setting up a different iTunes library for each family member:

Book II Chapter 1

Syncing and Backing Up Your iPhone

1. **Hold down the option key (Mac) or the shift key (Windows) and open iTunes.**

   A dialog gives you the options of creating a new library or choosing which you want to open.

2. **Select Create Library.**

   Type in a name and location for the library.

3. **Whenever you start up iTunes, hold down the Option (Mac) or Shift (Windows) key and to open your personal library.**

4. **Sync your iPhone with your library.**

Make sure you uncheck Copy Files to iTunes Media Folder When Adding to Library. On Mac, this is found under iTunes➪Preferences➪Advanced; on Windows, Edit➪Preferences➪Advanced.

Perhaps you have an iPhone for business and another one for your personal use. You can sync more than one iPhone with the same account and even sync different things to each. Give each iPhone a different name and when you open iTunes, choose the phone you want to sync from the pop-up source menu and then sync as outlined previously. iTunes remembers which sync goes with which phone.

Banking on Backups in Case Things Go Kerflooey

Sooner or later the backup you created using either iCloud or iTunes might come in handy. You may have to erase and reset your iPhone because it's gone haywire or maybe you had to send your iPhone in for repairs. The best case scenario is you got a new iPhone and want to restore your old data to your new phone. To load the backup file onto your iPhone, old or new, from iCloud:

1. **Choose Settings⌃General⌃Reset.**

2. **Tap Erase All Content and Settings.**

3. **When the Setup Assistant opens, tap Restore from iCloud Backup.**

4. **Sign in to iCloud with your Apple ID and password.**

   iCloud pushes the most recent backup to your iPhone.

If your backup is on your computer, and you use iTunes to back up:

1. **Connect your iPhone to the computer you usually use to sync.**

2. **Open iTunes, if it didn't automatically open (depends on how you set it up).**

3. **Click iPhone, or whatever you named it, in the devices pop-up menu in the upper right.**

4. **Click the Summary tab.**

5. **Click Restore Backup.**

   iTunes gives you a chance to back out of your choice or go ahead. Clicking Restore iPhone will erase your iPhone and re-install the most up-to-date operating system. You then must restore from a backup or start over with your iPhone. This is a drastic measure if you're having great problems with your iPhone or a good option if you plan to give your iPhone to someone else and want it to have a clean slate.

6. **If you see multiple backup files, choose the most recent one associated with your iPhone.**

7. **Sync your music, videos, podcasts, and books as we explained earlier in this chapter.**

If you like to keep things minimalistic, you can delete older backups. Go to iTunes⌃Preferences (Edit⌃Preferences on Windows), and click Devices. You see a list of your backups. Just clock the one or ones you want to delete then click Delete Backup. Poof! Gone.

Chapter 2: Apps 411: Browsing, Installing, and Managing Apps

In This Chapter

↙ **Searching for and installing apps**

↙ **Reviewing apps**

↙ **Updating apps**

↙ **Deleting apps**

↙ **Stopping by the Newsstand**

*W*ith about 700,000 apps (and counting!) available at the time of publication and more being released every day, there is truly an app for every task, interest, or necessity. We make some recommendations in this book's online bonus content, but to give you an idea, you can find apps for recipes, games, electronic readers, home banking, photo enhancement, conversion tools, flashlights, and music identification, not to mention profession-specific apps such as radiation dosage calculators for oncologists or turbine calculators for mechanics. (For more on how to access the online bonus content, see this book's Introduction.)

In this chapter, we tell you how the App Store works, give you tips for reading reviews to help you choose apps, show you how to install and delete apps and reinstall them if you deleted them by mistake, and make sure your apps are up to date. We also introduce you to Newsstand, which organizes apps for reading periodicals on your iPhone.

Discovering the Joy of Apps: "There's an App for That!"

A handful of apps are developed by Apple, and the rest are developed by third-party developers. You download apps from Apple's App Store, which you access either via your iPhone or other iOS device or via iTunes on your computer. The nice thing about the App Store is that it offers one-stop shopping. You don't have to shop from website to website for the best price or the latest version; everything is in one place. And Apple reviews the app before it goes up on the App Store, so it's been tested to work with your iPhone.

What's more, if you replace your iPhone with a newer model, lose your iPhone, or your iPhone or computer crashes before you've had a chance to back up the apps you've downloaded, the App Store has a record of everything you've downloaded and you can download your apps again (if they're still available) — without paying for them a second time. That's why you need an Apple ID to sign in to the App Store or iTunes, even to download free apps.

Free or for a price?

There are two kinds of apps: free and paid. Some of the coolest apps are free. Apps developers continue to sprout like mushrooms, and the relative ease with which an app can be written and distributed makes app programming, for some developers, a relaxing pastime. We like to divide the free apps into four types:

- **Stand-Alone Apps:** Found in all categories, these apps work on their own and can be games, financial management, recipes, or just about whatever you can think of.

- **Support Apps:** Vendors who provide an app that either is an iPhone version of their website or gives specific information. Home banking apps and real-time public transit information apps are two examples. Often, you find a link to the App Store on the website of the vendor or service provider.

- **Teaser or Intro Apps:** Pared-down versions of fee-based apps. One of Barbara's favorites, the iHandy Level, is the free app of a fee-based carpentry app suite that includes a protractor, plumb bob, ruler, and surface level for 99 cents each.

- **Revenue-Generating Apps:** These apps provide frameworks for the real meat of the app, such as magazine subscription apps or gambling apps. The app is free, but you pay for the content.

We think of paid apps in two categories:

- **Low-priced:** Most are just 99 cents and the highest runs $5. They run the gamut of categories. Some developers have become rich overnight with the idea that selling a lot for a low price is more effective than selling two at a high price. We're happy for their success and for the accessibility low prices provide.

- **Higher-priced:** More than $10. For the most part, these apps, such as scientific journals or GPS navigation tools, give access to costly, copyrighted information.

Double- (or triple-) duty apps

It seems we never go anywhere without one device or another — iPhone, iPad, or MacBook Air — and having the same apps and the same information about those apps on each device makes work, and life in general, easier. *Universal apps* make working on multiple devices a breeze because they work on all iOS devices (iPhone, iPad, iPod touch). A plus sign in the upper left corner of the price button indicates a universal app (see Figure 2-2). When you look at an app's Info screen, which we explain in just a few paragraphs (refer to Figures 2-3 and 2-4), tap the Details tab and scroll down to the Information section. Next to Requires you see which devices the app is compatible with.

Many iOS apps also have a Mac counterpart, often with more features, and are iCloud-enabled, which means you can create documents on one device, save them to iCloud, and open and edit them on another device. If you're a Windows user, you don't have to feel left out, you can access some of your documents through the iCloud.com website.

Searching for and Installing Apps

Now that you know a bit about what you're looking for, we tell you how to get your hands on some apps. You can enter the App Store through iPhone or iTunes doors.

Searching the iPhone App Store

With the hundreds of thousands of apps available, it's hard to know where to begin, let alone actually choose an app. Apple helps you by making some recommendations for apps, showing you bestsellers, best earners, and some Apple favorites. To begin navigating through the sea of apps on your iPhone, tap the App Store button on the Home screen, and a screen like Figure 2-1 appears. If you're familiar with the iTunes Store on a computer, you notice that the App store looks very similar on your iPhone. Across the bottom, you see five buttons:

- **Featured:** Shows Apple-recommended apps divided into sections. Ads automatically scroll across the top. You can scroll down to see the following

  - **New and Noteworthy:** Scroll horizontally through the icons or tap See All to see a complete list.

  - **Amazing on iPhone 5:** Here too, scroll horizontally through the icons or tap See All to view a complete list. This section changes periodically to promote seasonal or themed suggestions.

  - **What's Hot (not seen in the figure, scroll down a bit):** Here you find the most popular — that is, the most downloaded — apps, regardless of whether they are free or paid.

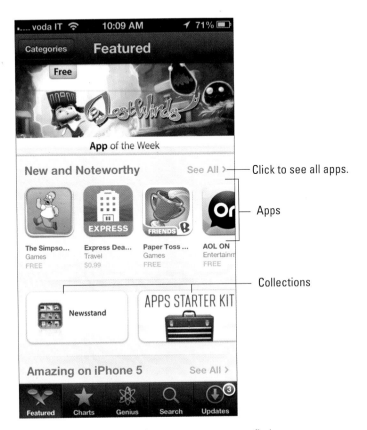

Figure 2-1: The App Store gives you many ways to find apps.

- **Collections:** In between the three sections you see rectangular icons that link to app collections. For example, tap on the Apps Starter Kit to see a list of apps that you might find interesting if you're an iPhone newbie or Education to see education-related apps.

There's also an Apps Made by Apple collection that's helpful to find apps like iBooks and Podcasts, which we recommend you add to your iPhone.

✔ **Charts:** Scroll horizontally through the icons in one of the three sections — Paid, Free, Top Grossing — or tap See All to view a complete list.

You see apps under Top Grossing that are free, and you may wonder how a free app can be top-grossing. Two ways:

- There's an app called Free App a Day that lets you make a wish that an app is free. If a single app gets enough wishes, it can be downloaded free for a limited time. The idea is that word gets out about how great the app is and people pay for it anyway after the free period is over.

- In-App Purchases: The app is free, but you then buy things within the app. For example, a poker game is free, but you buy 25 gold chips for $1.99.

✔ **Genius:** Gives you recommendations based on your purchasing and downloading history. Tap Turn On Genius to obtain the scrollable selection of recommended apps, as shown in Figure 2-2. The first time you have to agree to the iTunes Store terms and conditions. Here, too, you have a Categories button, but it reveals only categories that apply to the recommendations.

Book II
Chapter 2

Apps 411: Browsing, Installing, and Managing Apps

Figure 2-2: Genius makes recommendations for you based on your app purchase history.

Featured, Charts, and Genius screens have a Categories button in the upper left corner. Tap it to see a list of categories. Tap on one of the categories to see a list of apps in that category. Some apps fall into more than one category, in which case it shows up on two different lists. Some categories are divided into subcategories. Games and Newsstand are divided into subcategories.

✔ **Search:** You can search by the name of the app, if you know it, or by key words. The more words you type in the search field, the narrower your search results.

✔ **Updates:** Because the App Store knows which apps you've purchased and downloaded, it automatically sends you a notification when an update is available. The number you see in the badge on the Updates button is the number of apps that have updates. We talk about updates a little farther along in this chapter.

To learn more about an app, tap either an icon on the Featured or Charts screen or an item in a list in the See All, Genius, or Search screens. An Info screen opens, as seen in Figure 2-3. At the very top, you see the name of the app, the developer's name, the star ratings, and a button that displays either the price or "free." Three tabs let you view

- **Details:** Scroll horizontally through screenshots of the app, or scroll vertically to read a description, information about the app such as the version and age rating, which indicates the minimum age considered appropriate for this app: 4+, 7+, 12+, and 17+, as well as which devices it's compatible with, as mentioned earlier. You also find developer information, in-app purchases, the version history, and privacy policy. You may have to tap More or a disclosure triangle to read everything in the section, as shown in Figure 2-4.

Figure 2-3: The app's Info screen gives detailed information about the app, including a description, screenshots, and reviews.

Figure 2-4: Scroll down to see more information at the bottom of the Info screen.

  ✔ **Reviews:** You see the number of ratings and the average stars the app's been given as well as written reviews. You can also write a review yourself or tap a link to go to the app support page.

  ✔ **Related:** Scroll horizontally through a selection of other apps by the same developer or other apps that were purchased or downloaded by customers who purchased or downloaded this app. Tap any of the icons to reach that apps' information screen.

When you're choosing apps, read the description, which is written by the developer, to understand exactly what you should expect from the app. Then read the reviews with a discerning eye as to whether the app does what the description says it does, whether it's buggy, whether it's lame. Some reviewers write a bad review because they expected the app to do something that it never claimed to do. Look for a positive or negative consensus in reviews to help you make a downloading decision.

Installing from the iPhone App Store

If you decide to download the app, tap the Free or price button on either the Info screen or directly on the app in the See All list format, or in the scrollable ad that you see when you view Genius or Search results. The button changes to Install or Buy App. Tap the button. You may be asked to enter your Apple ID and password, as shown in Figure 2-5. (See Book II, Chapter 1 for setting up an Apple account if you haven't done so already.)

If you chose a paid app, you have to enter your credit card or PayPal account information, have your on-file charge card charged, redeem an iTunes or Apple Store card, or have a credit balance in your iTunes account. If this is the first time you've purchased something with this iPhone, you have to verify the account and payment information. A screen appears that asks for your payment information, where you must enter your credit card or PayPal information. Otherwise, you may tap None in the selection of

Figure 2-5: Type in your Apple ID and password when asked.

credit card options, redeem an iTunes or Apple Store card, and then purchase items against the iTunes account balance. A second screen may ask your security questions to verify that you are who you say you are. After you enter this information the first time, you don't have to do it again until your credit card expires, your iTunes balance reaches zero, or you change devices.

If you frequently download items from the iTunes store, you can associate a credit card with your iTunes account or purchase iTunes or Apple store cards. Tap Featured at the bottom of the App Store screen, scroll to the bottom, and tap Redeem. If asked, sign in with your Apple ID and password. Type in the code found on the back of the iTunes or Apple store card. Whatever your payment method, you always have a chance to Confirm or Cancel your purchase after you hit the price button.

After the App Store has the information it needs from you, and you have confirmed that you want to buy the app, the price or Free button reads Installing. You can continue shopping or tap the Home button and the button of the new app appears across the bottom. A Waiting or Loading progress bar appears beneath the app, as seen in Figure 2-6.

There are a few more things you should know about shopping at the App Store:

- You can't use store credits to give an app to someone as a gift. If you have both a store credit and a credit card on file and gift an app to someone, it will automatically be charged to your credit card.

- Although you can window-shop the App Store from your iPhone to your heart's content, you can only download apps up to 50MB in size from your cellular network. To download apps larger than 50MB, you have to have a Wi-Fi connection on your iPhone or go through the iTunes Store on your computer and then sync the apps to your iPhone.

- If you lose your Internet connection or for some reason the download is interrupted, the next time you have an Internet connection, the download starts again. If, instead, you open iTunes on your computer and sign in to your account with the same Apple ID you used to begin the download that was interrupted, iTunes completes the download.

Apps that find you

Sometimes an app finds you. A lot of information providers, like newspapers or radio broadcasts, service providers, such as banks and FedEx, and social networks, like Facebook or Pinterest, caught on to the power of apps right from the beginning and developed slimmed-down versions of their Internet offerings.

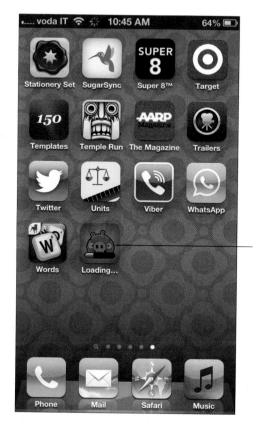

— An app is loading

Figure 2-6: After you tap Install and enter your Apple ID and Password, the download begins.

If you visit the FedEx website via Safari on your iPhone, you'll be prompted to download the FedEx app so you can track deliveries or request pickups. Barbara's bank sent her an e-mail invitation to download its online banking app. These apps give you direct access to the iPhone versions of their websites, which allow you to access the essentials without the extemporaneous fluff that takes a long time to load across a cellular data network.

Another way you can find apps for products and services you use frequently is to scan 2D barcodes, which are those one-by-one inch square graphic images that look like a labyrinth. You have to download a 2D barcode scanning reader such as QR Reader for iPhone or i-nigma QR. (QR stands for Quick Response.) After you have the reader app, you open the app and hold it over one of those barcodes. You are automatically sent to a mobile web page for the product or service associated with that barcode.

Shopping for Apps at the iTunes Store

If you do shop at the iTunes Store on your computer, you want to turn on Automatic Downloads so any purchases you make on one device, such as your computer or iPhone, are automatically downloaded to other devices linked to the same Apple ID.

To shop for iPhone apps from your computer, follow these directions:

1. **Open iTunes on your computer.**

2. **Click the iTunes Store button in the upper right corner.**

3. **Click the App Store tab at the top of the window or click and hold the tab to open a pop-up menu from which you can click a specific app category.**

4. **Browse and shop as you would for other media.**

Here's how to set up Automatic Downloads:

1. **Open iTunes on your computer.**

2. **Choose iTunes⇨Preferences and click the Store tab.**

3. **Under Automatic Downloads, check the type of media (Music, Apps, and/or Books) you want downloaded simultaneously to all devices.**

4. **Click OK.**

5. **On your iPhone, tap Settings⇨iTunes & App Stores and then tap On next to the items you want activated for Automatic Downloads (Music, Apps, and/or Books).**

Deleting Apps

You may tire of an app or find you downloaded an app that's a dud and you want to delete it. We explained this in Book I, Chapter 3, but here's a quick review. To delete apps from your iPhone, do the following:

1. **Press and hold any app on the Home screen until all the apps start wiggling.**

2. **Tap the X in the corner of the apps you want to delete.**

3. **Press the Home button when you're finished and the apps stand still.**

After you download an app, it remains associated with your Apple ID on iTunes. If you accidentally delete an app from your iPhone, you can download again from the App Store, as explained in later in this chapter.

If you want to rearrange how the apps appear on your Home screen, press and hold any app until they begin wiggling and then touch and drag them to new positions. See Book I, Chapter 3.

Updating and Upgrading Apps

An update is — almost always — an improvement to an app, usually to fix bugs. The App Store automatically checks for apps once a week, and also looks for updates whenever you sign in. Updates are free. You know you have updates when you see a numbered badge on the App Store button on your Home screen or on the Updates button at the bottom of the App screen. The number tells you how many apps have updates. Upgrades, on the other hand, may have a fee attached. For example, if you download the free, barebones version of an app but then want to upgrade to the full version, you'll probably have to pay for it. Or the free version may have third-party ads while the paid version is ad-free. Here we tell you the different ways you can find and install updates and upgrades.

Using iPhone's App Store to update

You can update one app at a time or update all the apps at once. Follow this procedure:

1. **Tap App Store on the Home screen.**

2. **Tap the Updates button on the bottom right corner of the App Store.**

   A list of apps that have updates appears, as shown in Figure 2-7. The version number is shown under the name of the app.

3. **Tap What's New (it's written quite small under the version number) to see what changes or fixes the update made or tap the app icon to open the Info screen.**

   A list of changes pops open.

4. **Tap the Update button on the Updates list or the Info screen.**

   OR

5. **Tap Update All on the Updates screen.**

   With Automatic Downloads, the apps in iTunes are updated as well.

Figure 2-7: The Updates screen shows you a list of which apps have updates available.

Using iTunes to update

You can see if updates are available from iTunes on your computer. Click the Library pop-up menu in the upper left of the iTunes window, and the number next to Apps indicates how many updates are available. Select Apps from the pop-up menu to open the Apps section of iTunes. A button at the bottom of the window tells you how many updates are available. Click that button to open the iTunes Store. The My App Updates window opens, where you can tap the Get Update buttons next to each individual app or click Download All Free Updates to get all the updates at once. If you didn't update the apps directly on your iPhone, they will be updated the next time you sync with iTunes.

Updating or upgrading from within the app

When a new version of an app is released, you are notified by the App Store on your iPhone and iTunes. Some apps let you know within the app that a new version is available. You might be playing a game and a notification appears telling you that a new version is available. Simply click the link that appears to get the new version.

Within the app you may also be invited to upgrade to the full or ad-free version. There might be a banner across the bottom that says something like "Click here to play ad-free." The link usually takes you to the App Store, and there's usually a fee involved if it's an upgrade, from either a barebones or ad-riddled free version to a paid-for full or ad-free version.

Buying more content

Earlier in this chapter, we mentioned add-ins like the chips you can buy so you can play the poker game. To keep things simple, add-ins are managed by the App Store. With our poker game example, after you've downloaded the app, you can purchase chips directly from within the app.

App Info and Settings

After an app is installed, you may want to find out more about the app or adjust some of the settings. On your iPhone, information such as the version number and links to the support site are usually found within the app by tapping an "i" or help button. Some app settings are managed on your iPhone under Settings. Tap Settings on the Home screen and scroll down to the bottom. The last section you see is the list of apps that have settings you can change. Each app has different settings so click through and play around with the settings for the apps that you have.

Other app settings are managed from within the app. There's no cut-and-dried rule to follow. You can visit the support page for an app to learn where the settings are and what they do. Again, we recommend playing a bit with the apps you have and trying different settings to make the app useful and enjoyable for you.

In iTunes on your computer, select Apps from the Library pop-up menu to display all your apps. Click an app icon, and then select File⇨Get Info. The app Info window opens, which has several tabs across the top. You're probably most interested in the Summary screen where you can see the version number of the app, its size and age rating, and when it was downloaded. You can also see what kind it is to determine if it works on both iPhone and iPad.

Reviewing Apps and Reporting Problems

We talked about how reviews can help you decide whether to purchase an app. After you purchase and use an app, you can contribute to the improvement of the app world by writing reviews and reporting problems. Your fellow app users will thank you and, at least in our experience, developers thank you, too, and quickly fix the problem. When you have a good or bad experience, write a quick review or at least give the app the appropriate number of stars. If you encounter a recurring problem, let the developer know. Here's how to submit reviews and problem reports on your iPhone and through iTunes.

On your iPhone

Open the App Store from the Home screen. Tap Search and locate the app you want to write a review for. You can only write reviews for apps that you have downloaded, whether free or purchased. Tap it to open the Info screen and then do the following to write a review:

1. **Tap the Reviews tab.**
2. **Tap Write a Review.**

   You may be asked to sign in to your Apple account.

3. **Tap the number of stars you want to give the app, and then fill in the form and write your review.**
4. **Tap Send to submit your review.**

If you're having a problem with the app, tap the App Support button, which opens the developer's website. Follow the links there to contact the developer about any problems you are having.

On iTunes

To write a review from iTunes, locate the app in the App Store section of the iTunes Store and click the Write a Review button just under Customer Reviews. Fill in the form that appears and click Submit. To contact the developer about a problem, click Report a Problem on the Write a Review form or click the App Support button next to the Write a Review button. If you are having a problem downloading or launching an app you recently down-loaded, go into your Purchase History from Store➪View.

Reinstalling Apps You Already Own

Mistakes happen. Computers crash. iPhones fall out of windows of moving cars. The result may be that you accidentally lose an app, could be a favorite game that you purchased or your online banking app. In any case, if you lose one app or all of them, the App Store knows what apps you already bought and lets you download them again (if they're still available from the App Store), free of charge. Here's how to do it on your iPhone:

1. **Tap App Store on the Home screen.**

2. **Tap the Updates button at the bottom right of the screen.**

3. **Tap Purchased at the top of the screen.**

   A list of apps you purchased appears.

4. **Tap All to see all apps you purchased or Tap Not on This iPhone to see apps you purchased that aren't on this iPhone.**

   There are three buttons you might see, as shown in Figure 2-8:

   • **Open** which opens the app

   • **Update** which means an update is available for the app

   • **iCloud icon** which means that you previously purchased the app but it isn't on your iPhone

5. **Tap the iCloud icon next to the app you want to reinstall.**

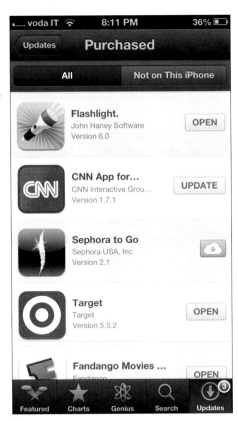

Figure 2-8: Access a list of purchased apps from the Updates screen.

The button changes to read "Installing" and the app is installed on your iPhone and has a New banner on its button on the Home screen.

On iTunes, the procedure is similar:

1. **Open iTunes on your computer and click iTunes Store.**

2. **Sign in to your account if you aren't already signed in.**

3. **Click Purchased in the Quick Links list.**

4. **Click the Apps tab and then click the iPhone tab.**

5. **Click Not on This Computer to see which apps are missing.**

6. **Click the iCloud button to download the app to your computer.**

    The app is downloaded to iTunes and automatically downloaded to your iPhone too, if you have activated Automatic Downloads in iTunes preferences, otherwise sync your iPhone with iTunes and the apps will be added to your iPhone.

Reading the News with Newsstand

You may have noticed the Newsstand button on the Home screen — it looks like a wooden bookshelf. This is really a folder in disguise that neatly organizes all your periodical subscriptions in one place. You find a publication's app (usually for free) by tapping the Newsstand button and then tapping Store. The Newsstand category of the App Store opens. (You can also reach it by opening the App Store, tapping Categories, and tapping Newsstand.) Scroll through as you would for any other kind of app as we explained previously. Tap the publication that interests you and tap Free to install the app.

The app icons appear like magazine covers or newspaper front pages on the Newsstand bookshelf, as shown in Figure 2-9. There are two ways to obtain issues:

 ✔ Tap Newsstand, and then tap the publication. Tap the Library button to see a list of subscription options as shown in Figure 2-10. Often you have the option of purchasing single issues or 3-, 6-, or 12-month subscriptions, as well as special issues.

 ✔ In the App Store, find the publications app, and then scroll to the bottom of the Info screen. Tap Top In-App Purchases to see what issues are available. Tap the issue you want to buy.

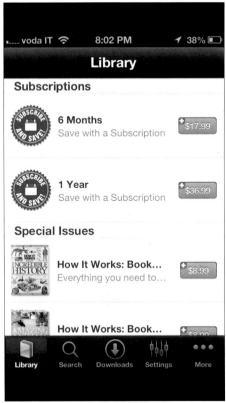

Figure 2-9: Newsstand stores your newspaper and magazine subscriptions in one place.

Figure 2-10: See subscription options from the publication's app.

When new issues are released, a badge on the Newsstand icon indicates their availability. Click on the publication on the Newsstand shelf to download and read the latest issue. If you want a publication to automatically push newly available content to your iPhone, go to Settings➪Newsstand and tap Automatic Content Download On for the publications you want to add this feature, as shown in Figure 2-11.

Because each publication app is just that, an app created by a third-party developer, there's no set rule for the publication interface. Different publications use different buttons, and you'll have to poke around and see what you can do and how the app works. The first time you open a publication after you subscribe, you may have to enter login information, which may be your Apple ID or may be a different user ID and password the publication asked you to create. Some publications give you a free iOS subscription if you subscribe to the print edition, and you would enter your subscriber information, usually culled from the mailing label on the print edition, in the Settings screen. You may have other options within the publications on Newsstand, as you can see in Figure 2-10, there's a Search and Settings option.

Newspapers usually show articles in streaming, meaning they are frequently updated and if you want to download an article to read later, you add it to a reading list in the app. Magazines, on the other hand, are usually downloaded to your iPhone, which means they occupy space. If you find you're running out of storage, see if the app offers a delete issue option so you can free up space. As a subscriber, you can download it again at a later date.

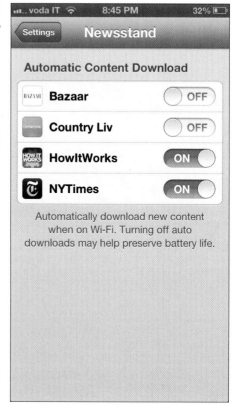

Figure 2-11: Go to Newsstand Settings to automatically download new content.

Chapter 3: Enhancing and Protecting iPhone with Add-ons

In This Chapter

- ✔ Considering neat-o iPhone add-ons and accessories
- ✔ Protecting iPhone with screen protectors and cases
- ✔ Tuning in to headphone and headset options
- ✔ Plugging in to cable and dock choices
- ✔ Touring in-car helper gizmos
- ✔ Pumping up the volume with external speaker add-ons

*E*ver since Apple introduced the first iPod, the so-called "iAccessories" market continues to come up with all kinds of add-ons and accessories for all things i — including, of course, your iPhone.

Just how big is the add-ons and accessories business? With so many categories and products to cover, we could literally fill an entire book. And with every new iPhone Apple releases, those new (and usually improved) add-ons and accessories hit the market, too. So instead of trying to cover every possible accessory category and type, we've selected just a few of our favorites to illustrate some of the most popular types of add-ons and accessories for your iPhone.

iPhone 5   iPhone 4S   iPh

one Accessories

Let's go shopping!

Although many iPhone (and iPod touch) cases, cables, docks, and other accessories may *look* similar or just seem like they'd work with some or all of the i-device products, they rarely do. This explains why Apple created the "Made for iPhone" label, which is what you want to look for when you're shopping for iPhone accessories. What's more, you want to note *which* iPhone model (or models) a particular product is designed to work with, so you can be sure the product works with *your* iPhone.

Taking Protective Measures

 iPhones are rugged little gizmos. Even so, the two most popular iPhone add-ons that most people buy for their beloved gadget are screen protectors and protective cases (which are not to be confused with iPhone cases that are all about glitz or fashion but offer zero or minimal actual protection).

Screen protectors

The iPhone screen is made of hardened glass that's so strong you can drag your car key back and forth across it and you still won't be able to scratch the glass.

Still, some iPhone owners swear by those sticky-backed screen protectors you can stick to your iPhone's screen to protect it from scratches. And while neither of us uses a screen protector on our iPhones, we both agree with two potential byproduct benefits of using a screen protector, which are

- **Minimizing smudges:** Certain screen protectors minimize how much of the finger oil smudges you see.

- **Preventing bits of glass from falling free if you shatter your iPhone's screen:** Joe can attest to this fact when, a few years ago, his iPhone 3G's screen shattered to bits when he knocked it off his desk and it landed face down on the floor. The screen was still able to function and respond to his finger taps, thanks to the ZAGG invisibleSHIELD screen protector he'd previously applied to the screen. Luckily, he could continue using the smashed-screen iPhone until he was able to replace it with a new iPhone. (Of course, had Joe enclosed the befallen iPhone in a protective case that offered cushioning around the front edges, the screen probably would have survived the short fall intact, screen protector be damned — more on protective cases in a moment.)

You can buy two main kinds of screen protectors:

- **Easy On/Off:** Semi-rigid, easy-to-apply or remove plastic screen protectors in either glossy or matte (anti-glare) finishes that don't always look so great because it's next to impossible to apply them without dust or air bubbles getting trapped beneath the surface when you first apply the screen protector.

- **Semi-Permanent:** Pliable, adhesive-backed plastic film protectors that require special handling and spraying your iPhone's screen with a special liquid to apply them to your iPhone's screen — but which benefit from a durable, fingerprint-hiding, permanent-feeling fit and finish that feels like they're part of iPhone's design, while minimizing or even completely eliminating any unsightly (read: distracting) dust particles or air bubbles from appearing beneath the surface.

Our favorite screen protector picks for the two categories described previously are

- **Screen Guard Anti-Smudge Overlay (www.belkin.com):** Smooth anti-smudge finish means obsessive types won't need to constantly polish their iPhone's screen to keep it looking clear and clean.

    Because some iPhone cases include a plastic screen protector, consider buying one of those two-for-one options if you're planning on buying a case as well, rather than laying out cash to buy both add-ons separately.

- **Zagg invisibleSHIELD (www.zagg.com):** Joe has applied the invisibleSHIELD — based on a clear, thin, and very durable military film originally made to protect U.S. military helicopter blades from high-speed damage — to numerous iPhones and iPads and has always been happy with the results. Choose from full-body or screen-only options (as shown in Figure 3-1), all of which come with a spray bottle of fluid used to help position the film, and a squeegee to squeeze out fluid and air bubbles.

**Book II
Chapter 3**

**Enhancing and
Protecting iPhone
with Add-ons**

Zagg recommends you don't touch your iPhone for 24 hours after you apply the invisibleSHIELD; however, in Joe's experience, applying the screen protector before bed allows sufficient time for the shield to dry and set overnight. That said, you should still be gentle with your iPhone the next morning and wait until later in the day or evening to really manhandle your gadget or outfit it with a protective case (which may pinch the edges) to ensure best possible results.

Figure 3-1: Zagg offers screen-only or full-body invisibleSHIELD options.

Cases

Of course, a screen protector won't protect your iPhone's screen from breaking if it's struck with considerable force — or even just on a corner or edge. To protect your iPhone's screen from breaking, your best bet is to buy a protective case or at the very least (for minimalist types), a bumper.

Protective cases generally come in four styles:

✔ **Bumper case,** which is sort of like a semi-rigid rubber-band that wraps the frame of your iPhone. The edges are well protected, and the case has holes for the volume buttons and connector ports. The bumper extends slightly beyond the front and back so that if your iPhone falls flat on its face, the bumper hits the ground first.

✔ **Minimal case,** which covers the back and sides of your iPhone, and usually the four corners, but not always the front face, which may leave your iPhone's screen vulnerable to breakage if it endures a forceful fall or impact.

✔ **Surrounded case,** which covers the back, sides, corners, and front edges of your iPhone, and provides a scant but potentially screen-saving lip and layer if your iPhone falls or is impacted facedown or on any edge or corner. Surround-type cases generally come in two styles:

  • One-piece construction that you squeeze your iPhone into

  • Two-piece, or "slider" construction that you slide onto either end of your iPhone until the inner edges meet in the middle (or nearly in the middle in some cases); or two-piece "snap" case construction that's typically a larger, fuller back and sides half, and a second front "frame" that snaps to the front of the back half to seal the full-case protection deal . . . er, design.

✔ **Wallet case,** which is styled like a miniature folio and typically features a few slots inside the front cover for stashing your ID, credit cards, and cash. (In addition to the two cases in the following section, be sure to check out Joe's favorite — the BookBook case for iPhone — in "Bonus Chapter 5: The Well-Informed Listener and Reader," which you can download from this book's companion website. For more on the website, see this book's Introduction.

Although Apple stopped producing a bumper case for iPhone, other manufacturers stepped in with their own models, such as the Scosche bandEDGE (`www.scosche.com`) shown in Figure 3-2, which is available for iPhone 4 and 4S and coming soon for iPhone 5. The bandEDGE provides reasonable peace of mind in the event you drop your iPhone and it lands on one of its vulnerable front edges — or even facedown. At the same time, the bandEDGE's lack of a back cover makes this case feel close to going naked — from your iPhone's point of view, of course.

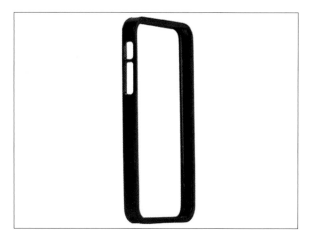

Figure 3-2: Scosche's bandEDGE bumper case offers the "bare" minimum protection.

Some minimal protection cases — which are so thin, they're sometimes referred to as *skins* — don't provide corner or front screen edge protection for your iPhone. As such, choosing one of those types of cases is more of a fashion over function purchase. To each his or her own!

Surround-type cases offer the best protection for your iPhone, with choices ranging from lightweight (yet still offering full protection) to thicker, heavier weight models designed to endure the most rugged conditions or environments — including falling from the sky, or landing in a puddle of water, as some of the choices below illustrate.

A few of our favorite surround type cases include the following:

✔ **Incase Crystal Slider (www.goincase.com):** This interesting looking case, shown in Figure 3-3, offers two great features in one: the all-round protection of Incase's standard Slider Case, with a lightweight and colorful minimalist look.

✔ **Grove Bamboo Case (www.grovemade.com):** Beautiful and better for the environment — that's what you get when you go with one of these handmade cases. Choices include plain or engraved, as shown in Figure 3-4. You can also send your own custom design, but be warned: The engraved or custom styles can take six or more weeks to arrive at your doorstep.

Figure 3-3: Full protection, minus the bulk and weight.

Figure 3-4: The eco-friendlier Grove Bamboo Case for iPhone.

✔ **Griffin Survivor Military-Duty Case for iPhone 5 (`www.griffin technology.com`):** Steer your web browser to a special video clip on Griffin's website (`www.griffintechnology.com/armored`) and watch in horror as an iPhone inside a Survivor case gets thrown down a paved street, flung across an icy creek, hurled down a hillside, bowled with on a concrete floor, and slammed into an office wall — all of which iPhone survives, intact. (It doesn't survive a car peeling out over it, however.) In other words, if you're the rough outdoors type (or just clumsy), consider the Military-Duty Case for iPhone 5, as shown in Figure 3-5.

Figure 3-5: Give your iPhone a reason to sing "I'm a Survivor!"

✔ **Moshi Overture (`www.moshimonde.com`) and Hex Axis Wallet:** Two styling wallet style cases for iPhone 4 models and iPhone 5 include the Moshi Overture and the Hex Axis Wallet, both shown in Figure 3-6. Each case has card and cash holders, while the Hex Axis Wallet one-ups the other case thanks to a clever built-in stand feature.

Figure 3-6: Two wallet cases: The Moshi Overture (left), and Hex Axis Wallet (right).

✓ **Lenmar Meridian iPhone 5 Battery Case (www.lenmar.com):** Although recent and new model iPhones feature rechargeable batteries that are mighty enough to see you through at least a full day of typical usage, some heavy-usage iPhone owners may have to carry their chargers so they can plug in and juice up their iPhone when the battery is running low. Or you can leave the charger home and opt for the Lenmar Meridian iPhone 5 Battery Case juice pack, shown in Figure 3-7, which pulls double-duty as both a protective case and an extra power source that can greatly extend your iPhone's uptime.

Figure 3-7: A protective case and battery booster in a single package.

Discovering Headphones and Headsets

iPhone 5's new bundled stereo EarPods with mic offer pretty good sound quality and the added bonus of letting you control a bunch of your iPhone's features, like answering and controlling phone calls and playing and pausing music and video. For most people, that's good enough.

But for some folks, spending extra to replace the bundled earphones is a must: for instance, audiophiles who want higher quality sound output (or make that input into the gray space between your ears), or frequent phone-callers who would like the hands-free convenience of making and receiving phone calls without wires getting in the way of their conversations. And ditto for anyone who enjoys (or depends on) listening to their favorite musical performers to help push them harder when they're working out or running without those dangling wires to get in the way of their own performance.

Some of our favorite headphone and headset choices include the following:

✔ **Bose SIE2i sport headphones (`www.bose.com`):** For outdoorsy types or runners (like Joe), They're sweat- and weather-resistant, stay comfortably yet securely in place without wobbling or bouncing no matter what terrain you're traversing. An included Reebok fitness armband holds your iPhone in place so you don't have to worry about dropping your beloved workout partner, and the built-in remote and mic makes it easy to answer that important call you're waiting for, or control music playback and volume. Work it!

✔ **Beats by Dr. Dre (`www.beatsbydre.com`):** It used to be just wearing white iPhone headphones made you stand out in a crowd (and in some cities, made you easy targets for mugging thieves!). Nowadays, the standard iPhone headphones are commonplace, and a new eye-catching brand has become the in sound "thang": Beats headphones. Designed for sound engineers, musicians, and those who take sound seriously, Beats was established in 2006 as the brainchild of legendary artist and producer Dr. Dre and chairman of Interscope Geffen A&M Records Jimmy Iovine. Prices range from $199 for the Beat Solo model, to $399 for Beat Pro, as shown in Figure 3-8.

**Book II
Chapter 3**

Enhancing and
Protecting iPhone
with Add-ons

Figure 3-8: High-end sound for those who take their music seriously.

✔ **Jawbone Icon HD (www.jawbone.com):** Small and light enough to stay in your ear without one of those annoying loops, the Jawbone Icon HD Bluetooth headset, shown in Figure 3-9, is equipped with advanced, military-grade noise cancellation technology that eliminates unwanted background noise when you talk on the phone. What's more, the headset's battery level appears in your iPhone's status bar — or tap the Icon HD's control button to get a spoken report on how much battery juice is left for handsfree chitchat.

Figure 3-9: The Jawbone Icon HD offers truly hands-free operation.

Hooking Up with Cables and Docks

You can never have too many connections, especially iPhone-friendly ones that enhance your iPhone's features. They let you do things like connect your iPhone to your TV to watch photo slideshows or videos you shoot with iPhone — or movies you buy or rent from the iTunes Store — just to name a few scenarios.

Some of our favorite cable and dock options you can buy for your iPhone include the following:

✔ **Apogee JAM Guitar Input (www.apogeedigital.com):** Connect the Apogee JAM Guitar Input into your iPhone (or iPad, as shown in Figure 3-10) and your guitar and record your jam sessions to GarageBand running on your iPhone; an input gain control knob makes it easy to pump up the volume — and green and red indicator lights make it easy to keep an eye on whether you're rocking within an agreeable range, or too hard to the point of un-harmonic distortion. Sweet!

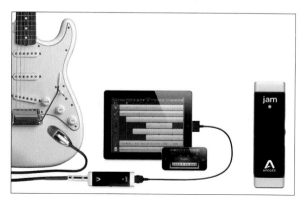

Figure 3-10: A full-on guitar jam in the palm of your hand.

✔ **Lightning to 30-pin Adapter (www.apple.com):** Happy you bought a new iPhone 5 to replace your earlier iPhone, but bummed your plug-in accessories won't work with the iPhone 5's new Lightning connector? No worries, you can buy one of two types of Lightning to 30-pin Adapters. The compact adapter is shown in Figure 3-11, and the other is a cabled adapter. With these adapters, you can use those 30-pin accessories you already own.

Figure 3-11: The Apple Lightning to 30-pin Adapter.

↙ **Apple AV Adapter and Cables (www.apple.com):** Plug the Lightning Digital AV Adapter or the Lightning to VGA Adapter into your iPhone, and then connect the adapter to your HDTV with an HDMI cable (sold separately) or your VGA TV or monitor, and va-va-voom: Your iPhone can now entertain the entire room on the big-screen. Show off what you see on your iPhone screen (be it a game of Angry Birds, or the latest blockbuster you rent or buy from the iTunes Store), while keeping your iPhone juiced to last through the entire performance, thanks to a second port on the adapter that accommodates your iPhone's charger cable.

Another awesome (and totally wireless) option for streaming your iPhone's video and music to your TV and sound system is Apple's AppleTV product, which we write about in Book V, Chapter 4.

Taking It Away with Car and Travel Accessories

It goes without saying (but we'll say it anyway) that neither of us advocates using your iPhone to carry on phone or text (!) conversations while driving — and we mean never, ever. If you need to send or reply to a text message, or make or answer a call, do yourself — and everyone in your car or on the road — a favor and pull over. (This public service announcement brought to you by "Common Sense.")

That unsaid rule said and out of the way, here are a few of our favorite iPhone accessories for the car (that don't have anything to do with using your iPhone while driving to participate in phone or text conversations):

↙ **Travel Stand (www.griffintechnology.com):** With handsfree landscape viewing and helpful headphone storage, Griffin Travel Stand for iPhone, as shown in Figure 3-12, turns your car's dashboard or airplane tray table into a personal movie theater (for passengers or flyers) or GPS navigator station. When the show's over, the stand's compact size makes it easy to slip in your pocket and take the show elsewhere.

Figure 3-12: A video stand with headphones storage for easy viewing on the go.

✔ **IOGEAR Solar Bluetooth Hands-Free Car Kit (www.iogear.com):** Pair your iPhone with IOGEAR's Solar Bluetooth Hands-Free Car Kit, shown in Figure 3-13, for hands-free placing and answering calls while keeping your eyes on the road and your hands on the wheel. A built-in solar panel harnesses the power of the sun for easy recharging.

Figure 3-13: Safer phoning on the road — the eco-friendlier way.

Book III

Communications Central: Calls, Messages, and the Web

The 5th Wave   By Rich Tennant

"Okay, the view's just up ahead. Everyone switch to 'America the Beautiful' on your iPhone playlist."

Impatient readers will probably open this mini-book first — caught you, didn't we? Each of the next four chapters focuses on an aspect of communications. Chapter 1 shows you how to make phone calls with your iPhone. You might be thinking, "How hard can that be?" It's not difficult, but there's a difference between making simple phone calls and using all of your iPhone's phone-calling features, such as FaceTime video calls and voice-controlled dialing. Chapter 2 is all about messaging. We explain how to send both SMS and MMS messages and manage them, and we tell you how they differ too. We show you how to use iMessages to send words and images to your other iOS and Mac friends across Wi-Fi and cellular data network without cutting into your SMS allowance. Wax your (key)board because the third chapter is an invitation to a web surfin' Safari. We present an in-depth study of navigating the web on your iPhone and managing the websites you use most often with bookmarks and web apps. Chapter 4 explains Mail: how to set up an e-mail account and how to write, send, receive, respond to, and manage e-mail messages. At the end of this minibook, you'll wonder how you ever communicated without your iPhone.

Chapter 1: Managing Phone and FaceTime Video Calls

In This Chapter

✔ Making and receiving calls

✔ Taking note of Phone notifications

✔ Listening to and managing voicemail messages

✔ Perusing and adjusting phone-related settings

✔ Creating and organizing favorites and contacts

✔ Juggling call options and conference calls

✔ Face-to-face video chatting with FaceTime

*W*e're guessing you've already made and received phone calls with your iPhone before you arrived at this chapter. You probably also listened to voicemail messages for calls you were unable to answer, and maybe you even changed the ringtone that plays when calls come in.

Even if you've already done some or all of those things, this chapter is all about maximizing your up-close-and-personal relationship with iPhone's phone-related features.

In this chapter, we introduce you to the Phone app you use to place a call or answer one, and we tell you how to politely decline a call that you can't respond to at that moment. We then show you how to listen to and manage your voicemails, and about the different ways iPhone notifies you when you miss a call. Next, we point out phone-related settings you may want to familiarize yourself with before you start making calls — especially if you're traveling overseas. At the end of the chapter, we tell you about two Phone features, call waiting and conference calls, and how to conduct face-to-face video chat calls using FaceTime.

Homing in on Phone

 Tapping the Phone icon on the Home screen brings up the image in Figure 1-1 and is indisputably the most obvious way to use your iPhone as, well, a phone.

Some not-so-obvious ways that can also land you on Phone screen include answering an incoming call, tapping a phone number in an e-mail or text message you receive to call that number back, tapping a number in the Contacts app, or by speaking the name or number you want Siri (iPhone 4S or later) or iPhone's Voice Control feature to dial on your behalf.

 We assume that your iPhone currently enjoys an active connection with your provider's cellular network, as indicated by the cell signal strength icon in the top left corner of iPhone's status bar. The more bars you see, the better the signal. If instead of bars you see No Signal or No Service, you won't be able to make or receive calls until you're once again in range of your provider's cellular network signal. To familiarize yourself with other icons you see in the status bar, check out Book I, Chapter 2.

The FaceTime Favorite icon

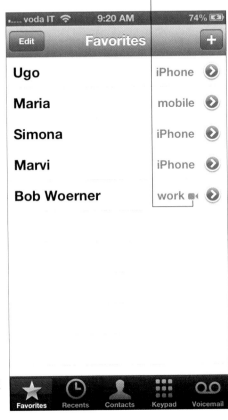

Figure 1-1: The Phone app: More ways to make calls than meets the eye.

However you reach the Phone screen, you always see the following icons at the bottom of the screen that activate Phone app's main features:

 ✔ **Favorites:** iPhone's version of speed dial, offering quick, one-tap dialing access to the fifty people you call the most.

 ✔ **Recents:** A roll-call list displays up to 75 of the most recent calls you placed, answered, missed, or hung up on.

 ✔ **Contacts:** Your personal phone book stored in the Contacts app. See Book IV, Chapter 1 to learn about the Contacts app.

✔ **Keypad:** An on-screen keypad that works like the physical keypads introduced in the '80s, for dialing phone numbers.

✔ **Voicemail:** Your inbox for listening to, replying to, managing, deleting, and getting more information about voicemail messages you receive.

We write about the first four of these Phone features (as well as using Voice Control) in the next section and cover Voicemail in the section "Visiting Voicemail."

Making Calls

iPhone lets you make calls a number of ways — from tapping out numbers the old-fashioned way using the on-screen keypad, to saying the number or name of the person you want to call out loud without having to bother touching the screen at all.

To simply make a phone call, tap the Phone app on the Home screen, and then tap one of the five buttons at the bottom of the Phone screen (refer to Figure 1-1).

Here's a quick rundown of the ways to make calls (all of which we cover in depth in the following sections):

✔ Tap Favorites, and then tap the contact you want to call.

✔ Tap Recents, and then tap the name or number you want to call.

✔ Tap Contacts, find and tap the contact you want to call to display his contact card, and then tap the phone number you want to dial.

✔ Tap Keypad, type the number you want to call, and then tap Call.

✔ Tap Voicemail, tap the name or number you want to call, and then tap Call Back.

✔ Press and hold the Home button to activate Siri (iPhone 4S or later) or Voice Control, and then say the name or number you want to call.

Using Favorites

Tapping Favorites displays the names of up to 50 people and organizations you deem important enough to score a spot on what is essentially iPhone's version of your speed-dial list, as shown in Figure 1-1. Both phone numbers and FaceTime contact information count against the total, and each number counts as one, so if you have a work number and a home number for the same person, that equals two favorites. You can add, edit, rearrange, remove, and — most importantly— make phone calls with Favorites.

Add a Favorite

1. **Tap the + (plus sign) button to display your contacts, and then search or scroll through your contacts to find the one you want to add.**

2. **Tap the contact you want to add to your favorites list, and then choose the phone number you want to associate with that contact's favored place on your list. (See Book IV, Chapter 1 to learn about Contacts).**

3. **A dialog asks if you want to add the number as a Favorite for Voice Call or FaceTime, as shown in Figure 1-2. Tap the one you want.**

   The person's name appears in your Favorites list. A description of the phone number associated with each favorite appears to the right of the contact's name, to indicate *mobile, home,* or another label you selected when you created or edited the person's contact card.

   A camera icon (refer to Figure 1-1) appears alongside any names you add as FaceTime Favorites, which we explain in the "Doing FaceTime Video Chat Calls" section later in this chapter.

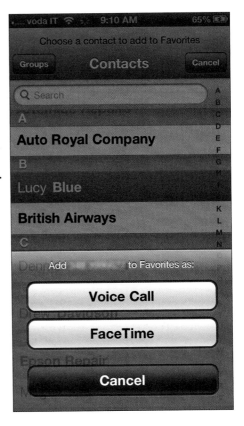

Figure 1-2: A number can be assigned as a FaceTime or Voice Call Favorite.

The + button doesn't appear after you've reached the Favorites list limit of 50 favorites. You'll need to delete an existing favorite from your list to make the + appear again so you can tap it to add a new favorite.

Call a Favorite

Tap a name in the list and the outgoing call is placed.

Delete or rearrange Favorites

1. **Tap the Edit button in the upper left.**

2. **Tap the red button to the left of a name you want to delete, and then tap the Delete button that appears to the right, as shown in Figure 1-3.**

   Your out-of-favor contact's name only vanishes from your Favorites list, but her card is not deleted from your saved Contacts.

3. **Next to a name you want to move to a new position in the list, tap and drag the rearrange button up or down your list and then let go to save your favorite in its new location.**

4. **Tap the Done button when you finish.**

Get More Info/Edit a Favorite

Tap the blue arrow to display a favorite's contact Info screen. The person's contact card displays any information you filled in for that contact, including phone numbers and e-mail addresses. We explain Contacts more in Book IV, Chapter 1, but you'll notice two things in Contacts after you add a person to your Favorites list:

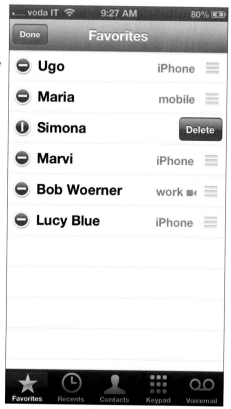

Figure 1-3: The Favorites edit screen.

- A blue star appears next to the phone number that's been saved in your Favorites list. Tap another number for that contact to add a second favorite number for that contact (for instance, one for Mom's mobile number, a second for her home number).

- Contacts already added to your favorites list with no second or remaining phone numbers to add won't appear in your contacts list when adding new contacts to Favorites (because you've already added them).

Using Recents

Tapping Recents displays a chronological list — also referred to as your phone's call log — of up to 75 of the most recent numbers your iPhone has called, received or missed calls from, or hung up on (more than one call from the same number counts as one of the 75), as shown in Figure 1-4. Tap the All tab to view every kind of incoming and outgoing call or tap Missed to see only those calls you didn't respond to for one reason or another.

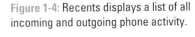

Here's how to interpret the information you find on the Recents list:

- Names indicate calls to or from people whose numbers are saved in Contacts.

- Phone numbers aren't associated with a person's contact card. (That doesn't mean you can't save a phone number in Contacts without a name — you can. But why you'd want to is anyone's guess.)

- The label next to the recent caller/callee's number — such as home, mobile, or other — is displayed if you assigned that label to the number in Contacts or the contact management app from which you imported the contact.

Figure 1-4: Recents displays a list of all incoming and outgoing phone activity.

- Calls you place are marked with the outgoing phone call icon.

- Missed calls are hard to miss on your list because they're the items displayed in red type.

- Incoming and outgoing calls from or to the same person or phone number are displayed together as one item in the list. The number in parentheses next to the name or number (refer to Figure 1-4) tells you how many calls were placed.

  Tap the blue arrow button to see detailed information about the call activity: the day and time (or consecutive times) a contact or phone number reached out to you (or you reached out to them), as shown in Figure 1-5. You also see any additional phone numbers, e-mail or street addresses, and other details from the contacts card in Contacts. A blue star appears next to any of that contact's phone numbers you designated as favorite.

Figure 1-5: Tap the blue arrow to see the time and duration of calls from the same number.

Book III Chapter 1

Managing Phone and FaceTime Video Calls

Make sure to tap the blue arrow when you want more information in either the Favorites or Recents list because tapping the name will initiate a call.

To remove items from the list, one at a time:

⯈ Swipe across an individual call and then tap the Delete button that deletes only that recent call from the list.

⯈ Tap the Edit button in the upper right. Tap the red and white minus sign that appears to the left of the call you want to delete, and then tap the Delete button.

To remove all the items from the Recents list, tap Clear in the upper left, and then tap Clear All Recents in the dialog that appears.

Tapping the Clear button clears *all* items from the Recents list even if you tap Clear while viewing only Missed calls.

Using Contacts

Tapping Contacts displays your iPhone's central directory for storing and managing contact "cards" containing the names, phone numbers, e-mail and street addresses, and other information, as shown in Figure 1-6. The Contacts you see in the Phone app are the same as those in the Contacts app.

Tap a contact card to display the contact's Info screen, as shown in Figure 1-7, and then tap the phone number you want to call to dial that number.

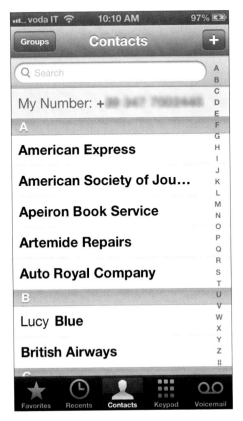

Figure 1-6: Contacts lists every contact "card" saved on your iPhone.

Figure 1-7: Tap a contact's phone number to call that number.

TIP

Tap the Add to Favorites button if you frequently call this contact.

You can search your contacts from the Contacts list three ways:

- Drag or flick up or down the list until you see the contact you want.
- Tap a letter in the A to Z index on the right edge to jump to contact names beginning with that letter, and then scroll through the list until you see the contact you want.
- Tap the Search field (tap the clock in the Status bar if you don't see it) and begin typing the name of the person or company you're searching for to display any contacts that match what you type, and then tap the contact that matches the one you're looking for, as shown in Figure 1-8.

You can also search for your contacts using Spotlight search, which you access by flicking the main Home screen to the far right; we tell you everything you need to know about using Spotlight in Book I, Chapter 3.

Tap the + button when viewing your Contacts list to create a New Contact card. When viewing a contact's info card, tap Edit to make changes to that contact. We write about creating, using, and managing Contacts in Book IV, Chapter 1.

Instead of adding contacts to your iPhone by hand, it's easier to fill up your Contacts list (if you haven't already done so) by syncing your iPhone with iTunes or iCloud. Learn about syncing in Book II, Chapter 1.

Using the Keypad

Tapping the Keypad displays the onscreen keypad. Tap the numbers of the phone number you want to call and then press Call to dial your number, as shown in Figure 1-9.

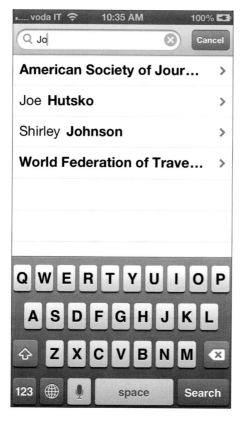

Figure 1-8: Homing in on contacts with the Search feature.

Figure 1-9: Dialing phone numbers the "old-fashioned" way.

Book III
Chapter 1

Managing Phone and FaceTime Video Calls

Tap the delete button to backspace over a number (or numbers) you mistyped.

Some nifty things you can do (and see!) when you're using Keypad include the following:

↳ Enter a "soft" pause by pressing and holding the * key until a comma appears in the phone number display. A soft pause is two seconds. You could use this feature if you call in for your voicemail at work and have to call the phone number, and then enter an access code, and then perhaps a passcode. Putting a soft pause between the phone number and each code gives the system time to receive the information and go to the next step.

↳ Enter a "hard" pause by pressing and holding the # key until a semicolon appears in the phone number display. A hard pause waits for your confirmation (tap the Dial button) before transmitting the next series of numbers. For example, when calling a company, you have to wait for the line to be answered before entering an extension.

↳ Paste a phone number you copied from another app into Keypad by tapping the display zone above the numeric keys, and then tapping Paste in the pop-up that appears.

↳ Press Call to bring up the last number you dialed, and then press Call again to dial it.

↳ See the contact name magically appear beneath a number you tap in if that number is on any contact's card.

 ↳ Tap the Add Contact button (to the left of the Call button) to either create a new contact card with the phone number you're typing, or to add the phone number to an existing contact, as shown in Figure 1-10.

Figure 1-10: Putting a new phone number to good use.

Using Voicemail

Voicemail

One of our favorite things about the Phone app's Voicemail feature is how *seeing* those messages in the voicemail inbox helps to remind us to call back any of those people we want to chat with.

Tap a name or number in the Voicemail list screen and then tap Call Back to call that person or phone number.

To learn about the other things you can do on the Voicemail screen besides returning phone calls, check out the section "Visiting Voicemail," later in this chapter.

Using Siri or Voice Control

Both iPhone's Voice Control and Siri (iPhone 4S or later) features are all ears when it comes to using your voice to make your iPhone do things for you — including making phone calls. In Book I, Chapter 3, we explain all the other things Voice Control and Siri can do for you. Here, we explain phone calls.

You can use Voice Control or Siri but not both at the same time, and you need either a cellular data or Wi-Fi Internet connection to use Siri.

Siri

Siri is a bit more intelligent than Voice Control, or perhaps she has better ears. Do one of the following to solicit Siri:

- ✓ Press and hold the Home button until the Siri screen opens
- ✓ Press and hold the center button on the EarPods controls until you hear a double-beep
- ✓ Press the Attention button on your Bluetooth headset
- ✓ Bring your iPhone to your ear, if you activated the Raise to Speak function, until you hear a double-beep

Speak your command, more or less as if you were talking with a person. You can give complex instructions, like "Call Lucy." Siri looks first in your Favorites for people named Lucy and then for Lucy's phone number. Siri responds along the lines of "Calling Lucy Blue's iPhone," as shown in Figure 1-11. If there is no Lucy in your Favorites, Siri asks for more information. Speak the requested information and Siri makes the phone call when she finds the number. If the person you want to call isn't in your Contacts or somewhere else on your iPhone, Siri can search the Internet for the number, and then connect you. You get the picture. If the person isn't available, you can ask Siri to send the person an e-mail.

**Book III
Chapter 1**

**Managing Phone
and FaceTime Video
Calls**

Siri requires a Wi-Fi or cellular Internet connection and can be slow to respond to your request — up to 10 seconds — depending on the type of Internet connection you have and because your request is sent to Apple's server, which processes the request, and then instructs Siri how to respond. If you use Siri only for making phone calls, Voice Control will probably be faster and more accurate.

Voice Control

Press and hold the Home button to activate Voice Control. The screen shown in Figure 1-12 opens (you'll also hear a double-tone sound). Say "Call" or "Dial," followed by the name of the person or phone number you want to call. A slightly robotic voice repeats your request aloud and then places your call for you.

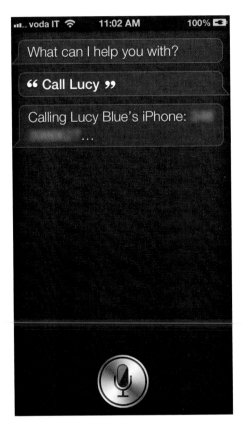

Figure 1-11: The Siri calling screen.

Figure 1-12: The Voice Control screen.

Even more ways to make calls

Besides using the Phone app, Siri, or Voice Control to make calls, you can also initiate calls by tapping phone numbers that appear on web pages you're browsing, in e-mail, notes, or text messages you receive, and in other near and possibly faraway places like the search results you turn up when you use Maps to locate a restaurant, business, or other organization. To make a call from Maps, tap the arrow next to the name on the map to open up an information screen, and then tap the phone number to make the call. (See the calling sequence for Maps in the two following figures.) Tapping a phone number in any app displays a dialog, which gives you the option to call the number, whereas pressing and holding on a number serves up even more options for doing things besides just calling the number, including sending a text message to the number, creating a new contact card for the number, or adding the number to an existing card already saved in Contacts, as shown in the figure.

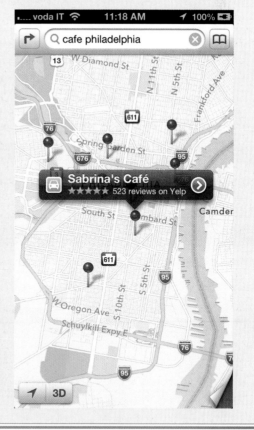

Ways Voice Control may respond to your request include the following:

- **No Match Found:** That's what the Voice Control robot says (followed by three tone sounds) if it can't find a phone number in Contacts that matches the name you said; or if it can't understand the phone number you gave it to dial for you. Either way, you can try again by immediately repeating the name or number (perhaps more slowly this time).

- **Multiple Numbers:** If a contact you're calling has more than one phone number, the Voice Calling robot says the contact's name aloud, and then rattles off the different phone numbers it finds for that contact, such as "home, mobile, or work." Say the one you want and Voice Control completes the call request.

- **Multiple Matches Found:** That's what Voice Control tells you if it finds multiple numbers for a name you say, such as "Call Joe;" Voice Control lists the names of contacts with the same name so you can pick one, or it asks you to be more specific.

Calling tips

Whether you're talking to Siri or Voice Control, when saying a person's name, you can differentiate between people who have the same first name by adding their last name, as well as say the specific phone number you want to call if you have more than one phone number for the person:

- Say "Call" or "Dial," and then say

  - "Joe Smith"

  - "Joe Smith at work"

  - "Joe Hutsko, mobile"

Sometimes your iPhone has trouble understanding you in a crowded place with a lot of ambient noise such as a party or street corner. If you are calling someone with a foreign name, say it with an English pronunciation. For example, Barbara's husband's name is Ugo (pronounced oo-go), but for Siri or Voice Control to understand, Barbara must say "call *hew-go*". One day Siri was convinced Barbara wanted to call someone named "google google" until finally Siri gave up and quite testily said, "Barbara, I don't understand."

When saying phone numbers you want to call, remember the following:

✔ Speak each number clearly and separately; for instance, if you want to call 555-6666, you would say "Call five five five, six six six six."

✔ If you're calling an 800 number, you can say "eight hundred," followed by the rest of the number you are calling.

The Voice Control and Siri features work even if your iPhone is locked, which is a handy feature — unless you misplace or lose your iPhone and someone picks it up and starts making international calls. To turn off the ability to make Voice Control calls when your iPhone is locked, go to Settings➪General➪Passcode Lock and turn off the Voice Dial option, as shown in Figure 1-13. (It will only be active if you have set up a Passcode.) When the Voice Dial feature is off, you can still use Voice Control or Siri when your iPhone is locked to do things like play or pause music or say "What time is it?" to hear the local time. If you say "Call Joe Hutsko," however, the ever-watchful genie that lives inside your iPhone politely responds, "Voice dialing is disabled."

Figure 1-13: Disable or enable the Voice Dialing or Siri feature when iPhone is locked.

Book III
Chapter 1

Managing Phone and FaceTime Video Calls

Answering Calls

Because you never know when you might get a call, mastering the art of answering calls (or rejecting ones you're unable or not in the mood to answer) is a useful iPhone talent to acquire sooner than later.

When you receive a call, your iPhone displays one of the incoming call screens shown in Figure 1-14, depending on whether your iPhone is locked (left) or awake (right). You'll hear your chosen ringtone and, if your iPhone is on your person — depending on how sensitive you are — you may feel it vibrating. If the information of the person calling you is saved in Contacts, you'll see the person's name (and photo, if you assigned a photo to that person's contact card). If the caller isn't one of your contacts, you either see the caller's phone number and name, or "Unknown" or "Blocked" if the caller has chosen to block their Caller ID from appearing when they place calls.

Figure 1-14: Two incoming call screens: One locked (left), the other not (right).

To answer an incoming call

✔ Drag the Slide to Answer button to the right (if your iPhone is locked)

✔ Tap Answer

To instantly quiet your iPhone's ringtone when you receive an incoming call, tap either volume button once, or press the Sleep/Wake button once. You can still answer the call but the ringing is muted. Double-click the Sleep/Wake button to send the call directly to voicemail.

If a second call comes in while you're engaged in another call, you see the screen as shown in Figure 1-15. Tap Hold Call + Answer to put your current call on hold and respond to the second incoming call.

If you want to end the first call and answer the second, your iPhone responds differently depending on whether you have a GSM (AT&T) or CDMA (Verizon, Sprint) iPhone.

- **GSM:** Tap End Call + Answer.

- **CDMA:** Tap End Call, and when the second call rings again, tap Answer.

We give you more details on juggling more than one call at a time in the section "Making Dual and Conference Calls."

Figure 1-15: Options for responding to a second incoming phone call.

When you answer an incoming call, the active call screen appears. We give you the full 411 on your options in the section "Managing Calls" a little farther along in this chapter.

Declining Calls

Sometimes, you just can't respond to a call or don't want to talk to the caller. iOS 6 gives you several options for declining phone calls and added two new functions: You have the option of declining a call but sending a message to the caller that reads "I'll call you later" or something to that effect, or you can opt to be reminded in an hour to call the person back. Here are your call-declining options:

- **Press the Sleep/Wake button twice (which sends the call to voicemail).**

- **Tap the Decline button (if your iPhone is awake).**

- **Tap Ignore to send a second call to voicemail and continue talking on the first call.**

- **Ignore iPhone's pleas to get your attention.** After a few moments, the call is automatically declined.

- **Touch and drag the Reply/Remind button on the right of either incoming call screen then tap one of the buttons, as shown in Figure 1-16:**

  - *Reply With Message:* Choose one of the options or tap Custom to create a specific response for that call. Go to Settings⇨Phone⇨Reply With Message to create different default replies. Tap in the field of the reply you want to replace and type your own reply, as shown in Figure 1-17.

  - *Remind Me Later:* Tap one of the options:

    In One Hour. You'll receive a notification in an hour to call the person whose call you declined.

    When I Leave, and then choose either Current Location, Get Home, or Get to Work to receive a reminder based on one of those three locations. Location Services must be turned on for the When I Leave feature to appear and function.

Answering or declining calls while using your iPhone's stereo headphones is merely a matter of working the remote button as follows:

- Click the center button once to answer a call, or twice to decline a call.

- Click the volume + or - buttons to adjust the volume level.

When you decline a call in any of the preceding ways, the caller hears your voicemail greeting, followed by the option to leave you a voicemail message. Ditto if someone tries calling you when your iPhone is turned off, Airplane Mode is turned on, or Do Not Disturb is activated and your phone is locked.

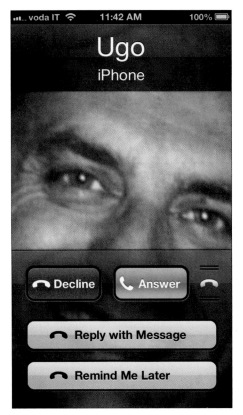

Figure 1-16: Decline calls with a polite message or remind yourself to call back.

Figure 1-17: Create your own default replies to calls you decline.

Activate Do Not Disturb by turning Settings➪Do Not Disturb➪On. Tap Settings➪Notifications➪Do Not Disturb to schedule a set daily time to be left undisturbed. See Book I, Chapter 4 for more details.

Managing Calls

In the previous sections, we tell you about (almost) every which way you can answer and make calls with iPhone. In this section, we tell you about the things you can do while you're engaged in an active call, such as adjusting the volume for your call or switching on iPhone's speakerphone, as well as neat stuff like using the active call screen to do other things while you're actively engaged in a call, and making or accepting a second call while you're on your current call, and then merging those two calls together so everyone can join the conversation.

When you make or answer a call, the active call screen appears as in Figure 1-18. The Active Call screen displays information about the person or business you're speaking with such as the phone number or name (if saved in Contacts), and the length of time you're engaged in your call from the moment you connected. You'll also see a photo of the person if you saved a photo with his contact card in Contacts.

The buttons you see have the following functions:

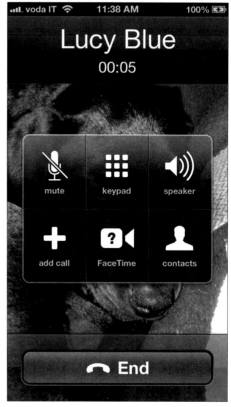

Figure 1-18: The active call screen.

 ✔ **Mute:** Tap Mute to prevent your caller from hearing sound on your end of the conversation, even though you can still hear your caller; tap again to turn off Mute.

 ✔ **Hold:** Press and hold the Mute button; the mute button changes into the Hold button; tap Hold again to turn off Hold. When you place a call on hold, neither you nor the person on the other end can hear the other.

 ✔ **Keypad:** Tap Keypad to display the keypad, and then tap any numbers or the * and # buttons to do things like respond to options when calling automated customer service phone numbers, or check your work voice-mail inbox.

 ✔ **Speaker:** Tap the Speaker icon to hear your caller's voice through iPhone's built-in loudspeaker.

 ✔ **Switch Audio Device:** You see this button in place of the Speaker button when you have a Bluetooth headset paired with your iPhone, which we explain in the section "Using Bluetooth headsets."

 ✔ **Add Call:** Tap Add Call to put one person on hold and call another and also to set up a conference call. We explain this is detail in the section "Making Dual and Conference Calls."

✔ **Use FaceTime:** Tap FaceTime to switch your current voice-only call to a FaceTime video chat call, which we write about in the section "Making a FaceTime Call," later in this chapter.

✔ **Contacts:** Tap Contacts to browse your contact cards to do things like find and share a phone number with the person you're currently speaking with, or choose another contact's phone number that you want to call while engaged in your current call.

Using Bluetooth headsets

When you make a call while you're connected to a Bluetooth headset you paired with your iPhone, the Audio Sources screen shown in Figure 1-19 appears while your call is being connected. Tap iPhone or Speaker if you want to switch to either of those audio sources instead of your Bluetooth device; or tap Hide Sources to display the active call screen, which automatically appears after your call is connected. (We tell you how to set up and manage Bluetooth devices in Book I, Chapter 2.) To change the audio source, tap the Audio Source button on the active call screen to display the Audio Sources options, tap the audio source choice you want to switch to, and then tap Hide Sources to return to the active call screen.

Press iPhone's volume up and down buttons to increase or decrease the volume level of your call. If you're using headphones or a Bluetooth headset, you can also press the volume + and - buttons on those listening devices to adjust the call volume.

Figure 1-19: Choosing your preferred audio source while making or managing a call.

Multitasking while on a call

Whenever a call is underway — whether you placed or answered the call — the active call screen is displayed (refer to Figure 1-18).

When you're engaged in an active call, you can switch to another app to do other things, like looking up recipe ingredients you jotted in Notes, or reading an e-book while you're stuck on hold. When you switch to another app while engaged in a call, the green pulsing active call banner shown in Figure 1-20 appears at the top of the screen. Tapping the active call banner returns you to the active call display.

Making dual and conference calls

While you're engaged in an active call, you can make a second call, or you can answer an incoming call (unless you've turned off your iPhone's call waiting feature, which we explain in the "Call Forwarding, Call Waiting, and Caller ID Blocking" section of this chapter). If you have a GSM-model iPhone, you can also initiate a conference call that lets you speak with up to five people at once.

The active call banner

Figure 1-20: The active call banner.

Making a second call

While on an active call, you can make a second call by doing the following:

1. **Tap Add Call to display your iPhone Contacts.**

2. **Scroll to find and tap to choose the contact you want to call, as shown in Figure 1-21.**

   You can tap the Favorites, Recents, and Keypad buttons at the bottom of the screen to use any of those options to add your second call.

   When your second call is established, the active multiple calls screen appears (refer to Figure 1-22).

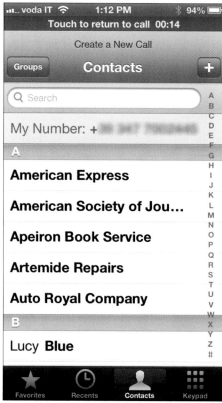

Figure 1-21: Choose the second person or number you want to call.

Figure 1-22: The active multiple calls screen.

3. **On a GSM phone, switch between your callers to speak privately with one or the other by tapping the caller's name at the top of the screen.**

    See the section "Activating Your iPhone" in Book I, Chapter 2 to determine which type of phone you have if you're not sure.

    CDMA phones only allow you to switch between calls if the second call was incoming.

4. **Tap End Call to hang up on the caller you're currently speaking with. Your other caller becomes your active call and you can press End Call when you're finished conversing with that caller.**

Answering a second incoming call

When you receive a second call, you can respond to the incoming call screen (refer to Figure 1-15) by doing one of the following:

✔ **Tap Ignore** to continue your current conversation without interruption. The second incoming call is sent to your voicemail.

✔ **Tap Hold Call + Answer** to put your current call on hold and answer your second incoming call. When you choose this option, the active multiple calls screen appears.

✔ **End Call + Answer** to disconnect with your current call and answer your second incoming call (GSM); tap End Call and then tap Answer when the second call rings through (CDMA).

Making a conference call

You initiate a conference call (see Figure 1-23) by making or answering a second call as described previously. After your second call is established, the multiple active calls screen appears (refer to Figure 1-22).

To turn your two calls into a conference call, and even add more callers to your two calls and turn those calls into a conference call, do the following:

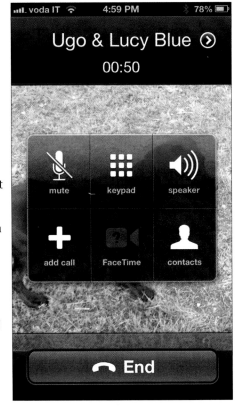

Figure 1-23: The Conference call screen.

1. **Tap Add Call to add a second person to a call you initiated and then choose the person you want to add from Contacts, Favorites, or Recents.**

   Or tap Hold Call + Answer to add an incoming call.

2. **On A GSM phone, you may have up to five people on your conference call. Repeat step one to add the third through fifth person to your current group call.**

3. **Tap Merge Calls to combine your two (or more) calls into a single Conference Call in which everyone can speak and hear everyone else.**

To merge calls on a CDMA phone, you must place the second call in order to merge with the first one.

The conference call screen shown in Figure 1-23 appears, grouping all of your active callers as a single item at the top of the screen.

Managing a conference call

When a conference call is underway, you can use the conference call screen to manage your conference call by doing the following:

✔ Tap the combined callers group at the top of the screen to display the Conference call screen, as shown in Figure 1-24.

✔ Tap the End Call button to the left of a caller's name or number to disconnect that caller from the conference call.

Figure 1-24: Juggle individual callers during a conference call.

✔ To speak privately with one caller in your conference call, tap the Private button to the right of the caller's name to speak that caller; your other callers are put on hold while you speak privately with a single caller.

Book III Chapter 1

Managing Phone and FaceTime Video Calls

Visiting Voicemail

For the times when you can't respond to a call, voicemail is a great way for your caller to let you know what she wants so you can respond when it's convenient for you. In this section, we explain setting up your voicemail greeting, and listening to and managing voicemail messages.

Tap Phone⬝Voicemail to display the Voicemail screen, as shown in Figure 1-25.

Recording and changing your greeting

If this is the first time you're visiting the Voicemail screen, iPhone prompts you to create a password and record your voicemail greeting. Repeating the same steps is how you change your voicemail greeting message whenever you want.

Tap Greeting to display the Voicemail Greeting screen shown in Figure 1-26, and then choose one of the following options:

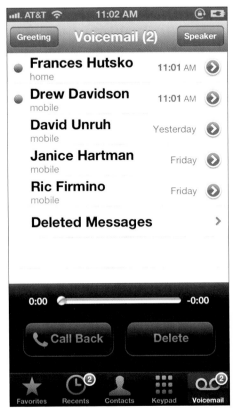

Figure 1-25: The Voicemail screen lists your voicemail messages.

✔ Tap Default if you want callers to hear your cellular provider's generic voicemail message (which says something like "the person you are trying to reach at" — your phone number — "is not available," followed by instructions on how to leave a message, yada yada yada).

✔ Tap Custom if you want to record (or change) a personal greeting message in your own words, and then tap Record to record your greeting; tap Play to listen to your greeting.

✔ Tap Save when you're happy with your choice, or tap Cancel if you've changed your mind, and you want to keep the existing greeting.

Go to Settings⇨Sounds⇨New Voicemail to designate the sound and vibration pattern you want to hear when you have a new voicemail message.

Listening to and managing voicemail messages

When you tap a voicemail message in the voicemail list to select that voicemail message, your selection is highlighted, the Call Back and Delete buttons become active, a tiny Play/Pause button appears on the left side of your selection, and the message's length is displayed to the right side of the playback scrubber bar beneath the voicemail message list, as shown in Figure 1-27.

Figure 1-26: The Voicemail Greeting screen.

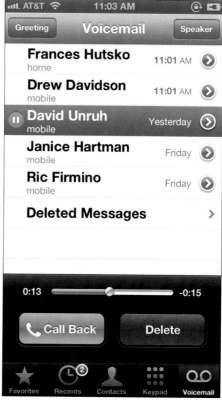

Figure 1-27: Listening to a voicemail message with the speakerphone turned on.

**Book III
Chapter 1**

Managing Phone and FaceTime Video Calls

Visual voicemail: Seen and heard

Visual voicemail is called that because you actually see your voice messages listed in a nice and neat stack just like your e-mail messages, whereas typical "non-visual" voicemail only appears . . . well, nowhere, because only visual voicemail messages can be seen and heard. If you've never had voicemail, you may be unfamiliar with what it's like to retrieve your voicemail messages the "old-fashioned way" by dialing into your voicemail mailbox; then pressing buttons on the keypad to skip, fast forward, rewind, and delete those messages as you listen to them one after the other — all of which visual voicemail lets you do with your fingertips. You can select the messages you want to hear and listen to them in the order you want. Better yet — ask Siri to read your list of visual voicemail messages to you.

Unfortunately, visual voicemail isn't a feature you always find on every iPhone. In some cases, you may have to pay an extra monthly fee for the feature. In other cases, the visual voicemail feature may not be offered by your carrier.

✔ To listen to and control playback of a voicemail message:

- Tap the Play button to listen to the message. A Pause button replaces the Play button. You can juggle between the two to play and pause playback.

- Drag the playhead in the scrubber bar to move to any location in the voicemail message.

- Tap the Speaker button to hear messages out loud through iPhone's speaker (rather than holding iPhone to your ear or listening through headphones).

✔ Tap Call Back to call the person who left you the selected message.

✔ Tap Delete to delete the selected voicemail message. When you delete a voicemail message, the message is removed from the Voicemail list screen, and is saved in the Deleted Messages folder, which is automatically created if it isn't already displayed.

Messages you've listened to remain in your voicemail inbox until your cellular carrier deletes those messages. This means that even if you delete a message, it may pop back into the Inbox at a later date. The length of time messages you've listened to remain in your voicemail box varies; check with your carrier.

✔ To display more information about the caller, tap the blue disclosure triangle on the right side of your selected voicemail message to display the Info screen.

Tap the Deleted Messages folder to display the Deleted screen, as shown in Figure 1-28.

When viewing the Deleted screen, you can

✔ Tap a voicemail message to select it, and then

• Tap Play to listen to the message

• Tap Undelete to move the message out of the Deleted Messages folder and back to the Voicemail messages screen

✔ Tap Clear All to remove all deleted messages from the Deleted Messages folder and back to the Voicemail messages screen.

Figure 1-28: The Deleted screen lists items in the Deleted Messages folder.

With Visual Voicemail at your service, the idea of ever going back to the old way of dialing in to your voicemail box and tapping buttons to skip through your messages seems like torture. That said, you can relive the past by pressing and holding the 1 button on the keypad to automatically dial into and begin listening to your voicemail messages, or by typing your own phone number and pressing Call, and then pressing * and entering your password to listen to your voicemail messages. Like we said, torture!

Taking Note of Phone Notifications

Using the Phone app puts you in control of placing and answering calls and voicemail messages when you want. iPhone works behind the scenes as your personal answering service, alerting you to missed calls or voicemail messages by displaying notifications and badges, as shown in Figure 1-29. Read more about notifications in Book I, Chapter 4.

You can set how your iPhone alerts you to incoming calls by going to Settings⇨Sounds, as explained in the "Perusing Phone Settings" section later in this chapter.

The different notification messages iPhone displays when you miss (or decline) calls or receive new voicemail messages include the following:

Figure 1-29: iPhone lets you know when you missed a call.

- ✔ **Missed Call:** Displays the phone number or name of one of your contacts whose call went unanswered.

- ✔ **Voicemail:** Displays the phone number or name of one of your contacts who has left you a voicemail message.

- ✔ **Missed Call and Voicemail:** Combines both types of notifications.

The different notification badges iPhone displays when you miss (or decline) calls or receive new voicemail messages are as follows:

- ✔ **Phone App Icon:** A red badge indicates the combined number of missed calls and/or new voicemail messages.

- ✔ **Reminder:** If you declined an incoming call by tapping Remind Me Later, a reminder notification shows up on your phone an hour after you declined the call.

If your iPhone is unable to receive calls because Do Not Disturb is activated, it's in Airplane Mode, is out of your cellular network range, or is powered off, notifications messages, badges, and sounds for any missed calls or voicemail messages won't appear until your iPhone is able to receive calls again.

Perusing Phone Settings

From the moment your iPhone is activated, you can use the Phone app to make, receive, and manage calls, and to listen to voicemail messages — all without ever needing to adjust (or even know about) any of your iPhone's many phone-related settings options.

We show you how to change a few phone-related settings throughout this chapter on a "need to know" basis; however, we encourage you to take a moment to get acquainted with the full spectrum of those settings.

By touring iPhone's phone-related settings options, you can maximize your awareness of every call-related feature, and potentially minimize the risk of incurring unexpected charges on your monthly phone bill, by acquainting yourself with certain options that can cost you an arm and a leg if you happen to turn them on without realizing the implications.

You find various Phone settings in the Settings app. For details on Settings⇨ General, which gives you options for usage tracking and accessibility, see Book I, Chapter 4. The specific Phone settings are explained in the next few sections.

Notifications

Tap Settings⇨Notifications⇨Phone to choose whether you want Phone notifications listed in the Notification Center and set the alert style you prefer: None, Banners (which appear at the top of the screen and then disappear automatically), or Alerts (which block your phone until you perform one of the actions). Choose whether you want the badge to appear on the Phone icon and whether you want to see notifications when the screen is locked. Read all about notifications in Book I, Chapter 4.

Sounds

Tap Settings⇨Sounds to choose your vibration, ringtone, and volume options, as shown in Figure 1-30. Choose when you want your phone to vibrate, if at all, by tapping Vibrate on Ring and Vibrate on Silent to the On or Off position. Tap Change with Buttons On so you can adjust the ringer volume with your iPhone's volume buttons. Tap Ringtone to choose the sound you want to hear for incoming calls. On the Ringtone screen, you can also select or create a vibration pattern. Remember to choose a sound for your New Voicemail, too.

See Book IV, Chapter 1 to assign special ringtones to specific contacts.

Phone

Tap Settings⇨Phone to adjust the following information, as shown in Figure 1-31.

- ✔ **My Number:** Displays your personal phone number. Although it's set automatically, you can tap the disclosure triangle and change it.

- ✔ **Reply With Message:** Change the default replies for calls you decline with this option. Refer to the section "Declining Calls."

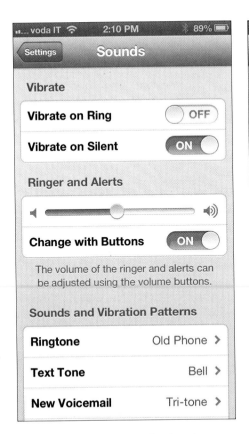

Figure 1-30: Sounds settings for choosing ringtones — and silent options, too.

Figure 1-31: Change the Phone app settings to suit you.

✔ **Call Forwarding, Call Waiting, Show My Caller ID (GSM models):** Turns those features on or off. See the next section to learn how to activate these features.

✔ **TTY:** To turn on iPhone's ability to connect to a Teletype machine to enable deaf or hearing-impaired users to communicate by reading and typing text (requires the iPhone TTY Adapter cable, sold separately; we write about all of iPhone's Accessibility features in Book I, Chapter 2).

✔ **Change Voicemail Password:** To change your numeric voicemail password.

✔ **Dial Assist:** To have iPhone automatically add proper prefix number when calling the U.S. from abroad.

✔ **SIM PIN (GSM models):** To turn on, choose, and change the secret code you can use to lock your iPhone's SIM card; when activated, you must type in the PIN code whenever you turn iPhone off then on again.

After three failed attempts to unlock the SIM code, you may need to type in a Personal Unlocking Key (PUK) code in order to unlock your iPhone; if so, contact your cellular carrier's customer service number to find out your iPhone's PUK code.

✔ **Carrier Services (depends on iPhone model and carrier):** One-touch speed-dial access for dialing up various phone account-related information like your current bill balance, data and minutes usage, and directory assistance.

Call Forwarding, Call Waiting, and Caller ID Blocking

Some phone-related settings you may want to take advantage of include call forwarding, call waiting, and caller ID blocking. To turn those features on or off for GSM model iPhones (like the ones that work with AT&T or the unlocked model you can buy at the Apple Store), tap Settings➪Phone, and then tap the setting you want to turn on or off. Refer to Figure 1-32.

You have to have cellular service when you turn Call Forwarding on, which means activate Call Forwarding before you go off into the wilderness with your iPhone. If you turn on Call Forwarding, a prompt appears so you can type in the phone number you want your calls forwarded to.

The call forwarding icon appears in the Status Bar when you turn on the Call Forwarding feature on GSM model iPhones.

Don't forget to turn Call Forwarding off when you no longer want your calls sent to another number; otherwise, you'll be wondering why your iPhone doesn't ring anymore.

Caller ID blocking only works for phone calls; your ID still appears when you make a FaceTime call. It doesn't really matter because the person you're calling is going to see who you are anyway.

To turn those features on or off for CMDA model iPhones like the ones that work with Verizon, use the Phone app's Keypad to type in the appropriate special code below for the particular feature you want to manage:

▸ **Call Forwarding on:** Type *72 followed by the phone number you want your calls forwarded to, and then tap Call.

▸ **Call Forwarding off:** Type *73, and then tap Call.

▸ **Call Waiting off for a call you are about to make:** Type *70, and then type the number you want to call and tap Call.

▸ **Block Caller ID for a call you are about to make:** Type *67, and then dial the number you want to call and tap Call.

On CMDA model iPhones, you can only turn off call waiting and caller ID blocking on a per-call basis, but you can't turn either feature off for all calls the way you can with GSM model iPhones.

Doing FaceTime Video Chat Calls

iPhone 4 and later models offer the FaceTime function, which lets you speak with and see a person who is also using a device that can make and receive FaceTime calls, as shown in Figure 1-33.

A big change came to FaceTime with the release of iOS 6: You can make FaceTime calls with your iPhone 4S or 5 (but not 4) over the cellular network. This is great news for those of you (like Barbara) who are often out of Wi-Fi range, but want to make FaceTime calls.

AT&T users have to sign up for AT&T's Mobile Share data plan and it's unclear how much that really costs for FaceTime calls. Even if you have a contract with another carrier, using FaceTime on the cellular network cuts into your data transfer allowance. If you have a cap on your data allowance, you'll want to keep track of how much you're consuming so you don't go over your monthly limit and incur additional charges. A 45-minute FaceTime call consumes roughly 65 megabytes.

FaceTime calls other iPhones with the phone number or e-mail address, but uses an e-mail address to call FaceTime-enabled Macs, iPod touches, or iPads. And if one of those devices is calling your iPhone, they use the e-mail address associated with your FaceTime ID.

To use FaceTime, both parties need to be connected to a Wi-Fi network (iPhone 5 users can also use FaceTime with a cellular data connection by going to Settings⟳FaceTime⟳Use Cellular Data ON) and meet one of the following requirements:

a. You and the person you want to FaceTime with are both using iPhone models that offer the FaceTime feature, and that feature is turned on in Settings⟳Phone⟳FaceTime. (The FaceTime feature is turned on by default; additionally, the FaceTime feature can also be turned off in Settings⟳General⟳Restrictions.)

b. Your iPhone meets the preceding requirement, and the person you want to connect with is using another FaceTime-capable device, such as an iPad 2 or later or a fourth generation iPod touch or later, or a Mac with FaceTime.

Making a FaceTime call

As we mention in the "Managing Calls" section, you can switch an existing voice call to a FaceTime call, or you can initiate a FaceTime call by first making a call using any of the methods we show you in the "Making Calls" section.

Some things to consider when making FaceTime calls:

✔ **During a Call:** Tap the FaceTime button in the active call screen to switch your voice call to a video chat call.

✔ **Using Favorites or Recents:** The FaceTime camera icon indicates phone numbers and names that you can tap to call using FaceTime.

✔ **Using Keypad:** Type the phone number you want to call using FaceTime, and then tap Call; tap the FaceTime button once the call is in progress.

✔ **Using Voicemail:** Tap the More Information button on an item in your Voicemail list, tap the FaceTime button, and then tap the e-mail address or phone number you want to call.

✔ **Using Contacts:** Tap the contact you want to call, tap the FaceTime button, and then tap the e-mail address or phone number you want to call.

✔ **Using Voice Control or Siri:** Press and hold the Home button and then say "FaceTime" followed by the name or number of the person to call.

✔ **Caller ID Block:** Your phone number appears when you make a FaceTime call even if you have activated your iPhone's Caller ID Block feature (which we write about in the section "Call Forwarding, Call Waiting, and Caller ID Blocking," earlier in this chapter.)

The FaceTime Failed message appears if a person you try to call isn't using a FaceTime-capable device or FaceTime is turned off on that device.

When your FaceTime call is established, the active FaceTime call screen appears as shown in Figure 1-32.

Accepting a FaceTime call

The FaceTime incoming call screen appears when you receive an incoming FaceTime call invitation, as shown in Figure 1-33.

Tap Accept or Decline to answer or decline the FaceTime invitation. You can also touch and drag the Reply/Remind button to use that feature as explained in the section "Declining Calls."

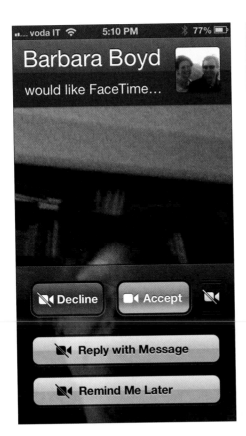

Figure 1-32: The active FaceTime call screen, live and in-person (virtually speaking).

Figure 1-33: An incoming FaceTime call invitation.

Managing a FaceTime Call

When you're engaged in a FaceTime video chat call — that you initiate or accept — the active FaceTime call screen appears. The person you're connected with fills up most of iPhone's screen, while your own mug appears in a tiny window that you can drag to whichever corner you want.

During an active FaceTime call, you can do a bunch of neat things, including the following:

✔ **Changing to Landscape View:** Rotate your iPhone sideways to view your caller in Landscape mode.

✔ **Switch Cameras:** Tap the Switch Cameras button to switch your live video feed from iPhone's front-facing camera to the higher-resolution rear-facing camera. You can use this feature to show off things around you, like the snoozing kitty in your lap, or the snowstorm coming down outside your office window. Tap the Switch Cameras button again to switch back to iPhone's front-facing camera and its focus on you.

✔ **Mute Your Sound:** Tap the Mute icon to squelch the mic on your end of the video chat conversation. When you mute your mic, you can still hear sound from the person on the other end of your chat, and they can still see your video. Tap Mute again to allow yourself to be heard again.

✔ **Pause Your Video:** Tapping Home and switching to another app puts your FaceTime video on hold; the person on the other end will still hear you, but you won't see each other while you're away from the FaceTime screen; tap the banner that appears at the top of iPhone's screen (as you would in a regular phone call) to return to your FaceTime call, where you'll be both seen and heard once more.

✔ **Capture a Screenshot:** Press Home and Sleep/Wake at the same time to capture a screenshot of your FaceTime chat; iPhone saves your screenshot in the Photo app's Camera Roll album. (You can capture a screenshot this way in other apps, too, not just in FaceTime.)

Adjusting FaceTime settings

Just like Phone and most of the other apps on your iPhone, FaceTime has a few settings that you can adjust to your liking. Tap Settings⊏FaceTime to see the screen as in Figure 1-34. You can do the following:

✔ **Tap** the toggle switch to turn FaceTime Off or On.

✔ **Apple ID:** You must be signed in for FaceTime to work; if you try to tap FaceTime On and it doesn't work, tap your Apple ID, enter your password in the screen that follows, and then confirm the phone number and e-mail address where you can be reached via FaceTime.

When you are signed in to your Apple ID account, the following choices appear:

- *Change your Location*

- *View your Apple ID account*

- *Sign Out*: If you sign out, you'll have to sign in again to use FaceTime.

↙ **FaceTime Access:** Tap the e-mail addresses with whom you want to share FaceTime requests. Tap the disclosure triangle to the right to remove the e-mail completely from the list. Tap Add Another Email to do that.

↙ **Caller ID:** Choose either your phone number or e-mail address as the identification that appears on the device of the person you're calling when you initiate a FaceTime call.

↙ **Use Cellular Data (scroll down to see this option):** Tap On to use FaceTime with both Wi-Fi and cellular data; tap Off to use only Wi-Fi for FaceTime calls.

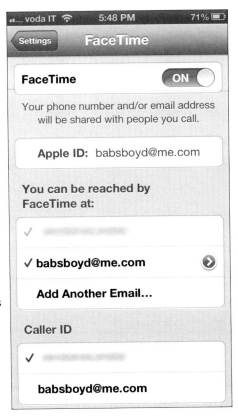

Figure 1-34: Choose the e-mail others can use to reach you via FaceTime.

International Calling Options

Depending on which iPhone model you own, you may be able to use your iPhone while you're traveling overseas. Again, using this feature is typically a very costly proposition, and again, your best plan is to contact your provider before you take off. If it turns out you can use your iPhone while traveling overseas, we recommend turning off the data roaming feature. Tap Settings➪General➪Cellular➪Cellular Data to disable that feature and only use Wi-Fi, when available, for your data functions. You can still make and receive phone calls and send and receive text messages, although often with a roaming surcharge above and beyond your regular phone plan cost. For example, Barbara sends SMS for 10 cents a message when at home and 75 cents per message when overseas, so she tries to limit her text messaging when travelling.

Chapter 2: Sending and Receiving Text and Multimedia Messages

In This Chapter

✓ **Setting up for SMS and MMS messages**

✓ **Using iMessage to text iOS devices and Macs**

✓ **Sending and receiving messages**

✓ **Managing messages**

*A*mong the teen and preteen set, text messaging is almost an obsession. Even if you're beyond the teen set, messaging is a quick and efficient way to keep in touch — you don't have to worry about bothering the person you want to contact, you can respond to others at your convenience, and you have a written record of your exchange.

As with other apps, you have more than one way to perform the task at hand. In this chapter, we show you the different ways you can send messages — traditional SMS and MMS as well as iMessage messages, which you exchange with your i-device — and Mac — user friends. With iMessage, you can begin an exchange (called a *conversation* in Messages lingo) on one device, say your iPhone while you're at the bus stop, and then continue it on another, such as your Mac or iPad, when you get home. Because "the media is the message," we show you how to add photos, video, voice memos, and links to your messages. With all this communicating, we close the chapter with how to manage the messages you've been sending and receiving.

Before all that, however, we're going to give you a quick run-through of the settings for the Messages app.

Reviewing Messages Features and Adjusting Settings

To understand the Messages features and settings, you should familiarize yourself with the parts of a message, as shown in Figure 2-1.

- **To field:** Enter names, phone numbers, or e-mail addresses of people you want to send messages to.

- **Text and Subject fields:** Type your message here; the Subject field within the Text field is a feature you can turn on or off in Settings⫺Messages.

- **Camera button:** Tapping the Camera button lets you add photos or videos to your messages.

- **Character count:** This keeps track of how many characters your message contains. Again, this is a feature you can switch on or off in Settings. (Some service providers limit the length of text messages; if yours does, this option helps you write messages within the limit.)

Setting up Messages settings

By now, you're probably familiar with the Settings app. It's where you turn the features for the other iPhone apps on or off. The settings for Messages let you personalize the way iPhone alerts you that you have messages and offers some options for composing messages.

To open Settings for messages, tap Settings⫺Messages. You'll have to scroll down because Messages is a little way down the list after General. You see what's shown in Figure 2-2.

- **iMessage:** Tap this toggle switch on to activate the iMessage service, which lets you exchange messages with other iOS devices, such as iPhone, iPad, and iPod touch, as well as Macs running Mac OS X 10.8 Mountain Lion, for free (over Wi-Fi). We explain this service in the "Addressing, Writing, and Sending Text Messages and iMessages" section of this chapter.

- **Send Read Receipts:** When turned on, people who send you messages will be notified when you read their sent message.

- **Send As SMS:** If iMessage is unavailable, your message is sent as an SMS text message. Your cellular service plan may charge an extra fee for SMS.

- **Send & Receive:** Add additional e-mail addresses where you want to receive iMessages (in addition to your mobile phone number). Tap Send & Receive. The iMessage screen opens. Tap Add Another Email. The keyboard appears where you can type in the e-mail address you wish to add. Tap Messages at the top when you finish.

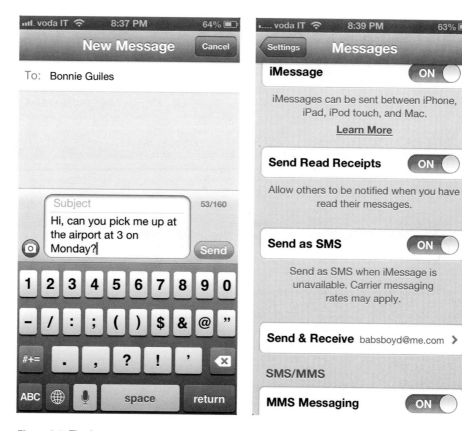

Figure 2-1: The features of a new message.

Figure 2-2: The Messages Settings screen.

Book III
Chapter 2

Sending and
Receiving Text
and Multimedia
Messages

Scroll down to see the last four choices:

- **MMS Messaging:** With this feature on, you can send and receive photos, video, and voice memos and insert a subject line in the text field. You may have to enter information from your cellular service provider in the MMS section of Settings⇨General⇨Cellular⇨Cellular Data Network, and there may be an additional charge to send MMS.

- **Group Messaging:** If you turn this on, you can send one SMS/MMS message to several people, although responses come back only to you. This option isn't available in all areas.

- **Show Subject Field:** With this switch on, a subject line appears before any text messages that you write — just like e-mail. However, this turns an SMS (Short Message Service) into an MMS (Multimedia Message Service). If you're sending to someone who doesn't have MMS capabilities, they may not receive your message. If you leave the subject field blank, it remains an SMS, or you can just keep this setting off.

✔ **Character Count:** iPhone conveniently splits messages longer than 160 characters into multiple messages so people with phones that have limited text capabilities can still receive messages from you. The kicker is that each section of the message counts as one message, meaning one three-part message is billed as three messages. Turn this switch on and a character counter appears to the right of the text-entry field in the New Message screen so you can keep an eye on the length of your message. If you are sending an SMS to another iPhone, you can write a whole novel and the message still counts as just one message, but your thumbs might be tired.

Change switches from on to off, or vice versa, with a simple tap. No swiping needed.

New message alert

You can choose the audible alert you want to hear when someone sends you a message, or choose none if you prefer only a visual alert:

✔ To change the alert sound for Messages, tap Settings⟳Sounds⟳Text Tone. A list of potential alert vibrations and tones appears.

✔ To set the vibration that occurs when a message arrives, tap Vibration and then select a vibration style from the list that appears. You can also tap Create New Vibration to create a custom vibration or tap None to hear only a text tone without a vibration when a new message arrives.

✔ To preview the sounds, tap the names on the list. Tap the name of the sound that you want to hear when a new message arrives or tap None. A checkmark indicates the sound you've chosen.

✔ Tap Sounds in the upper left corner, and then tap Settings in the upper left corner to return to the Settings screen, or press the Home button to return to the Home screen.

Addressing, Writing, and Sending Text Messages and iMessages

Sending text messages, or texting, is a fast and easy way to, well, send a message to a person or a group of people. You can ask your spouse to pick up milk and bread on the way home or send a phone number to a colleague, and neither of them has to write anything down because they have your messages to refer to. You can let your whole family know that your plane landed safely after flying through a tempest on the way to Hawaii.

What's more, Messages recognizes phone numbers or contact names associated with iOS devices, such as an iPhone, iPad 2 or later, or iPod touch. When you tap the contact name of someone who uses an iOS device, Messages uses the associated e-mail address to send the iMessage. When you know you want to send a message to someone with an iPad or iPod touch or a Mac with OS X Mountain Lion installed, which don't have phone numbers, choose the e-mail address. Like magic, Messages sends your outgoing text message as an iMessage. iMessages travel over the cellular data network or a Wi-Fi Internet connection so you don't pay an SMS fee, although you do use your data allotment if there's no Wi-Fi. If an Internet connection isn't available, your message is sent as a normal SMS or MMS, as long as you turned that option on in Settings⇨Messages⇨Send as SMS On.

To send a message:

1. **Tap the Messages icon on the Home screen.**

2. **Tap the Compose button in the upper right corner. It's the one that looks like a pencil and piece of paper.**

   A New Message screen opens.

3. **Address and write your message as explained in the following section.**

4. **Tap the Send button.**

Addressing and writing your message

When you open a New Message screen by tapping the Compose button, the keyboard is active and the cursor is in the To field, where you fill in the name or number of the person you want to send your message to. You can address your message in one of three ways:

- Tap the 123 button in the lower left corner of the keyboard to change the top row of letters to numbers. Type the phone number.

- If the person you want to send the message to is stored in Contacts, begin typing the recipient's name in the To field. Names of people in Contacts that begin with the same letters show up as a list from which you can choose. Your choices narrow as you type more letters. (See Figure 2-3.) The phone number is listed under the contact's name and if a contact has more than one phone number, his name is listed with each phone number. You can see that Don Boyd has four phone numbers.

TIP

Even if you have selected to view only one group in Contacts, Messages consults all your contacts when you begin typing a few letters. See Book IV, Chapter 1 to learn about Contacts.

**Book III
Chapter 2**

**Sending and
Receiving Text
and Multimedia
Messages**

Make sure you choose a cell phone number. Text messages can be sent to some service providers who offer SMS support.

🖝 If you want to send a message to another iOS device or Mac, type the e-mail address that your recipient uses and the message will be sent as an iMessage. You know you're sending an iMessage because you see New iMessage written across the top of the message (as shown in Figure 2-4) instead of New Message. The bubble around the name in the To field and incoming text bubbles are blue. If the recipient begins to write a response immediately, you see an ellipsis while she's typing a response to your sent message, much like a chat exchange.

Figure 2-3: Begin typing the first letters of your recipient's name and Messages searches Contacts to find matches.

Figure 2-4: Send unlimited iMessages to other iOS devices and Macs — for free!

To use iMessage, you must activate iMessage (Settings➪Messages➪ iMessage On) and have an active Internet connection.

✏ Alternatively, tap the plus sign (+) button in the upper right corner, which opens Contacts. Find the name you want by doing one of the following:

- Scroll through the list until you find the name of the person you want to send a message to.

- Tap the first letter of the name in the alphabet that runs down the right side of the screen to jump to names beginning with that letter. Scroll through that section to find the person you're searching for.

- Tap the magnifying glass icon at the top of the alphabet list. The cursor blinks in the Search field. Type the name of the person you're looking for. As with any Search field, matches pop up when you type the first letter and diminish as you narrow your search by typing more letters.

When you open Contacts from Messages, you see your active groups. Tap the Groups button to open more groups. (You only see this button if you have groups in Contacts.)

✏ After you've found it, tap the name of the person you want to send a message to. If the contact has just one phone number, when you tap the name, you automatically return to the New Message screen and the name of the recipient will be in the To field. If the contact has more than one phone number or also has an e-mail address, the contact information opens. Tap the number you want to send the SMS to, or the e-mail address you want to send the iMessage to, and you'll bounce back to the New Message screen.

✏ If you want to send your message to more than one person, just tap the plus sign (+) button and repeat the preceding steps to add a person from the contact list or type in a phone number.

From Contacts, you can tap the Text Message button on the Info screen of the contact to open a New Message screen with your chosen contact in the To field. From your Favorites list, tap the blue arrow button on the right, and then scroll down and tap the Text Message button, which takes you to a New Message screen.

Book III Chapter 2

Sending and Receiving Text and Multimedia Messages

Writing your message

After you've entered the names of the message recipients, tap return. The cursor moves to the text field:

1. **Type your message.**

   Any features you activated for the keyboard in Settings, such as Auto-Correction or Enable Caps Lock, are active in Messages.

Messages remembers the keyboard you use to write messages to different contacts. If you write some messages in English with the English keyboard and some in Chinese using the Chinese keyboard, after a couple exchanges in Chinese, Messages automatically "remembers" that you write in Chinese with that contact and opens with that keyboard; likewise for your English messages. It means one less tap for you.

If you make a mistake and need to edit your message, the Text field has the same functions for typing as other apps, as explained in Book I, Chapter 3.

To avoid accidentally hitting Send when you're aiming for the letter o or p, write your message before filling in the To field. The Send button is activated only after a recipient's name or a phone number has been entered. This tip only works when you are initiating a thread, not when responding to a message.

2. **When you've finished typing your message, tap the Send button and it's on its way.**

   You'll see a progress bar at the top of the screen, as shown in Figure 2-5, and hear a whooping sound when the message has been sent.

If you use an iPhone 4S or later and have activated Siri, tap the Dictation button to the left of the space bar if

Figure 2-5: The Sending progress bar shows your message is on its way.

you prefer to dictate your message instead of typing it. (Refer to Book I, Chapter 3.)

Add the Emoji language in Settings⟹General⟹Keyboard⟹International Keyboards to insert smiley faces and hearts in your messages.

Receiving and Replying to Text Messages

Ding-ding! You've got a message. If you're doing other things, a notification shows the name or phone number of the sender along with a line of the message. Or maybe not. You set your preferred way of being notified of new messages in Settings. Go to Settings⟹Notifications and click Messages. Select your notification choices as explained in Book I, Chapter 4. You may be notified of new messages in one or more of the following ways:

- A notification banner appears at the top of the screen and discreetly fades after a few seconds.

- An alert calls for your undivided attention and you must choose to close it or reply before it leaves you alone.

- On the Lock screen, if more than one notification appears, you can drag across the notification to unlock your iPhone and go directly to the app the notification came from.

- A numbered red badge appears on the shoulder of the Message icon on the Home screen, letting you know how many unread messages you have.

- Drag your finger down from the Status Bar to open the Notifications Center and view Messages there, if you activated that option in Settings ⟹Notifications⟹Messages.

- In the Message list, unread messages have a blue dot next to them.

After you read a message, the badge on the Messages icon on the Home screen disappears, or displays a lower number, the blue dot in the Message list goes away, and the Notification in the Notification Center disappears.

After you've received a message, you'll want to read it and maybe respond. Here's how to read your messages:

1. **If you didn't read the message as soon as it arrived, tap Messages on the Home screen. An unread message has a blue dot next to it.**

**Book III
Chapter 2**

**Sending and
Receiving Text
and Multimedia
Messages**

In the Messages list (refer to Figure 2-6), you'll see the name or number of the person or entity who sent the message, the time, day, or date it was received (depending on how long ago it was sent), and the first two lines of the message.

After an exchange begins, you see the last message exchanged regardless of who sent it, so if you sent a response to someone, you see the first two lines of your response next to the name of who sent the message.

2. **Tap the message and a message screen opens, displaying the whole message. The text of incoming iMessages is in a blue bubble; that of an SMS is in a green bubble.**

You can choose to reply with a message or call the person back.

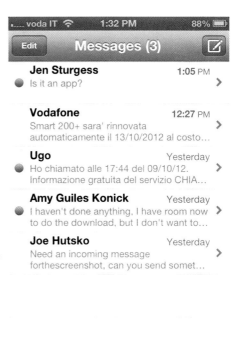

- To call, just tap the Call button at the top of the screen. If you don't see the Call button, tap the status bar to automatically scroll back to the top.

Figure 2-6: The Messages list shows read and unread messages you've sent and received.

- To communicate via FaceTime, tap the FaceTime button. We explain FaceTime in Book III, Chapter 1.

- To reply, tap once in the Text field. The keyboard opens. When you've finished writing your message, tap Send. As with a message you initiated, you see a Sending progress bar and, if you chose a sound in Sound settings for Sent Mail, you hear a tone indicating that the message has been sent.

If you're writing a message and need to refer to something in the incoming message, or earlier in the conversation, you can scroll through the conversation. To free up more of the screen, touch the background (a non-message part of the screen) just above the text field and flick down to hide the keyboard, giving you more viewing room to scroll through the conversation. Tap in the text field to bring the keyboard back.

When your iPhone is unable to receive incoming calls, it's also unable to send or receive messages. Whether it's in Airplane mode, is out of range of your carrier's cellular network, or is powered off, notifications, badges, and sounds for any new SMS or MMS messages won't appear until your iPhone is able to receive calls — and messages — again. If you try to send a message and it doesn't reach its destination, an alert badge that looks like an exclamation point appears on the Messages icon on the Home screen. (iMessages still work if you have Wi-Fi service.)

A received message has information about a person or company that you can store in Contacts. To add a new name and phone number or new information to an existing contact, do the following:

1. **From within the message, tap the button at the top right of the screen.**

   If the person the message is from already exists in Contacts, the button on the upper right of the screen reads Contact. Tapping that button takes you to the Contact Info screen of the person where you can edit the information.

   If Messages doesn't recognize the number the message came from, the button reads New Contact.

   A message rectangle opens, giving you the option to Create New Contact or Add to Existing Contact.

2. **To add a person or entity, choose Create New Contact.**

   You are bounced to a New Contact screen that is partially filled out with the name and number. You can fill in the other information if you like. Save by tapping Done. You are then returned to the message where you began.

3. **To add a new number to an existing contact, tap Add to Existing Contact.**

   This brings up the All Contacts screen, where you select the name of the Contact you wish to add this information to. Tap on the name of the desired Contact and type in the new information.

SMS and MMS are acronyms for Short Message Service and Multimedia Messaging Service, respectively. These are the protocols used for transferring text and multimedia with cellular phone technology.

Book III
Chapter 2

Sending and
Receiving Text
and Multimedia
Messages

Sending and Receiving Multimedia Messages

Now things get fun. You probably want a way to share the photos and videos that you take with your iPhone and to send multimedia messages. MMS is a quick way to do that when e-mail isn't an option, and you can send media to your iMessage friends, too.

Capturing and sending a video or photo

Say you're taking a walk and find a stray puppy along your way. You want to take a picture and send it to your spouse with a clever message about the new addition to the family. Here's how:

1. **Tap Messages on the Home screen, and then tap the Compose button.**

2. **Fill in the To field as described in the previous section.**

   If your recipient uses iOS 5 or later, your MMS may be sent with iMessage if the iMessage requirements are met.

3. **Tap the Camera button.**

   Three buttons appear — Take Photo or Video, Choose Existing, and Cancel (if you changed your mind about the pup). See Figure 2-7.

4. **Tap Take Photo or Video to open the camera and then tap the Camera button at the bottom of the screen.**

   The photo, or video, is taken and a Preview screen opens. You have the option of retaking the photo, by tapping Retake in the lower left corner, or using the photo, by tapping Use in the lower right corner.

5. **If you don't like the photo, tap Retake and try again, and again, and again until you have a photo or video you like.**

Figure 2-7: Tap Take Photo or Video to insert a new image.

6. **If you're the next Ansel Adams and got a great shot on the first take, tap Use. Either way, when you take a photo you like, tap Use.**

Messages opens and, instead of New Message, the screen now reads New MMS at the top. You see your photo or video in the Text field and the cursor blinking under the image, as shown in Figure 2-8.

7. **Type your message and tap Send.**

You see a Sending progress bar and, if you chose a sound in Sound settings for Sent Mail, you hear whatever sound you chose when the message has been sent.

If the Camera button is grayed and inactive, make sure MMS Messaging is On in Messages Settings. You can still send photos and video with iMessage when MMS Messaging is Off.

You can also open Camera, take your photo or video, and send an MMS from Camera. Full details are in Book V, Chapter 1.

Figure 2-8: A new message becomes a new MMS when multimedia files are inserted.

Book III
Chapter 2

Sending and
Receiving Text
and Multimedia
Messages

Copying and sending existing videos, photos, and voice memos

Sometimes you already have a multimedia file — that is a photo, video, or voice memo — on your iPhone. There are two ways to send that file via MMS. Your first option is from within Messages, the second option is from the Photos or Voice Memos apps. The procedure is virtually the same, only your point of departure changes.

✓ Tap Messages on the Home screen, and then tap the Compose button. Address your message as explained previously. Tap the Camera button to the left of the Text field. A screen appears asking if you want to Take Photo or Video or Choose Existing. Tap Choose Existing and the Albums screen opens showing a list of your Albums. Tap the Album where the photo or video you wish to send resides, and then tap the photo or video you want to send. A Preview screen opens, allowing you to choose that image or cancel. Tap Choose and you return to the New Message screen. Add a written message. When the message is ready, tap Send.

✓ To send directly from the Photos app, tap Photos on the Home screen. The Album list opens. Tap the Album that contains the video or photo you want to send, and then tap the photo or video you want to send. Three icons appear at the bottom of the screen, as shown in Figure 2-9. Tap the Action button, which is the first one on the left, and tap the Message button. A New Message screen opens. Address, write, and send your message as previously explained.

Figure 2-9: Tap the first button on the left to place a photo or video into your message.

✓ To send a recording from Voice Memos, tap Voice Memos on the Home screen. Tap the List button on the lower right corner to open the Voice Memos list. Tap the memo you want to send. Tap Share and then tap the Message button, as shown in Figure 2-10. The New Message screen opens. Address the message and type in an accompanying message in the Text field, and then tap Send.

As with most things, you have to pay a price for messaging. Depending on the phone plan you have, you may pay a per-message fee for sending and receiving SMS or MMS, usually around 20 cents, or you can opt for a bundled flat fee for a limited, or sometimes unlimited, number of messages per month. One message to 25 recipients doesn't count as one message but 25 messages, so keep your plan in mind when doing group sends to avoid unpleasant end-of-the-month invoice surprises. And remember iMessages are free — that is, part of your cellular data plan, not your SMS/MMS plan.

If someone sends you an image or video, you might want to save it outside Messages. When you receive an MMS, tap the image in the speech bubble. It opens on the full screen. Tap the Action button and choose Save Image (or Video). The image or video is saved to the Camera Roll on your iPhone.

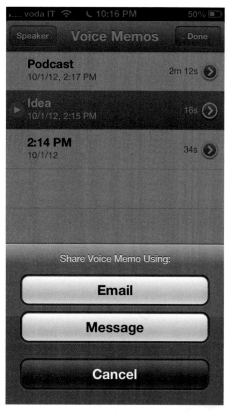

Figure 2-10: Tap the Message button to send a Voice Memo in a message.

Sending map locations, web page links, and more

Say you've made dinner plans with friends, but they need directions to the restaurant. Combining Maps and Messages, you can send the address and directions directly and avoid the hassle of explaining how to get there:

1. **Tap Maps on the Home screen and search for a location by typing the address or name of the business or restaurant in the Search field.**

2. **When you find the address, tap the blue and white arrow to see the information about the location you're searching for.**

3. **Scroll to the bottom of the Info screen and tap the Share Location button.**

Book III
Chapter 2

Sending and
Receiving Text
and Multimedia
Messages

4. **Tap the Message button that appears as shown in Figure 2-11.**

   The New Message screen opens with a link to the map location you were browsing.

5. **Address, write, and send the message as detailed earlier in this chapter.**

Figure 2-11: Map location links are sent via MMS.

From other apps, a Messages button appears when you tap the Action button, for example, in Safari, when you're browsing a web page, tap the Action button, tap Messages, and a New Message appears with a link to the web page. Address the message and tap Send. Likewise, for an audio or video clip you found in Podcasts, tap the Action button on the Info screen and send a message. Same goes for things you find in the iTunes and App Stores. Sharing has never been so easy!

Receiving links to locations or websites is just as easy as sending them. If you receive messages that have URLs embedded in them, the links are active, which means you can just tap them, right in the message, and Safari opens to the linked page or Maps to the location or iTunes to the album, and so on.

Saving, Deleting, and Forwarding Messages

Like a packet of love letters tied in a pink ribbon, some messages are worth saving. You may want to delete others even before they've been read. And some, you'll want to share with your best friend.

As you send and receive messages, they stack up in reverse chronological order within the Messages app — what we've been referring to as the Messages list (refer to Figure 2-6).

Ongoing conversations

Incoming and outgoing messages exchanged with the same person are called *conversations* — notice that the icon for Messages is a conversation bubble. You see the name of the person you have exchanged messages with in the Messages list. Tap on that name and you see all the messages you've exchanged with that person that you haven't deleted. Received messages are shown in grayed conversation bubbles on the left. Sent messages are on the right in green or blue conversation bubbles, as shown in Figure 2-12.

SMS, MMS, and iMessage messages are all listed in Messages and sometimes all three types appear in a conversation with the same person. This happens when you send a message to someone who has iMessage capabilities, but you don't have a Wi-Fi or cellular data connection.

Only the most recent message is shown in the Messages list, whereas the most recent 50 messages are shown in the conversation. You can download older messages by tapping

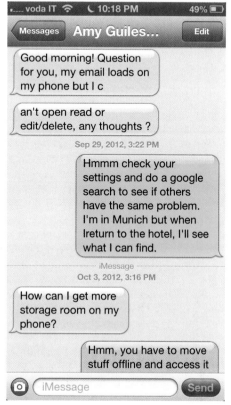

Figure 2-12: Received message conversation bubbles are on the left; sent messages are on the right.

the button. The newest message is displayed at the bottom — Messages opens to show this message — so if you scroll to the top of the screen, you can read from top to bottom and follow the conversation as it occurred.

Deleting messages

Text messages often contain information of fleeting importance, so you probably don't want to keep them and clutter up your Messages list. You can choose to delete some or all of the messages in a conversation. In this section, we show you several ways to delete messages.

If you want to delete some of the messages in one conversation, tap the Edit button in the upper right corner. Circles appear to the left of each portion of the conversation. Tap the circle next to the part you wish to delete and it becomes a white checkmark in a red circle, as shown in Figure 2-13. Two

Book III
Chapter 2

Sending and
Receiving Text
and Multimedia
Messages

options are highlighted at the bottom of the screen: Delete or Forward. To delete the portion of the conversation that you checked, just tap Delete. If you want to clear the whole conversation, tap Clear All at the top of the screen on the left. This only clears the conversation; the name or phone number remains in your Message list and new messages from that contact show up in the Message list under that person's name.

If you want to clear a single message, do this from the Messages list. You can use either a two-step method or a three-step method. After a message is deleted, it's gone, so if you want an extra step to think about what you're about to delete, use the three-step method:

✓ Tap Edit and red circles with hyphens appear next to each message. Tap the circle next to the message you want to delete. The circle rotates 90 degrees and a Delete button appears to the right of the message, like you see in Figure 2-14. Tap the Delete button and poof! The message is

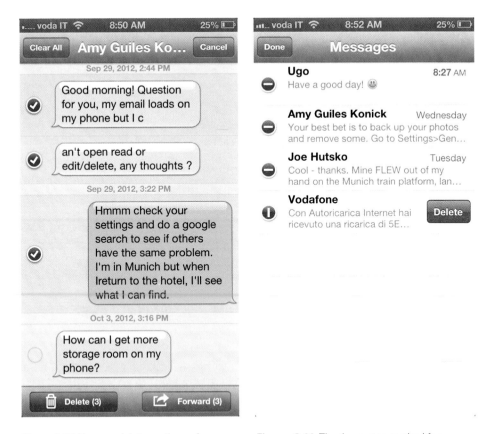

Figure 2-13: You can delete portions of a conversation.

Figures 2-14: The three-step method for deleting messages.

gone. When you've finished deleting messages, tap Done to return to the Messages list.

✔ If, on the other hand, you don't worry about deleting something by mistake, use the two-step method. Swipe across the entry for the message you want to delete. A Delete button appears next to that message, as in Figure 2-15. Tap the button and the message is deleted.

Forwarding messages

You may receive information from one person that you'd like to pass on to another. Rather than retype or copy and paste the information, you can forward the portion of the conversation that has the information to someone else. To forward a message, follow these steps:

1. **Choose the message you want to forward from the Messages list.**

   If the message is part of a conversation, open the conversation by tapping the message from the list.

2. **Tap the Edit button and transparent circles appear next to the message or messages that make up the conversation.**

3. **Tap the circle next to the message(s) you want to forward.**

   The red circle with the white checkmark appears.

4. **Tap the Forward button in the bottom right corner.**

   A New Message screen opens with the message you wish to forward in the text box.

5. **Insert a phone number or a name from Contacts in the To field and tap the plus sign (+) button if you want to add additional recipients.**

6. **Tap Send when you're ready to send the message.**

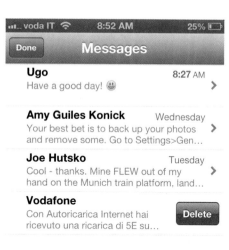

Figure 2-15: The message-deleting two-step.

Book III
Chapter 2

Sending and
Receiving Text
and Multimedia
Messages

The Sending progress bar opens at the top of the page. If you chose a sound in Sound settings for Sent Mail, you hear whatever sound you chose when the message has been sent.

You can search for text within messages in the Messages list by using the Search box at the very top of the list. Just type the specific word or phrase you're searching for and tap the magnifying glass.

Chapter 3: Surfing the Web with Safari

In This Chapter

- ✓ Touring Safari's features
- ✓ Opening and viewing web pages
- ✓ Sharing web pages
- ✓ Organizing bookmarks
- ✓ Adding web apps and clips to your Home screen
- ✓ Adjusting general and security settings

*R*eady to surf the web with Safari? If your answer is yes, you've come to the right place. We begin this chapter with a guided tour of iPhone's Safari web browser, pointing out basic features and ways you use Safari to browse web pages. We then walk you through actually opening and viewing pages, showing you neat things along the way, like zooming in and out of web pages, using Reader for distraction-free reading, or turning your iPhone sideways for a wider, toolbar-free view of a web page — and for easier typing when you need to fill in web forms.

After getting your feet wet with a little basic web surfing, we show you how to juggle multiple web pages you want to view, how to control video and audio content, how to save images to your iPhone's camera roll, how to view documents, and how to create bookmarks for web pages you often visit so you can view those web pages with a few taps of your finger.

Near the end of our surfin' safari, we show you the ins and outs of using Safari's Search feature to find web pages you're looking for — and to find things on those web pages you've found. And finally, we conclude this chapter by giving you a rundown of Safari settings you may want to adjust to make your web surfing experience smoother — and safer.

If web browsing is old hat to you, you may want to skip ahead to the "Playing Favorites with Bookmarks" and "Accessing Websites from the Home Screen" sections, which explain some nifty features you may not be familiar with.

Surfin' Safari Tour

There's no time like the present to take a quick tour of the Safari screen so that we'll be on the proverbial same page. The Safari screen is divided into three zones: the title bar, the web page, and the toolbar. Refer to Figure 3-1 for the following explanations:

- ✓ **Title Bar:** The name of the web page you're viewing runs across the top and beneath it you see the following, from left to right:

  - • **Address field:** Displays the web address's URL (which stands for Uniform Resource Locator); the Address field is also what you tap to make the keyboard appear, so you can type in a web page address you want to open and view.

Figure 3-1: The Safari web browser screen displaying a web page.

- **Stop/Reload button:** A dual-purpose button you can tap to stop a web page from loading, or to reload a web page to see any new information that may have been updated on that web page, such as breaking stories on a news web page.

- **Search field:** What you tap to make the keyboard appear, so you can type in a name of a person, place, or anything you're searching for, such as a restaurant, a weather report, or the name of your favorite *For Dummies* author.

If you don't see the title bar, tap the Status bar at the top of iPhone's screen to make the title bar appear. If you don't see the Status bar, turn your iPhone to portrait orientation.

- **Web page:** Below the title bar, you see the bulk of the web page content. The beauty of web pages is that no two are exactly alike — which can also be the frustrating thing about web pages. Many websites have both full and mobile versions, so what you're used to seeing on your computer, beyond being smaller, might look completely different on your iPhone. Refer to Figure 3-2 and check out the sidebar, "A tale of two web pages," to get the rundown of the difference.

- **Toolbar:** At the bottom of the screen, you find the toolbar that displays buttons for the following functions:

  - **Previous/Next:** Previous goes back to the previous web page you viewed; Next moves you Forward to the web page you just left when you pressed Previous. (One or both buttons may be dim until you navigate away from the current web page you're viewing.)

  - **Action:** Displays options for sharing or doing something with the current web page you're viewing, including creating a bookmark that links to the web page, adding the page to your Reading List, creating a Home screen icon for the web page, sharing the web page via Mail or Messages, tweeting the link with Twitter or posting it to Facebook, copying the link, or printing the web page.

  - **Bookmarks:** Displays the Bookmarks screen, which holds a list of links that give you quick access to web pages you want to revisit. Reading List, (viewing) History, and iCloud tabs are listed in Bookmarks too. We dedicate a whole section to bookmarks later in this chapter.

  - **Web Pages:** Lets you scroll through up to eight open web pages and move quickly from one to another.

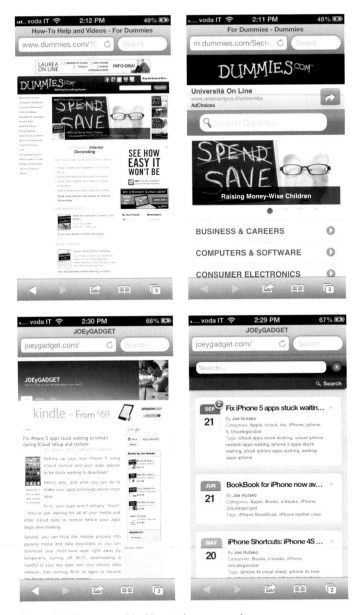

Figure 3-2: Two ways of looking at the same web pages.

A tale of two web pages

The first and third web pages shown in Figure 3-2 are miniature versions of the same "desktop" versions of what the web pages look like if you view them using your computer's web browser, whereas the second and fourth web pages are the "mobile" versions of those same web pages, respectively.

The notion behind "mobile" web pages is that they minimize graphics and much of the other extraneous "stuff" that normally appears on the desktop version of the web page, so as to make it easier for you to navigate those web pages on your mobile device, in this case, your iPhone. Some web pages gauge whether the web browser you're using is a desktop browser or a mobile browser, and automatically present one or the other, based on your browser. Other times, you type in a specific mobile web page address like `mobile.ny-times.com` to access the mobile version of that web page. Sometimes typing the mobile address for a web page using your computer's browser has no effect and the desktop version of the web page opens anyway and vice versa: Sometimes typing the full desktop version of a web page on your iPhone ignores your wish and forces you to view the mobile version of the web page.

Other times, you get the best of both worlds: A web page that automatically opens the mobile version when it detects you're using an iPhone gives you the option to switch to the desktop version of that web page if you so desire. You usually find this at the bottom of the page with a toggle switch, as shown here, or with a Full Site link.

Taking the idea of an iPhone-savvy website one step further, many companies have created *web apps* — specific iPhone apps that let you view information from their website via a special app that offers other features. We discuss them toward the end of the chapter.

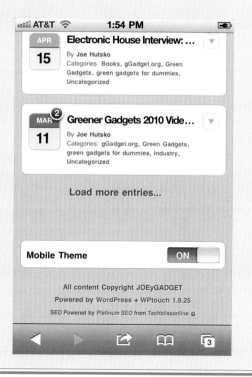

Opening web pages

Now that you know what to expect, we take you through the different ways of opening web pages, switching from one to another, searching, and a bunch of other things you can do in Safari. Your iPhone needs to be connected to a Wi-Fi network or your cellular provider's data network in order to follow along with all of the Safari goodness contained within these pages. Start with these steps:

1. **Tap Safari on the Home screen.**

   The Safari screen appears, and you see either a blank screen or the last website you viewed the last time you used Safari.

2. **Do one of the following:**

   Tap Address Field: The keyboard appears; type in the web address of a web page you want to view, and then tap Go. Safari then displays the web page for the address you typed in.

   Tap the Bookmarks button: Tap a web page bookmark you want to open. Safari displays the web page for the bookmark you tapped. See the section "Playing Favorites with Bookmarks" for details.

   Tap Search: The keyboard appears; type a word, name, phrase, ZIP code, or whatever you're searching for. A list of search results appears; tap the result that seems closest to what you seek to open the web page. See the section "Searching Tips and Tricks" for more information.

   If you don't see the Address and Search fields at the top of the Safari screen, tap the Status bar at the top of iPhone's screen to instantly scroll to the top of the web page and reveal the Address field.

3. **Interact with the web page in the following ways, which we explain in detail in the section "Viewing Web Pages," or repeat Step 2 to go to another web page:**

   Tap links, buttons, or other elements that take you to another spot on the web page, to a web page on the website you're accessing, or to another web page on another website.

   Tap fields to type in information.

   Save images.

   Tap a link to upload an image.

   Tap a phone number.

   Tap a street address.

Safari keyboard tips and tricks

Notice anything *strange* about the keyboard when you were typing in the web address you want to open? Strange how, you ask? Oh, you know, just little things — like that fact that there's no spacebar key!? Before you begin worrying your iPhone's keyboard may be hexed, we can assure you there *is* a method to this seemingly keyboard-oversight madness. Because you can't have spaces in a URL address, your iPhone intelligently eliminates the space-waster on the keyboard that appears when you tap in the address field.

Here are a few other tips and tricks that can help you maximize your Safari keyboard experience, while minimizing how much typing you actually have to do:

✔ **Skip the www:** If you know the URL, type it without the "www" in the Address field and Safari presents a list of potential matches, tap the match. If there's no match, tap the Go button and Safari tries to connect with what you typed. If that doesn't work, it will add the "www" and try again. Same goes for the ".com" suffix.

✔ **Type www sometimes:** You may *want* to type **www** when you're typing in certain website addresses in order to open the full-size versions instead of the mobile version. Case in point: Typing www.nytimes.com opens the full-size web page, but typing nytimes.com opens the mobile version of the web page (refer to Figure 3-2 near the beginning of this chapter to see what we're talking about).

✔ **Press to complete:** Tap and hold the .com button to display a list of alternate completion options, and then drag your finger to the one you want and let go to fill in that choice (.net, .edu, .org, .com, or one of the other choices).

✔ **Landscape keyboard:** Rotate your iPhone sideways to display the wider-reaching landscape keyboard for easier, more accurate typing.

✔ **Use AutoFill:** Use Safari's AutoFill feature to automatically fill in common fields such as name, address, and phone number fields, e-mail address fields, and user name and password fields. We tell you about AutoFill later in this chapter.

You don't need to tap the erase button to clear the Address field before you type the web page address you want to open. Tap the Address field and begin typing the web address you want to open; the field is automatically erased. (Don't tap and hold, which will insert a blinking cursor allowing you to edit the existing URL address.)

Stopping and reloading web pages

Whichever way you choose to open a web page, after Safari actually begins loading the web page, a trio of visual cues appears to let you know Safari is processing your request. Those cues include a blue progress bar in the Address field, the Reload button changing to the Stop button, and the twirling network activity icon in the status bar.

You can stop or reload a web page by doing one of the following:

- ✔ Tap the stop button if you want to instantly stop loading a web page that seems to be taking forever.

- ✔ Tap the reload button to reload the web page and display any new information that may have been added to the web page since you began viewing it (such as the latest-breaking news on a news web page).

Viewing Web Pages

When the web page appears, you're free to move about the cabin — er, we mean view the web page — in any number of free-ranging ways.

Using fullscreen and portrait views

When it comes to viewing web pages, Safari lets you have it both ways: portrait orientation view (taller than it is wide) and landscape orientation view (wider than it is tall), as shown in Figure 3-3. Switching between these views is merely a matter of turning your iPhone sideways or upright, depending on whether you want to view your web page in landscape or portrait view, respectively.

In landscape view, Safari gives you the fullscreen option. Tap the fullscreen/ normal screen toggle switch that shows up to the right of the web pages button in the toolbar when you turn your iPhone to landscape orientation. The toolbar disappears completely and all your iPhone screen real estate is dedicated to the web page; the title bar is pushed out of view, but you can scroll up to see it. Fullscreen view is particularly useful when you want to watch video on a web page.

The Fullscreen toggle switch

Figure 3-3: Rotating iPhone sideways displays the landscape view, here in its full-screen glory.

 If you see the Portrait Orientation Lock icon in the top-right corner of the status bar, turning your iPhone on its side won't switch your web page to the wide-screen landscape view. To turn the Portrait Orientation Lock feature off or on, double-click the Home button, and then slide the recent apps icon list at the bottom of the screen to the right. Tap the Portrait Orientation Lock icon to toggle that feature on or off.

Using Reader

If you see a Reader button in the Address Field, you can view the article in Reader. Reader displays the text of the article on a plain white page without any of the ambient noise that surrounds it on the web page itself, as shown in Figure 3-4.

Tap the Font button in the upper-left corner to change the size of the text. Tap the Action button to reveal the same tasks that appear when you tap the Action button from a web page view, such as sharing, printing, or saving the article to your Reading List. Tap Done when you finish reading.

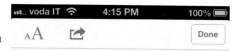

Brain connectivity predicts reading skills

Reading ability in children seems to be linked to the strength of connections in the brain.

JGI/J. Grill/Getty

The growth pattern of long-range

Figure 3-4: Reader makes reading web articles easier.

Scrolling web pages

One thing you do a lot of when you're viewing a web page is scrolling — up, down, and sometimes all around — to see all of the information on the web page. In rare instances, you may also come across a web page that contains a scrollable frame of text *within* the web page — which is referred to as a *text frame*.

Ways you can scroll a web page you're viewing include

- ✓ **Scrolling carefully:** Drag a web page up or down, or sideways; don't worry about accidentally tapping something on the web page — as long as you drag your fingertip as soon as you touch the screen, Safari interprets your gesture as a scroll (or flick) rather than a tap.

- ✓ **Scrolling quickly:** Flick up or down to scroll in those directions more quickly.

- ✓ **Scrolling instantly to the top:** Tap the status bar at the top of iPhone's screen to instantly scroll to the top of a web page.

- ✓ **Scrolling inside a text frame:** Drag two fingers up or down in a text frame within a web page to scroll just the text in that frame up or down.

Zooming web pages

Using Safari's zoom view features can make scrolling web pages (and text frames within web pages) easier on your eyes — and fingertips.

Fortunately, many web pages automatically display an easier to read mobile version of themselves when they detect you've opened the web pages using a smartphone like the iPhone, which means you typically won't need to (or won't even be able to) zoom in or out of the contents of those web pages.

Other times, a web page may not offer a mobile viewing option, which means you're faced with viewing the full-size version of the web page that is designed to be viewed with your computer web browser program.

Thankfully, Safari's zoom in and out features make it easy to narrow your focus on just the section of a full-size web page that you want to view.

Ways you can zoom in and out of web pages include the following:

- ✓ **Double-tap zooming:** Double-tap a column on a web page to zoom in to or out of that column, as shown in Figure 3-5.

- ✓ **Spread and pinch zooming:** Spread two fingers apart or pinch together to zoom out or in to a web page.

To quickly reset a web page to its original size, double-tap anywhere on the screen to home in on a column, and then double-tap again to zoom all the way out to the full-screen view.

Although you can always zoom in and out of any full-size web page on iPhone's screen, not all mobile versions of certain websites allow zooming.

Figure 3-5: Zooming in on a web page with a double-tap — or a pinch.

Navigating Web Pages

There's a reason it's called the World Wide Web. Web pages contain links to other web pages that contain more links and all those links weave a web of pages that seems infinite. One tap leads to another tap, and pretty soon you've spent your whole morning learning about the habits and habitats of the great tit bird that you saw in your garden that morning. Barbara refers to it as the Internet vortex, but Safari's navigation features can help you stay the course as you wind your way from web page to web page, as we explain in the following subtopics.

Going back, forward

Before we tell you about the many types of links you can tap to joyfully (or frustratingly) lose yourself in the web, it can help to know up front how to use Safari's Previous and Next navigation buttons to move backward or forward through web pages.

Using Safari's Previous button, you can always backtrack one or two or ten or more steps to return to whatever web page you started on before you wound up getting inadvertently lost (or (un)intentionally sidetracked). And using Safari's Next button, you can repeat your steps forward to the farthest web page you visited before you backtracked *away* from that farthest point by tapping the Previous button.

- ✔ Tap Previous to go back to the previous web page you viewed.
- ✔ Tap Next to go forward to a page you were viewing before you tapped the Previous button.

Using Safari's History feature, which we explain a little farther along in our mutual journey through this section, is another (often more direct) way you can go back to a web page you previously visited.

Book III Chapter 3

Surfing the Web with Safari

Juggling multiple websites

You have two choices for what happens when you tap a link. Select your choice by tapping Settings⇨Safari⇨Open Links, and then choosing one of these:

- ✓ **In New Page:** A web link you tap for a different website, shifts the Safari page you're viewing to one side, and opens a new Safari page window to display the different website you tapped the link for. Links that are for web pages within the same website do not open a new Safari page. The Previous/Next buttons work only within the same website. To access different Safari pages, you have to tap the Web Pages button and flick between them.

- ✓ **In Background:** A web link you tap replaces whatever web page you're viewing with the web page the link you tapped leads to. The Previous/Next buttons take you back and forth between all the web pages you visited.

With either choice, you can always open a new Safari page window on your own by tapping the Web Pages button. To switch between and close the multiple web page windows you open, you also use the Web Pages button.

The number of web pages you have open in Safari is displayed on the Web Pages button, although you won't see a number when you have only one web page open. (Refer to Figure 3-1.)

Tap the Web Pages button to display the Web Pages screen, as shown in Figure 3-6.

You can open and work with up to eight Safari pages at a time.

A thumbnail image of the web page you were viewing appears in the center of the Web Pages screen with that page's title above the thumbnail. Dots beneath the thumbnail indicate how many web pages you have open.

Figure 3-6: The Web Pages screen.

Things you can do when viewing the Web Pages screen include the following:

✔ **Open a new web page:** Tap New Page to create and open a new, blank Safari web page, and then use one of the methods described in "Opening web pages" earlier in this chapter to open a web page you want to see.

✔ **Switch between web pages:** Flick left or right to see thumbnails and titles of other open web pages, and then tap the web page you want to view to open that web page.

✔ **Close a web page:** Tap the red X button in the upper-left corner of a web page thumbnail to close that web page.

✔ **Close the Web Pages screen:** Tap Done to close the Web Pages screen.

Revisiting history with History

The Previous button is great for going back three or four links, but more than that and it can be tiresome. Sometimes you want to go back to a web page you viewed a few hours ago or even a few days or weeks ago. Thanks to Safari's History feature, you can do just that. Think of the History feature as a kind of virtual bag of popcorn, which drops a kernel of popcorn for every web page you visit, so you can instantly teleport your way back to any given kernel of popcorn (er, web page) without having to actually tap the Previous button a zillion times to retrace your steps.

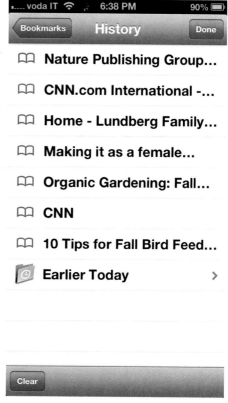

Book III
Chapter 3

Surfing the Web
with Safari

Opening previously viewed web pages

To view your Safari web history, press and hold the back button or tap Bookmarks, and then tap the History folder to view your web history activity, as shown in Figure 3-7. Tap any item in the list to reopen that web page you previously visited.

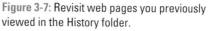

Figure 3-7: Revisit web pages you previously viewed in the History folder.

To help keep the History screen neat and manageable, Safari creates folders for web pages you visited earlier in the day, and for web pages you visited earlier in the day and before today.

Tap any of those folders to view web pages you previously visited, and then tap any of the items listed to revisit that web page.

If you don't see the History folder shown in Figure 3-8, that means you previously navigated to another Bookmarks folder; tap the Bookmarks button in the upper-left corner to back your way out of whatever folder you're in until you see the History folder, and then tap the History folder to view your Safari web history. Or just tap and hold the back button!

Although the History folder is stored inside Safari's Bookmarks folder, you can't save a Bookmark in the History.

Erasing your web history

On the History screen (refer to Figure 3-7), you may have noticed the Clear button in the lower-left corner. By tapping that button, you can wipe out your entire Safari web browsing history in one fell swoop if you're the sort of person who'd rather not keep a record of your web browsing around.

To clear your Safari web history, tap Bookmarks⇨History, and then tap the Clear button in the lower-left corner. The red Clear History button appears, giving you a moment to reconsider whether you really want to wipe out your web history. Tap Clear History if you really do, or tap Cancel if you change your mind and you want to keep your web history on hand.

If you don't want to leave a trace of your web surfing on your iPhone, you can turn Private Browsing on in Settings⇨Safari; however, this deactivates the Previous and Next buttons.

Tapping into Web Page Links

When you open and view a web page, more often than not, you wind up tapping a link on that web page, which takes you to another web page. For instance, when you view the *New York Times* web page, you scroll up and down the list of news stories, and then you tap the web page link for the news story you want to read, and then *that* web page replaces the one you were viewing with the news story.

Web links aren't limited to opening other web pages, however. The following things may occur, too:

- Display a graphic or photo or a photo slideshow you can tap through to view a series of photos

- Open a PDF document file

- Display a form with fields you can fill in with information, such as your shipping address on a shopping site, or your e-mail address, so you can receive a weekly newsletter from a museum you're fond of

✔ Play an audio file, such as a news story, a podcast, or a song

✔ Play a video file, say a movie trailer or a friend's dog catching a Frisbee

✔ Open another app, which you must exit (by double-pressing the Home button) to return to Safari

In the remainder of this section, we also tell you about interacting with the different types of links you might encounter, such as phone numbers, e-mail, and location addresses. We tell you how to view and do things with content-rich web links, such as saving photos or graphics to your iPhone's Photos app, or opening other apps to view the contents of a link, like Word or PDF documents, or a PowerPoint presentation.

When you see words or phrases in blue with the text of an article, tap the text to open a link to another web page related to the word or phrase you tapped.

Working with basic links and forms

By now, you know all you need to do to open a web page link is tap it, and that linked web page replaces the one you're viewing, or it opens a new Safari page screen to display the linked web page.

Pressing and holding on a web page link displays the link's information and options dialog, as shown in Figure 3-8.

The web page link's full web address (URL) appears at the top of the dialog, and below the web address are buttons you can tap to do the following things:

✔ **Open:** Opens the web page link.

✔ **Open in New Page:** Forces Safari to open the web page link in a new Safari page screen instead of replacing the web page screen you are viewing (see "Juggling multiple websites" earlier in this chapter).

✔ **Add to Reading List:** Places the link in your Reading List so you can come back later and read

Figure 3-8: The web page link info and options dialog.

whatever it is that interests you on this web page. This is a type of temporary bookmark; in fact, Reading List is found in the Bookmarks list.

✔ **Copy:** Copies the web page address to the clipboard so you can paste the web address elsewhere, like in a note in the Note app, or in a text message in the Messages app.

✔ **Cancel:** Closes the web page information and options screen.

Filling in forms and fields

When it comes to filling in forms, Safari serves up some useful helpers to make tapping out type and numbers using the keyboard as easy as possible.

Tap a field and begin typing. If you're having trouble seeing the field you're typing in, you can zoom in and out of the web page even while the keyboard is displayed. Turning your iPhone to landscape view makes the keyboard slightly larger.

Tap Next to move the cursor to the next field in the form, as shown in Figure 3-9. Tap Previous if you need to go back to a prior field you filled in. Tapping either of those two buttons repeatedly quickly moves you from field to field. You can also scroll down to tap into any other fields you need to complete.

Tap Done when you finish filling in the form fields.

Using AutoFill to do the typing for you

Safari's AutoFill feature automatically fills in common fields with your personal information with a single tap instead of requiring you to fill in those fields individually. Another common type of information Safari can automatically fill in for you is user names and passwords.

To turn on Safari's AutoFill feature and options, tap Home, and then tap Settings⟳Safari⟳AutoFill to display the AutoFill settings screen, as shown in Figure 3-10.

Tap Use Contact Info On and Safari fills in online forms with your personal information. Where that personal information comes from in the first place is answered by the My Info option, just below the Use Contact Info switch. You should see your own name in the My Info option field. That means Safari copies the information you have saved in the name, address, phone number, and e-mail address fields of your own Contacts card and pastes those bits

Figure 3-9: When filling out forms, Safari helps you "tab" between fields with the Next and Previous buttons.

of information into the appropriate fields when you tap AutoFill on a web page form.

If you don't see your name in the My Info option field, tap that field to display your Contacts, and then locate and tap your own Contacts card name to select it as the card you want to use for the My Info option.

Saving user names and passwords

Tap the Names & Passwords option On if you want Safari to remember any user names and passwords you type to access certain web pages. The first time you type your name and password on a web page that requires that information, Safari displays a pop-up message, asking if you'd like to save the password. Tap Yes if you would, Never for This Website if you never-ever-ever want to save the password for the web page, or Not Now, if you don't want to save the password right now, but you want to keep your option of saving the password open the next time you visit the web page.

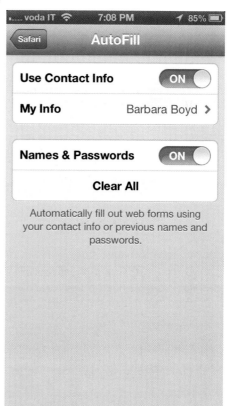

Figure 3-10: Safari's AutoFill settings screen.

Some websites have a Remember Me option for usernames and passwords that works if you accept cookies, in which case Safari doesn't ask if you want it to remember because the website takes care of that. (See the section "Adjusting General and Security Settings" at the end of this chapter to learn about cookies.)

To wipe out any saved user names and passwords now (before you turn the option on) or in the future (by coming back to this setting), tap Clear All, and those saved user names and passwords are history.

Pop-ups, pick-lists, check boxes, and radio buttons

Sometimes you encounter on-screen controls and gizmos on certain web pages, such as pop-up menus and pick-lists you tap and scroll through to select predetermined information such as the state you live in or a quantity of something you may be ordering. You may also come across check boxes and radio buttons on certain websites. Tap these boxes or buttons to mark or unmark your selection.

Using these digital doodads, like the pop-up and pick-list shown in Figure 3-11, is usually pretty self-explanatory: Tap to display the pop-up menu, and then scroll up or down the list and tap your choice.

Tapping the Upload button on sites like Flickr or eBay opens two choices for uploading photos: Take Photo or Video, which opens the Camera app and uploads the image directly from Camera to the website, or Choose Existing, which opens Photos allowing you to select the image you want to upload.

Opening app web links

Sometimes a web link you tap closes the Safari screen and opens another app to display the contents of the

Figure 3-11: Tap a pop-up menu and then flick to scroll up and down lists.

link you tapped. For instance, you might be viewing the website for your favorite store and find they have a special iPhone app; when you tap that link, the App Store opens so you can download the app.

Whenever you leave Safari and a web page you were viewing to use another app, you can always go back to that web page by pressing Home, and then tapping Safari or pressing the Home button twice to open the recent apps bar, and then tapping Safari.

Using phone and e-mail address links

When you encounter phone number and e-mail address web links, you can use those links to call the number you see, or create an e-mail message using the e-mail address you see. You can also send a text message or add the phone number or e-mail address to a contact card you have saved on your iPhone, or create a new contact card using either or both of those links.

Tapping into Phone links

Tap a phone number link you want to dial, and then tap Call in the pop-up screen that appears, as shown in Figure 3-12. The Safari screen closes and the active call screen appears as your iPhone places your call.

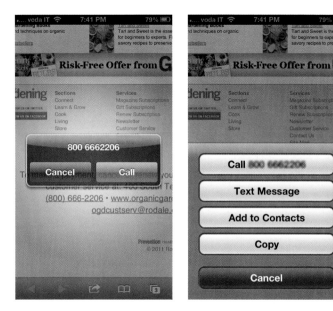

**Book III
Chapter 3**

Surfing the Web
with Safari

Figure 3-12: Tap a phone number link to dial, or press and hold to see more options.

To do other things with a phone number link, press and hold on the phone number to display phone number link options screen, and then choose one of the following options:

- **Call:** Dials the phone number.

- **Text Message:** Opens a new text message and pastes the phone number into the To field.

- **Add to Contact:** Opens an Info screen in Contacts where you can choose to Create a New Contact or Add to (the number) an Existing Contact. After you choose one, either a New Contact screen opens or your

Contacts list opens. Scroll through to find the contact to which you want to add the number.

✔ **Copy:** Puts the phone number in the clipboard so you can then open another app, and then tap and hold where you want to insert the number. Tap Paste when the option is offered.

Phone numbers and e-mail addresses are underlined so you know they are *hot links,* that is, a link that performs an action other than opening a web page.

Employing e-mail links

Tap an e-mail address you want to use to send an e-mail message, and a new message appears with the address already filled in the To field. Complete your new e-mail message and then tap Send. The e-mail message screen closes and your Mail inbox appears. Tap the Home button, and then tap Safari to return to Safari.

To do other things with an e-mail address link, press and hold on the e-mail address to display the e-mail link options screen, and then choose one of the following options:

✔ **New Message:** Creates a new e-mail message with the e-mail address you tapped already filled in the To field.

✔ **Add to Contacts:** Opens an Info screen in Contacts where you can choose to Create a New Contact or Add to (the number) an Existing Contact. After you choose one, either a New Contact screen opens or your Contacts list opens. Scroll through to find the contact to which you want to add the number.

✔ **Copy:** Copies the e-mail address to the clipboard so you can paste the e-mail address into another app such as Notes or Messages.

Opening photo, video, audio, and document links

Sometimes links you tap on a web page open photos, or play music or audio, or a video. Typically Safari figures out how to handle these other kinds of content all by itself, by playing an audio or video you tap, or by opening a common type of document file using iPhone's built-in Quick Look feature.

You can usually save photos and graphics files to the Camera Roll album in the Photos app, and sometimes you may want to choose to open a file you're viewing with another app you have installed on your iPhone.

For instance, you may want to open a Word document using Pages, QuickOffice, or Documents to Go if you have either of those apps installed on your iPhone. That way, you can save and edit the file, rather than just viewing the file using iPhone's built-in Quick Look feature, which lets you view common file types like Word docs, Excel spreadsheets, and PDF files.

Some of the other kinds of content, like streaming video or audio files, let you watch or listen to those kinds of files using Safari's built-in video and audio player features, but you can't save the files on your iPhone.

Opening streaming video and audio links

When you tap a streaming video or audio link on a web page, Safari opens and begins playing the link with its built-in video or audio player feature, also shown in Figure 3-13. The player displays all of the controls you need for starting, pausing, stopping, rewinding, fast forwarding, and adjusting the volume of the content you're watching or listening to.

Figure 3-13: Safari's built in video (left) and audio (right) player features.

When you're watching video content, those controls typically disappear after a few moments, so you can enjoy the video without having those distracting controls blocking your view.

A few things you can do when you're watching video content include

- Tap the screen to make the video controls reappear after they disappear

- Double-tap the screen when you're watching a video in portrait mode to zoom in or out

- Rotate your iPhone sideways to watch a video in landscape, fullscreen mode to enjoy the fullest possible view

Sometimes instead of seeing a thumbnail of a video on a web page, you may see a message informing you that your web browser requires Adobe Flash to view the video. Unfortunately, viewing Flash videos with Safari isn't possible because of Apple's choice to not support Flash on iPhone.

Your iPhone supports the video playing features of the web page creation language known as HTML5, which supports embedded QuickTime video playback, or Apple's own QuickTime video feature. The good news is that more and more websites are using HTML5 to create or revise their web pages. And, Adobe has released a software tool that developers can apply to their Flash videos, which makes them viewable on an iPhone, although this tool doesn't enable Flash-based games.

Saving photo and graphic files

Most of the time, you can save a photo or other graphic image file you encounter on a web page to the Camera Roll album in the Photos app, your iPhone's resident photo management app that we discuss in Book V, Chapter 1. Press and hold on a photo or other kind of image file to display the Safari options screen, and then tap Save Image to save that image file to the camera roll in the Photos app or Copy to place the image in the clipboard and then paste it in another app, as shown in Figure 3-14. If the image you tap is actually a link, you'll see more options, such as Open, Open in New Page, Add to Reading List, and Copy.

A bit of copyright "fine print" you ought to keep in mind: Although it's generally acceptable to save any photo or other kind of image file for your own viewing pleasure, you're generally not permitted to use those photos or other image files to share with others — on your own website, or in a magazine you write for, for instance — without the express consent/permission of the person or organization who owns the rights to those image files you may have saved to your iPhone.

Viewing and opening document files

Often you can view certain document files you may encounter on your web adventures. Tapping on a document link on a web page you're viewing prompts Safari to try to open the document file using its built-in Quick Look feature, as shown in Figure 3-15. The Quick Look feature can display a number of popular document file types, including Microsoft Word, Excel, and PowerPoint documents, and PDF documents.

Sometimes you may want to open a document you're viewing using another app you have installed on your iPhone. To open a document using another app, tap the Open In <*appname*> button on the right to use the default app displayed on that button, or tap the Open In button on the left (refer to Figure 3-15) to display other apps on your iPhone that you can use to open the app. Tap the button that corresponds to the app you want to use to open the document. Safari closes and the app launches and loads the document.

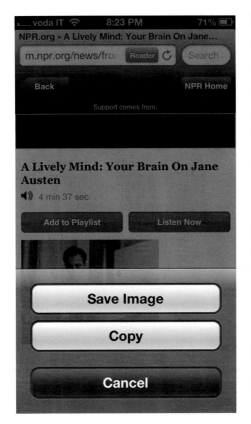

**Book III
Chapter 3**

Surfing the Web
with Safari

Figure 3-14: Choose Save Image to copy a photo from a web page.

Figure 3-15: The Quick Look feature displays documents quickly, or you can open them in another app.

Acting on Web Page Links

The action button in the toolbar at the bottom of the Safari screen lets you do many things with the web page you're viewing. Say you want to send someone an e-mail with a link to a web page you want them to look at or you want to post a link to Facebook. Or maybe you want to copy a web page link so you can paste it in another program such as Notes, for instance, where you might be creating a list of favorite recipe web pages. You can do all of those things and more directly from the web page you're browsing. Follow these steps:

1. **While viewing a web page in normal or Reader mode that you want to share, print, or copy, tap the Action button at the bottom of the screen (at the top of the screen in Reader mode).**

   The screen as shown in Figure 3-16 appears.

2. **Tap your sharing method of choice from the following:**

   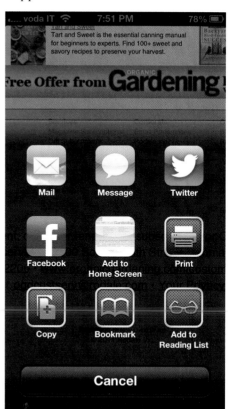

   • **Mail:** A new message appears with the web page address pasted into the body of the message; complete the message as usual and then tap Send.

     If you share an article from Reader, the entire article will be pasted in to the Mail message.

   • **Message:** A new text message, which may be SMS or iMessage depending on the recipient, appears with the web page address pasted into the body of the message; complete the message as usual and then tap Send.

   • **Twitter:** Write something to accompany your link, and then tap Send.

Figure 3-16: Tap the Action button to see your sharing options and more.

- **Facebook:** Write something to accompany your link, and then tap Post.

- **Print:** Select a printer if your printer isn't selected, tap the plus sign to print more than one copy, and then tap Print.

  You may have noticed we didn't mention Add to Home Screen, Copy, Bookmark, or Add to Reading List. We discuss those later in this chapter.

  After each of these actions, your message disappears into the ether and the web page you were viewing appears front and center once more.

- **Copy:** The web address is copied to the clipboard so you can paste it to another app. Return to the Home screen or the multitasking bar to open another app and paste the link. Double-press the Home button to open the multitasking bar and tap Safari to return to the web page you were viewing.

3. **Continue what you were doing in Safari.**

You can also print other types of content you can open and view in Safari, such as PDF (Portable Document Format) or Microsoft Word docs, Excel spreadsheets, and photos — in other words, anything iPhone's QuickLook feature can open and display on the screen, you can print to an AirPrint-enabled printer.

Playing Favorites with Bookmarks

Much like their paper counterparts save your place in a book, electronic bookmarks save your place, or places, on the web — it's a way of easily returning to a website or specific web page whenever you want. Even better, bookmarks you save in Safari on your Mac or Windows PC (or Internet Explorer on your Windows PC if that's your preferred web browser) and iPhone and other iOS devices sync so you find the same bookmarks on all your devices. This back and forth magic happens almost instantly if you have an iCloud account set up on your iPhone, and if you've turned on the sync bookmarks setting for that account. It also happens when you sync your iPhone with your computer using iTunes, either cabled or with Wi-Fi, if that's your preferred syncing method.

We tell you how to sync bookmarks and all kinds of other stuff between your iPhone and your computer in Book II, Chapter 1.

Viewing, opening, and creating bookmarks

To view a bookmarked web page, tap Bookmarks to display the Bookmarks screen (refer to Figure 3-17), and then tap the bookmark you want to open that web page. Your iPhone comes with some pre-installed bookmarks to get you started. You also see the following:

- **Reading List:** Store articles you want to read later here.

- **History:** A list of web pages you viewed on your iPhone.

- **iCloud Tabs:** A list of web pages you're viewing on other devices.

- **Bookmarks Bar, Menu, and folders:** Correspond to those you have in these places on your computer, and you can add to any of these places from your iPhone.

You may need to scroll down your list or tap a folder stored in the Bookmarks list to find the bookmark you want to open.

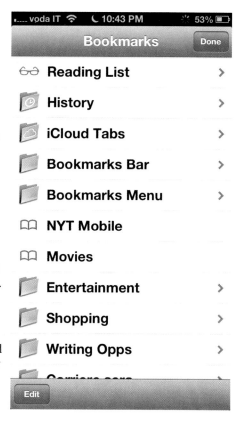

Figure 3-17: Bookmarks mark your favorite web pages so you can return in a tap.

Adding bookmarks

To create a new bookmark for a web page you're viewing, do the following:

1. **Tap the Action button to display the Action option screen, and then tap Bookmark to display the Add Bookmark screen.**

   The keyboard appears, and the blinking cursor is positioned at the end of the web page name.

2. **(Optional.) Edit the name of the website if you don't like the name that's automatically created for the bookmark, as shown in Figure 3-18.**

   You might want to use something more descriptive or shorter so the whole name appears in the Bookmarks list.

3. **(Optional.) Tap the disclosure triangle on the right of the Bookmarks folder button to choose a different folder than the one that's already chosen.**

4. **Tap Done or Save to save your new Bookmark.**

Organizing bookmarks

The number of bookmarks you have can get out of hand quickly if you want to remember and revisit many web pages. Placing bookmarks for similar web pages together in folders makes your browsing easier and saves you from scrolling through hundreds of bookmarks to find the one you want. Deleting bookmarks you don't use anymore is also a good idea. For example, if you plan a vacation to Los Angeles, you might place bookmarks about L.A. museums, hotels, and restaurants in one folder for easy access. When you return from your trip, you could delete the whole folder or move the restaurants to a Restaurants bookmark folder and delete the rest — you get the idea.

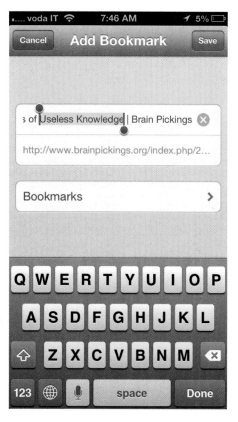

Figure 3-18: The Add Bookmarks screen.

You create new folders in the Bookmarks list or delete or rearrange folders and bookmarks using the Bookmarks edit feature. Tap Bookmarks, and then tap Edit to display the Bookmarks edit screen. You can do the following:

✓ **Rearrange your bookmarks:** Tap the Rearrange button to the right of a bookmark, and then drag the bookmark up or down the list and release your finger to drop the bookmark in its new location.

✓ **Delete a bookmark or bookmark folder:** Tap the red – (minus) sign to the left of a bookmark or folder you want to say goodbye to, and then tap the Delete button. The bookmark or folder (and all the bookmarks filed inside) disappears.

✓ **Create a new bookmark folder:**

1. Tap New Folder, and then type a name for your new bookmark folder in the Title field that appears.

The folder lands in the top level of the Bookmarks list. To place a folder inside another folder, on the Bookmarks Bar, or Bookmarks Menu, tap the disclosure triangle next to the Bookmark button then tap where you want it to go. A checkmark lets you know where that folder will be placed.

2. Tap the folder button in the upper-left corner to save your new folder and return to the Bookmarks screen.

⤴ Rename or move an existing folder by tapping the folder, and then following the same steps for creating a new bookmark folder.

⤴ Tap Done when you're finished editing the Bookmarks list, and Safari returns you to the web page you were viewing before you started tweaking your bookmarks.

Saving to read later

If you've spent any time on the web, you probably know how many things you find that you'd like to read but you don't have the time when you find it. If you're like us, in the past, you used bookmarks to save those places you wanted to come back to later, only to find you had so many bookmarks they were no longer manageable, or that you had bookmarked a website but the content you wanted to read had changed when you returned.

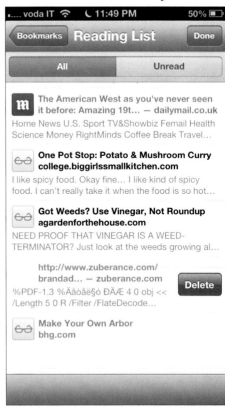

The Reading List function of Safari takes care of those problems as it stores articles or web pages you want to read later. To save an article or web page to your reading list, while you're on the page, tap the Action button and then tap Add to Reading List.

To view an article in the Reading List, tap the Bookmarks button on the toolbar and then tap Reading List (if you don't see Reading List, tap the Bookmarks button in the upper left corner to return to the main Bookmarks screen). The title, source, and the first two lines of the article appear in the list, as shown in Figure 3-19, so you don't have to decipher cryptic bookmark names.

Figure 3-19: Reading List puts articles and web pages you want to read later all in one place.

Tap the All or Unread tabs at the top to view everything in Reading List or only the things you haven't read yet. Unread articles in the All list have bold titles. Tap an article and it opens in Safari.

Articles remain in Reading List until you remove them by swiping across and then tapping the Delete button (refer to Figure 3-19).

In iOS 6, you can read articles in your Reading List offline and, like bookmarks, Reading List items sync between devices so if you put something on your Reading List on your iPhone, you find it on your iPad and computer – how great is that?

Opening iCloud tabs

With iCloud, you hardly notice when you move from one computing device to another — except for the screen size. As long as you're signed in to the same iCloud account on all your devices, tabs you open in Safari on your computer or other iOS device are visible on your iPhone, and vice versa.

Tap the Bookmarks button in the toolbar and then tap iCloud Tabs to see the tabs you have open on other devices, as shown in Figure 3-20. On your computer or iPad, click or tap the iCloud icon in the Safari toolbar at the top of the window or screen.

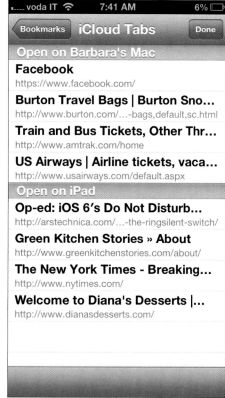

Figure 3-20: See the web pages you're browsing on other devices on your iPhone.

Accessing Websites from the Home Screen

Instead of bookmarking sites you visit frequently, you can have a button on your Home screen that taps in directly to the website or web page. There are two ways to go about this: web apps and Web Clips. Here we explain both.

Web apps

Many websites, from those of news outlets like *The New York Times*, to stores such as Target, or your bank, display a link that reads Download the iPhone App. When you tap this button or link, the App Store opens and gives you the opportunity to download an app for that site. (See Book II, Chapter 2 to learn about downloading and installing apps.) When you use the web app, you see the content of the website, but usually see other functions as well that help you navigate and interact with the information that website provides. Or you might have a streamlined version of the main service that website offers. Like apps in general, there's no hard, fast rule for how and what they present, so the best thing to do is explore.

Figure 3-21 shows an example: Barbara can go to her bank's website and sign in to her account or use the bank's web app, which has an easier sign-in procedure and eliminates extraneous information.

Figure 3-21: Web apps are site-specific apps that give you added features related to the services offered.

Web Clips

If you visit a particular web page often and there's no web app available, you can create a Home screen icon, called a Web Clip, for that web page. The Web Clip appears on the Home screen, just like your iPhone's app icons.

Tapping the Web Clip automatically opens the web page. If you want Safari to open to a specific "Home page," create a web clip for that page.

To create a Web Clip:

1. **Open the web page for which you want to create a Web Clip.**

   You can zoom in to a particular column on the web page you want to add to your Home screen, and when you tap the icon on the Home screen, Safari opens the web page to that same section — very handy for tracking just a column of information, like the daily menu special at your favorite diner.

2. **Tap the Action button to display the Action options screen, and then tap Add to Home Screen.**

   The Add to Home screen appears, displaying a name and icon for the Web Clip you want to add to the Home screen.

3. **Edit or type a new name for your Web Clip — nine letters is optimal if you want to see the whole name under the icon.**

4. **Tap Add.**

   Safari closes and ushers you to the Home screen where your new Web Clip has been added.

If you don't see the Add to Home Screen button in Step 1, that's because your iPhone's Home screen is filled to capacity, in which case you'll need to delete an app or Web Clip you have saved on your Home screen. Alternatively, you can make more space by moving one or more Home screen icons into folders that occupy only one icon space themselves and can hold up to 16 icons (12 on iPhone 4S and earlier) inside them. We show you how to add, remove, and organize Home screen icons and folders in Book I, Chapter 3.

**Book III
Chapter 3**

**Surfing the Web
with Safari**

Searching Tips and Tricks

Safari's Search field is the place to go to whenever you want to find something on the web or on the web page you're viewing. When you first begin using your iPhone, Google is the search engine that Safari uses to find things you search for using the Search field.

If you'd rather depend on Bing or Yahoo! to carry out your web searches, you can change your search engine choice by tapping Settings on the Home screen, and then tap Safari↪Search Engine and pick your preferred search engine. We tell you about the rest of Safari's settings at the end of this chapter.

Searching the web

To Search the web using Safari's search feature:

1. **Tap the Search field to display the keyboard, and then begin typing the word, name, phrase, ZIP code, or whatever you're searching for.**

   As you type, a list of suggested search words appears, based on web pages you may have already visited, or bookmarked, or one which your chosen Search engine provider thinks may match what you're looking for.

   A list of matches on the web page you were viewing also appears in the lower part of the screen under the On This Page heading; you may have to scroll down to see it.

   At this point, you can do one of the following:

2a. **Tap one of those suggested matches if it matches your criteria.**

2b. **Ignore those suggested matches that appear and finish typing what you're looking for in the Search field, and then tap the Search button.**

   Either way, Safari displays a list of search result links that you can then tap to explore any of those possibilities.

 You can use Spotlight Search to search from the left-most Home screen. Type your search criteria and then tap Search Web (or Search Wikipedia if you want to search www.wikipedia.org instead of the web at large). The Home Search screen closes and Safari displays a list of web (or Wikipedia) links that match the word or phrase you typed.

Searching on a web page you're viewing

Sometimes you want to find something on a web page you're currently viewing (that you maybe even found by searching for that web page in the first place). Instead of scrolling up and down a web page to hunt down a word or phrase, you can use Safari's search feature to locate and highlight the word or phrase on the web page for you.

To find a word or phrase on a web page you're viewing:

1. **Tap the Search field, and then type some or all of the word or phrase you're looking for.**

   As you type, a list of suggested web page matches appear, but you can ignore those because you're already on the web page you want to be on.

2. **Flick the list of suggestions up toward the top of the screen.**

The keyboard closes, and at the bottom of the suggestions is another list under the heading On This Page, followed by the number of matches found on the web page you're viewing.

3. **Tap the item beneath On This Page to display those matches on the web page.**

A yellow highlight appears around the word or phrase that matches what you're looking for, as shown in Figure 3-22.

4. **(Optional) Tap the previous and next arrows on the lower right to display other highlighted matches (if more than one match was found), and continue to move around until you find what you're looking for on the web page.**

5. **Tap Done to close the On This Page search screen buttons and view the web page.**

.ıll.. voda IT 🛜 8:38 AM 36% 🔋

Millikan have done out of sheer curiosity in the effort to understand the construction of the atom has released forces which may transform human life; but this ultimate and unforeseen and unpredictable practical result is not offered as a justification for Rutherford or Einstein or Millikan or Bohr or any of their peers.

Further:

" With the rapid accumulation of 'useless' or theoretic knowledge a situation has been created in which it has become increasingly possible to attack practical problems in a scientific spirit. Not only inventors, but 'pure' scientists have indulged in this sport. I have mentioned Marconi, an inventor, who, while a benefactor to the human race, as a matter of fact merely 'picked other men's brain.' Edison belongs to the same category. ———— Highlight

[...]

Ehrlich, fundamentally speculative in his curiosity, turned fiercely upon the problem of syphilis and doggedly pursued it until a solution of immediate practical use — the discovery of salvarsan — was found. The discoveries of insulin by

Done   1 of 7 Matches   ◄   ►

Figure 3-22: Finding what you're looking for on a web page you're viewing.

You can ask Siri to search for you if you have an iPhone 4S or later. Press and hold the Home button until you hear Siri ask how she can help you, and then speak your request or question.

Adjusting General and Security Settings

In the sections before this one, we occasionally ask you to check out or adjust a particular Safari setting, like turning on the AutoFill feature, for instance. In this section, we give you a complete rundown of Safari's settings and feature options.

Press the Home button, and then tap Settings⟶Safari to display the Safari Settings screen, as shown in Figure 3-23.

The 411 on Safari's settings is as follows:

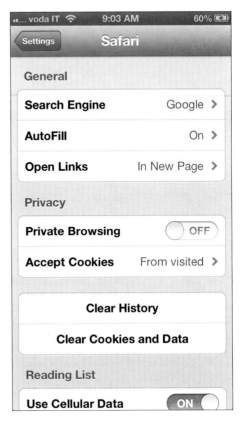

- **Search Engine:** Tap and choose your preferred Search provider.

- **AutoFill:** Tap to activate and adjust the AutoFill features described in the earlier section, "Using AutoFill to do the typing for you."

- **Open Links:** Tap this button to choose what you want Safari to do when you tap a link in a web page. See the section "Juggling multiple websites" for a full explanation.

- **Private Browsing:** With Private Browsing On, Safari doesn't keep a history of websites you visit. This is convenient if you share your iPhone with others and don't want your secret web habits revealed.

Figure 3-23: Safari's settings screen.

- **Accept Cookies:** Cookies are bits of information certain websites store, so those websites can know and remember certain things about you. Tap and choose whether you want to receive cookies Never, From Visited, or Always. From Visited is the choice we recommend so that websites you go to can remember things like your ZIP code for giving you the weather forecast and so on. Choosing Never may result in some websites not functioning properly, and choosing Always also allows sites you didn't visit but that appeared via pop-ups to grab and store information about your Internet activity.

- **Clear History, Clear Cookies and Data:** Tapping either of these erases their respective saved files from your iPhone. Clear History wipes out Safari's memory of any websites you visited. Clear Cookies and Data erases any crumbs of cookie information you may have typed in to certain websites, like your ZIP code.

✔ **Use Cellular Data:** Downloads articles to Reading List using your cellular data connection (when Wi-Fi isn't available) so you can read them offline.

If you're concerned about your cellular data limits and consumption, turn this option off.

Scroll down to see the following options not shown in Figure 3-22.

✔ **Fraud Warning:** Turn this on if you want Safari to warn you if what seems like a legitimate website you want to open may in fact be a potentially harmful site.

✔ **JavaScript:** Turned on, this feature allows websites to present information and options in fancy ways, with things like pop-up buttons, swirling graphics, and interactive features that won't appear or work if you turn this feature off.

✔ **Block Pop-ups:** This feature does its best to prevent any annoying pop-up advertisements from getting in the way of your web browsing experience.

✔ **Advanced:** Opens the following two choices:

- **Website Data:** Tap to view any databases that are automatically created by certain websites so those websites can speed up your web browsing experience when you use them. You may see databases for `mail.google.com`, for instance, if you use Safari to read your e-mail. Tapping a database item listed in the Databases screen displays more information about how much, and the maximum amount of, space that database is taking up on your iPhone. Tapping Edit allows you to delete items one by one from the list, whereas tapping Remove All Website Data clears the list completely.

- **Web Inspector:** Website developers turn on this feature to help them troubleshoot problems the web pages they create may run into. Average Joes like you and me can keep this option turned off.

If you want to keep advertisers' snooping eyes from gathering information about your web habits (to then offer you things they think you should buy from them), go to Settings⟳General⟳About. Scroll to the bottom and tap Advertising, and then tap Limit Ad Tracking On.

Book III
Chapter 3

Surfing the Web
with Safari

Chapter 4: E-mailing Every Which Way You Can

In This Chapter

✓ Configuring your e-mail account

✓ Using Mail

✓ E-mailing from other apps

✓ Adjusting your e-mail account settings

✓ Playing Fetch with your e-mail

Although the popularity of text messaging, Twitter, and Facebook as communication tools might make you think e-mail is going the way of the dinosaurs, it's still a much-used, efficient way to send and request information, make reservations, keep in touch with family and friends who live far away or, sometimes, are just down the hall in another room. With a little web research, you can find the name of the CEO of your favorite company and send her a message about how much you like the latest model of the doohickey they've released. You can also complain directly to the head of research, development, and manufacturing when your beloved doohickey breaks a week after you bought it.

With your iPhone, you have e-mail at your fingertips. In this chapter, we're assuming (always dangerous, we know) you already have an e-mail account — in fact, we know you do because you got one when you set up your iCloud account, right? We show you how to configure your e-mail account in the Mail app so you can access your e-mail from your iPhone. Then, we explain the ins and outs of Mail — writing and sending a new message, receiving and replying to a message, and saving and deleting messages. We tell you about Mail's new VIP inbox that assures you don't miss any messages from important folks. We also go over initiating an e-mail from other apps such as Notes, Maps, and Photos. Then we take a look at the account settings you can change. Your iPhone comes with preset choices for these features that probably are fine for 90 percent of users, but for the remaining 10 percent and the purely curious, we explain all the settings one by one.

Configuring Your E-Mail Account

Before you can actually send and receive e-mail messages, you have to configure your account. If you established the iCloud account while setting up your iPhone, you already have a configured e-mail account — although iCloud may not be your only e-mail account. You can set up your e-mail by yourself on your iPhone or connect your iPhone to your computer and use iTunes to sync the e-mail account information from your computer to your iPhone. We explain how to configure an e-mail account directly on your iPhone, and then show you how to do so with iTunes if that's your preferred method.

Configuring your e-mail account on iPhone

You can configure your e-mail account directly on your iPhone with a series of taps. Apple has been kind enough to insert the technical stuff needed to access some of the most used e-mail services. For the following e-mail services, you need to have just your e-mail address and password handy:

- ✔ iCloud
- ✔ Google Mail
- ✔ Yahoo!
- ✔ AOL
- ✔ Windows Live Hotmail

Setting up an iCloud account

If you set up an iCloud e-mail account when you created your Apple ID, you have either an @iCloud.com or an @me.com. And, you may have already turned on your iCloud account when you set up iCloud syncing (refer to Book II, Chapter 1). If not, we explain it here.

If you have an @me.com or an @mac.com e-mail account that you set up some time ago, you received an e-mail from Apple in October announcing that your existing account is now an iCloud account and you have been assigned an e-mail address with an @icloud.com suffix although mail sent to your existing @me.com or @mac.com address still arrives. If you sign in with one of the former accounts, you are automatically signed in to the new @icloud.com account as well.

Follow these steps to set up your iCloud e-mail on your iPhone:

1. **Tap Settings on the Home screen, and then tap Mail, Contacts, Calendars.**

   You have to scroll down — it's right below iCloud.

2. **If you have no e-mail account, the Add Account screen opens directly, as shown in Figure 4-1.**

   If you see iCloud in the Accounts list and Mail is listed beneath it, as in Figure 4-2, you can skip ahead to the "Using Mail" section.

   If you see iCloud but Mail isn't listed or you don't see iCloud at all but want to add it, tap Add Account and go to Step 3.

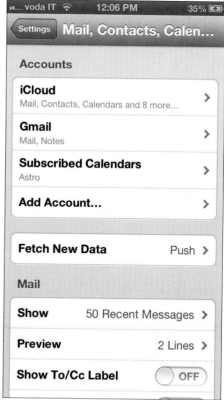

Figure 4-1: The Add Account screen.

Figure 4-2: The Mail, Contacts, Calendars settings show which accounts you have set up on your iPhone.

3. **Tap iCloud, if you have an @me.com or @mac.com account.**

   iCloud uses your @me.com or @mac.me e-mail address.

4. **Type in the e-mail address and password associated with your Apple ID and then tap the Next button.**

   If you don't have an Apple ID, click Get a Free Apple ID and follow the on-screen instructions to set one up.

   Your account is verified.

5. **The iCloud screen opens.**

   A message asks if you want iCloud to use the Location of Your iPhone. We suggest you tap OK. Find My iPhone is explained in Book I, Chapter 4.

   On the screen shown in Figure 4-3, you have a series of options and toggle switches that turn those options on. Turning an option on means that the information in that app is shared between your iPhone and iCloud and any other devices you access iCloud with, such as an iPad, Mac, or Windows PC. Any time you make changes to one of them on one device, the changes go up to the iCloud and rain down on the other device.

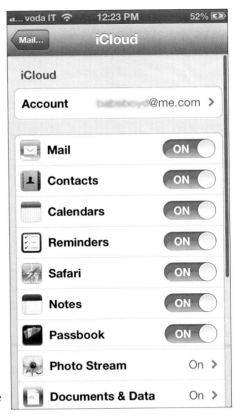

Figure 4-3: Tapping Contacts, Calendars, Reminders, and Safari On automatically merges their contents with iCloud.

   ✔ **Mail:** Turn this on and you receive your iCloud mail on your iPhone.

   ✔ **Contacts, Calendars, Reminders, and Safari:** Turn these switches on and information in these apps, previously synced with your Mac or Windows PC, is merged with iCloud. The information is consequently updated on all devices when changes are made on one device.

   ✔ **Notes:** New notes or changes to existing notes are sent to all devices.

- **Passbook:** Store cards and boarding passes are stored here, as explained in Book IV, Chapter 3.

- **Photo Stream:** When on, sends up to 1,000 of the most recent photos taken in the past 30 days in Photos on your iPhone to iCloud. (See Book V, Chapter 1 for details.)

- **Documents & Data:** Allows apps to store documents and data in iCloud, as explained in Book II, Chapter 1.

- **Find My iPhone:** This app allows you to find your phone if it's lost or stolen. (Gasp!) It also allows you to use iCloud to erase the data in iPhone remotely and lock it in the tragic event that your iPhone is stolen or lost. All this is explained in detail in Book I, Chapter 4.

Google Mail, Yahoo!, AOL, and Windows Live Hotmail accounts

Apple has already put the incoming and outgoing server information for the most popular e-mail providers on iPhone. If you use Gmail, Yahoo!, AOL, or Windows Live Hotmail, do the following:

1. **Tap Settings on the Home screen, and then tap Mail, Contacts, Calendars. You might have to scroll down — it's right below iCloud.**

2. **Tap Add Account.**

3. **The Add Account screen opens.**

   Refer to Figure 4-1.

4. **Tap the name of the account you use; for example, Google Mail, also known as Gmail.**

5. **The Google Mail (or Yahoo! or AOL or Windows Live Hotmail) screen opens, as shown in Figure 4-4.**

   Filling in the Name field is optional (Windows Live Hotmail doesn't even have one). Type

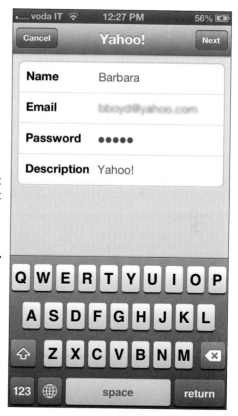

Figure 4-4: Type your name, e-mail address, and password in the designated fields.

your e-mail address in the Address field and your password in the Password field.

6. **Tap the Next button in the upper-right corner.**

   The Google Mail (or one of the others) screen opens. You have three options to consider turning on or off, depending on the services you use:

   • **Mail:** This connects you to your e-mail account so that messages download to your iPhone in the Mail app and you can send messages from your e-mail account in Mail.

   • **Calendars:** When you turn this on, you have the option of keeping or deleting existing calendars on your iPhone. The Keep On My iPhone option may cause duplicates. After you turn this feature on, changes you make to your calendar on your computer are synced to your iPhone, and vice versa.

   • **Notes:** If you turn this on, you see notes you write in Notes within your e-mail account on Mail. This is handy if you frequently e-mail notes from Notes.

   After you're happy with the settings, tap Save.

The Description field is automatically filled in with Google Mail, Yahoo!, AOL, or Windows Live Hotmail, but if you tap there, you can change it. For example, we set up two Gmail accounts: one for personal e-mail exchanges and another for newsletter subscriptions. This way, we don't have to weed through a dozen or more daily newsletters to find more important messages. In the Description field, we named one Friends and the other Subscriptions, and then tap the mailbox in the Mailboxes list to view only those types of messages. See the "Multiple inboxes" section for more information.

Setting up Microsoft Exchange

Microsoft Exchange is often used in a corporate setting where a company-specific server manages the employees' e-mail. If you use Microsoft Exchange, you might need to ask your network administrator for the server name, and then follow these steps to set up a Microsoft Exchange account on your iPhone:

1. **Tap Settings⟷Mail, Contacts, Calendars⟷Add Account⟷Microsoft Exchange.**

   The first Exchange screen opens and requests your e-mail address, password, and a description, which is optional.

2. **Fill in the information requested and tap Next.**

3. **The second Exchange screen opens as shown in Figure 4-5. Fill in the requested fields.**

   You may have to ask your network administrator for some of the details.

4. **Tap Next.**

   If Microsoft Auto Discovery didn't fill in the server address, type it in. It will be something like *exchange.company.com*.

5. **The Exchange account opens with options for Mail, Contacts, and Calendars. Turn Mail On to have e-mail from your Exchange account accessible from your iPhone.**

   Turn on Contacts and Calendars as well if you want to access that information from your Exchange account. See Book IV, Chapter 1 and 2 to learn more about Contacts and Calendars.

Setting up other IMAP and POP accounts

If you or your company uses another e-mail provider, it's probably an IMAP — Internet Message Access Protocol or POP — Post Office Protocol account. iOS 6 is pretty clever at finding the account and setting it up based on just your e-mail address and password, which we explain here:

1. **Tap Settings on the Home screen, and then tap Mail, Contacts, Calendars.**

   You have to scroll down — it's right below iCloud.

2. **The Add Account screen opens (refer to Figure 4-2); tap Add Account if you don't see it.**

Figure 4-5: Fill in the Microsoft Exchange screen to add Exchange to your e-mail accounts.

Book III
Chapter 4

E-mailing Every Which Way You Can

3. **Tap Other at the bottom of the list.**

4. **Tap Add Mail Account, the first button on the screen.**

   A New Account screen opens.

5. **Fill in your name, address (your e-mail address), your password, and a description if you want something different than what is automatically entered. See Figure 4-6.**

6. **Tap Next and your account is verified (refer to Figure 4-6).**

7. **Your iPhone automatically recognizes if it's an IMAP or POP account and presents the appropriate choices, as shown in Figure 4-7.**

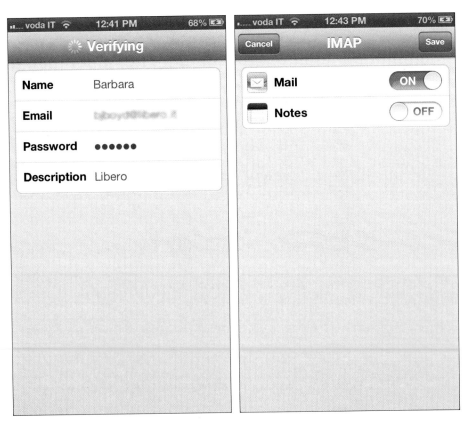

Figure 4-6: Fill in the requested information in the New Account screen.

Figure 4-7: Set up IMAP and POP accounts on your iPhone.

8. **Tap the options, such as Mail or Notes, to the On position to have that data accessible from your iPhone.**

9. **Tap Save.**

    The account is added and appears in the list of accounts in Settings⟹ Mail, Contacts, Calendars.

Depending on the type of service, you may be asked for other information during the setup: for example, Host Name, which is usually something like *mail.providername.com*, the User Name, which is the name you gave when you signed up for this e-mail service and is often the part of your e-mail address before the @ (at) symbol, your password, and the Outgoing Mail Server Host Name. You can find this information on the website of the provider on the page that references iPhone or smart phone setup, or ask the tech support person or network administrator at your office.

Configuring your e-mail account with iTunes

We recommend you set up your e-mail accounts on your iPhone without going through iTunes, but if you're more comfortable with a cable and computer, we don't want you to feel excluded. You may have done this already if you connected your iPhone to iTunes (see Book II, Chapter 1), but here are the steps:

1. **Connect your iPhone to your computer with the USB cable or turn on iTunes Wi-Fi sync in Settings⟹General and connect both your iPhone and your computer to the same Wi-Fi network.**

2. **Open iTunes.**

3. **Click the name of your iPhone under Devices in the source list on the left side of the window.**

4. **Click the Info tab at the top of the window.**

5. **Scroll down to Sync Mail Accounts.**

6. **Select the mail accounts you wish to sync to your iPhone.**

    Only the account information, not the messages that are present in that account, are synced.

7. **Click the Sync button on the bottom right of the window.**

That's it. You can disconnect your iPhone and begin using Mail right away.

POP goes the message

IMAP services keep your messages on the e-mail or Internet service provider server, even after you've read them, whereas POP services only store your messages temporarily. After you've downloaded them, they're no longer on the server, unless you change the settings in your Mail program that you want to leave them on the server after being downloaded.

Most web-based e-mail service providers, such as iCloud, Google Mail, Yahoo!, or AOL use IMAP. IMAP is convenient if you want to read e-mail messages on both your iPhone and from a computer in a different location, although you do need to delete messages now and then so your mailbox doesn't fill up and reject new incoming messages.

Other e-mail service providers use POP, which is convenient because the messages are literally on your iPhone or on your computer if you've downloaded them there first. After you download the messages, they reside where you first read them. You can configure both your computer and iPhone to leave the messages on the server after you've downloaded them so you can access them from the other device at a later time. We explain that just a bit further on in this chapter under "Incoming Settings."

Using Mail

iPhone's Mail app works like most e-mail programs. Terms we've come to know and love for printed material that is delivered to our homes and offices — mail, inbox, carbon copy — are used to describe electronic material that is delivered to our homes and offices via our computers, iPhones, and other devices. We start by explaining how to create and send a message, and then tell you about replying to, forwarding, filing, and deleting messages. Next, we go through the ways you can view and organize messages. Lastly, we show you how to search messages.

Creating and sending e-mail messages

To create and send an e-mail message, just follow these steps:

1. **Tap the Mail button on the Home screen.**

   The Mailboxes screen opens, as seen in Figure 4-8.

2. **Tap the inbox for the account you want to send the message from.**

3. **Tap the Compose button in the lower-right corner of the screen.**

   A New Message screen opens. The cursor is blinking in the To field.

You can tap the Compose button in the lower-right corner of the Mailboxes screen. The message will be sent from the default mailbox you establish in Settings⟹Mail. We show you how to change the outgoing e-mail address from within the message in Step 5.

4. **In the To field, type the e-mail address of the person you want to send the message to.**

   If the person you want to send the message to is stored in Contacts, begin typing the recipient's name in the To field. Names of people in Contacts that begin with the same letters show up as a list from which you can choose. Your choices narrow as you type more letters.

   Referring to Figure 4-9, the e-mail address is listed under the contact's name and if a contact has more than one e-mail address, his name is listed with each address and the type of address appears to the left.

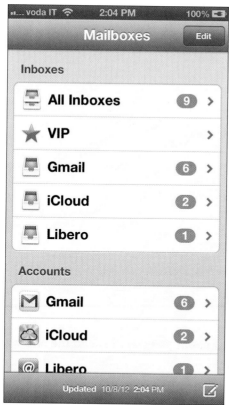

Figure 4-8: The Mailboxes screen lists the inboxes and accounts on your iPhone.

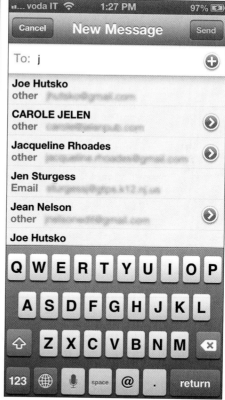

Figure 4-9: Type the first letters of the name of the person you want to send a message to find the e-mail address in Contacts.

Book III
Chapter 4

E-mailing Every
Which Way You Can

Entries with a blue and white arrow next to them are e-mail addresses that you received messages from or sent to. Tap the arrow to show the Recent screen, as in Figure 4-10. From here you can create a new contact, add the e-mail address to an existing contact, or delete the entry from the Recent history — tap the button for the task you want to do.

When you find the name you want, tap it. If you want to add another recipient, repeat the previous step.

To open Contacts and choose the recipients from there, tap the plus sign button on the right of the To field. Contacts opens. Scroll through the list and tap the names of the desired recipients. You can access all your contacts or just specific groups by tapping the Groups button.

5. **If you want to send a Cc — Carbon Copy, or Bcc — Blind Carbon Copy, to other recipients, tap the Cc/Bcc field.**

The field expands into three fields: Cc, Bcc, and From. Fill in the Cc and/or Bcc fields the same way you fill in the To field.

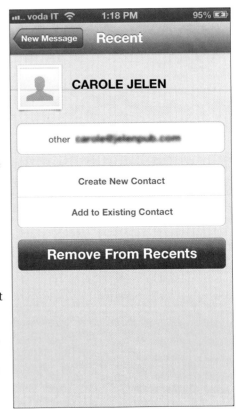

Figure 4-10: E-mail addresses you recently used but that aren't in Contacts appear in the list of potential addresses too.

If you want to change the address from which the message is sent, tap the From field and choose the account you wish the message to be sent from, as seen in Figure 4-11.

6. **When you finish addressing the message, tap Return.**

   The cursor moves to the Subject field.

   TIP You can move names from one address field to another, such as from To to Bcc, by touching and dragging them where you want.

7. **Type the subject of the message, and then tap Return or tap directly in the message field.**

   The cursor moves to the message field.

8. **Type your message and then edit it.**

   Double-tap a word to highlight it and activate grabbers. Tap Select to select the word or Select All to select the entire text and then, optionally, grab the blue grabbers to highlight the word or words you want to format, and then do the following:

   • Tap the Cut, Copy, or Paste buttons if you want to perform those editing actions on your text.

Figure 4-11: Tap Cc/Bcc to expand the field and type in an additional address or change the From address.

Book III
Chapter 4

E-mailing Every Which Way You Can

   • Tap the arrows on the right or left ends of the button bar to see more options.

   • Select just one word, and tap Suggest to see a list of spelling corrections or tap Define to see a definition.

- Tap **B/U** to open a button bar with bold, italic, and underline options, which you tap to format the selected text.

- Tap Quote Level to open a button bar that offers an increase (indent) or decrease (outdent) option. Tap the one you want to use.

- Tap Insert Photo or Video to open your Camera Roll in the Photos app and choose an image or video to attach to your message.

Repeat the process to apply more than one formatting option to the same text or to remove the format. (Refer to Figure 4-12.)

9. **Tap the Send button.**

The word *Sending* and a turning gear appear at the bottom of the screen, and then a sending progress bar opens. Faster than you can put a stamp on an envelope, your message is on its way. If you've turned on the Sent Mail alert under Settings⇨Sounds, a rushing sound confirms your message has been sent.

Figure 4-12: Format text with in-message editing buttons.

If you're composing a message and have to stop midway, you can save it as a draft. Tap Cancel in the upper-left corner. Three buttons appear, as in Figure 4-13. You can choose to Delete Draft, and the message disappears forever. Choose Save Draft, and the message goes into your Drafts inbox to be opened later and modified. Choose Cancel to return to the message and continue writing. Tap and hold the New Message button to see a list of Drafts waiting to be completed.

You can ask Siri to compose and send e-mail messages (as long as you use an iPhone 4S or later, Siri is turned on, and you have an Internet connection). Press and hold the Home button or bring your iPhone up to your ear and tell Siri who you want to send a message to, and then start dictating. See Book I, Chapter 3 to learn more about Siri. Unfortunately, Siri can't read your messages to you — yet . . .

Replying to, forwarding, filing, printing , and deleting messages

iPhone has several ways of letting you know you've received a message. If Badge App Icon is turned on in Settings⇨Notifications⇨Mail, the Mail icon on the Home screen wears a badge showing the number of unread messages you have. If the Notification Center and Alert Styles are selected in Settings⇨Notifications⇨Mail, you are alerted that way. Also, an audible alert plays if you turned on New Mail alerts under Settings⇨Sounds. See Book I, Chapter 4 to learn more about notifications settings.

Figure 4-13: You can save a message in the Drafts file to finish writing it later.

Book III
Chapter 4

E-mailing Every Which Way You Can

To refresh your inboxes, drag down from the top of the screen (just below the Status Bar or you'll open the Notifications Center) an expanding droplet appears and then becomes a spinning gear. Mail checks for any new messages. (Refer to the end of the chapter to learn how to adjust the Push and Fetch settings.)

To read your messages, tap Mail on the Home screen. The Mailboxes screen opens, as shown in Figure 4-14.

✔ To access all your incoming messages, tap All Inboxes. If you have only one e-mail account on your iPhone, this is the only inbox you'll see.

✔ To access the messages in one specific inbox, tap the name of that inbox. A list of the messages opens, as shown in Figure 4-14. Unread messages have a blue dot next to them. The gray To label indicates that Barbara was a direct recipient of the message. The gray Cc means Barbara

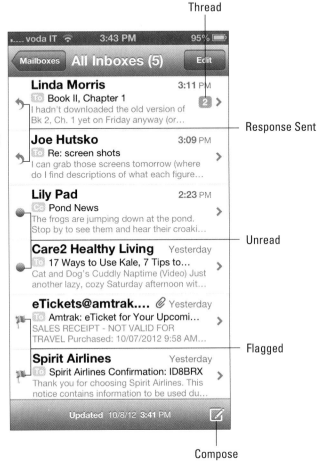

Figure 4-14: Messages are listed in reverse chronological order within a mailbox.

was receiving a copy of the message. We explain how to activate this feature in the section, "Adjusting E-Mail Account Settings."

✔ An e-mail exchange you have with the same subject line, whether with the same person or not, is called a *thread*. A thread is created when you send or receive a message and a reply is then received or sent. Turning this feature on in Settings⫶Mail (which we get to a bit later in this chapter) puts related messages, the so-called thread, together. In the main message list, as shown in Figure 4-14, you see the most recent message of the thread and a number to the right of the message tells you how many messages the thread contains. Tap that message and you see the thread of messages, as shown in Figure 4-15. The number of messages in the thread appears at the top of the screen; a curved arrow to the left of a message means you responded to that message.

✔ Tap on the message you want to read, and it opens as in Figure 4-16.

You have several options from the message screen:

✔ Tap the up and down triangles in the upper-right corner to read the next or previous message.

✔ Tap the Flag button to add a colored flag to the message so it stands out in the Inbox message list (refer to Figure 4-14). Or mark a message as unread, in which case the blue dot reappears next to the message in the list, as if you'd never opened it.

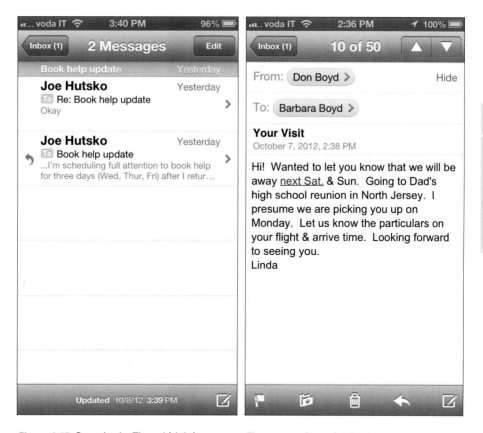

Figure 4-15: Organize by Thread (right) groups related messages together in a sublist.

Figure 4-16: A received message.

Book III
Chapter 4

E-mailing Every
Which Way You Can

✔ Tap the File button, and a screen opens as shown in Figure 4-17. Tap the folder where you want the message to reside. To file the message in a different mailbox, tap Accounts, and then tap the folder to which you want to move the message. If you change your mind, tap Cancel.

If you want to see the other folders for a specific account, tap on the name of the e-mail provider in the Accounts list. You may have to scroll down if you have more than six e-mail accounts. Here you find the folders where you filed your message in the previous section.

✔ Tap the trashcan button to delete your message. Tap one of the two buttons that appear: a Delete Message button and a black Cancel button.

✔ If Archive Messages is on, you won't see a trashcan button. Activate or deactivate the Archive Messages feature in Settings➪Mail, Contacts, Calendar➪*Account Name*.

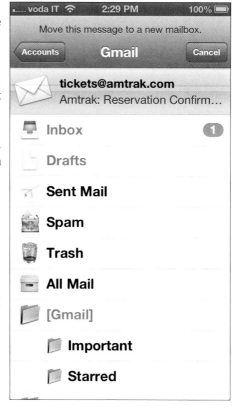

Figure 4-17: Choose the folder where you'd like to file the message.

✔ Tap the Forward button, and the options as shown in Figure 4-18 appear.

✔ **Reply:** Tap to reply to the sender of the message. When you finish writing your message, tap Send.

✔ **Reply All (if there are other recipients besides you):** To send a reply to the sender and to all addresses in the To or Cc list, tap this button. When you finish writing your message, tap Send. The entire message is placed in the body of your reply.

If you want to include only a portion of the message you are replying to or forwarding, highlight that portion before tapping the Reply or Forward button.

✔ **Forward:** To forward a copy of the message to someone else, tap the Forward button. If there are attachments, Mail asks you if you want to include the attachments. After you make this choice, the message window opens with the cursor blinking in the To field. Address the message as explained previously. Write something in the message field, and then tap Send. The Re in the subject field changes to Fwd so the recipient knows this is a forwarded message.

✔ **Print:** To print the message, you must have access to an AirPrint-enabled printer. Do the following:

  1. **Tap Print.**

     The Printer Options screen opens.

  2. **Tap Select Printer.**

     iPhone looks for available printers. When one is found, you return to the Printer Options screen.

  3. **Increase the number of copies you want printed by tapping the plus sign to the right, or leave it at the default of one copy.**

  4. **Tap Print.**

     Your message is printed.

✔ **Compose:** The last button on the right is the compose button, which takes you to a New Message screen to write a new message.

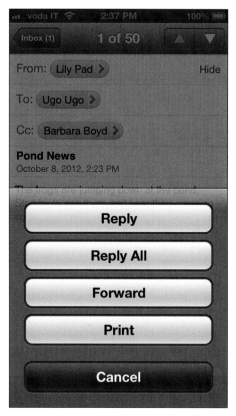

Figure 4-18: Tapping the Forward button gives you four options.

Book III
Chapter 4

E-mailing Every Which Way You Can

You can receive e-mail attachments and view many of them. Attachments you can read include PDF files, images files such as JPEG, TIFF, and GIF, and iWork and Microsoft Office files. You can forward any kind of attachment, even those you can't open with iPhone.

Tap and hold an image attachment, and then tap Save Image to save it to your Camera Roll.

Working with multiple messages

You may want to delete multiple messages, move several from the inbox to another folder, or flag a selection of messages or mark them as unread, all at once. Here's the way to do that:

1. **Tap Mail⇨All Inboxes or one of the account-specific inboxes.**

2. **Tap the Edit button in the upper-right corner.**

   Empty circles appear to the left of each message.

3. **Tap the circle next to the messages you want to delete, move, or mark.**

   A white checkmark in a red circle appears.

4. **After you've selected all the messages you want, tap the appropriate button: Delete, Move, or Mark, as shown in Figure 4-19.**

   Tapping Move opens the filing options (refer to Figure 4-16). Tapping Mark lets you flag the messages, in which case a little flag waves next to the message in the message list, or mark them as *unread*, which replaces the blue dot next to the message that indicates unread messages. Repeat the steps to Unflag or Mark as Read messages that are flagged or marked as unread.

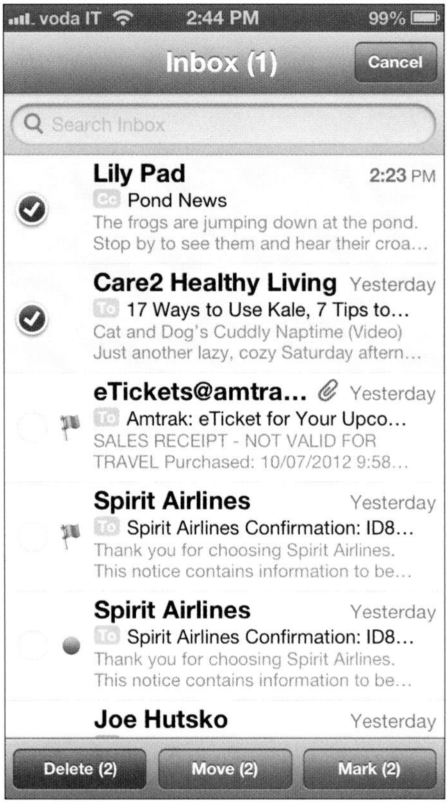

Figure 4-19: Tap Delete, Move, or Mark when managing messages.

---

voda IT   2:44 PM   99%

Inbox (1)   Cancel

Q Search Inbox

✓ **Lily Pad**   2:23 PM
Pond News
The frogs are jumping down at the pond.
Stop by to see them and hear their croa...

✓ **Care2 Healthy Living**   Yesterday
17 Ways to Use Kale, 7 Tips to...
Cat and Dog's Cuddly Naptime (Video)
Just another lazy, cozy Saturday aftern...

eTickets@amtra...   Yesterday
Amtrak: eTicket for Your Upco...
SALES RECEIPT - NOT VALID FOR
TRAVEL Purchased: 10/07/2012 9:58...

Spirit Airlines   Yesterday
Spirit Airlines Confirmation: ID8...
Thank you for choosing Spirit Airlines.
This notice contains information to be...

Spirit Airlines   Yesterday
Spirit Airlines Confirmation: ID8...
Thank you for choosing Spirit Airlines.
This notice contains information to be...

Joe Hutsko   Yesterday

Delete (2)   Move (2)   Mark (2)

5. **You can also swipe on the message in the list to make a red Delete button appear.**

   Tap the Delete button and the message is deleted.

The thing is, just because you clicked Delete, your messages still aren't really deleted. They've been moved to the trash. To truly take out the trash or delete your messages from you iPhone, follow these steps:

1. **Tap Mail then the name of the account in the Accounts list, not the Inboxes list.**

2. **Tap the Trash button, which looks like a trashcan.**

   If Archiving is on, instead of the trashcan, you see an archival box icon.

3. **Tap Edit.**

   The red Delete All button is activated.

4. **Tap Delete All.**

   Your messages are truly deleted.

But wait! What about that Move and Mark buttons?

1. **Follow Steps 1 through 3 above.**

2. **Tap in the empty circles to the left of the messages you want to remove from the trash, flag, or mark as unread.**

   The Move and Mark buttons are then activated.

3. **Tap the Move button to put the selected messages in the folder you want or the Mark button to flag or mark the messages as unread.**

Book III
Chapter 4

E-mailing Every
Which Way You Can

Tapping into in-message links

An incoming message contains much more than just the written message. Take a look at these features:

✔ Tap the blue bubble with the name of the sender or one of the other recipients of the message. A screen opens that gives you an option of creating a new contact or adding this e-mail address to an existing contact (refer to Figure 4-20).

Tap a sender's name to add that person or company to the VIP list. Any incoming messages from that address automatically go to the VIP inbox so all your most important messages are grouped together.

✔ Phone numbers, e-mail addresses, and website addresses that appear blue and underlined are active links. Tap the phone number, and an option of calling that number appears. Tap the e-mail address, and a New Message screen opens. Tap a website address to open the page in Safari.

✔ Tap Hide/Details, next to the sender's name, to hide or show the recipients of the message. When there are a lot of recipients, it's helpful to tap Hide so you can see more of the message in the opening screen.

✔ If you receive an invitation from a calendar app that uses the iCalendar format, tap on the file and the Event Details open. Tap the Add to Calendar button at the bottom of the screen and then choose the calendar where the event should be inserted. For more details about sending and receiving event invitations, see Book IV, Chapter 2.

✔ Zoom in on the message by spreading two fingers on the screen.

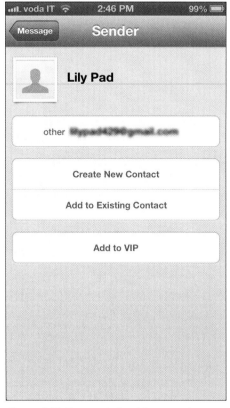

Figure 4-20: The sender's address can be added to Contacts or the VIP list.

 If you follow a link and move from Mail to Safari, you can return to Mail by tapping the Home button twice to open the recent apps bar. Tap the Mail button to return to the open message you were most recently reading.

 If you return to the Home screen or flip to another app with multitasking, Mail (or any app for that matter) remains where it was. Say you're reading a message and then remember a phone call you have to make. You finish the call and then tap the Mail button. Mail opens on the message you were reading, not the first Mailboxes screen. To return to the Mailboxes screen, tap the back button in the top-left corner of the screen.

Multiple inboxes

You can skip this section if you have one e-mail account. If you do have just one e-mail account, you may be wondering why you would have more. Sometimes it's as simple as having a work e-mail address and a personal e-mail address. Beyond that, say you manage the tennis league. A separate e-mail address is useful to represent the team when corresponding with sponsors and opposing team representatives. We mentioned earlier that we have one e-mail address for newsletters we subscribe to and another for personal e-mail exchanges. If you already have more than one e-mail account or are thinking of adding another, read on.

When you tap Mail on the Home screen, the first screen that opens shows a list of inboxes and a list of accounts. You can choose All Inboxes to see a chronological list of all the messages you've received. Tap an account-specific inbox and you see a list of messages from that e-mail account only. For example, tap Google Mail to see only messages that have been sent to your Google Mail address.

You can turn an account off by going to Settings➪Mail, Contacts, Calendars. Tap the name of the account you want to turn off. Tap the Mail button off. This is handy if you're going out of town and want to limit the messages that arrive on your iPhone.

Searching messages

There are times when you know who sent you an e-mail, you know it arrived sometime between last Thursday and Friday, you know the subject was something about a train, but you cannot find the message. Thankfully there's Spotlight, iPhone's searching tool that works with Mail, as well as many other apps such as Contacts, Reminders, and Messages. To use Spotlight:

1. **From within a mailbox — it can be All Inboxes, a specific mailbox, or even the Trash box — tap the status bar at the top of the iPhone screen or scroll up until you see the Search field with the magnifying icon on the left.**

2. **Tap in the Search field.**

   The keyboard opens as seen in Figure 4-21. Note that the gray text in the Search field reads *Search Trash*. This tells you where the search will take place. It would say *Search Inbox* if we were searching in the inbox.

3. **Type in the word or phrase you are searching for.**

4. **Choose the field you want to search: From, To, Subject, or All.**

   The search looks in the field you selected, and a list begins to appear with the first letters you type. The choices narrow as your type more letters.

   To search the body text of your messages as well, tap All, type your criteria, and then tap the Search button on the keyboard.

5. **Tap the message or messages you want to read from the list that appears.**

Figure 4-21: Spotlight searches for messages within Mail.

E-mailing Notes, Web Page Links, Map Locations, Pictures, and Videos

One of the great things about the Mail app is its flexibility and bandwidth. It's the backbone for sending so much more than just e-mail messages. With iOS 6, you can access Photos directly from the message you're composing, which makes inserting photos and videos super easy. Here we show you how to send photos and video another way as well as how to e-mail other types of information from different places.

The process for each type of object is the same: open the app, open the thing you want to send, tap the action button, and then tap the E-mail button. We'll take you through each one anyway, to clear up any little tweaks that might differ from app to app.

E-mailing notes

We love Notes. While Reminders is a terrific to-do list and deadlines tool, Notes is a quick substitute for the proverbial cocktail napkin or matchbook cover — drinking and smoking are so yesterday anyway. Plus, you can e-mail Notes you write. Here's how:

1. **Open Notes from the Home screen.**

2. **Tap the note you want to e-mail.**

3. **Tap the Action button at the bottom of the page.**

4. **Tap the Mail icon.**

   An e-mail message opens with the title of your note in the Subject field. The cursor is blinking in the To field.

5. **Address the message as explained at the beginning of this chapter.**

   You can also change the Subject field and write something in the message field in addition to your note text, if you want.

6. **Tap Send.**

Sending web page links

How many times have you swirled down into the Internet vortex and found something that you absolutely had to tell your best friend about? If you surf the Internet from your computer, you probably know about the Mail Link to this Page option. It exists on iPhone too. You just need to take three steps:

1. **From Safari, tap the action button at the bottom of the screen while you're looking at the page you want to send.**

2. **Tap the Mail icon.**

   A new e-mail message opens that contains a link to the page you were viewing.

3. **Fill out the new message as explained previously and tap Send.**

You can learn more about Safari in Book III, Chapter 3.

Sending map locations

We explain the Maps app in detail in Book IV, Chapter 3. Follow this procedure to send a map location from Maps with Mail:

1. **Open Maps from the Home screen.**

2. **Tap the Location Services button in the lower-left corner to pinpoint your current location.**

   Or

   Type the address you want in the Search field at the top of the screen.

   Or

   Tap the Bookmarks button in the upper-right corner to choose a location from your Maps' bookmarks or list of recent search results and then tap the address you want in one of these lists.

3. **Tap the blue and white arrow to the right of the location banner.**

4. **Scroll down the screen and tap the Share Location button.**

5. **Tap Mail button.**

   A new e-mail message opens with the address as the subject. In the Message field, the name of the location or address is blue and underlined, which means it's an active link in the e-mail you send. A vcf (Vcard) file is also attached. Recipients with HTML-enabled e-mail just need to tap or click on the link to be taken to the indicated location in Maps. Tapping the vcf file opens a contacts card which contains links to maps as well as the locations website, if one exists.

6. **Fill in the address of the recipient in the To field, type in any message you want to accompany the location link, and then tap Send.**

Sending photos and videos

You can send photos and videos from your iPhone using Mail. It's a great way to quickly send an image without having to sync to your computer to send. We explained inserting photos and videos in Step 8 of the section "Creating and sending e-mail messages." Here we explain how to send images from Photos:

1. **Open Photos from the Home screen.**

2. **Choose the photo or video you want to send from one of the albums.**

3. **Tap the Action button.**

4. **Tap the Mail button.**

   A new message opens with your image inserted.

5. **Fill in the To and Subject fields.**

   Write a message to accompany the image if you'd like.

6. **Tap Send.**

To send multiple photos in one e-mail, tap Camera Roll or the album that contains the photos, and then tap Edit in the upper right corner. Tap the photos you want to send (a red and white check mark appears on the selected thumbnails). Tap Share, and then tap the Mail button and proceed with filling out the message.

Size matters: Your cellular service provider may have a limit on the file size that you can send across the cellular data network. Likewise, your recipient's e-mail server may restrict the size of incoming messages (usually 5MB) and your photo won't reach its destination.

Adjusting E-Mail Account Settings

When you set up your e-mail account on iPhone, you've pretty much set up everything you need with regard to the technical information about the account. However, if you have more than one e-mail account on your iPhone or you absolutely have to know every detail about your iPhone, knowing your way around the settings might be helpful. We're going to take you through the e-mail settings options, one by one, so you get your mail how and when you want.

First we go through the settings that are specific to the Mail app and affect how your inboxes and messages appear and behave. Then we go through the more technical aspects of managing your e-mail account.

Settings for message presentation

These options have to do with the local management of your messages. Tap Settings⇨Mail, Contacts, Calendars and scroll to see the Mail settings, as shown in Figure 4-22. We explain each one in the following list:

✓ **Show:** Tap this button and choose how many messages you want to see in your inbox and outbox on Mail. If you have 100 messages to download but have chosen 50 to see, you'll see the first 50 to start. As you file or delete the messages, others from the 100 are added to the box. If you receive or send a lot of messages, you may want to choose one of the higher limits.

✓ **Preview:** Tap this button to choose how many lines of a message you want to see in the list of e-mail messages. You may choose from zero (None) to five lines.

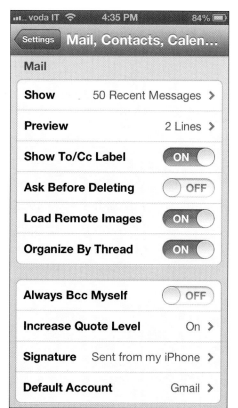

Figure 4-22: The Mail settings section of Mail, Contacts, Calendars screen.

Book III
Chapter 4

E-mailing Every
Which Way You Can

✔ **Show To/Cc Label:** This puts a small label next to the subject line in the list of messages in your inbox. *To* means that the message was sent directly to you; *Cc* means you were sent a copy of the message whose primary recipient was someone else.

✔ **Ask Before Deleting:** If you're prone to accidentally tapping the trash-can button when you don't want to, turn this on so that iPhone asks if you want to delete a message before it's actually deleted.

✔ **Load Remote Images:** Remote images reference an image on a web page that Mail would have to access, which gives the hosting site an opportunity to log your activity. You can save cellular time, and increase your privacy, by turning this off, which leaves you the option to manually open the images.

✔ **Organize by Thread:** This turns threading on or off.

✔ **Always Bcc Myself:** A Bcc is a blind carbon copy, meaning the recipients of your message don't see this name on the list of recipients, but the person who receives the Bcc sees all the (non-Bcc) recipients. If you turn this switch on, you receive a Bcc of every message you write.

✔ **Increase Quote Level:** Tap this option On and when you respond to a message, the original message will be indented. In an exchange, each time a response is sent, the text is indented more.

✔ **Signature:** This is the line (or lines) that appears at the end of e-mail messages you write. The default is *Sent from my iPhone*. Tap the button, and a screen opens where you can type a new signature line. Tap Per Account to customize the signature line for each e-mail account you use, as shown in Figure 4-23.

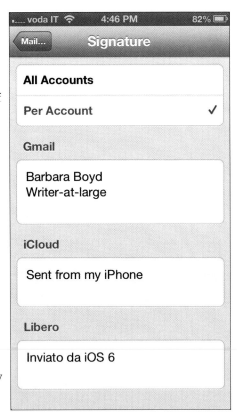

Figure 4-23: Write a custom signature line for your outgoing e-mail messages using the Signature feature.

✏ **Default Account:** The default account is used to send messages from other apps, like Maps or Safari. This is also the account your messages will go from if you tap the Compose button on the main Mailboxes screen and don't change the From field in outgoing messages. If you have multiple e-mail accounts, tap this button and choose the account you want to be the default account.

You can't type an active link to your web page, however, you can copy one from Safari and then paste it to your signature so people who receive messages from you can access your website directly from your e-mail message.

Account-specific settings

Some settings are specific to each e-mail account and are represented in a slightly different order for each account, but the titles and functions are the same. You may have to tap through several screens to reach your final destination. For example, tap Settings⇨Mail, Contacts, Calendars⇨iCloud⇨ Account and then Mail in the Advanced section at the bottom of the screen to find the Outgoing Mail Server or Settings⇨Mail, Contacts, Calendars⇨ Gmail⇨Account, and at this level you find the Outgoing Mail Server. On either account, tap the Advanced button beneath Outgoing Mail Server to find other settings, such as Mailbox Behaviors. Any time you see an arrow in the right end of a field, you can tap it to see more information. Here are what the settings you find mean and how you might want to use them.

Outgoing Mail Server

This feature controls which server your mail is sent from. If you have only one e-mail account on your iPhone, leave this alone. You can skip down to the next subheading.

If you have more than one e-mail account on your phone, each one has an assigned outgoing mail server. This is called the Primary Server for that account. You have the option of turning on the outgoing server associated with another e-mail account so that if the primary outgoing mail server of one e-mail account doesn't work, iPhone tries one of the other servers. If you look at Figure 4-24, Gmail uses the `smtp.gmail.com` server to send mail. If that server is down and Barbara's trying to send a message, iPhone uses `smtp.libero.it` to send it because that server is turned on in the list of Other SMTP servers.

These are the steps for managing your outgoing mail servers. If you have just one e-mail account or use preset accounts such as iCloud or Gmail, you'll probably never need to fuss with these settings. If you have more than one account and set up under Other, take a look to see how it works:

1. **Tap Settings⇨Mail, Contacts, Calendars.**

   The Mail, Contacts, Calendars screen opens.

2. **Tap the name of the account you want to work on under the Accounts list. We use Libero, Barbara's IMAP account, as the example.**

3. **Tap the Account button.**

4. **Tap the SMTP button under Outgoing Mail Server.**

   The SMTP screen opens, and you see which outgoing servers are used for sending your mail. (Refer to Figure 4-24.)

5. **Tap Add Server at the bottom of the list of servers.**

   An Add Server screen opens.

6. **Type in the Host Name, for example,** `smpt.verizon.com`. **Then type in your user name and password.**

7. **Tap Save.**

Figure 4-24: If your primary server is down, iPhone attempts to send messages with a secondary server.

The From address on your e-mail is the one associated with the server that sends the message. For example, if your work server is down and you've set your personal Gmail account as the secondary server, the e-mail is sent from your Gmail account. Your colleagues, clients, or CEO see the e-mail as coming from `hotdiggitydog@gmail.com` rather than `johnsmith@ab12.org`.

Mailbox Behaviors

This setting controls where your draft and sent messages are stored, either on iPhone or on the mail server. Depending on your e-mail service provider, you may also have the option of when the deleted items are ultimately deleted; for example, immediately, a week after they've been removed, or once a month. Refer to Figure 4-25. In iCloud, you have four options for deleting messages from the server:

- ✔ **Never:** Messages remain on the server after you've deleted them manually. This means you may access them on another device.

- ✔ **After One Day/Week/Month:** Messages are deleted from the server after one day, seven days, or one month, whether you've read them or not.

Gmail only lets you choose where drafts are stored but doesn't let you choose when deleted messages are removed. Other accounts may or may not give you the same choices — you have to poke around in the deeper levels of the settings screens.

Even if your provider lets you manage different mailboxes, the process is the same:

1. **Tap Settings⇨Mail, Contacts, Calendars.**

   The Mail, Contacts, Calendars screen opens.

2. **Tap the name of the account you want to work on.**

3. **Tap the Account button.**

4. **Tap the Advanced button.**

   The Advanced screen opens and is similar to Figure 4-25. There may be fewer (or more) options depending on your service provider.

5. **Tap Drafts Mailbox.**

   This setting controls where your draft messages are kept.

6. **Tap Drafts under On My iPhone if you want to keep your draft messages on your iPhone.**

Book III
Chapter 4

E-mailing Every
Which Way You Can

Figure 4-25: The Advanced features allow you to manage where your draft and deleted messages are stored and adjust the pathway for incoming mail.

A checkmark shows up next to Drafts, as shown in Figure 4-26.

7. **Tap Drafts (or another folder if you want) in the list under On the Server if you want your draft messages to be stored on the server.**

If you have large draft files, perhaps with multimedia attachments, it may be more convenient to store them on the server so as not deplete the memory on your iPhone.

8. **Repeat Step 7 for Sent Mailbox and Deleted Mailbox.**

9. **(Optional) Tap Remove under Deleted Messages to set how soon messages are removed from the server after you delete them.**

10. **Tap the button in the upper-left corner to return to the previous level. Continue tapping the upper-left button until you reach the Settings screen. Tap Done if you see it along the way and have made changes. Press the Home button to go to the Home screen.**

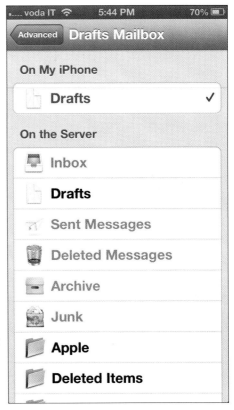

Figure 4-26: A checkmark indicates where you've chosen to store your draft messages.

The S/MIME option, which you may see, lets you add certificates for signing and encrypting outgoing messages. To install certificates, you need a profile from your network administrator or from a certificate issuer's website on Safari or sent to you in an e-mail.

Configure your computer e-mail program to leave messages on the server as well. Go to the Preferences or Tools menu and follow the instructions for your particular e-mail program.

Incoming Settings

The Incoming Settings section (refer to Figure 4-25) gives you limited options for encrypting incoming e-mail and changing the path it comes in on. You probably shouldn't change these settings unless instructed to do so by a technical support person from your cellular provider or a network administrator at your place of employment. In fact, iCloud doesn't even give you the option of changing them because they're preset by Apple. Here, we go through the settings briefly, but remember: You probably don't want to change them.

1. **Tap Settings⬄Mail, Contacts, Calendars.**

2. **Tap the name of the account you want to work on.**

3. **Tap the Account button.**

4. **Tap the Advanced button.**

5. **Turn Use SSL (Secure Sockets Layer) on or off.**

    Ideally, this setting is on as it encrypts incoming messages, making them unreadable to shady types who want to "eavesdrop" on your e-mail conversations.

6. **Tap Authentication to establish the mode in which your account needs to be verified.**

    Password is the most common type of authentication used for iPhone-supported e-mail accounts. If your service provider uses one of the other types — MD5 Challenge-Response, NTLM, or HTTP MD5 Digest, you'll be given the necessary information when you sign up.

7. **The last two, IMAP Path Prefix and Server Port, should really be left alone unless you are instructed to change them by a technician.**

8. **Tap the back buttons in the top-left corner to return to the Settings screen you want or press the Home button to go to the Home screen.**

Using Push and Fetch

Going back to the Mail, Contacts, Calendars screen, you see a button called Fetch New Data. Think of the Mail app as the dog and your incoming e-mail messages as the ball. The mail server throws — the terminology is *pushes* — your messages and iPhone catches — or downloads — them. Alternatively, the messages are on the server and Mail goes and fetches them when told. Once again, you have the option of turning Fetch and Push on or off. Here's how to activate or deactivate Fetch:

1. **Tap Settings⬄Mail, Contacts, Calendars⬄Fetch New Data.**

    The Fetch New Data screen opens, as seen in Figure 4-27.

2. **Turn Push on and new data is pushed to your iPhone from the server.**

   Whether Mail is open or not, messages arrive in real-time in your mailbox and you hear an audible alert as they arrive, if you've established one.

3. **Choose a frequency for Fetch.**

   Tap one of the four time choices.

   If you turn Push off or use an application that doesn't support Push, your iPhone automatically downloads messages at the frequency you chose.

4. **Scroll down the screen and tap the Advanced button.**

   A screen opens that lists the e-mail accounts you have set up on your iPhone (refer to Figure 4-28).

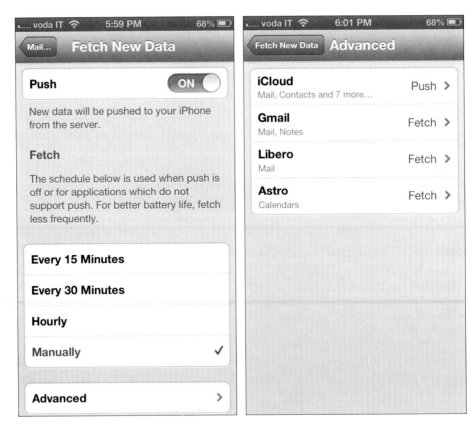

Figure 4-27: Fetch New Data lets your iPhone play catch with incoming e-mail messages.

Figure 4-28: You can choose to retrieve incoming messages using Push, Manual, or Fetch settings.

5. **Tap the name of the account you want to manage.**

   A screen opens with the schedule options available. Buttons for Push, Fetch, and Manual or, if Push isn't supported, for Fetch and Manual appear in list.

6. **Tap the option you want:**

   Push: To automatically retrieve new messages as they arrive in your inbox on the server.

   Fetch: To check for messages at the interval you previously established.

   Manual: To check for messages only when you open the Mail app or when you drag down below the status bar to refresh your inbox.

7. **Tap the back buttons in the top-left corner to return to the Settings screen you want or press the Home button to go to the Home screen.**

Book IV

Making iPhone Your Personal Assistant

The 5th Wave   By Rich Tennant

iPhone

"In fact it does come with a compass."

As much as we believe they make the office or small business run more smoothly and efficiently, secretaries and administrative assistants seem to be rare outside of a large corporate setting. (If you are a secretary or admin, we tip our hats to you.) If you don't have a secretary, your iPhone can be a fair substitute. And, if you are one of the blessed secretaries out there, your iPhone can help make your job easier too.

Chapter 1 of this minibook is about keeping in touch. We show you how to import contacts to your iPhone from existing sources and then how to keep all your devices in-sync and up-to-date. Chapter 2 reviews the Calendar, Reminders, and Clock apps that came with your iPhone and gives you tips for scheduling your time, making to-do lists, remembering tasks, and being on time. Chapter 3 is chock full of apps that help you get where you need to go, namely Maps, Compass, and the new Passbook app that manages boarding passes and store cards. We also introduce you to the Weather app so you know if you need an umbrella where you're going. The Calculator and Stocks apps are covered in Chapter 3 so you can add up the profits from your investments. We present the Notes and Voice Memos apps in the last chapter so you can say goodbye to ideas scribbled on the border of the newspaper. This minibook could be your gateway to the paperless office!

Chapter 1: Perfecting Your People Skills with Contacts

In This Chapter

- ✓ Adding existing Contacts
- ✓ Creating new Contacts
- ✓ Adding Twitter and Facebook friends to Contacts
- ✓ Linking contacts from different sources
- ✓ Viewing Contacts
- ✓ Searching Contacts
- ✓ Contacting a Contact

*L*ike it or not, the multiple technological devices we have — for example, home and work computers, tablet, e-book reader, and iPhone — let us connect with people in an instant. All those devices, however, can mean multiple places where we store phone numbers, e-mail addresses, birthday and anniversary dates, and other information associated with the same person. Contacts gives you an easy way to keep information about your friends, family, colleagues, service providers, and your favorite ice cream vendor in one place. And if you have more than one device, you can share that information across all your devices.

The Contacts app on your iPhone replaces your old tattered, coffee-stained address book and more. Contacts is malleable and, unlike its paper predecessor, has unlimited lines so you can add birthdays, anniversaries, and even notes about the person or entity. And when information changes? No need for correction fluid or an eraser: With a few taps, you can change as much and as often as you wish. If you already have an iPhone-compatible electronic address book, you can transfer the data to your iPhone by syncing your iPhone and your computer. This also means if you have a lot of data to enter or change, you can type it in on your computer then sync with your iPhone.

In this chapter, we begin by explaining how to sync your existing electronic address book with Contacts on your iPhone. If you read Book II, Chapter 1, you learned about syncing, but we go through the specifics for Contacts here. We explain the editing procedures for a single contact: adding a new contact, making changes, even deleting a contact. We show you how to search for a contact, too. We conclude this chapter with the interactive aspects of Contacts, including adding your Twitter and Facebook friends to Contacts, sharing your contacts with someone else, and communicating with your contacts via phone, Facetime, e-mail, and text messages.

Adding Existing Contacts

You probably have some form of electronic address book on your computer. If you don't, skip over this section and go directly to creating new contacts, in which case you create your address book in the Contacts app on your iPhone. Your existing contacts could be in one or more of the following places:

- ✔ On your Mac in Contacts, Address Book, Entourage, or Outlook.

- ✔ On your PC in Microsoft Outlook, Windows Address Book, or Windows Contacts.

- ✔ Online in Microsoft Exchange, Yahoo!, or Google.

- ✔ On the SIM card of a previous cell phone (refer to the sidebar at the end of this section).

The easiest way to transfer your contacts from an old iPhone to a new iPhone is to use your iCloud, Gmail, Yahoo!, or Exchange account. That way, anything you already have saved to any of those accounts automatically restores to your new iPhone. Alternatively, use iTunes to sync your old iPhone's latest backup data to your new iPhone. In this section, we go through importing your contacts from these different applications into Contacts on your iPhone. We begin with the simple sync with iTunes and iCloud and then go to more specific imports from Microsoft Exchange, Google, Yahoo!, LDAP or CardDAV formatted data, and a SIM card. At the end of this chapter, we explain adding contact information from incoming phone calls, voicemail, messages, and vCards attached to e-mail.

If you use IBM Lotus, you need a third-party contact management app such as DejaOffice (www.dejaoffice.com) to sync your contacts to your iPhone.

If you use Windows, you can sync with just one application. On a Macintosh, you can sync with multiple applications.

Importing contacts from iTunes

Although we recommend you use iCloud to keep all your data up-to-date, if you have spotty Internet service or for whatever reason prefer manual syncing, follow these steps to import a copy of your electronic address book from your computer to your iPhone:

1. **Connect your iPhone to your computer with the USB connector cable.**

2. **Open iTunes, if it didn't open automatically.**

3. **Click on your iPhone in the upper right of the iTunes window.**

4. **Click the Info tab, and then select the box next to Sync Contacts.**

   If you use Outlook, you must first change the preferences from within Outlook. Click Outlook⇨Preferences. Select Sync Services from the list on the left. Click Synchronize Contacts with Address Books. Click OK. A dialog appears, asking how you want to synchronize your data; choose accordingly.

5. **Click All Contacts if you want to sync all the contacts in your electronic address book.**

   Or

   Click Selected Groups, as shown in Figure 1-1 and choose which of the groups of contacts in the list you want to sync. (Groups correlates to Categories in Outlook and other Windows address book applications.)

Figure 1-1: Sync all your contacts or a selected group.

6. **If you have added contacts to your iPhone but haven't assigned them to a group, select the check box next to Add Contacts Created Outside of Groups on This iPhone To and choose which group you want those contacts to go into.**

   Leave it unchecked if you just want those contacts to remain part of All Contacts and not part of a group.

7. **Click Sync.**

   If you made changes to your syncing criteria, the Sync button reads Apply. Click Apply.

The next time you connect your iPhone to your computer to perform a sync, the settings you chose will be used.

Accessing your contacts from iCloud

We explain how to set up an iCloud account in Book II, Chapter 1. Essentially, iCloud stores your data, such as contacts, calendar information, your iTunes media library, photos, and documents on a remote server — called a *cloud* — that pushes data updates to your iPhone and any other computers or devices with iOS 5 or later you have associated with your iCloud account. To sync Contacts on your iPhone with your computer and other iOS devices via iCloud, do the following:

1. **Tap Settings⟳iCloud.**

2. **Tap Contacts ON, as shown in Figure 1-2.**

   If your screen doesn't look like Figure 1-2, go to Book II, Chapter 1 to set up an iCloud account.

3. **If you previously synced the contacts on your iPhone with your computer, perhaps with iTunes, a message appears letting you know that the contacts you previously synced with your computer will be merged with iCloud. Tap Merge.**

   Any changes you make in Contacts on your iPhone or on other devices associated with iCloud, such as your computer, iPad, or iPod touch, are automatically pushed to all devices. You will never have conflicting information again!

If you do turn on Contacts in iCloud, a message at the bottom of the Contacts portion of the Info screen lets you know that you are syncing your contacts with iCloud. You can still sync with iTunes, but you may create duplicate records.

If you want to use iCloud with your Windows PC, download the iCloud Control Panel for Windows app from Apple (www.apple.com/icloud/setup/pc.html).

Adding and syncing Microsoft Exchange contacts

Particularly in a corporate setting, some of your contacts, such as the company directory, may be in Microsoft Exchange. As long as the technical support folks in your office will give you the access information, you can sync the contacts from Microsoft Exchange with your iPhone. Microsoft Exchange uses over the air (or OTA) syncing to import and exchange information between the Contacts app on your iPhone and the contact data stored in the Microsoft Exchange cloud.

You can still sync with iTunes if you have different contact data on your computer, like your friends and family, whose information obviously isn't stored on your company server. That makes your iPhone a one-stop source for all your contact information.

Figure 1-2: Turn Contacts On in iCloud to automatically sync Contacts on your iPhone with other devices using iCloud.

Follow these steps to set up the account on your iPhone:

1. **Tap Settings⇨Mail, Contacts, Calendars.**

   The Mail, Contacts, Calendars screen opens.

2. **Do one of the following:**

   1. If you set up a Microsoft Exchange account when you first set up your iPhone or when you set up e-mail as explained in Book III, Chapter 4, tap the name of that account in the list that appears.

   2. Turn Contacts On with the toggle switch in the account screen.

Book IV
Chapter 1

Perfecting Your
People Skills
with Contacts

Or

1. Tap Add Account to set up a new account.

2. Tap Microsoft Exchange.

3. Fill in the requested information.

4. Tap Next.

   After the information you entered is verified, you'll be asked to turn on a series of switches to establish which types of things you want to sync. Turn on Contacts. (Turn on the others such as Mail, Calendars, Bookmarks, or Notes if you want to sync those with Exchange.)

   You now see Microsoft Exchange in the list of accounts on the Mail, Contacts, Calendars settings screen.

3. **Tap the Save button in the upper-right corner and you return to the Mail, Contacts, Calendars settings screen.**

4. **Tap Fetch New Data.**

5. **Tap Push On.**

   Anytime changes are made to the contacts on the server now associated with your Microsoft Exchange account, those changes are pushed to your iPhone.

6. **If your server doesn't support push, or you want to conserve battery power, select a default fetch interval — every 15 or 30 minutes, or hourly.**

   Your iPhone contacts the server for new data at the interval you select.

Importing Yahoo! contacts

Apple has made importing your contacts from Yahoo! simple. Referring to Figure 1-1, notice the last two options in the Contacts section: Sync Yahoo! Address Book contacts and Sync Google Contacts.

If you already set up an e-mail account for Yahoo!, as explained in Book III, Chapter 4, you need only select the box next to Sync Yahoo! Address Book contacts and then click Configure. Agree to let iTunes access your information from Yahoo!. Type in your Yahoo! ID and password, and then click OK. When you click Apply, your Yahoo! contacts and your iPhone contacts sync.

If you need to set up a Yahoo! account on your iPhone, follow these steps:

1. **Tap Settings on the Home screen, and then tap Mail, Contacts, Calendars.**

2. **Tap Add Account.**

3. **Tap Yahoo! on the Add Account screen.**

4. **The Add Account screen opens.**

    Filling in the Name field is optional. Type in your e-mail address in the Address field and your password in the Password field.

5. **Tap the Next button in the upper-right corner.**

    The Yahoo! screen opens.

6. **Tap the Contacts switch On.**

Yahoo! Address Book is stored on a remote server, so you have to have an Internet connection to access it.

Importing and syncing with Google Contacts

Although your iPhone Settings offer a preset way to add a Google account, that account includes Gmail, Google Calendars, and Notes but not Google Contacts. Google gives you two ways to manage your Google account information, including Contacts, on your iPhone. You can set it up as a Microsoft Exchange account or as a CardDAV account. We find the second option easier, but if you work in an enterprise environment, using Exchange might be your best bet. Here's how to set up a Google/Exchange account. In the next section, we explain setting up CardDAV accounts.

1. **If you have contacts on your iPhone and don't use iCloud, sync your contacts between your iPhone and iTunes so that iTunes has a backup.**

2. **On your iPhone, go to Settings⇨Mail, Contacts, Calendars.**

3. **Tap Add Account.**

4. **Tap Microsoft Exchange. (Yes, Microsoft Exchange.)**

    The Exchange screen opens.

5. **Type your Google e-mail address and password in the Email and password fields.**

    Change the description to Gmail if you like.

6. **Tap Next.**

    Your account is verified.

7. **In the Exchange screen that appears, type** m.google.com **in the Server field, as shown in Figure 1-3.**

8. **Type your Google Mail address in the Username field.**

9. **Tap Next.**

Your account is verified.

10. **Tap Contacts On in the Exchange Account screen.**

While you're there, you can tap Calendar and Mail On as well if you use those services.

11. **Tap Save.**

12. **You can do one of the following to keep your contacts synced:**

• If you have contacts on your iPhone that you want to keep, choose the Keep On My iPhone option when prompted, which keeps existing contacts on your iPhone and continues to sync them with iTunes or iCloud. This option keeps both the Google contacts and any existing contacts in sync.

• If all your contacts are on Google, choose Delete Existing Contacts and the Google contacts sync with your iPhone as the All Contacts group.

13. **The sync begins automatically if you have Push enabled; otherwise, open Contacts and the sync will begin.**

Figure 1-3: Use Exchange to sync Google Contacts with your iPhone.

If you set up iTunes Wi-Fi Syncing (see Book II, Chapter 1), your Contacts are synced when your iPhone is connected to a power source, up to once a day. If you use iCloud, changes are synced automatically and a backup is created when your iPhone is connected to a power source, to the Internet via Wi-Fi, and in sleep mode.

Configuring LDAP or CardDAV contacts accounts

LDAP (Lightweight Directory Access Protocol) and CardDAV (Card Distributing Authoring and Versioning) are Internet protocols that allow access to data on a remote server. Multiple users can access the same information, so it is often used in business and organization settings. The difference between the two is that LDAP data remains on the server — you access it from your iPhone via an Internet connection, but it isn't synced to your iPhone. CardDAV data is synced over the air to your iPhone, and, depending on the way the server is set up, you may be able to search the server for contact information.

If your employer uses an LDAP or CardDAV supported contacts program that you want to access or sync with your iPhone, you can add an LDAP or CardDAV account. You'll need some account information from your IT department or network support person:

 ✔ **Server:** This has your company or organization information.

 ✔ **User Name:** This is your identification.

 ✔ **Password:** A password is required.

 ✔ **Description:** This name shows up on the list of accounts on the Mail, Contacts, Calendars settings screen.

After you've gathered the necessary information, set up the account on your iPhone by following these steps:

1. **Tap Settings⇨Mail, Contacts, Calendars.**

2. **Tap Add Account.**

3. **Tap Other.**

4. **In the Contacts section, tap Add LDAP or Add CardDAV Account, whichever is indicated.**

5. **Type in the information requested.**

   For Google, type **google.com** in the Server field.

6. **Tap the Next button in the upper-right corner.**

   After your account information is verified, make sure Contacts is turned On, and the contacts data are added to your iPhone.

7. **Tap the Save button in the upper-right corner and you return to the Mail, Contacts, Calendars settings screen.**

   When you open Contacts, your contacts are automatically synced.

8. **Tap Fetch New Data.**

   The Fetch New Data screen opens.

9. **If your server supports push notifications, Tap Push On.**

   Anytime changes are made on the server where the contacts reside, that change is pushed to your iPhone, and vice versa.

10. **If your server doesn't support push or you want to conserve battery power, select a default fetch interval — every 15 minutes, every 30 minutes, or hourly.**

    Your iPhone contacts the server for new data at the interval you select.

Book IV
Chapter 1

Perfecting Your People Skills with Contacts

Copying SIM card contacts the SIM-ple and not-so-SIM-ple way

Although your iPhone doesn't store information on the SIM card, if you are transferring to iPhone from another cellular phone, you may have contact information on the old SIM card that you want to transfer.

If your old device is an Android or other non-iPhone smartphone that uses a micro-SIM card, you can typically pop out your new iPhone 4 or 4s's micro-SIM and pop in your old one to copy those contacts to your new iPhone. (Go to Settings➪Mail, Contacts, Calendars➪Import SIM Contacts.) Ditto if your old device uses a nano-SIM card and you're moving to a new iPhone 5, which also uses a nano-SIM card.

If your old phone's SIM card isn't the same type of SIM card in your new iPhone — whether iPhone 4 or 4S, or iPhone 5 — you may still be able to copy any contacts from your old smartphone by connecting it to your computer and using special data export software that may either come with your old phone, or is available to download from the phone manufacturer's website, or by using a third-party smartphone data transfer program. Check your smartphone's manual or search the manufacturer's support site to see if they offer a software application you can download to export your contacts from your old phone so you can copy them to your new iPhone.

A DIY solution for making your too-big micro-SIM fit in your much smaller nano-SIM slot is to carefully cut the micro-SIM down to nano-SIM size. Search Google on those terms, and you'll turn up a slew of how-to videos on how to do exactly that.

Another option: Check out the nifty third-party program PhoneView for Mac (www.ecamm.com), which offers super-simple drag-and-drop backing up and transferring of contacts (and all sorts of other iPhone data) between old iPhones and new iPhones, and even between iPhones and iPads (handy for transferring your Angry Birds progress between iOS devices so you don't have to replay all those levels you already beat).

If your contacts are in another program, you can try exporting them as vCards (the file will have a .vcf suffix) and then importing them into Address Book (OS X 10.7 or earlier), Contacts (OS X 10.8 or later), or Entourage or Outlook 2011 on the Mac or Outlook or Windows Address Book on a Windows PC. Follow the previously outlined procedure for syncing.

Adding your Facebook and Twitter contacts

Both Twitter and Facebook have been integrated in iOS 6, which means you can add any contacts you have in either of those social networks to Contacts. Instead of opening the profile of each member of your high school class to copy and retype their e-mail addresses and phone numbers, with just a few taps, you can import the information to Contacts directly from Twitter and Facebook. Follow these steps:

1. **Tap Settings⇨Facebook.**

   The Facebook settings screen opens.

   If you don't have the Facebook app installed, tap the Install button to download it from the iTunes Store.

2. **Tap in the User Name field and type in your user name.**

3. **Tap in the Password field and type in your password.**

4. **Tap Sign In.**

   A disclaimer appears that explains what happens on your iPhone when you sign in to Facebook. Essentially, information about your Facebook friends will be downloaded to Contacts; Facebook events will sync to your Calendar; you can post status updates and images directly from the Photos app; and Facebook-enabled apps will work with your permission.

5. **Tap Sign In again to accept these conditions. You can change the settings after you sign in if you don't want these things to happen.**

6. **The Facebook settings screen reappears with Calendar and Contacts options, as shown in Figure 1-4.**

7. **Tap Contacts On.**

8. **Tap Update All Contacts to provide Facebook with information from your Contacts, which allows it to update matching contacts.**

Tap the Groups button, and then tap All Facebook to see or hide your Facebook friends in Contacts.

To add Twitter user names and profile photos to your contacts, Tap Settings⇨Twitter, sign in to your Twitter account, and then tap Update Contacts.

Figure 1-4: Turn Contacts on to see your Facebook friends in Contacts.

Unifying contacts

When you import or access contacts from different sources, you may find you have more than one information record for the same contact. Contacts links contacts that have the same name, and creates a unified contact. A unified contact doesn't merge the information but does display all the information for one person on one record. If you make changes to one record, that information syncs with the source it came from, but doesn't change on records from other sources. This means if you change the e-mail on a contact in Google, the information is updated on the Google server and on your devices that access the Google server but it isn't changed on the record that comes from Facebook. You can manually link contacts and change which one is the top unified contact by doing the following:

1. **Tap a contact that has more than one record, and then tap Edit.**

2. **Tap the Link Contact field at the bottom of the Info screen.**

   Your list of contacts opens.

3. **Tap the name of the contact you want to link to the first contact.**

   You can link two or more contacts with the same name or with different names, such as a personal card and a company card or two partners at the same business.

4. **Tap the Link button in the upper-right corner.**

   The Info screen now reads Unified Info.

5. **Tap Done.**

   Scroll down to the bottom of the unified info screen to see the list of Linked Contacts, as shown in Figure 1-5. The unified card shows all the information you have about that person. Click one of the sources to see only the information from that source.

6. **To use a different name for the unified card, tap the name you want to use and then tap the button that reads Use This Name For Unified Card.**

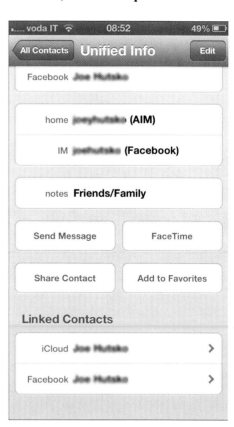

Figure 1-5: Link contacts from different sources and view them in one Unified Info screen.

The names on the individual contact records don't change but the unified card shows the name you selected.

7. **To unlink contacts, tap Edit, and then tap the minus sign next to the source you want to unlink.**

Creating New Contacts

We find ourselves adding new friends and businesses to Contacts frequently, and when we're out and about, the iPhone is our device of choice for adding those new contacts. You, too, probably want to add new friends, colleagues, and acquaintances to Contacts on your iPhone, and then transfer the new information to your computer and other iOS devices automatically if you use iCloud or the next time you perform a sync with iTunes. Contacts stores much more than just names, addresses, and phone numbers. You can add a photo of the person, a birthday or anniversary — which nicely links to Calendar — e-mail addresses, websites, and whatever kind of field you want to invent, like favorite color or namesake holiday date. In this section, we show you how to create new contacts, fill in the contact info with everything you know about the person, make changes, and, well, delete them if things go bad in the relationship, for whatever reason.

Filling in name, address, phone number, and more

Follow these steps to fill in basic information about your contacts:

1. **Tap Contacts on the Home screen or in the Dock within the Phone app.**

   1. If you want the new contact to be part of a group, tap the Group button at the top of the screen. You won't see this button if you don't have any groups.

   2. Deselect all but the group you want the new contact to be part of. You can only add to a group that resides on your iPhone not a remote group such as Facebook.

      A checkmark indicates which group is active, as shown in Figure 1-6. Even if you add a contact to a group, it is part of both All Contacts and All on My iPhone.

   3. Tap Done.

2. **Tap the plus sign in the upper-right corner.**

   A New Contact screen opens.

3. **Tap in the field that reads First.**

   The cursor appears in that field and the keyboard opens.

4. **Type in the first name of your new contact.**

   Not all contacts have first and last names and you are not obligated to fill in any field that you don't have information for. If you just have the name and phone number of a company, you can fill in only those fields.

5. **Tap Return to move from one field to the next.**

   Continue typing in the information you have for your contact.

If you have contacts from more than one account, for example a Microsoft Exchange account as well as contacts on your iPhone, select the default account where new contacts will be saved by tapping Settings➪Mail, Contacts, Calendar and then tap Default Account in the Contacts section. Tap the account you want to use or On My iPhone to automatically place new contacts on your iPhone.

The following sections describe fields that have specific functions.

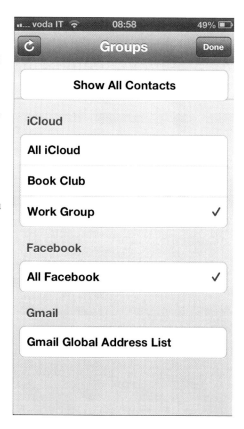

Figure 1-6: The Groups screen lets you choose which contacts you want to view and where to add new contacts.

Phone, E-mail, and URL fields

The Phone, E-mail, and URL fields behave the same way, but their behavior may seem a bit peculiar at first. Here we give you a few tips to help you understand them:

- As soon as you begin typing in the first field, say, phone number, a minus sign appears to the left and a new field is added beneath it. You can type a second phone number in this new field. As soon as you begin typing in the second phone number field, a third one appears. This happens with the Phone, E-mail, and URL fields. Don't worry: Those empty fields won't clutter up the final view of your contact's info screen. You only see the blank field in Create or Edit mode.

✔ Notice that there's a line between the field name and the empty field for Phone, E-mail, and URL. You can change the field name of these fields by tapping on the field name to the left of the line. A Label list opens. Click the label you want to associate with the phone number, e-mail, or URL that you type in the adjacent field.

✔ Scroll down to the bottom of the Label list and you see Add Custom Label. Tap this and you can enter a label of your own for the field.

You can memorize a phone number with an extension so when you dial from Contacts you don't have to enter the extension. Type the phone number, tap the +*# button, and then tap Pause. The keypad returns and you can type the extension. When you tap Done, a comma appears between the phone number and extension. You can add more than one pause if the system needs more time between dialing the number and typing the extension. If you tap Wait and enter the extension, when you make the call, you have to tap Dial again at the appropriate time after the initial call is made and the extension will then be dialed.

Ringtone, Vibration, and Text Tone fields

You can assign a special sound or vibration so that when a contact calls or sends a text message, you know by the sound who is calling or who the message is from:

✔ **Tap Ringtone.** A list opens from which you choose the ringtone you want to hear when that contact calls.

✔ **Tap Vibration.** A list gives you options for the vibration you want associated with that contact. Click Create New Vibration to record your own custom vibration.

✔ **Tap Text Tone.** A list opens to choose the sound you hear when that contact sends you a text message. Tap Buy More Tones to access the ringtone section of the iTunes Store and download tones that can be used for ringtones or text tones.

You can only have one ringtone, one vibration, and one text tone per contact. You can't assign a different ringtone for each number associated with a contact.

Add New Address

You can tell how little importance is given to our physical addresses anymore. This field is at the bottom of the list like a rarely used option. To add an address, tap the plus sign to the left of the field or in the blank field. The field expands as shown in Figure 1-7. Type in the address.

Book IV
Chapter 1

Perfecting Your People Skills with Contacts

Here, too, as soon as you begin typing a second field opens, so you can add a second address. And, tapping on the field name to the left, you can change the field name so it reflects which address it's associated with, like work or home or even a custom field, like cabin or boat slip.

Add Field

The last field has options that can be added to the previous fields. Tap on the plus sign or in the empty field and the list of Add Field options opens. After one of the options is used, it no longer appears in the Add Field options list.

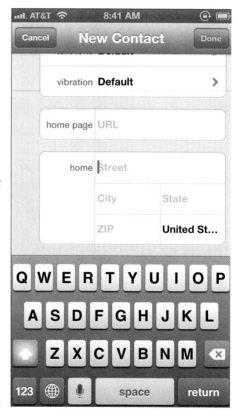

Figure 1-7: The Add New Address field expands so you can type in the street address, city, state, ZIP, and country.

- The first six field options are related to the name of the contact:

  - **Prefix:** Adds a field before first name where you can type in a title such as Mr. or Princess.

  - **Phonetic First Name and Phonetic Last Name:** Are inserted immediately after the First or Last Name fields so you can type in a phonetic spelling of the names that are pronounced differently than they are spelled.

  - **Middle:** Adds a field between the First and Last Name for a middle name.

  - **Suffix:** To add common suffixes like M.D. or Jr.

  - **Nickname:** Comes right before company.

- **Job Title and Department:** Are inserted before Company.

- **Twitter/Profile:** You can add multiple social network profile user names to each contact. Tap Twitter to add a Twitter user name. Tap Profile to add a user name for Facebook, Flickr, LinkedIn, Myspace, Sina Weibo, or a custom service. After tapping the Profile option, the Info screen reopens. Tap the field label to the left of user name to choose which social network you want.

✔ **Instant messenger:** After tapping this option, you return to the Info screen. Enter the User Name and then tap the field below it to reveal a list of ten IM services plus an option to add a custom service. Tap the service you use to instant message with this contact. You can also edit the name of this field by tapping on the field name on the left. The options are Home, Work, Other, or Add Custom Label.

✔ **Birthday:** Tap birthday and a rotor opens, as shown in Figure 1-8, so you can choose the month, day, and year of the contact's birth date. A birthday that is added to a contact appears in Calendar if you activate the Birthday calendar. Read more about Calendar in Book IV, Chapter 2.

✔ **Date:** The first field name that comes up is Anniversary for this field, after which you can add as many other important dates related to this contact as you want. Use the rotor to put in the date you want. Like the Phone, E-mail, URL, and Address fields, as soon as you add this field, a blank one appears beneath it. You can also edit the name of the field by tapping on it and choosing other or adding a custom label.

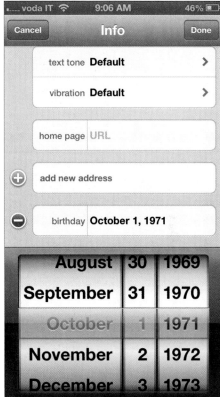

Figure 1-8: Use the rotor to set your contact's birthday.

✔ **Related People:** Add people who are related to the Contact, such as parent, spouse, sibling, partner, assistant, or manager. After tapping the option, you return to the Info screen. Tap the field label to reveal a list of choices for the type of relation, and then type in the name or the relation or tap the blue and white arrow to choose someone else from your Contacts list. Related People are not the same thing as Linked Contacts. Refer to the earlier section, "Unifying Contacts" to learn how to view contacts from different sources on one screen.

Create a New Contact for yourself including your own related people and then specify which is your card by going to Settings⮑Mail, Contacts, Calendars⮑ My Info, which opens Contacts. Choose the contact you created for yourself. The My Info card is used by Siri, Reminders, and other apps to understand commands like "Remind me upon arriving Home" or "Call my sister." Specify the My Info card for Siri by going to Settings⮑General⮑Siri⮑My Info.

Each time you add a custom label, that label is added to the list beneath whatever options Contacts gives you for that field. If you add a lot of custom labels, the Add Custom Label button is all the way at the bottom — just scroll down to find it. You can delete custom labels from the list by tapping the Edit button. Tap the minus sign that appears next to the label you want to delete, and then tap the Delete button. If the custom label was being used on a contact, it will be replaced by a generic label.

Adding photos

The first thing you see on the New Contact screen is a field in the upper-left corner called Add Photo. This lets you add a photo of the contact and when a call comes in from any of the phone numbers of that contact, the photo appears on your Home screen. You have two ways to add photos:

1. **Tap Add Photo.**

   A dialog appears, which gives you the option to take a photo or choose an existing photo.

2. **Tap Take Photo.**

   The Camera app opens. Book V, Chapter 1 talks all about the Camera, but here's a quick rundown.

   1. Aim the camera at the subject you want to photograph, and tap the Switch Camera button if you see yourself instead of your subject. When you're satisfied, tap the green camera button or the volume up button.

   2. If you like the shot, you can resize it by pinching or spreading your fingers on the image and drag to move it to a pleasing position.

   3. If it's just not right, tap Retake, and try again. Refer to Figure 1-9.

   4. When you like the result, tap Use Photo.

      You see the photo you took in the photo field on the Contact Info screen.

   Or

   Tap Choose Photo.

The Photos app opens.

1. Tap the album where the photo you want to use is stored.

2. Tap the photo you want to use.

3. Move and scale as explained in Step 2 previously.

4. When you like the photo, tap Choose.

   The photo is saved to the New Contact screen.

The data in Contacts in the Phone app is the same data as in the Contacts app — just two ways to reach the same information.

Adding contacts from phone calls and messages

If you receive a phone call or message from a number that isn't in Contacts, or make a call to a number that isn't in Contacts, you may want to add that number to an existing contact or create a new contact. Here's how:

1. **After you finish a conversation, tap Phone⇨Recents.**

   A list of recent incoming and outgoing calls appears.

2. **Tap the blue and white arrow to the right of the number you want to add, it can be from a call you received or one you initiated.**

   An Info screen opens, as shown in Figure 1-10.

3. **Tap Create New Contact.**

   A New Contact screen opens. Type in the information you have and select a special ringtone if you want.

   Or

4. **Tap Add to Existing Contact.**

   The Contacts screen opens.

Figure 1-9: Take a photo of your contact and adjust it until it's just right.

Book IV
Chapter 1

Perfecting Your
People Skills
with Contacts

5. **Search for the contact you want to add the number to and add the number in the appropriate field.**

6. **Tap Done.**

To create a new contact or add a number to an existing contact from the keypad, when you call a new number:

1. **Tap Phone⇨Keypad.**

2. **Enter the number you want to call, but don't tap Call.**

3. **Tap the plus sign to the left of the Call button.**

   A dialog gives you three choices:

   • Create New Contact

   • Add to Existing Contact

   • Cancel

4. **Tap the button for the action you want to take.**

5. **Follow the procedure for creating a new contact or adding a number to an existing contact.**

6. **Tap Done.**

To create a new contact or add a number to an existing contact from a received message:

1. **Tap Messages on the Home screen.**

2. **Tap the message that came from an unidentified number.**

3. **Tap Add Contact and follow steps 3 through 6 as outlined previously.**

Figure 1-10: Add the phone number from a recent call to an existing contact or create a new one.

If you have numbers that you call frequently, you can add them to the Favorites list on the Phone app. Open the contact you call frequently and tap the Add to Favorites button at the bottom of the Info screen. If there's just one phone number, the contact is added automatically. If there are multiple numbers, a dialog shows all the numbers and you tap on the number you want to add to the Favorites list in Phone.

Editing and Deleting Contacts

People move, change jobs, phone numbers, and names, and you want to keep Contacts current with the state of affairs. The point of departure for editing and deleting contacts is the same:

1. **Tap Contacts on the Home screen or in the dock of the Phone app.**

2. **Tap the name of the contact you want to edit or delete.**

3. **Tap the Edit button in the upper-right corner.**

4. **Tap in the field you want to edit.**

   The keyboard opens so you can make your change.

   Scroll to the next field you want to edit and make any other changes.

5. **To delete a field, tap the red and white minus sign to the left of the field.**

   If you want to delete a field that you added from the Add Field selections, tap that field, tap the X that appears to the right, and then tap Done. When the field is empty, it will no longer appear on the Contact Info screen.

6. **To add an additional phone, e-mail, website, or address, tap in the blank field below the last filled-in field.**

7. **To add a field, tap the Add Field field at the bottom of the screen and proceed as explained previously in the "Creating New Contacts" section.**

8. **Tap Done in the upper-right corner.**

   The corrected contact info screen appears.

To delete a contact, tap the name of the contact, tap edit, and then tap the Delete Contact button at the bottom of the edit screen.

Changes and deletions you make are automatically pushed to your computer if you use over-the-air syncing, or they will be synced with iTunes the next time you perform a Wi-Fi sync or connect your iPhone to your computer. If you use iCloud, changes sync to all devices logged in to your iCloud account.

Sorting Contacts

You can adjust the sort order and the display order in Settings ➪Mail, Contacts, Calendars and scroll down to the Contacts section (refer to Figure 1-11). The settings apply to groups and All Contacts.

Book IV
Chapter 1

Perfecting Your
People Skills
with Contacts

✔ **Sort Order:** Tap to open options for choosing to sort your contacts by first name and then last name, or vice versa.

✔ **Display Order:** Tap to open options for viewing your contacts by first name followed by last name, or vice versa.

You can mix and match the options in four different ways, for example, you can sort by last name and then display by first name, whatever makes the most sense to you.

Searching Contacts

You can search Contacts in three ways. Each time you open Contacts from another app, which we talk about in the next section, the search and find process is the same. Tap Contacts on the Home screen and choose either All Contacts or the group you want to search in:

✔ Scroll through the list until you see the name you want. If you scroll very fast, tap to stop the scrolling, and then tap on the name you want.

Figure 1-11: Sort and display contacts in the order you want.

✔ In the index that runs down the right side of the screen, tap the letter that corresponds to the initial letter of the name of the person you're looking for. Then scroll through that section of the alphabet to find the person.

✔ Open Spotlight Search by tapping the status bar at the top of the screen or by tapping the magnifying glass icon above the A in the index. Tap in the Search field to open the keyboard. Begin typing the name of the person you want to find. A list of possible matches appears. The more you type, the fewer the choices. Contacts looks at the first letters of first names, last names, and words that are part of a company name. If you type "Jo," first names like **Jo**e or **Jo**anne come up, last names, like **Jo**hnson and **Jo**nes appear, and companies or organizations such as **Jo**lly Ice Cream and Association of Writers and **Jo**urnalists show up as well. (Refer to Figure 1-12.)

Whichever way you choose to search, when you find the name you are looking for, tap on the name to either open the Contacts info screen or to add that name to the To field in the program you're sending from.

If you are searching for a contact that you know is in Contacts but can't find it, make sure you are looking in the right group or switch to the All Contacts view to search your entire address book.

When you search in Spotlight Search from the Home screen, Contacts is included in your search. Read more about Spotlight Search in Book I, Chapter 3.

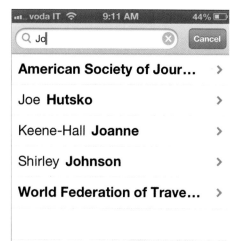

Figure 1-12: Spotlight Search matches the first letters of first and last names and words in a company name.

Sending One Contact to Another

Say a friend compliments you on your new haircut and asks for your stylist's name and phone number. You can dictate the name and number or write it down on a scrap of paper, or you can send the information directly from Contacts:

1. **Open the contact you want to share.**

2. **Tap the Share Contact button at the bottom of the screen.**

3. **Choose to send the information by e-mail or message.**

   A new message screen opens.

4. **Fill in the address and tap Send.**

   The information is sent in vcf or vCard (Versit Consortium Format), which is a file format for electronic business cards.

A Share Contact button on the Info screen also opens when you tap the blue and white arrow on the Recent Calls list.

Calling and Messaging from Contacts

Although you use Contacts to manage information, you can also generate communications directly from a Contact Info screen. Tap the contact you want to connect with and then do one of the following:

✔ Tap a phone number to call the person.

✔ Tap an e-mail address to open a pre-addressed New Message in Mail. Type in a subject and message, and tap Send.

✔ Tap FaceTime at the bottom of the Contact Info screen to initiate a FaceTime video chat.

✔ Tap Send Message at the bottom of the Contact Info screen, as shown in Figure 1-13, and then choose the correct phone number (or e-mail address if sending to a device with iMessage) to send a message. A New Message in Messages opens, addressed to the contact. Type your message and tap Send.

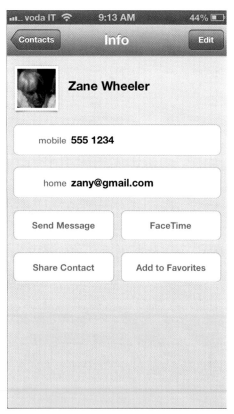

You can also access Contacts from communication apps that use the information in Contacts — Phone, Mail, and Messages. Contacts also appears when you want to send things from non-communication apps like Photos and Safari. We take you through the process for each one in their respective chapters, but after you learn to send things to a contact from one app, you pretty much know how to send them in any app. Ah, the beauty of iPhone!

Read about each of the apps that use Contacts in the following chapters:

Figure 1-13: Connect directly from the Contact Info screen in Contacts.

✔ **Mail:** Book III, Chapter 4.

✔ **Messages:** Book III, Chapter 2.

✔ **Notes and Voice Memos:** Book IV, Chapter 4.

✔ **Photos:** To send still images and video, see Book V, Chapter 1.

✔ **Safari:** To send links to web pages, see Book III, Chapter 3.

✔ **Maps:** To send links to a specific map or directions, see Book IV, Chapter 3.

Chapter 2: Managing Your Time with Calendar, Reminders, and Clock

In This Chapter

✓ **Adding and syncing existing Calendars**

✓ **Viewing and hiding Calendars**

✓ **Creating, changing, and deleting Calendar events**

✓ **Sharing Calendar through iCloud**

✓ **Remembering with Reminders**

✓ **Using Clock to help pass the time**

*S*ometimes it seems the more technology advances in the name of making our lives easier, the more complicated and busy our lives become — or maybe we just take on more because we can. Whatever the reason, we all have a lot to remember and the three apps explained in this chapter can help.

The Calendar app on your iPhone helps you keep track of appointments, birthdays, and deadlines along with fun things like parties and vacations. Calendar syncs with calendars on your computer and other iOS devices as well as remote calendars you subscribe to. When you receive invitations, Calendar inserts the event on the right day and time. We begin this chapter by explaining how to add and sync your existing electronic calendars to your iPhone. Then, we show you Calendar's different views and settings. Next, we look at creating and editing events on your iPhone, how to respond and add event invitations, and how to search for an event.

The second app we explain is Reminders, the list-making, automatic reminding app that's great for simple shopping lists as well as projects that have tasks with deadlines. While we're on the subject of time, we explain the Clock app too. You learn that it's not just your ordinary clock but a world clock, alarm, stopwatch, and timer.

Adding and Syncing Existing Calendars

The Calendar app consists of one or more calendars and events on those calendars. You can create blank calendars on your iPhone and then fill in the events as you schedule them and you can also sync events from calendars you keep in other places, such as your computer or on a remote calendar such as Google, Yahoo!, or a Microsoft Exchange calendar that resides on your company's server and is shared among colleagues at work. First we explain how to create a calendar on your iPhone, and then, for those of you who do have an existing electronic calendar, we explain how to add that calendar to your iPhone and keep all your calendars synced in the future.

Adding a calendar on your iPhone

Even if you sync calendars from other computers or remote servers, chances are, sooner or later you'll want to create a calendar on your iPhone. Follow these steps:

1. **Tap Calendar on the Home screen.**

2. **Tap the Calendars button in the upper-left corner.**

   A list of your local and remote calendars appears.

3. **Tap Edit in the upper-left corner.**

4. **Tap Add Calendar.**

   (If you turned the Calendar option on in iCloud, you find this in the iCloud section.)

   The Add Calendar screen opens.

5. **Type a name for the calendar and then tap a color you want to use to identify events in this calendar, as shown in Figure 2-1.**

6. **Tap Done.**

   The Edit Calendars screen appears and you see your new calendar in the list.

7. **Tap Done in the upper-left corner to return to the main Calendars list.**

Figure 2-1: Create new calendars directly on your iPhone in the Calendar app.

8. **Tap Done — once more — in the upper-right corner to view your events.**

   See the section "Viewing and Hiding Calendars" later in this chapter for more information.

Adding calendars from other sources

We recommend using iCloud to keep your calendars in sync, and we cover the basics of syncing in Book II, Chapter 1; here, we focus only on syncing calendars. iPhone's Calendar app supports the following electronic calendars:

- **Macintosh:** Calendar (iCal, if you're using OS X Lion or earlier) and MS-Outlook sync with iCloud or iTunes. You can sync more than one calendar application on your iPhone with a Macintosh.

- **Windows:** Outlook 2007 and 2010 sync with iCloud or iTunes. Windows limits syncing to one calendar application.

- **Both platforms:** Microsoft Exchange, Google, Yahoo!, and CalDAV accounts with over-the-air syncing.

If you access calendar information from a remote server, like Microsoft Exchange, iCloud, a CalDAV server, Google Calendar, or an iCalendar subscription (we explain each of those in just a little bit), you have to have an account on both your iPhone and your computer.

On a Macintosh, set up an account in Calendar:

1. **Click Calendar⇨Preferences and then click Accounts.**

2. **Click the plus sign at the bottom left of the window to add an account.**

3. **Fill in the information requested, and then click Create.**

If you're using Microsoft Exchange, you're probably in a corporate setting with your computer already set up. Go to the section "Adding and Syncing Microsoft Exchange Calendars" for instructions to set up your iPhone.

Importing calendars from iTunes

If you set up iTunes Wi-Fi Syncing (see Book II, Chapter 1), your Calendars are synced once a day when you connect your iPhone to a power source and to the same Wi-Fi network your computer uses, so you can skip this section. If you don't use Wi-Fi syncing, follow these steps to import a copy of your electronic calendar from your computer to iTunes:

1. **Connect your iPhone to your computer with the USB connector cable or to the same Wi-Fi network as your computer.**

2. **Open iTunes, if it didn't open automatically.**

3. **Click on your iPhone in the top-right of the iTunes window.**

4. **Click Sync Calendars.**

   If you use Outlook, you must first change the preferences on your computer. Click Outlook⟷Preferences. Click the Sync Services icon and then check the box next to Calendar.

5. **Click All calendars if you want to sync all the calendars that appear in the list below.**

   Or

   Click Selected Calendars and choose which of the calendars in the list you want to sync.

6. **Select the check box next to Do Not Sync Events Older Than 30 Days.**

   You can change the time period (30 days is the default). If you want to have an historic record of your calendar on your iPhone, type in the number of days history you want. A shorter period of time takes less time to sync.

7. **Click Sync in the lower-right corner.**

   If you made changes to your syncing criteria, instead of Sync you see Apply. Click Apply.

The next time you connect your iPhone to your computer to perform a sync, the settings you chose are used.

Accessing Calendar from iCloud

We explain how to set up an iCloud account in Book II, Chapter 1. Essentially, iCloud stores your media, documents, and data on a remote server — called a *cloud* — that pushes data updates to your iPhone and any other computers or iOS devices you have associated with your iCloud account. To sync Calendar on your iPhone with your computer and other iOS devices via iCloud, do the following:

1. **Tap Settings⟷iCloud.**

2. **Tap Calendars on, as shown in Figure 2-2.**

   If your screen doesn't look like Figure 2-2, go to Book II, Chapter 1 to set up an iCloud account.

3. **If you previously synced the calendars on your iPhone with your computer, perhaps with iTunes, a message appears letting you know that the calendars you previously synced with your computer will be merged with iCloud. Tap Merge.**

   Any changes you make in Calendar on your iPhone or on other devices associated with iCloud, such as your computer, iPad, or iPod touch, are automatically pushed to all devices. You will never have conflicting information again!

If you do turn on Calendar in iCloud, a message at the bottom of the Calendars portion of the Info screen lets you know that you are syncing your contacts with iCloud. You can still sync with iTunes, but you may create duplicate records.

If you want to use iCloud with your Windows PC, download the iCloud Control Panel for Windows app from Apple (www.apple.com/icloud/setup/pc.html).

Adding and syncing Microsoft Exchange calendars

If you use Microsoft Exchange, you use over-the-air or OTA syncing to import and exchange information between the Calendar app on your iPhone and the Microsoft Exchange calendar. When you use this option, you no longer need to sync with iTunes; in fact, doing so may cause duplicate calendar entries. However, you do need to set up an account on your computer, as explained previously. Follow these steps to set up the account on your iPhone:

1. **Tap Settings⇨Mail, Contacts, Calendars.**

   The Mail, Contacts, Calendars screen opens.

Figure 2-2: Turn Calendars on in iCloud to automatically sync Calendars on your iPhone with other devices using iCloud.

2. **Do one of the following:**

   1. If you set up a Microsoft Exchange account when you first set up your iPhone or when you set up e-mail as explained in Book III, Chapter 4, tap the name of that account in the list that appears.

   2. Turn Calendars on with the toggle switch in the account screen, as shown in Figure 2-3.

   Or

   1. Tap Add Account to set up new account.

   2. Tap Microsoft Exchange.

   3. Fill in the requested information.

   4. Tap Next.

      After the information you entered is verified, you'll be asked to turn on a series of switches to establish which types of things you want to sync. Turn on Calendars. (Turn on the others such as Mail, Contacts, Bookmarks, or Notes if you want to sync those with Exchange.)

Figure 2-3: Turn Calendars on in the account screen if you want to use the calendar feature of Microsoft Exchange.

   You now see Microsoft Exchange in the list of accounts on the Mail, Contacts, Calendars settings screen.

3. **Tap the Save button in the upper-right corner and you return to the Mail, Contacts, Calendars settings screen.**

4. **Tap Fetch New Data.**

5. **Tap Push On.**

   Anytime you make a change to the calendar on your computer that's associated with your Microsoft Exchange account, that change is pushed to your iPhone, and vice versa.

If you use over-the-air syncing, such as iCloud or Microsoft Exchange, the Sync Calendars in iTunes option is disabled. You can choose to sync both with OTA and iTunes, but doing so means you run the risk of having duplicate entries. Our advice: Stick with OTA-only to ensure you're truly in sync across all of your devices.

Configuring CalDAV calendar accounts

CalDAV is an Internet protocol that allows access to data in the iCalendar format on a remote server. Multiple users can access the same information so it is often used in business and organization settings. If your employer uses a CalDAV supported calendar program, and you want to access that calendar from your iPhone, you can add a CalDAV account. You'll need some account information from your IT department or network support person:

- ✔ **Server:** This has your company or organization information.

- ✔ **User Name:** This is your identification.

- ✔ **Password:** A password is required.

- ✔ **Description:** This name shows up on the list of accounts on the Mail, Contacts, Calendars settings screen.

Armed with this information, set up an account on your computer as explained at the beginning of this section. Next, set up the account on your iPhone by following these steps:

1. **Tap Settings⇨Mail, Contacts, Calendars.**

2. **Tap Add Account.**

3. **Tap Other.**

4. **Tap Add CalDAV Account in the Calendars section.**

5. **Type in the information requested.**

6. **Tap the Next button in the upper-right corner.**

   After your account information is verified, the calendar data is added to your iPhone.

7. **Tap the Save button in the upper-right corner and you return to the Mail, Contacts, Calendars settings screen.**

8. **Tap Fetch New Data.**

   The Fetch New Data screen opens, as shown in Figure 2-4.

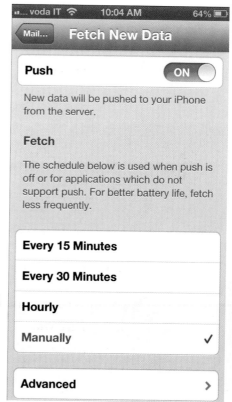

Figure 2-4: The Push feature sends calendar updates to your iPhone as they happen on the remote server.

9. **If your server supports push notifications, Tap Push On.**

   Anytime you make a change to the calendar on your computer that's associated with your iCloud or Microsoft Exchange account, that change is pushed to your iPhone, and vice versa.

10. **If your server doesn't support push (or you want to conserve battery power — Push is power hungry), select a default fetch interval — every 15 minutes, every 30 minutes, or hourly.**

    Your iPhone contacts the server for new data at the interval you select.

Importing Google and other calendars

The Google suite of programs, such as Google Mail, Google Calendar, or Blogger, is so popular that Apple has integrated syncing between your iPhone and Google. Same goes for Yahoo!. If you use Google or Yahoo! calendars, all you need is your e-mail address and password. To set up an account on your iPhone, follow these steps:

1. **Tap Settings on the Home screen, and then tap Mail, Contacts, Calendars.**

2. **Tap Add Account.**

3. **Tap Google Mail or Yahoo! on the Add Account screen.**

4. **The Add Account screen opens.**

   Filling in the Name field is optional. Type in your e-mail address in the Address field and your password in the Password field.

5. **Tap the Next button in the upper-right corner.**

   The Google Mail or Yahoo! screen opens.

6. **Tap the Calendars switch On.**

   The calendar you added shows up as one of your calendars in the Calendar app. By default, only the primary Google calendar is synced to your iPhone, so if you don't see the calendar you're looking for, log into the Google account (you can do this on your computer if you want) where the calendar resides, and then go to `www.google.com/calendar/iphoneselect`. Select the calendar from the list that you want to sync to your iPhone and click Save. Tap the Calendar button on the Home screen and you find the additional Google calendar in the calendar list.

 If you have multiple Google Calendars, you might find Google Sync to be a better way to manage your calendars. Follow the instructions in Book IV, Chapter 1 for "Importing and Syncing with Google Contacts" and turn the Calendar option on.

If you create a remote calendar account on Microsoft Exchange Active Sync, the calendar data syncs between Exchange and the remote server. The data, but not the account information, syncs to your iPhone and shows up in the calendar list From My Mac/PC.

Adding Facebook events to Calendar

Facebook is integrated in iOS 6 so any events on Facebook — birthdays, class reunions, store promotions — are pushed to Calendar. Although some have complained about the overt presence of Facebook in iOS 6, you can follow these steps to activate this feature, or not:

1. **Tap Settings⇨Facebook.**

   The Facebook settings screen opens.

   If you don't have the Facebook app installed, tap the Install button to download it from the iTunes Store.

2. **Tap in the User Name field and type in your user name.**

3. **Tap in the Password field and type in your password.**

4. **Tap Sign In.**

   A disclaimer appears that explains what happens on your iPhone when you sign in to Facebook. Essentially, information about your Facebook friends is downloaded to Contacts; Facebook events sync to your Calendar; you can post status updates and images directly from the Photos app; and Facebook-enabled apps work with your permission.

5. **Tap Sign In again to accept these conditions. You can change the settings after you sign in if you don't want these things to happen.**

6. **The Facebook setting screen reappears with Calendar and Contacts options.**

7. **Tap Calendar On.**

   Even if you turn this feature on, you can hide the Facebook Events calendar, as explained in the later section, "Viewing and Hiding Calendars."

Subscribing to iCalendar (.ics) calendars

One of the strong points of Calendar is the ability to access calendars created by other people and see those events on your iPhone. You may learn about these events through electronic invitations — invitations that are sent via e-mail — or from a public calendar site where you can search for published calendars. Apple maintains a page of downloadable calendars at www. apple.com/downloads/macosx/calendars/.

An iCalendar or .ics file is the standard file type for exchanging calendar information. Calendar, Outlook, and Google Calendar support the .ics standard.

If you receive an e-mail with an invitation to either an event attached, the invitation probably has the .ics suffix. You simply click that attachment, either from the e-mail message on your computer or on your iPhone, and then choose one of the following responses:

- **Accept** the invitation and the event is automatically added to your calendar. The next time you sync, the event is copied to your other devices. (If you use OTA syncing, the event syncs automatically.)

- **Decline** to refuse the invitation.

- **Maybe** to postpone your decision to attend the event or not.

Whichever response you choose is sent to the person who sent the invitation.

If you receive a list of events in Mail, tap the calendar file within the message. When the list of events appears, tap Add All. Choose the calendar where you want to add the events, and then tap Done.

If you receive an invitation to a calendar, you can choose to Decline or Join Calendar. If you decline, an e-mail informs the sender of your decision. If you join, an e-mail informs the sender of your decision and the calendar is added as one of your calendars in Calendar. You can choose to view or hide that calendar's events by selecting or deselecting it in the calendars list.

To subscribe to published, public calendars, you can search a site like http://icalshare.com/ or Google Calendars and subscribe to the calendars that interest you. Some organizations post a subscription link on their website so you can automatically receive notifications of their events. To add a calendar subscription on your iPhone, do one of the following procedures:

1. **Tap Safari on the Home screen.**

2. **Type the URL for the calendar sharing site you want to use, for example,** http://icalshare.com/.

3. **Find the calendar you want to add, and then tap the Subscribe to Calendar button.**

4. **Tap the appropriate response, such as Subscribe or Add Calendar, in the dialogs that appear.**

5. **The calendar is automatically added to Calendar and appears on the calendar list.**

If the calendar you want to add isn't part of a service like iCalShare, have the URL of the shared calendar handy and follow these steps:

1. **Tap Settings⇨Mail, Contacts, Calendar.**

2. **Tap Add Account.**

3. **Tap Other.**

4. **Tap Add Subscribed Calendar (near the bottom of the screen.)**

5. **Type in the server address for the calendar on the Subscription screen, as seen in Figure 2-5.**

6. **Tap Next.**

   The server address is verified and a Subscription screen appears. You may have to enter a username and password to have access to the calendar. Some calendar providers ask you to use SSL (secure socket layer) for security reasons. See Book III, Chapter 4 to learn how to turn SSL on in Mail.

7. **The calendar appears on the calendar list in the Calendar app.**

If you want to delete the calendar, go to Settings⇨Mail, Contacts, Calendars⇨Subscribed Calendars. Tap the calendar you want to delete, and then tap Delete Account.

You can make changes to the event in Calendar, but the changes are not reflected on the source calendar (such as Google Calendars), which is stored on a remote server and accessed on the Internet.

Viewing and Hiding Calendars

You now have one or multiple calendars on your iPhone. Calendar neatly puts the data in four formats: in portrait (vertical) view, Calendar displays a month-at-a-glance, a day-at-a-glance, and List, which is a scrollable list of your events and appointments. Turn your iPhone to the landscape (horizontal) position to see several days at-a-glance — 5 on an iPhone 5, 3 and a half on earlier models. To choose which calendars you want to see

Figure 2-5: You can subscribe to public calendars that use the iCalendar standard.

1. **Tap Calendars on the Home Screen.**

2. **Tap the Calendar button in the upper-left corner.**

   A list of your calendars opens, as shown in Figure 2-6.

3. **Tap the name of the calendar you want to see or hide.**

   If there's a checkmark next to the name of the calendar, events in that calendar show up in the four views. Note that the Calendars are color-coded. Events shown in List and Day views are color-coded to respond to the calendar they come from.

4. **Tap Show All Calendars if you want to see all events.**

5. **Option: Tap the blue and white arrow to the right of the calendar, do one of the following, and then tap Done:**

   • *Edit* the color of the calendar by tapping the color you want to associate with that calendar's events.

   • *Delete* a calendar by scrolling to the bottom of the screen and tapping the Delete Calendar button.

6. **Tap Done.**

   Calendars opens to the view you most recently used.

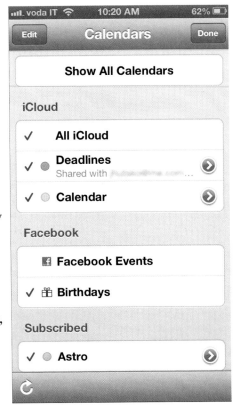

Figure 2-6: The Calendar list shows you the calendars you sync with and those you subscribe to.

List, Day, Week, and Month views

When you open Calendar from the Home screen, you see one of the screens as shown in the upcoming figures. The buttons on the screen, from top to bottom, work as follows:

✓ **Calendars:** Takes you to the list of your calendars.

✓ **Plus Sign:** Tap this button to add an event to your calendar. We explain that in detail in the next section.

✔ Between the Calendar and Plus Sign buttons, you see the number of calendars shown. In Figure 2-7, you see "3 Calendars," which means the events you see come from three different calendars, as selected on the Calendars screen in the previous procedure. You see All Calendars if you choose Show All Calendars or just the name of the calendar if you selected only one from the Calendars screen.

✔ **Left and right arrows (day and month views only):** In Day view, these arrows move a day before (left) or a day ahead (right). If you tap and hold the arrow, the day changes quickly. The arrows on Month view work the same but take you from one month to the previous or next; tap and hold moves quickly through the months.

✔ **Today:** Tap on the Today button at the bottom of the page in any of the views, and today is highlighted. If you make an appointment on a day two weeks in the future, tapping Today quickly takes you back to today rather than scrolling through with the arrows at the top.

✔ **List:** Opens the List view as shown in Figure 2-7. You see five or six events. If you have a busy day, you may see only one day. If you have just one or two things each day, you see more days. The colored dot to the left of the event corresponds to the calendar it comes from. You can scroll up and down this list to see what you did or what's coming up.

✔ **Day:** All-day events are shown at the top, and then you see a list of the day's appointments, much like a paper agenda or planner that you may be used to using. Scroll up and down the day's appointments to see different hours of the day. The background color of the event corresponds to the calendar it comes from.

✔ **Month:** Days with appointments have a dot under the number. If you click on a day other than today, the day you click is blue and today is gray.

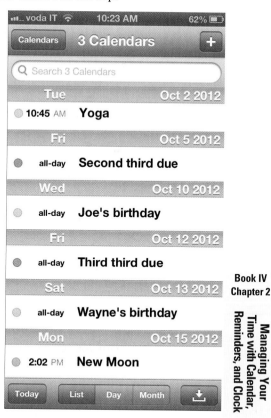

Figure 2-7: You can scroll through the List view to see your appointments and events.

✔ **Invitations Inbox:** A red numbered badge appears on this button when you receive invitations; the number indicates how many invitations. Click on the button and the invitation opens. We talk about responding to invitations in the "Responding to meeting invitations" section later in this chapter.

To view several days of your calendar together, as shown in Figure 2-8, rotate your iPhone to landscape view and you see a multiday calendar. Swipe left and right to scroll to previous and upcoming days. Swipe up and down to scroll from morning to evening. All-day events are posted at the top of the day. Multi-day events are highlighted across all the days of the event.

Figure 2-8: Turn your iPhone to landscape view to see a week-at-a-glance calendar.

Showing birthdays

If you use Contacts, you probably know that you can include a birthday as part of the contact information. (We explain Contacts in Book IV, Chapter 1.) Calendar links to Contacts and can display the birthdays on your calendar.

Scroll to the bottom of the Calendars list screen. You find the Other section and Birthdays. A checkmark indicates that Birthdays is selected; tap Birthdays if it isn't selected. Tap Done. Birthdays are automatically inserted as all-day events. If you turned Calendar On in the Facebook Settings, you also see a Birthdays option in the Facebook section of the Calendars list screen (refer to Figure 2-6).

You now see birthdays in the List and Day views and a dot on the date in Month view. The gift icon is next to the event so you know it's a birthday.

You can set a default alert time for birthdays by tapping Settings⟷Mail, Contacts, Calendars⟷Default Alert Times⟷Birthdays and choosing when you want to receive an alert that someone's birthday is near (from a week before to the day of).

If you use birthdays from Contacts and add the birthday as an event, it shows up twice on your calendar.

Creating, Changing, and Deleting Calendar Events

As work and life styles evolve, we tend to use Calendar on our iPhones more than our computers. (Of course, every entry is synced to our computers and devices with iCloud.) In this section, we show you how to create new events and change or delete existing ones. We explain setting up repeating events and alerts so you don't miss any important scheduled encounters, and we discuss how to respond to invitations.

Filling in who, what, where, and when

If you're familiar with Calendar on a Mac (iCal in OS X 10.7 and earlier), creating events in Calendar will be a breeze. Even if you use Outlook or another calendar program, Calendar is pretty straightforward. Here's how to add an appointment or event:

1. **Tap Calendar on the Home screen.**

2. **From List, Day, or Month Calendar view, tap the plus sign button in the upper-right corner to open the Add Event screen.**

   In Day or Month view, press and hold the time or day where you want to add an event until an Add Event screen appears.

3. **Tap the first field, where you see Title and Location.**

   The keyboard appears.

4. **Type in the name of the event or appointment in the Title field.**

5. **Tap Return, and then type in a Location or something else pertinent to the appointment. This field is optional.**

6. **Tap the field with Starts, Ends, and Time Zone.**

   The screen as in Figure 2-9 opens, with the Starts field highlighted.

7. **Using the rotor, set the date and time the appointment begins.**

8. **Tap the Ends field. Set the date and time the appointment ends.**

9. **If it's an all-day event such as a meeting or anniversary, tap the All-Day switch to On.**

   The rotors change and show only the month, day, and year. If the event is more than one day, say a conference or vacation, choose the beginning and ending dates.

The advantage to using the all-day feature instead of setting the beginning time to 8 a.m. and the ending time to 8 p.m. is that in Day view, the event shows up at the beginning of the day rather than as a highlighted event over the course of the whole day. This way, you can add specific appointments during the course of the all-day event. In List view, All-Day appears next to the event title.

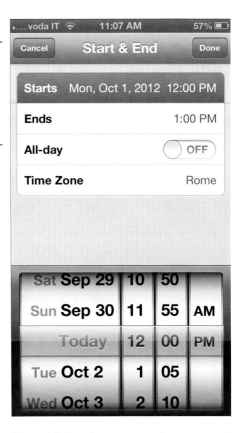

Figure 2-9: Use the rotor to set the starting and ending date and times for your event.

10. **Tap the Time Zone field if you want to set the event in a time zone other than your own.**

    A field opens where you type in the name of a large city that resides in the time zone you want to use. Tap the city from the list when a match appears.

11. **Tap Done.**

    You return to the Add Event screen.

12. **Tap the Calendar field.**

    The Calendar screen opens.

13. **Tap the calendar you want to put this event on if it's different than what is shown in the field. You choose the default calendar under Settings, which we explain a few sections ahead.**

    This is the only thing you can't edit at a later date. If you want to move this event to another calendar, you have to create a new event and choose a different calendar.

14. **Tap Done.**

You can stop here or you can add some more details to your event with the remaining fields: Repeat, Alert, and Notes. You can even add attachments or links to websites in Notes. If you use an over-the-air calendar like iCloud or Microsoft Exchange, you also have the options of indicating if you're busy or free during the event and of inviting people to your event.

Setting up a repeating event

The default repetition setting for a new event is Never. If your event is one-time only, skip this. For yearly events like an anniversary, or weekly events, such as a tennis lesson, the repeat function is handy.

You only have to enter the information once and Calendar takes care of the rest, saving you the hassle of both remembering to re-enter the event the next time it's coming around and of re-typing the information. Here's how:

1. **Tap Repeat on the event you created.**

   If it's an event that you created previously, open that event and tap Edit in the upper-right corner.

2. **Choose the frequency with which you want the event to repeat.**

3. **Tap Done.**

   You return to the Add Event screen but another field is added under Repeat: the End Repeat field.

4. **Never is the default, which you probably want to leave for events such as anniversaries. Your tennis lesson may be seasonal, so tap the End Repeat field.**

5. **Use the rotor to choose the date the event ends.**

6. **Tap Done.**

Adding Alerts

If you have a lot on your plate — and who doesn't? — alerts can be a big help. Your iPhone beeps (or vibrates if the Ring/Silent switch is set to Silent) and sends a notification message at the interval you select, from five minutes to two days before your event.

Even if your iPhone is sleeping and/or locked, Calendar wakes your iPhone. You hear the beep and the notification appears, as shown in Figure 2-10. Slide the slider bar to view the event. When you sync your calendars, alerts sync to the corresponding calendar on your computer, and vice versa.

You can even receive two alerts, so you can be reminded of your dear Aunt Sybil's retirement dinner two days before the event, giving you time to get a gift, and then again, the day of the dinner. Follow these steps:

1. **Tap Alert on the Add Event screen or the Edit screen, if you want to add an alert to an event you already created.**

2. **Tap how long before the event you want to receive an alert.**

3. **Tap Done.**

You return to the Add Event screen, but another field is added under Alert, the Second Alert field.

4. **Tap Second Alert if you want to receive two alerts for the same event.**

5. **Tap how long before the event you want to receive a second alert.**

6. **Tap Done.**

Go to Settings➪Notifications➪Calendar to choose the alert sound and style. Tap None for one or both types of alerts if you don't want to receive a visual or audible notification. To learn more about the Notification Center, go to Book I, Chapter 4.

You can set default alerts for events or all-day events by tapping Settings➪ Mail, Contacts, Calendars➪Default Alert Times. Then tap Events or All-Day Events and choose when you want to receive an alert. This gives you an alert for all of those kinds of happenings, so if you have a lot of events, setting up default alerts may be more a cause of confusion than a reminder. In that case, you may want to only assign individual alerts to your most important events.

Figure 2-10: Alerts are received even if your iPhone is locked or sleeping.

If you have an alert scheduled during a time that Do Not Disturb is turned on, you won't receive the alert — unless your iPhone is awake when the alert time occurs.

Adding Notes

Adding a note to an event is a great way to remember things associated with that event: for example, if you need certain files for a meeting, or want to save the phone number of the person you're going to meet or the confirmation number for a flight. To add a note:

1. **Tap Notes on the Add Event screen, or Edit screen if you want to add an alert to an event you already created.**

2. **Type in the information you want.**

Or

Copy and paste to the Notes field from a contact, website, note, or an e-mail: Switch to the app that contains information you want to copy.

Copy that information. Double-click the Home button to open the process bar and tap Calendar. You return to the Notes screen where you left off. Press and hold in the field until the magnifying loupe appears. Lift your finger, and then tap Paste. Voila! The information you copied is now in the note of your event.

3. **Tap Done.**

Indicating your availability

If you post an event to an over-the-air calendar such as one in iCloud or Microsoft Exchange, you can indicate that you are free, or busy, during the event that you post by tapping Availability on the Add Event screen, and then tapping Busy or Free, as appropriate. Tap Done.

Inviting people to your event

If you use an over-the-air calendar, like iCloud or Microsoft Exchange, or use Mail on a Mac, you can invite people to your event directly from Calendar. Make sure you accurately complete the details of your event before sending it to the invitees. Then follow these steps:

1. **Tap Invitees.**

   The Add Invitees screen opens.

2. **Type in the e-mail addresses of the people you want to invite or tap the plus sign on the right.**

   Contacts opens. Scroll the list or tap the letters down the right side or use the Search function to find the name you're looking for.

3. **Tap the name of the person you want to invite.**

   You return to the Add Invitees screen and the name appears in the space at the top.

4. **Repeat steps 2 and 3 to add more people.**

5. **Tap Done in the upper-right corner.**

   An event invitation is automatically sent to your invitees.

Figure 2-11 shows a completed Add Event screen.

Of course one of the easiest ways to add an event is to call on Siri. Press and hold the Home button until Siri appears and then speak the details of your event, such as "Set up a meeting with Joe on Thursday at 3 p.m." or "Create a repeating event every Tuesday from 10:15 to noon." Siri asks the necessary questions to send invitations, add locations, and even edit events at a later date.

Editing and deleting events

Meetings get cancelled, appointment times and dates get changed, and in the old pen and paper calendar world, we used a lot of correction fluid. You can swiftly edit or delete appointments and events on your iPhone without inhaling those nasty fumes.

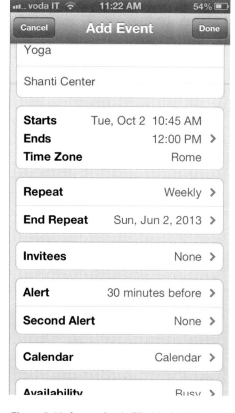

Figure 2-11: A completely filled-in Add Event screen.

1. **Tap Calendar from the Home screen.**

2. **Locate the event you want to change or delete from one of the views. We find List or Day easiest.**

3. **Tap the event you want to work on.**

   An Event Details screen opens, as you see in Figure 2-12.

4. **Tap Edit in the upper-right corner.**

   The Edit screen opens, which looks like the Add Event screen except it's filled in.

5. **Tap in the field you want to change.**

6. **Make changes using the same techniques you use to enter data in a new event.**

7. **Tap Done.**

If you want to delete the event, instead of editing as in Step 5, tap the red Delete Event button at the bottom of the screen. Two buttons pop up, Delete Event and Cancel. Tap the appropriate one.

Responding to meeting invitations

Meetings are a fact of life in large and small business. Once upon a time, we used the phone to invite people to meetings, but e-mail and electronic calendars have changed that. You can receive and respond to meeting invitations on your iPhone if you have enabled calendars on Microsoft Exchange or iCloud.

You receive four types of notifications when someone sends you an invitation:

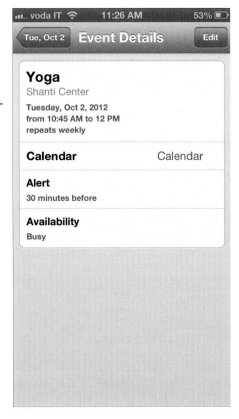

Figure 2-12: The Event Details screen shows information about events you created.

- ✔ **Notification box:** An alert beep sounds and a notification box gives you minimal details about the event and the choice to close the box or view the complete details of the event. You can turn New Invitation Alerts off in Mail, Contacts, Calendar Settings.

- ✔ **On your calendar:** The meeting appears on a gray background with a dotted line around it.

- ✔ **On the Calendars screen:** A numeric alert badge appears in the inbox on the lower-right corner.

- ✔ **On the Home screen:** A numeric badge appears on the Calendar button.

Tap the inbox on the Calendars screen to view invitations received. Tap on the invitation to open the details, see Figure 2-13. You have three response choices:

- ✔ **Accept:** This puts the meeting on your calendar at the indicated date and time. Your name is added to the list of attendees.

- ✔ **Maybe:** On both your calendar and the sender's calendar, the meeting appears tentative if you select Maybe.

- ✔ **Decline:** This sends a response to let the person know you won't be attending. Nothing is added to your calendar and the invitation is deleted from your iPhone.

Tapping Add Comments in any of the three responses and typing a response sends an e-mail to the sender; otherwise, your response is sent with an empty e-mail.

If you receive an invitation in an e-mail, it shows up as an attachment with an .ics suffix, which indicates the iCalendar standard. Tap on the attachment and the Event Info screen opens. You can then add the event to your calendar and respond.

Sharing Calendars

Just as you can subscribe to other's calendars on servers like iCalshare.com, you can share calendars you create on iCloud with other people who have an iCloud account. Sharing calendars lets other know what you're up to or gives others the possibility to post events on your calendar. Follow these steps to activate sharing:

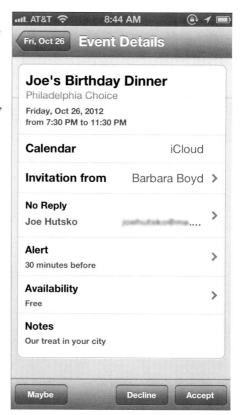

Figure 2-13: You can Accept or Decline an invitation, or choose Maybe while you think about it.

1. **Tap Calendar on the Home screen.**

2. **Tap the Calendars button in the upper-left corner.**

3. **Tap the blue and white arrow to the right of the calendar you want to share. It must be an iCloud or Microsoft Exchange calendar.**

   Tap Edit⟳Add Calendar if you want to create a new calendar, and then tap Done.

4. **To share the calendar with one or more specific persons, tap Add Person.**

   An Add Person message screen opens; it looks like an e-mail message.

5. **Type in the name of the person you want to share the calendar with or tap the plus sign to choose someone from your Contacts list.**

   Add as many names as you wish.

6. **Tap Add.**

   The Edit Calendar screen appears and the name or names of the people you share with appear in the Shared With list.

7. **Tap View and Edit to grant or remove calendar editing privileges to the person, as shown in Figure 2-14.**

8. **Tap Edit Calendar to return to the previous screen.**

9. **Scroll to the bottom of the screen to find the Public Calendar option.**

10. **Tap On to allow anyone to subscribe to a read-only version of your calendar.**

11. **Tap Share Link, as shown in Figure 2-15, to send an e-mail or message to people you want to invite to subscribe to this calendar or copy the link to post it elsewhere such as a Twitter or Facebook or your blog.**

12. **Tap Done.**

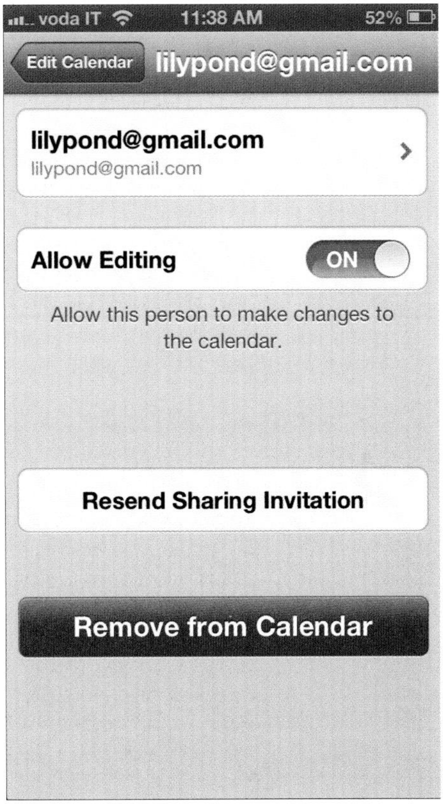

Searching Calendars

You can click on a date to see what events and appointments you have scheduled, but what if you know you have a dentist appointment but can't remember the exact day? You can search in Calendar to find the missing event. Calendar searches in the title, location, notes, and invitees fields of calendars that are active — those you have selected in the Calendars list. Follow these steps:

Figure 2-14: Grant editing privileges to people with whom you share your calendar.

1. **Tap Calendar on the Home screen.**

2. **Tap the List button at the bottom of the screen.**

3. **Tap the Spotlight Search field at the top.**

    The cursor appears in the field and the keyboard opens.

4. **Begin typing a keyword from your appointment.**

    Matches come up as soon as you type the first letter. The results narrow as you type more.

5. **Tap the Search button in the bottom-right corner to close the keyboard.**

6. **Tap the event you were searching for when you see it on the list.**

   The Event Details screen opens.

7. **If that isn't the event you were looking for, tap the Search button on the top left to return to the search screen and try again.**

8. **Tap Cancel when you've finished.**

Adjusting iPhone's Calendar Settings

You can change five Calendar settings from the main Settings app on your iPhone. To access them, tap Settings⇨ Mail, Contacts, Calendars. Scroll down to the bottom of the screen. The Calendars settings are in the last section, as shown in Figure 2-16. You can adjust five items:

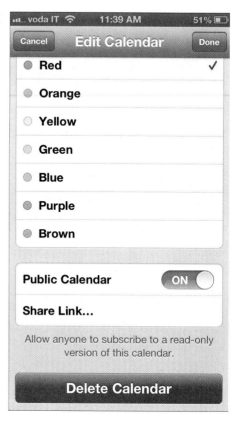

Figure 2-15: Let others subscribe to your calendar to stay informed of your events.

✔ **New Invitation Alerts:** When this is set to On, you receive an alert when a new invitation arrives from a remote calendar, such as Outlook. If you're feeling overwhelmed by the number of meeting invitations you receive, tap this setting Off.

✔ **Time Zone Support:** Time Zone Support is turned On when you first use your iPhone. The time zone that your iPhone is set to appears next to the Time Zone Support button. Events and alerts you enter in Calendar maintain the time you enter, regardless of what time zone you're actually in. We recommend that you leave it that way because switching between On and Off changes the times on events you already created.

To change your time zone, tap Time Zone Support on the Mail, Contacts, Calendar Settings screen. The Time Zone Support screen opens. Tap the switch On and then tap Time Zone. The Time Zone screen opens with a keyboard. Begin typing the initial letters of the city or country of the time zone you want to use. A list of potential cities appears and the results narrow as you type more letters. Tap a city that's in the time zone you want. You return to the Time Zone Support screen. Tap the Mail button in the upper-left corner to return to the Settings screen.

Turn Time Zone Support off and your events reflect the local time of your current location. The times for events you already created change. For example, an event at 9:30 a.m. in London changes to 2:30 a.m. when you land in Atlanta.

🗸 **Sync:** Appears if you use an OTA calendar. Choose how much event history you want to include when you sync your events. Tap to open the Sync screen and choose 2 Weeks Back; 1, 3, or 6 Months Back; or All Events. If you sync using iTunes, you set up the historical syncing timeframe on the Info window.

🗸 **Default Alert Times:** Set alerts for all birthdays, all events, or all all-day events. See the section "Adding Alerts" earlier in this chapter for the steps to use this feature.

🗸 **Default Calendar:** Choose which calendar you want as the default. Any new events you create automatically are placed on the default calendar, unless you change it on the Add Event screen. Tap Default Calendar. The Default Calendar screen opens, which displays the calendars that are available. Click the calendar you want. A checkmark appears to the right of the selected default calendar.

Figure 2-16: Customize Calendar to your liking in Settings.

Remembering with Reminders

Reminders is a listmaker's electronic dream come true. Reminders is a catch-all for your To Do lists, neatly divided into categories you want to add. You create lists of tasks and then have Reminders send you an alert based on a time or location. There's even a Completed list so you have the satisfaction of seeing things checked off your list. And, Reminders automatically syncs via iCloud with the Reminders app on your other iOS devices or Mac and Outlook on your Mac or Windows PC. Just remember to turn Reminders On in Settings⇔iCloud.

If you don't want to sync Reminders with iCloud, your Reminders lists will sync across iTunes as part of the Calendar sync — they appear in the list of Calendars in the iTunes Info panel when you connect your iPhone to your computer.

Creating new Reminders tasks

We prefer to ask Siri to add new tasks to our Reminders lists (see Book I, Chapter 3), but if you don't have an Internet connection or your connection is slow, you can create them by yourself. Here's how to "manually" create new Reminders:

1. **Tap Reminders on the Home screen.**

   The Reminders screen opens. The first time you open Reminders you see a blank list: Go to Step 3.

2. **After you create multiple lists (refer to the section Creating Reminders lists), tap the Lists button in the upper-left corner and do one of the following:**

   • Tap the list you want to add the task to.

   • In the scrolling calendar at the bottom of the screen (refer to Figure 2-17), tap the date you want the task to expire on.

3. **Tap the first blank line on the lined piece of "paper" or tap the plus sign in the upper-right corner.**

   The keyboard appears.

4. **Type the task you want to remember.**

   The task appears in the list with a check box to the left and a disclosure arrow to the right.

5. **Tap the disclosure arrow.**

   The Details screen opens.

6. **Tap each item to specify how you want Reminders to help you remember this task. Figure 2-18 shows a completed task.**

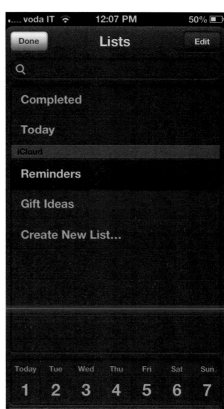

Figure 2-17: Add a task by choosing a list or a date.

- *Remind Me On a Day:* Tap On and tap the date to open a rotor that allows you to specify the date and time. You also have the option to Repeat at an interval you select.

- *Remind Me At a Location:* Tap On. If you want to be reminded of the item when you leave or arrive at your current location, tap either When I Leave or When I Arrive, and then tap Done. If you want to use a different location, tap the address that appears. The Location screen opens. Tap the address to open Contacts and choose an address there or tap Enter an Address and type in a specific location. Tap Details in the upper left corner after you choose the location. You return to the Details screen. Tap Done after you have specified a Day or Location (or both) to return to the Details screen. The Location option only works with iPhone 4 or later and works better if you use a street address.

Figure 2-18: Add details about your task so Reminders knows where and when to remind you.

Tap Show More to see the following:

- *Priority* lets you set the task as a low, medium, or high priority.

- *List* gives you the option to specify in which list you want to keep the reminder. See the next section, "Creating Reminders lists."

- *Notes* is where you can type in any additional details about the reminder.

7. **Tap Done when you finish with each item to return to the previous screen.**

8. **Go to Settings⇨Notifications to choose the alert tone and style you want Reminders to use.**

To rearrange, edit, or delete items in a list do the following:

✏ To rearrange the order of items in your list, tap the Edit button in the upper-right corner and then tap and drag the list button to the right of each item to move it up or down in the list.

✏ Edit a task by tapping the disclosure arrow to the right of the task to open the Details screen.

✏ Delete an item by swiping across the task and then tapping the red Delete button.

✏ Delete an item by tapping Edit and then tapping the red and white minus sign to the left of the item.

✏ Or, tap the disclosure arrow to the right of the task and then tap Delete at the bottom of the Details screen.

Creating Reminders lists

Reminders comes with two lists: Reminders and Completed. You can add other lists and then create new Reminders on the lists you want. To view the existing lists, tap the List button at the top left of the screen and then tap the list you want to view. Notice that your lists on iCloud are grouped under an iCloud heading. To add or delete a list, follow these steps:

1. **Tap Reminders on the Home screen to open Reminders.**

2. **Tap the List button in the top-left corner to open the Lists screen.**

3. **Tap Edit in the upper-right corner.**

4. **To create a new list, tap Create New List.**

    The keyboard opens.

    Type in the name of the list and then tap Done.

5. **To delete a list, tap the red and white minus sign to the left of the list name in the list.**

6. **Drag the list button to the right of the items to rearrange their order.**

7. **Tap Done to return to the Lists screen and then tap the list you want to view (refer to Figure 2-17).**

When you complete a task, tap the check box to the left of the task on the list and the task moves onto the Completed list, which you reach by tapping the List button and then tapping Completed in the list of lists. You can also view completed tasks for a specific list by tapping Completed at the top of the list. You may have to scroll up to see Completed.

If you want to see all your tasks for one day tap the List button at the top of the screen and then tap Today at the top of the list or tap a date in the scrollable calendar at the bottom of the screen.

Search in Reminders by tapping the List button. Type a few words of the task you're looking for in the search field or use Spotlight Search from the Home screen. Or just ask Siri to find a reminder for you.

Using Clock to Help Pass the Time

Your iPhone has not one but four time tools: a world clock, an alarm, a stopwatch, and a timer. If you keep your iPhone by your side, you can pretty much eliminate every other clock-like gadget in your home. With the Clock app, you can do things like use the world clock to make sure you don't call your cousin in Mongolia at 2 a.m. Or, set an alarm to wake you up in the morning and separate alarms to wake your children in time for school. Help your friend track trial times for the 100 meter dash. Set a timer for the cake you've put in the oven and to turn off your iPhone's Music, Video, or Podcasts app when you fall asleep. We take you through each of these marvelous clock features, one by one.

Adding clocks from around the world

When you tap the Home button to wake your iPhone, you see the time on the screen. You set that time on the World Clock function of your iPhone's Clock app. You can also set up clocks from other time zones to keep you informed of what time it is in your overseas office or in the country where your sister is studying.

You only see four or five clocks at a time (depending on your iPhone model), but you can scroll down the list and have as many clocks as there are time zones.

Follow these steps:

1. **Tap Clock on the Home screen.**

2. **Tap the World Clock button in the bottom-left corner.**

3. **Tap the plus sign in the upper-right corner.**

   The search field opens with a keyboard below.

4. **Begin typing the city or country that you want to add a clock for.**

   If I type **S**, both Scotland and San Rafael come up, as does Detroit, U.S.A. The more letters you type, the narrower your search results.

5. **Tap the city you want to add.**

If you don't see the exact city you were searching for, tap one that's in the same time zone.

6. **The World Clock screen returns, as shown in Figure 2-19.**

   You see the city you chose added to the list. The clock has a white face if it's daytime in that city and a black face if it's night.

7. **To rearrange the order of the clocks, tap the Edit button in the upper-left corner.**

8. **Tap and hold the reorder button on the right, and then drag the clock to the position you want.**

9. **When the clocks are in the order you want, tap Done.**

10. **To delete a clock, tap the Edit button in the upper-left corner.**

11. **Tap the red button on the left.**

    A delete button appears on the right.

12. **Tap Delete.**

13. **Tap Done after you finish.**

Figure 2-19: World clock shows clocks from multiple time zones.

Setting Alarms

Some of the things we like about the Alarm function are that you can have multiple alarms, choose the days an alarm should repeat, select the sound you want it to have, and add a snooze function. If you want the alarm to vibrate only, leave your iPhone in Ring mode but turn the volume completely down.

Keep in mind that the alarm sounds even when your iPhone is in Silent mode.

Here's how to set alarms:

1. **Tap Clock on the Home screen.**

2. **Tap the Alarm button at the bottom of the screen.**

3. **Tap the plus sign in the upper-right corner.**

The Add Alarm screen opens.

4. **Use the rotor to set the time you want the alarm to sound.**

5. **Tap Repeat if you want to create a repeating alarm.**

   You can choose any day of the week or a combination of days, which means you can have a Monday through Friday alarm, which is labeled Weekdays on the alarm list, whereas a Saturday/Sunday alarm is labeled Weekends.

6. **Tap Back after you choose the days you want the alarm to repeat.**

7. **Tap Sound to choose the sound you want for your alarm.**

   Choose a sound from the list — scroll down to see all the options, which include ringtones you purchased or created. You can buy more tones by tapping the button at the top of the list, which takes you to the iTunes store.

   A neat new feature of iOS 6 is using a song for an alarm sound. Tap Pick a Song and then tap the song you want from the music collection on your iPhone. You can add more than one song and assign a different song to different alarms.

8. **Tap Snooze On or Off.**

   Snooze lets you tap the alarm off when it sounds. After ten minutes, it sounds again.

9. **Tap Label to name your alarm.**

   The Label screen opens with a field and keyboard. Click the X on the right end of the field to delete the default Alarm label, type the name you want, and then tap Done.

10. **Tap Save.**

   The alarm is added to the list of alarms on the Alarm screen.

To make changes to an existing alarm, tap the Edit button on the top left of the screen, and then tap the name of the alarm you want to change. The Edit Alarm screen opens, which is the same as the Add Alarm screen but has the information of the selected alarm.

To delete an existing alarm, tap the Edit button. Tap the red button to the left of the alarm time, and then tap the Delete button that appears on the right. Tap Done after you finish.

When you set an alarm, the alarm icon, which looks like a clock, appears in the status bar at the top of your iPhone's screen.

Timing events with Stopwatch

You can use the Stopwatch to time single events such as a speech or laps. Tap Start to start counting.

To time one thing, let it run until the action stops, and then tap Stop.

To time laps, tap Lap each time the runner or swimmer or bicycle rounds the bend.

The large numbers continue giving a cumulative time; the smaller numbers above show the lap's duration.

When you tap Lap, the laps are listed below with each lap's time, as shown in Figure 2-20. If you tap Start again, the count resumes from where it left off.

Tap Reset to zero the count and erase the lap times.

Counting down to zero with Timer

Figure 2-20: Time laps with the Stopwatch.

While the Stopwatch starts counting from zero, the timer counts down to zero. You can set the time from one minute up to 23 hours and 59 minutes, after which, you're better off setting an alarm. After you set the timer, you can go on to do things with other apps, even press the Sleep/Wake button. The timer continues to countdown in the background and sounds when the time's up. To set the timer:

1. **Tap Clock on the Home screen.**

2. **Tap the Timer button in the lower-right corner.**

3. **Turn the rotor to set the length of time you want to pass before the timer sounds.**

4. **Tap When Timer Ends to choose the "time's up" sound.**

   Scroll through the When Timer Ends list and tap the sound you want. Tap Buy More Tones at the top of the list to go to iTunes and buy additional sounds.

5. **Tap the Set button in the upper-right corner.**

6. **Tap the green Start button on the Timer screen.**

To use the Timer as a Sleep Timer while you're listening to audio or watching a video, as shown in Figure 2-21:

1. **Tap When Timer Ends.**

2. **Scroll to the very bottom of the screen and tap Stop Playing.**

3. **Tap Set.**

   The Time screen appears.

4. **Turn the rotor to set the length of time you want to enjoy your media.**

5. **Tap Start.**

   The countdown begins.

6. **Click the Home button.**

7. **Tap Music, Podcasts, or Videos depending on the type of media you want to listen to or watch.**

8. **Tap your selection.**

9. **Tap the Play button to begin playback.**

10. **Whatever you are listening to or watching is turned off when the timer stops.**

Figure 2-21: The Timer works as a regular timer on its own or as a sleep timer with iPhone's Music, Videos, and Podcasts apps.

Chapter 3: Tapping into Maps, Compass, Passbook, Weather, Calculator, and Stocks

In This Chapter

✓ Adjusting iPhone's location settings and services

✓ Seeking, finding, and sharing points of interest

✓ Getting directions

✓ Orienting yourself with Compass

✓ Checking in with Passbook

✓ Talking about the Weather

✓ Doing the math with Calculator

✓ Tracking investments with Stocks

Your iPhone comes with more than 20 apps installed. Some, like Phone, Mail, and Messages, help you communicate. Others, like Music, Video, and the Camera are about doing things for fun or leisure. The apps we talk about in this chapter are best described as information resources. Tools can help you do something you already do, but with more ease and sometimes better performance.

The apps in the first part of the chapter help you navigate to a destination, get your bearings, check-in at your location, and find out ahead of time how to dress for where you're going. What are we talking about? With Maps, just type in beginning and ending points and a mapped out route appears turning your iPhone into a GPS navigator that guides you to your destination.

The Compass app can be a handy ally when you want to know which way is north by northwest, whereas the Weather app can help you decide whether you ought wear a raincoat or apply sunscreen. Passbook keeps your boarding passes and store cards ready to use at the tap of a finger.

The last part of the chapter is dedicated to number crunching apps: Calculator and Stocks. Whether you want to tackle basic math problems or complicated scientific equations, Calculator helps you find the solutions. The Stocks app is a great tool for checking daily price quotes and tracking the historical performance of your investments.

Because the apps we cover here are stand-alone tools, don't feel obliged to read this chapter from start to finish (although we're always happy if you do). We go through them one by one and give you all the ins and outs, tips, and tricks so you get the most out of each app.

Adjusting iPhone's Location Settings and Services

Before we go into using Maps and Compass, we want to show you how to turn Location Services on. Without Location Services, Maps can give you directions from one address to another and the Compass can give you magnetic north. However, if you want to know where you are, or want true north, you have to turn on Location Services in Settings. Maps uses your location to give you the best local information available, whereas the Compass uses your location to identify true north. We give you a simple explanation about the difference between true north and magnetic north when we talk about Compass.

Other apps use Location Services too. For example, the Camera geotags photos, adding where the photo was taken to the date and time of the photo. (Everything about the Camera is explained in Book V, Chapter 1.) Reminders uses Location Services to process your location-based alerts. The first time an app wants to use Location Services, a notification message appears asking if you want to allow the app to use your location. You can choose yes or no. If you don't want the Camera to put your location on your photos, just tap no when Camera asks to use your Location. You can change these settings at any time, as explained in the third step here:

1. **Tap Settings on the Home screen.**

2. **Tap Privacy⟳Location Services, and then tap the toggle switch On.**

   The Location Services list, as seen in Figure 3-1, opens and displays all apps that can use your location in one way or another.

   When Location Services is on, its icon appears in the status bar. This is good to know because it consumes battery power, so don't leave it on if you're not using it.

3. **Turn Location Services on or off for each app.**

   The Location Services icon next to apps indicate the following:

- *Purple icon* the app has recently used your location.
- *Gray icon* the app has used your location in the last 24 hours.
- *Purple outlines icon* the app uses a geofence, which is a limit to the location and is used by apps like Reminders to alert you when you leave or arrive at a specified address.

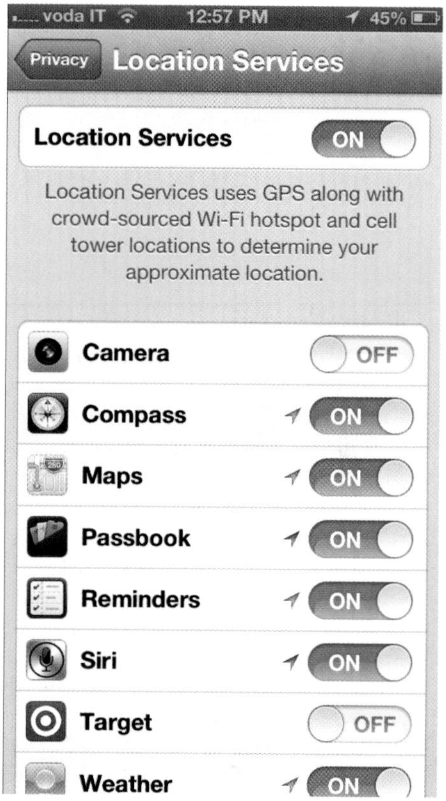

Location Services must be on for Find my iPhone to work. This should be a strong incentive to use a passcode to lock your iPhone. Otherwise, whoever "finds" your iPhone could just turn off Location Services and render Find My iPhone useless.

Getting There from Here with Maps

With Maps, you can do normal things that maps do — like find out where you are, if you're curious (or lost); or home in on a street address you want to go to. Or you can use Maps to accomplish loftier goals, like charting a course from your home to your vacation destination. What's more, with Maps, you can find rest stops, outlet malls, historic sites, and hotels along the way.

In this section, we tell you how to find your present location and how to find an address you know. Then we'll show you how to find a service, such as a restaurant or bookstore, near a location. We talk about how to get directions from one place to another, and finally, how to share or save the locations and directions you use.

Figure 3-1: You can turn Location Services on for specific apps.

Finding yourself

With Location Services on, Maps can tell you where you are. Tap Maps on the Home screen to open Maps, and then tap the Tracking button in the lower-left corner. If you have Location Services turned off, a notification message gives you the option of turning it on so Maps can find you.

Your exact location is the blue dot on the map, like you see in Figure 3-2. If there is a pulsing circle around the blue dot, your location is approximate; the smaller the circle, the more precise your exact (or nearly exact) location. If you're walking or driving, the blue dot moves along the map as you move along the road (or hiking trail or beach surf — you follow our point).

Change the orientation and size of the map by doing the following:

- Double-tap the Tracking button and a flashlight beam shines from the blue dot, lighting the way your iPhone is oriented. The Tracking button at the bottom of the screen changes to a flashlight icon, as in Figure 3-3.

- Use your thumb and forefinger to rotate the map.

- Tap the Compass button that appears in the upper-right corner to return to a north-facing orientation.

- Drag one finger around the screen to move the map up, down, or sideways.

- Double-tap with one finger to zoom in.

- Double-tap with two fingers to zoom out.

- Pinch and spread to zoom in and out.

Figure 3-2: The blue dot indicates your present location and follows your every move.

Maps combines the GPS (Global Positioning System), Wi-Fi, and cellular network data to determine your location and then uses TomTom and other mapping services to display locations and calculate routes.

Seeking and finding locations

Instead of finding a street name on a list, and then flipping a large unwieldy piece of thin, easily ripped paper, otherwise known as a map, to look for quadrant K-5, Maps lets you type in the address you seek. As fast as your Internet connection allows, the equivalent of quadrant K-5 appears on your iPhone screen. You can also find addresses from Contacts and from bookmarks that you set up in Maps. Follow these steps to map-folding freedom:

1. **Open Maps from the Home screen.**

2. **Tap the Spotlight search field at the top of the screen.**

   The keyboard opens.

3. **Type one of the following:**

   - *An address* in the form of a street name and number or an intersection, with the city and state or just the name of a city or town.

   - *A neighborhood or landmark*

   - *The name* of a person or business that's stored in your Contacts.

   A list of potential matches from Contacts and the Maps database appears; if you see the address you seek in the list, tap it to open a map showing that location.

4. **Tap the blue Search button in the bottom-right corner.**

   A red pin on the map indicates the address you seek. The address is written on a flag attached to the pin.

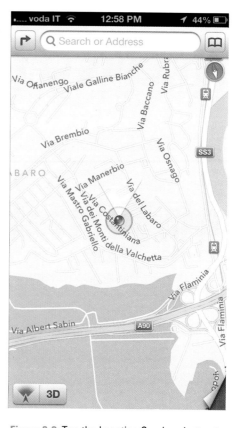

Figure 3-3: Tap the Location Services button to determine the direction you're facing.

To view and use an address you've recently used, select one from a Maps bookmark (see the next section for how to set up bookmarks), or open your Contacts list, do the following:

1. **Open Maps from the Home screen.**

2. **Tap the Bookmarks button to the right of the Spotlight search field.**

3. **Tap the Bookmarks button at the bottom left of the screen to use a bookmarked location.**

   A list of bookmarks opens.

   Or

   Tap the Recents button at the bottom in the center of the screen to use an address you've recently accessed.

   A list of recently used addresses opens.

   Or

   Tap the Contacts button at the bottom right of the screen to choose a person or business from Contacts.

   Your All Contacts list appears. Scroll through the list to open the Info screen that contains the address you seek.

4. **Tap the address you wish to use.**

   A map opens and a red pin indicates the address or location you're looking for.

You can blunder around an unfamiliar city looking for a place to eat until you stumble upon an appealing restaurant, or you can rely on Maps, which uses Yelp! to make suggestions for eateries and the like. Follow these steps to find sites and services quickly and easily:

1. **Open Maps from the Home screen.**

2. **Tap the Tracking button to find something near your current location, otherwise Maps searches for something near the last location you worked with.**

3. **Tap the Spotlight search field at the top of the screen.**

   The keyboard opens so you can type what you're looking for, say, *pizza* or *museums Prague*.

4. **Type your criteria in the Search field.**

   As you begin typing, Spotlight lists potential matches of locations (which have a red pin next to them) and words, which have a magnifying glass icon next to them.

5. **If your desired search word appears before you finish typing, you can tap that. If not, finish typing and then tap the Search button in the bottom-right corner.**

   Red pins appear on the matches in your vicinity or in the city you specified.

6. **Tap one of the pins.**

   A flag opens, giving the name and address of the location.

7. **Tap the arrow on the right end of the flag.**

   A Location screen opens that shows an aerial view of the map and the distance of the location from your current location (determined by Location Services), along with information like the phone number and address of the selected site, the site's web address, or a link to Yelp!, as seen in Figure 3-4. When available, you'll also see a Reviews and Photos button that give you reviews to read and photos to look at of the location.

   Tap the web page address to find out more about the location you found, such as a menu for the pizza

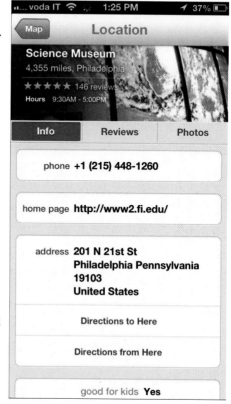

Figure 3-4: The Info screen shows information about a location you select.

parlor or special exhibits at the museum, or tap the phone number to call and make a reservation. (Maps also integrates with OpenTable to make reservations.)

If you have an iPhone 4S or later, press and hold the Home button and ask Siri to find whatever you're looking for for you.

Marking, saving, and sharing points of interest

Often you may find yourself using a couple of locations repeatedly as your starting point or destination. Instead of retyping the address each time you want to use those locations, you can set up bookmarks in Maps for those locations.

Maps bookmarks make it easy to return to frequently used addresses. Or, you may find a great restaurant that you want to add to Contacts and send to a fellow foodie friend. Here's how to bookmark, save, and share locations:

1. **Tap the flag attached to the pin, which indicates the address you want to bookmark, add to Contacts, or share with someone.**

   If there's no flag, tap the pin to open one.

2. **Tap the arrow on the right end of the flag.**

   An Info screen opens (refer to Figure 3-4).

3. **Tap one of the buttons at the bottom of the screen; you might have to scroll down to see them.**

   - **Add to Contacts** gives you the option of creating a new contact or adding the information to an existing contact. Choose the task you wish to do. See Book IV, Chapter 1 for complete details on using Contacts.

   - **Share Location** lets you send the information about this location to someone via Mail or Message or post the location to Twitter or Facebook (you must be logged in to your Twitter or Facebook account). Tap the button for your preferred means of sharing and the corresponding app opens: a New Message screen opens in Mail or Message, a Tweet opens in Twitter, or a status update appears for Facebook. See Book I, Chapter 4 to learn about Twitter and Facebook settings, Book III, Chapter 2 to learn about Message, and Book III, Chapter 4 to learn about Mail.

   - **Add to Bookmarks** brings up an Add Bookmark screen where you type in a name for this location's bookmark, and then tap Save.

 If you want a clean slate, you can clear your bookmarks by opening the list and tapping Edit, and then tap the red and white minus sign followed by the delete button, or simply swipe across the bookmarked address and tap Delete. Remove recent locations by tapping Recents and then tapping the Clear button.

Dropping a pin

If there's no pin on the location you want to save or share, tap the curled page button and tap Drop Pin. A purple pin shows up on the map with a flag that reads *Dropped Pin*. Why would you want to do that? Say you find yourself in front of a closed bookstore that has a first edition a friend of yours has been looking for, and you want to remember to tell your friend where this store is. Tap the Tracking button, the blue dot shows where you are. Drop a pin on your location; a flag shows the address of the pin. If the pin isn't exactly where you want it, zoom in on the map (double-tap with one finger), drag the pin, and then let go on the exact spot you want to mark. Tap the blue arrow button to display options you can tap to do things with the bookstore's location, like add the location to your Contacts or Bookmark the location, get directions, or share the location with your friend. To remove the pin, tap Remove Pin. That's exactly what happens when you return to the Map screen — out of sight, out of mind.

If you still prefer your maps on paper, tap the curled page button and then tap Print. See Book I, Chapter 2 for details about printing.

Getting directions

Rather than asking a stranger at a gas station where the intersection of First and Pine is, only to find he said "left" when he should've said "right," you can ask Maps to show you the way. With iOS 6 and an iPhone 4S or later, Maps provides voice-guided navigation just like a GPS navigator — one less gadget to cart around. Follow these steps for getting directions:

1. **Find an address in one of the three ways detailed previously.**

   The pin with the flag indicates the sought-after address.

2. **To get directions to the address from your current location, tap the Quick Driving Directions button on the left end of the pin's flag.**

   Or

   Tap the disclosure arrow on the right end of the flag and go to Step 3.

   Or

   Tap the Directions button in the upper-left corner and go to Step 4.

   An Info screen opens.

3. **You can obtain directions to and from this location by tapping one of the buttons:**

   Directions to Here: The Directions screen opens as seen in Figure 3-5. Current Location is the default for the starting point.

   Directions from Here: The Directions screen opens; however, Current Location is the default ending point or destination.

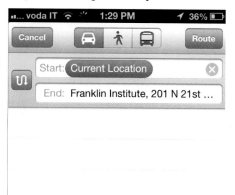

Figure 3-5: Fill in the starting point and destination you want on the Directions screen.

Book IV
Chapter 3

Tapping into Maps, Compass, Passbook, Weather, Calculator, and Stocks

Swap the Start and End points of the Directions by taping the Swap button.

4. **If you want to use your Current Location as your starting or ending point, tap the Route button in the bottom-right corner or tap in the field that contains Current Location.**

   Current Location is highlighted.

   1. Tap the circled X on the right end of the field to clear the field.

   2. Type in the address you wish to use.

   3. Tap the Next button on the bottom right.

      The cursor moves to the other field, which has the previously established address. You can change it with the keyboard if you want.

If you want directions and travel time for walking between destinations, tap the pedestrian button at the top of the screen. Tap the bus button to open the App Store and see a list of apps associated with the public transportation available for the area of your chosen directions, which you can download and use to search for a public transportation solution.

Figure 3-6: You have three map views to choose from.

5. **Tap the Route button in the bottom or upper-right corner.**

6. **The screen displays a map showing the route from your starting point to your destination, or from your destination back to your starting point, if you prefer.**

   The distance and estimated travel time are displayed above the map. If more than one route is available, Maps displays alternate routes, assigning a number to each. Tap the route you want to follow.

7. **Tap the curled page button to select and change how you see the map.**

   You see the screen shown in Figure 3-6.

TIP

If you ever wanted to take flight like a bird and swoop among the tall buildings of some of the world's most famous cities, tap the 3D or Flyover button next to the Tracking button to see the your standard view map in 3D or a hybrid or satellite view in Flyover mode (requires iPhone 4S or later). Zoom in until the 3D or Flyover button is active, as shown in Figure 3-7. The 3D or Flyover button is gray if the services are unavailable.

8. **Choose one of the following views:**

   - **Standard** shows you a map. This is the default view.

   - **Hybrid** shows the street names on a satellite view.

   - **Satellite** shows a satellite view.

9. **Tap Show Traffic.**

   This feature is only available in some locations.

   The roads on the map pulsate with red, yellow, green, or gray highlights to show you traffic conditions.

   - **Red** dots shows where traffic is heavy and stop and go.

   - **Orange** dots means traffic is moving slowly.

   - **Markers** indicate road work or an accident.

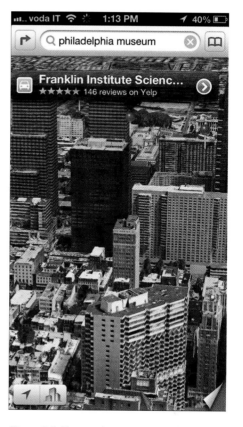

Figure 3-7: Flyover gives you a 3D satellite view.

10. **Tap the Start button in the upper-right corner.**

    If you have an iPhone 4S or later and an active Internet connection, point-to-point directions are dictated to you as you move along the route.

    In Map, Satellite, or Hybrid view, Maps zooms in to the first step of the list.

11. **Swipe across the green indications to move from one step to the next.**

    A circle indicates the intersection of the turn or road change at each step. The following taps give you different views along the way:

- Tap the Overview button to see the indications from starting point to destination.

- Tap the List button (next to the Tracking button in Overview) to see a list of the point-to-point directions, as shown in Figure 3-8.

- Tap any item in the list to see that point on the map.

Tap Overview, and then tap Resume to return to the point-to-point instructions.

12. **If you want to change your starting point or destination or the whole route, tap the End button in the upper-left corner and start over.**

Setting Maps' settings

You have a few choices of how Maps gives you directions. Go to Settings➪ Maps and tap your choices for the following:

- ✓ **Distances:** Choose miles or kilometers.

- ✓ **Map Labels:** Turn the toggle switch On to see labels in English or Off to see labels in the local language.

- ✓ **Label Size:** Choose between small, normal, and large for the labels on the map that identify street names, cities, and locations.

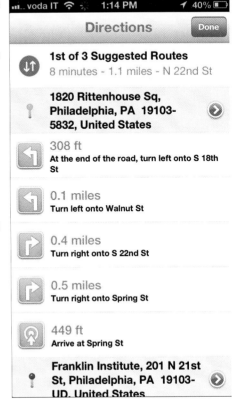

Figure 3-8: The List view shows you the written directions from your starting point to your destination.

On the Info screen, fields that appear are active and information that's available on your iPhone is filled in. For example, if an address you are using is associated with a person in Contacts for whom you also have a phone number and e-mail, those fields appear. If the location is unknown, only the Directions to Here and Directions from Here buttons appear, along with the Add to Contacts, Share Location, and Add to Bookmarks. Activate these options by tapping on the associated button:

- ✓ **Phone numbers:** Places a call to the phone number.

- ✓ **Addresses:** Returns you to the Maps screen.

- ✓ **Web page addresses:** Opens the webpage in Safari.

- **E-mail:** Creates a new Mail message.

- **Directions to Here and From Here:** Displays the Directions screen.

- **Add to Contacts:** Displays option to Create New Contact or Add to Existing Contact.

- **Share Location:** Displays option to create a new e-mail or message containing the location.

- **Add to Bookmarks:** Displays the Add Bookmark screen so you can save the address in Maps' bookmarks.

- **Report a Problem:** Lets you help Apple improve the Maps app. Tap this button and then choose from four problems: Information is incorrect; Pin is at incorrect location, Place does not exist, or My problem isn't listed. Tap the one you want, and then tap Next. Answer in the associated questions on the subsequent screen, and then tap Send.

Orienting Yourself with Compass

iPhone uses a built-in magnetic field sensor — a magnetometer — to give compass readings. The first thing we explain is how to calibrate the Compass to cancel the interference and get Compass back on course. We show you how to read the Compass, and explain the difference between true and magnetic north and how to select one or the other.

Calibrating your iPhone for greater accuracy

When you first open Compass, a notification message appears indicating that you should calibrate your iPhone. Any time iPhone detects some interference, usually something with a magnetic field or an electronic device like a cell phone or stereo, you see a message asking you to calibrate your phone. Simply move your iPhone in a big figure eight pattern a few times until the Compass itself appears.

Getting your bearing

Whether to determine the direction you're facing, for example to make sure your plants are on the east side of your house to get the morning sun, or find the direction you want to go, Compass is a great tool. After the Compass is calibrated, hold your iPhone (face-up, of course) so the back of your hand is parallel to the ground.

The red arrow on the Compass points north, the direction your iPhone is pointing is written in white above the compass. Move around, and the compass rotates and the headings change. When you have Location Services turned on, your geographic coordinates are displayed below the compass, as shown in Figure 3-9.

Book IV
Chapter 3

Tapping into Maps,
Compass, Passbook,
Weather, Calculator,
and Stocks

What's really helpful is that Compass links to Maps. If you want to see where you are on a map, tap the Location Services button in the bottom left corner. Maps opens and the blue dot indicates your location.

Double-tap the Location Services button to open the flashlight beam that shows you the direction you're facing. If you want to know the address, drop a pin and the address appears in the attached flag.

Choosing between true north or magnetic north

Compass gives accurate readings of both true north and magnetic north, and both are valid indications. True north, which is a GPS bearing linked to the geographical location of the North Pole, works when Location Services is turned on.

Magnetic north, on the other hand, depends on the Earth's natural magnetism, which changes based on your physical location. It works when Location Services is both on and off. Because magnetic north changes at different latitudes, it can be a few to many

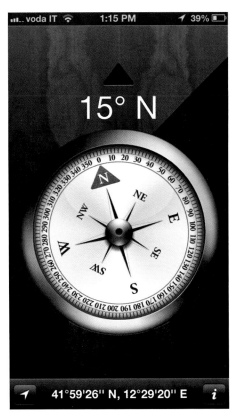

Figure 3-9: The Compass shows both the heading and the geographic coordinates for your location.

degrees different than true north and even south of your latitude. This difference is called *declination*. In some places, declination is less than one degree so it barely alters your bearings. Keep in mind, however, if you're hiking in the wilderness on a trail with 10 degrees of declination, those seemingly minor ten degrees can result in you being miles off course after several hours of continuous hiking. Technically speaking, to achieve the most accurate results, you have to know the actual declination degrees you're traversing for your current location to calculate the difference between magnetic north and true north. Localized trekking maps often have declination degrees on them, so you can adjust the orientation of your map when using true north. To choose between the two:

1. **Tap Compass on the Home screen.**

   The Compass opens (refer to Figure 3-9). When Location Services is on and GPS is available, you see your coordinates at the bottom of the screen.

2. **Tap the Information button in the lower-right corner.**

   The screen flips and you have the choice of True North (dimmed if Location Services is off) and Magnetic North.

3. **Tap your preferred north, and then tap Done in the upper-right corner.**

   The Compass screen returns.

Figure 3-10: The App Store neatly groups all Passbook-enabled apps together in one list.

Checking-in with Passbook

In the ongoing effort to eliminate paper, Passbook steps in to provide electronic versions of boarding passes, movie tickets, coupons, and store cards.

Obtaining passes

Before you can use Passbook, you have to install Passbook-enabled apps on your iPhone. Follow these steps to do that:

1. **Tap Passbook on the Home screen.**

2. **Tap the App Store button at the bottom of the screen.**

   A list of apps that support Passbook appears, as shown in Figure 3-10.

3. **Tap the Free button next to the Passbook apps that interest you to install the app on your iPhone.**

4. **Tap Install App.**

5. **Type in your Apple ID Password if requested.**

   The app is downloaded and the button now reads Open.

In addition to Passbook apps, you may receive e-mail with a link or find URLs on websites that download coupons (www.coupons.com has many) or special offers to Passbook. Tap these links and the associated barcode or qr-code is downloaded to Passbook, as shown in Figure 3-11. Show the coupon to the cashier when you check out to take advantage of the offer.

After you download one boarding pass, coupon, or store card to Passbook, you may not see the App Store button on the Passbook screen, and you have to go directly to the App Store to download Passbook-enabled apps.

Getting on board

The fun and practical side of Passbook is using the passes. When you're ready to use one of the Passbook-enabled apps, just tap the app on the Home screen and do one of the following:

- Tap the Add to Passbook banner and then tap the Add button on the coupon or follow the onscreen instructions to insert your username or number and password.

- For boarding passes, proceed with online check-in and then tap Download Boarding Pass to Passbook option, as shown in Figure 3-11. Figure 3-12 shows a Lufthansa boarding pass.

..... Vodafone.de 📶   00:47   88% 🔋

| Home | Info & Service | Entertainment |

Check-in > Flight overview

Choose "Resend mobile boarding pass" or change data below.

Passenger Data

1.   Barbarajane Boyd
     ◆ **** 4Y6

Flight Data

Flight Sun 30 September 12

19:25   Munich
21:00   Rome Fiumicino

LH 1850 / Economy

Barbarajane Boyd
Already checked-in
Seat: 11F

Display mobile boarding pass

Download Boarding Pass to Passbook

Figure 3-11: Passbook-enabled apps have banners or buttons to copy your card or boarding pass information into Passbook.

After the passes are in Passbook, you need only tap the appropriate one and scan it at the check-in counter or cash register. This means all you need is your passport and iPhone at the airport and when you reach the cash register at your favorite store, instead of shuffling a deck of store cards, just tap Passbook and then tap the appropriate card. In no time, you're on your way down the tarmac, points are added to your account, or discounts are applied to your purchase.

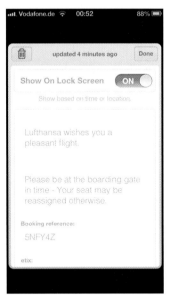

Figure 3-12: The front and back of a Lufthansa electronic boarding pass.

Managing passes

Most of the passes in Passbook have options for notifications as well as some information about how the pass works. Tap the Information button in the lower-right corner of the pass to see the "back side" of the pass, refer to Figure 3-12. You can choose to see the pass on the lock screen so when you get to the airport or store, the pass appears on your lock screen (as long as Location Services is on and you have a data connection). You can also eliminate a pass by tapping the Delete (the trash can) button in the upper-left corner of the pass.

Talking About the Weather

As much as our lives is conducted indoors, in offices, restaurants, shopping malls, cars, buses, and homes, we haven't completely lost interest in Mother Nature. Weather forecasts occupy a portion of every newscast, and there are countless weather websites, not to mention the numerous all-weather cable channels.

iPhone's Weather app is updated hourly and gives you the current temperature and the forecast for six days for cities across the country and around the world.

Adding, removing, and reorganizing cities

Weather uses Location Services to provide the forecast for your current location, but you may want to add other cities and locales too. Say you have to go on a multi-city book tour and want to know what the weather will be like in each city. You can add the cities you'll be going to and then quickly flip through each day to see whether to expect sunny skies in your upcoming stop. Follow these steps:

1. **Tap Weather on the Home screen.**

2. **Tap the Information button in the bottom right corner.**

   The screen as shown in Figure 3-13 opens.

3. **Tap the F or C button at the bottom of the page if you want to switch between Fahrenheit and Celsius temperature readings.**

4. **Tap the plus sign in the upper-left corner.**

5. **A screen opens with a search field and keyboard.**

6. **Type in the name or zip code of the city you want to add.**

   A list opens with possible matches.

7. **Tap the name of the city you want to add.**

   The city now appears in your list.

To delete a city from your list:

1. **Tap Weather on the Home screen.**

2. **Tap the Information button in the bottom-right corner.**

3. **Tap the minus sign to the left of the name.**

   A Delete button appears to the right of the name.

Figure 3-13: Add, delete, and reorder the cities you want Weather forecasts for.

4. **Tap the Delete button.**

   The city disappears from the list.

   If you tapped the minus sign by mistake, tap it again to cancel.

5. **Tap the Done button in the upper-right corner.**

   The weather screen returns.

 You can also determine the order you want to view the forecasts for each city. For example, you want to put the cities in the order that you'll be visiting them on your multi-city book tour. Touch and hold the reorder button, and then drag the city to the position on the list. Drag the names of the cities around until they are in the order you like.

Viewing current and upcoming conditions

After you've added and organized the cities and tapped Done, the weather screen returns, as shown in Figure 3-14. Each city on your list has its own weather forecast screen.

Flick left or right to move between screens. If you have Location Services on for the Weather app (Settings⇨ Privacy⇨Location Services), the first screen shows the forecast for your current location. The white dots at the bottom of the screen tell you how many cities you have forecasts for. Notice that the Location Services icon appears to the left of the dots.

The background is blue when it's daytime in that city and black when it's nighttime. On an iPhone 5, the current temperature is the biggest number at the top of the page; then you see the day's hourly forecast running horizontally across the middle and a list of the next five-days' forecast with the weather symbols we're used to: sunny, partly sunny, cloudy, thunderstorms, and so on. Swipe the hourly forecast left or right to see the conditions earlier or later in the day. On an iPhone 4S

Figure 3-14: Weather gives you the current temperature and a six-day forecast.

**Book IV
Chapter 3**

Tapping into Maps,
Compass, Passbook,
Weather, Calculator,
and Stocks

or earlier, swipe down on the daily forecast to open an hour by hour forecast for the next 12 hours.

You can add your local weather to the Notification Center by tapping Settings⊏>Notifications⊏>Weather Widget and then tap the Notification Center option on. When you pull down the Notification Center, you'll see the local forecast. Tap on the forecast in the Notification Center and the Weather app opens.

If you want more information, tap the Yahoo! button in the bottom-left corner. This opens the Yahoo! weather page in Safari and gives you more detailed weather information such as humidity, wind, and sunrise and sunset times along with links to websites with news and other information about that city.

Doing the Math with Calculator

The Calculator app on your iPhone is really two calculators: a basic four-function calculator that you use for addition, subtraction, multiplication, and division, and a scientific calculator that is capable of performing trigonometric calculations, logarithms, square roots, and percentages.

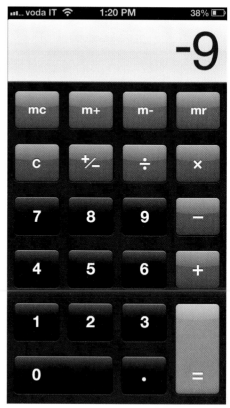

Doing basic addition, subtraction, multiplication, and division

Even if you remember your times tables, there are times when you reach for a calculator and you don't have to reach any farther than your iPhone. The basic four-function calculator opens when you tap Calculator. Follow these steps:

1. **Tap Calculator on the Home screen or you might find it in the Utilities folder on the Home screen.**

   The Calculator opens, as shown in Figure 3-15.

Figure 3-15: The four-function Calculator adds, subtracts, multiplies, and divides.

2. **Tap the numbers and operations you want to perform.**

   A white outline appears around the operation key you tap to remind you which operation is active.

You can copy and paste numbers from the Calculator results display to another app by pressing and holding on the display until the Copy/Paste button appears. You can also paste a number from another app into the calculator display to use it in a calculation. See Book I, Chapter 3 to learn about editing functions and commands.

The four buttons just below the display are for memory commands:

- **mc** clears any numbers you have in memory.

- **m+** adds the number on the display to the number in memory.

- **m-** subtracts the number on the display from the number in memory.

- **mr (memory replace)** uses the number you put in memory in your current calculation. The button is outlined in white when a number is stored.

Switching to a scientific view

Most cell phones have calculators today, but iPhone offers a full-function scientific calculator too. To open the scientific calculator, turn your iPhone to landscape view, as seen in Figure 3-16. (If you have locked your iPhone in Portrait view, this won't work until you unlock it: double-tap the Home button and swipe right to find the Orientation Lock button.)

You may not need the trigonometric and parenthetical grouping functions; however, the percentage function, which can quickly calculate discounts and markups, is useful even for non-astrophysicists.

If you have two vendors vying for your business and Vendor A offers a 3.475 percent discount over Vendor B's offer, you can quickly determine how much that percentage means in dollar and cents savings.

Type in the total amount and then the minus sign, followed by the amount of the percentage off and the percent sign. A quick press of the equals sign, and you have the final, discounted price: for example, 45000 — 3.475% = 43,436.25.

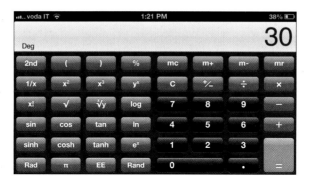

Figure 3-16: Turning your iPhone to landscape view opens the scientific calculator.

Tracking Investments with Stocks

Whether you have a single mutual fund or a sizeable portfolio managed by a financial advisor, keeping an eye on your investments is usually a good idea. And that's exactly the idea behind iPhone's Stocks app, a simple yet powerful tool you can tap into to display and track activity for the stocks and funds you're interested in for the time interval you want. First we show you how to add the companies you want to watch and put them in an order that you like. Next, we show you how to manage the viewing options Stocks offers.

Adding, deleting, and reordering stocks, funds, and indexes

Stocks comes with the U.S. (Dow Jones, NASDAQ, S&P 500) and foreign (FTSE/UK, DAX/German, HSI/Hong Kong, N225/Japan) index listings along with Apple, Google, Yahoo!, and Vanguard Natural Resources share activity already specified, as seen in Figure 3-17.

The first thing you want to do is add your personal stock or fund holdings or those that you're interested in watching for potential investments and delete any loaded ones that don't interest you. Here are the steps to follow:

1. **Tap Stocks on the Home screen.**

2. **Tap the Information button in the bottom-right corner.**

   The Stocks screen opens.

3. **Tap the plus sign button in the upper-left corner.**

   A search field opens with a keyboard.

4. **Type a company name or a stock identification code.**

   Stocks searches and a list of possible matches appears.

5. Tap the stock you wish to add to your list.

The screen returns to the list. The stock or fund you chose is added to the bottom of the list.

6. Repeat Steps 3, 4, and 5 to add as many stocks as you wish.

7. Tap the Done button in the upper-right corner.

The current price screen returns.

To delete a stock or index from your list:

1. Tap Stocks on the Home screen.

2. Tap the Information button in the bottom-right corner.

3. Tap the minus sign to the left of the name.

A delete button appears to the right of the name.

4. Tap the Delete button.

The stock or index disappears from the list.

If you tapped the minus sign by mistake, tap it again to cancel.

5. Tap the Done button in the upper-right corner.

The current price screen returns.

Figure 3-17: Stocks shows market activity for U.S. and foreign indexes as well as individual corporate share prices.

You can arrange the stocks and indices in any order you want, such as putting those you're most interested in at the top.

Touch and hold the reorder button, and then drag the stock to the position on the list. Drag the names of the stocks around until they are in the order you like.

The three buttons at the bottom of the Stocks information page let you choose how you view market fluctuations: by percentage changes, by price changes, or by market capitalization.

The market fluctuations appear on a green background if there's been a price increase and on red if there's been a decrease. The information lags about 20 minutes behind actual market activity.

Scrolling through views and news

After you establish the stocks and indices you want to follow, you may want to look at some historic data or see what the press has said about that company today.

Referring to Figure 3-17, the screen is divided into two zones: The top holds the list of stocks and indices you follow (six appear at a time, but you can scroll to see the other companies on your list).

The lower zone shows information about whichever stock or index you select from the upper zone. This zone scrolls left to right. After the price activity section, there's a graph that shows historic activity from one day up to two years. Scroll to the next screen to see a vertically scrollable list of news stories related to the stock or index highlighted in the upper zone — tap a news headline to open the complete article in Safari or tap and hold to add the article to Reading List. That's one information-packed screen!

Turn on the Stock Widget in Settings⟳Notifications and a ticker tape of your chosen markets, stocks, and funds appears in the Notification Center.

Monitoring investment performance over time

But wait, there's more. Go back to the graph that shows historic activity. There are seven time intervals at the top. Tap any of those intervals and the graph expands or contracts to show price fluctuations from today back to the date that corresponds with the interval you chose.

To display a more detailed view, turn your iPhone to landscape view, as in Figure 3-18. The graph for the interval you were viewing in portrait view appears with the greater detail that increased landscape size allows. This screen is interactive. For example, if you choose the one week view, touch on a day and a yellow vertical line shows the price for the day you are on.

Touch and drag the yellow line left and right and you see price fluctuations at intervals throughout the day. If you knew an announcement was made at a certain time on a certain day, you could see how soon after the announcement a change in the share price appeared. In the three month, six month, and one year views, the detail gives the daily closing price; in the two year view, the daily closing price is given for every other day; in the five year view, every year; and in the 10 year view, every other year.

Touch and hold on the screen to bring up the yellow line, and then drag left and right to see the price for different days. If you put two fingers on the screen at once, two vertical, yellow lines bracket a time interval and the share price change in that period is shown.

Move your fingers in and out to shorten and lengthen the time interval. In landscape view, when you flick from left to right, you see the graph for the same interval for each of the stocks and indexes on your personalized list.

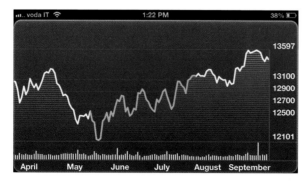

Figure 3-18: Turn Stocks to landscape view and the share price fluctuation graph becomes interactive.

Book IV
Chapter 3

Tapping into Maps,
Compass, Passbook,
Weather, Calculator,
and Stocks

Chapter 4: Creating and Sharing Notes and Voice Memos

In This Chapter

✏ **Creating, viewing, managing, and sharing notes**

✏ **Adjusting Notes settings**

✏ **Syncing existing Notes**

✏ **Recording, playing, managing, and sharing voice memos**

✏ **Syncing Voice Memos with iTunes**

*A*re you the note-taking type who goes through little yellow sticky notes faster that a chimp in a peanut factory? Do ideas pop into your head that you don't remember later because those sticky notes and a pen aren't within reach? And even if they were close at hand, you wouldn't be able to use them, anyway, because you're doing something like driving or working out?

If you answered yes to any or all of those questions, you're in good company. This chapter is all about using two of your iPhone's most useful apps — Notes and Voice Memos. Using this dynamic duo, you can capture your every thought on the fly, as neatly typed out notes that you type or dictate to Siri, or as recorded audio files captured using your iPhone's built-in mic (or your stereo headphone's mic) that you can listen to later.

In this chapter, we talk about syncing your notes and voice recordings with your computer using iCloud or iTunes, and we describe which computer programs you can use to access and share those notes or voice recordings.

Taking Note of Notes

Notes is a super-simple app you can use to keep track of lists, ideas, and any other kind of note you'd normally scribble down on a sticky pad or cocktail napkin. Notes you create are stored on your iPhone and, optionally, synced with your computer and other iOS devices through iCloud, Gmail, or another IMAP account.

To get started, tap the Notes app icon on the Home screen to launch Notes. The main Notes screen shows a list of any notes already saved in Notes, as shown in Figure 4-1.

You may see one or more notes listed even if you hadn't previously created notes using the Notes app. That's because Notes displays any notes that are copied to your iPhone when you sync your iPhone with iTunes (if you have that option turned on). Notes can also come from any e-mail accounts set up on your iPhone if you've turned on the Notes option in those e-mail accounts' settings. When the Notes option is turned on, you see an Accounts button appear in the upper-left corner of the Notes window. We write about syncing Notes and e-mail accounts in the section "Evaluating Your Notes Sync Options" later in this chapter.

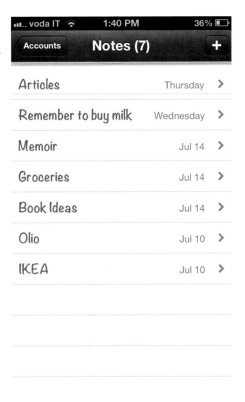

Figure 4-1: A list of notes you have saved in the Notes app.

Creating a new note

Tap the plus sign (+) button to create a new note. The keyboard appears, ready to capture your brilliant thoughts, as shown in Figure 4-2.

Turning your iPhone sideways displays the landscape mode keyboard, which can help increase your typing speed and accuracy — although it does decrease the number of lines you see as you write your note. If the wider keyboard doesn't appear when you turn your iPhone sideways, double-click the Home button

Figure 4-2: Typing with a narrow focus, or a wider point of view.

and flick the bottom of the screen to the right, and then tap the orientation lock button to unlock the orientation lock feature.

Tap Done to save your note and hide the keyboard.

Tap Notes to return to the notes list.

Press and hold the Home button to activate Siri. When Siri is ready, just say "create a note" and when asked, dictate your note.

Searching and managing your Notes list

Notes are listed in chronological order, with the newest (or most recently edited) note appearing at the top of the list, and the least recently modified note relegated to the bottom of the list. Notes titles are automatically generated based on the first 30 characters of each note's first line; if you enter a return in the first line, only the word (or words) before the return appear in the title.

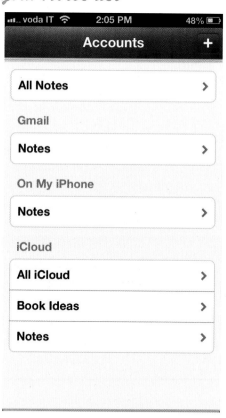

Figure 4-3: Accounts displays e-mail accounts for which you have Notes turned on.

When viewing the Notes list, you can do the following:

✔ Swipe left or right across a note title to display the Delete button, and then tap Delete to delete the note.

✔ Tap Accounts, (refer to Figure 4-1), to display any of the notes you sync with iCloud or e-mail accounts for which you turned on the Notes sync setting in Settings⇨Mail, Contacts, Calendars. When viewing the Accounts list, as shown in Figure 4-3, you can do the following:

• Tap All Notes to display a list of all of your notes saved and synced with all of your e-mail accounts.

• Tap an e-mail account name to display only the notes stored and synced with that specific e-mail account.

• Tap a folder in the iCloud section to see Notes in that folder. (This option is available if you use Notes on a Mac with iCloud.)

- Tap the plus sign (+) to create a new note that will be saved in your default e-mail account's Notes data when you press Done to save the note.

✔ Tap plus sign (+) to create a new note.

✔ Tap a note to view the note or do other things with the note.

✔ When viewing a list of notes or a note itself, tap the status bar at the top of iPhone's screen or drag your finger down the list to reveal the Search field, and then type in the first few characters of whatever you're looking for to display the titles of any notes matching your search criteria; tap the note title to view that note.

If you have selected Notes in Settings⇨General⇨Spotlight Search, any searches you perform from the Spotlight Search Home screen will search in Notes too.

Browsing, editing, deleting, and e-mailing Notes

Notes you create can contain regular and accented letters, numbers, and symbols (in other words, any of the alphanumerical stuff you can type with the keyboard), but not pictures, audio clips, videos, or other non-alphanumeric information.

When viewing a note, as shown in Figure 4-4, you can do the following:

✔ To add more text or edit a note, tap where you want to begin typing or touch and hold where you want to begin editing, and then type or edit to your heart's content. (See Book I, Chapter 3 for editing tips.)

✔ Shake your iPhone when the keyboard is displayed to display the Undo Typing message; tap Undo to, well, undo what you just did. Shake again to display the Redo Typing option and tap Redo to redo what you undid.

✔ Tap the left and right arrow buttons to flip to the previous or next note.

Back   Action   Delete   Forward

Figure 4-4: Take action or delete your note.

✔ Tap the Delete button (the trashcan) to delete your note.

✔ Tap the Action button to print or copy your note or send the note in an e-mail or message, as shown in Figure 4-5, and then

- Begin typing the name of the person you want to send the note to; a list of suggested recipients saved in Contacts appears. Tap the one you want to select, or continue typing in the intended recipient's e-mail address if it isn't one you have saved in Contacts.

- Add any additional recipients to the To field (or Cc/Bcc fields if you chose e-mail) if you want to send your note to more than one person.

If you've set up more than one e-mail account on your iPhone, tap the Cc/Bcc: to display the hidden From: field. Tap the From: field to display a list of all your e-mail accounts, and then tap the one you want to use to send your message.

Figure 4-5: Print or share the contents of your note.

- Edit or add any additional text to the Subject field and/or in the body of the e-mail or message if you want.

- Tap Send to send your e-mail or message.

Changing the Notes font

To change the Notes font, tap Settings (from the Home screen), and then tap Notes to display your font choices (three at the time of this writing), as shown in Figure 4-6. Tap the choice you like the most.

If you have activated several keyboards for different languages, when you choose a symbol or line-based language such as Japanese, the line width used by Notes changes automatically to use a finer pen that accommodates the lines and symbols. Even when you switch back to a letter-based language, the typeface remains with fine pen writing.

If the Default Account option appears beneath the Font list, that means at least two (or more) of your e-mail accounts are already configured to sync with Notes. Tap Default Account to display those e-mail accounts, and then choose the account you want Notes to use to sync new notes you create. You won't see the Default Account option if none or only one of your e-mail accounts is configured to sync with Notes.

TIP

If you want to store some Notes only on your iPhone, create at least one note before turning Notes on in iCloud (or turn Notes off in iCloud, create a note, and then turn it back on). You then see an On My iPhone section in the Accounts list (refer to Figure 4-3) and you can make this the default account if you want in the Notes Settings.

We write about syncing your notes with your e-mail accounts, and with e-mail programs on your computer, in the next section.

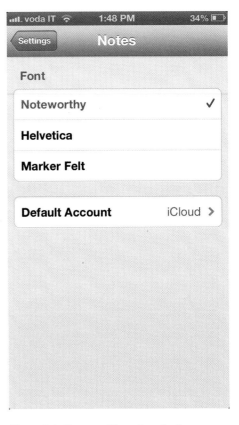

Figure 4-6: Choose a Notes font that's more your type.

Evaluating your Notes sync options

Notes you choose to sync with iCloud appear on your computer and your other iOS devices. Those you sync with your e-mail accounts appear on both your iPhone and on your computer's e-mail program (Outlook, Google Mail, or Yahoo!). If you are using a Mac OS prior to Mountain Lion, Notes will continue to sync with Mail.

You can sync your iPhone's notes two different ways, and understanding these ways can help you choose the best method for you:

  ✓ Using iCloud to sync Notes to all your devices, including your iPhone, your computer, and any other iOS 5 or later devices like iPad or iPod touch. Go to Settings⟶iCloud and tap the switch by Notes to On.

We write about using iCloud to sync your Notes and other information in Book II, Chapter 1.

✔ Syncing Notes with your e-mail accounts. Go to Settings⇨Mail, Contacts, Calendars, and then tap the account you want to sync Notes with. Tap the switch next to Notes On (see Figure 4-7) to automatically sync your notes over-the-air. AOL, Gmail, Yahoo!, and Hotmail e-mail accounts all offer the option to turn on the Note sync option, but syncing with any of them is a one-way way affair. When you log in to each respective e-mail service's website, you see notes you created on your iPhone; however, notes you create on those websites don't get synced back to your iPhone. We write about configuring e-mail accounts in Book III, Chapter 4.

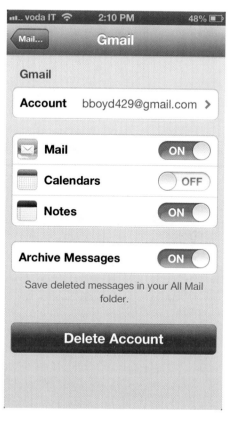

Figure 4-7: Notes can sync with your iPhone's e-mail accounts.

Speaking of Voice Memos

Once upon a time, people carried portable cassette tape recorders to capture the spoken word and other audible stuff like interviews, live music events, and baby's first words ("Mama?" "Dada?" "iPhone?"). Thanks to iPhone's Voice Memos app, you can quickly and easily record, listen to, edit, and share those kinds of out-loud sounds without the hassle of juggling clunky cassette tapes.

And so, because we're big believers in the adage "actions speak louder than words," rather than listening to more introductory words by yours truly, why don't you act on recording and listening to *your* spoken words and other sounds with Voice Memos?

Speaking of your first action: Tap Voice Memos on the Home screen (it may be in the Utilities folder) to launch the app, as shown in Figure 4-8.

Recording voice memos

Although that big silver thing that takes over most of the main Voice Memos screen *looks* like a mic, it doesn't actually record your voice or other sounds.

That function is handled by your iPhone's built-in mic, or by the mic built into the EarPods that came with your iPhone if you have those plugged in.

Other mic-enabled options for recording audio with Voice Memos include external mics designed to plug into your iPhone's Lightning or Dock Connector, and wireless Bluetooth headsets and headphones that let you cut the proverbial cord altogether (thus freeing your hands for flailing, gesticulating, or whatever).

Figure 4-8: Step up to the mic.

At bottom center of the Voice Memos screen is the sound level meter; the needle twitches in response to any sounds the mic picks up, whether you're actually recording those sounds. (Go on, don't be shy, say "hello" or "testing one, two, three" to your iPhone right now to see the meter in action.)

For optimal recording quality, Apple recommends a recording level between the -3 and 0-decibels (dBs) zone. Translation: As you're speaking, move your iPhone (or headphone mic) closer or farther from your mouth, or lower or raise your voice, or use a combination of both, to try to keep the recording level meter needle in or as close to that optimal-quality sweet spot between the black 3 and the red 0.

On the meter's left is the record button, and on the right, the voice memos list button. Both buttons change to other buttons when you begin recording, as you will see in the next breath.

To record, pause, continue, and stop recording a voice memo:

✔ Tap the record button or press the center button on your EarPod or headphone controls to begin recording your voice memo.

When you begin recording, four things happen at once to let you know your live recording session is underway: A single-chime sound plays, the record button changes to a pause button, the voice memos list button changes to a stop button, and a pulsing red banner with a recording length timer appears at the top of the screen, as shown in Figure 4-9.

If you go to the Home screen, switch to another app, or lock your iPhone while you're recording a voice memo (or you pause a memo you're recording), the red banner stays stuck at the top of the screen so you don't forget about your recording, as shown in Figure 4-10. Tap the red banner to return to Voice Memos.

Figure 4-9: Live, from New York! (Or wherever you are!)

Figure 4-10: Voice Memos can keep recording even if you switch apps or lock your iPhone.

Book IV
Chapter 4

Creating and Sharing Notes and Voice Memos

✔ To stop or pause recording, do one of the following:

- Tap the stop button or press the center button on your EarPods or headphone to stop recording.

  A double-chime sound plays, the left and right buttons return to their original functions, and the red banner and recording length timer disappear.

- Tap the pause button to pause recording.

  The red banner stops pulsing and the recording length timer freezes in time, the left button changes to the record button, and the right button changes to the memo list button.

✔ To resume or stop a paused recording, do one of the following:

- Tap record to resume recording your voice memo.

  Recording resumes, as in the very first bullet of this section; you can repeat this process of pausing and resuming your recording as many times as you want until you decide to tap stop, or press the center button on your EarPods, to end your recording session.

- Tap the voice memos list button to stop recording your voice memo.

  A double-chime sound plays, and then the voice memos list appears and your newly recorded voice memo begins playing — and what lucky timing, at that. The voice memos list is what we tell you about in the next section.

You *shouldn't* hear the chime and double-chime sound effects that play when you start and stop recording a memo if iPhone's ring/silent switch is switched to silent mode. We say *shouldn't* because in some countries or regions, the recording sound effects play even when the ring/silent switch is set to silent. Our guesstimate as to why those sound effects may still be heard even when iPhone is set to be quiet? To offer some kind of audible warning to anyone within earshot that you may be recording anything they say. (However, whether anything hypothetical persons may say can or will be held against them in a court of law, is not for me to say. We can only speculate.)

Listening to voice memos

The voice memo list displays your voice memos in chronological order, from newest to oldest, refer to Figure 4-11. To access the voice memo list from the main Voice Memos screen, tap the voice memo list button (refer to Figure 4-8). To return to the main Voice Memos screen, tap the Done button.

To listen to, pause, and control play of a voice memo:

- Tap a voice memo in the list to select the voice memo, and then tap the Play button that appears to the left of the voice memo's title.

  As your voice memo begins playing, the scrubber bar with a scrolling playhead button appears, and the play button turns into a pause button.

- Tap the Pause button to pause listening to your voice memo, as shown in Figure 4-11, and then press Play to resume.

- Drag the playhead left or right in the scrubber bar while the voice memo is playing or paused to move backward or forward.

- Tap the Speaker button if you want to hear your voice memos out loud through your iPhone's built-in speaker. (By default, your voice memos play through your iPhone's receiver speaker, or through your headphones, if you have those plugged in.)

Figure 4-11: Pausing a voice memo.

- To select another voice memo, tap the one you want to listen to, and then use the play, pause, and scrubber playhead button as previously described to listen to your selected voice memo.

To delete a voice memo:

1. **Tap a voice memo to select it, and then tap the Delete button.**

   The Delete Voice Memo and Cancel buttons appear, giving you a moment to consider whether you really want to delete your selected voice memo.

2. **Tap Delete Voice Memo to say goodbye to your selected voice memo, or tap Cancel if you've had a sudden change of heart and you want to keep your voice memo.**

Deleting a voice memo instantly erases the voice memo from your iPhone. But that doesn't necessarily mean the voice memo is gone forever — if you've turned on the voice memos sync option in iTunes, which copies all of your recorded voice memos to your computer's iTunes library and stores them there even if you later decide to delete those synced voice memos from your iPhone. Of course, voice memos you record and then delete before syncing with iTunes are gone forever. We tell you how to sync your voice memos with iTunes later in this chapter.

Naming, trimming, and sharing voice memos

Voice memos are automatically titled with the time the voice memo was recorded. Beneath the title, you'll see the voice memo's recording date, and the recording length number to the right is the voice memo's length. Tap the disclosure arrow button on a voice memo in the voice memo list to display the Info screen for your selected voice memo, as shown in Figure 4-12.

To close the Info screen and return to the voice memos list, tap the Voice Memos button.

The Info displays the full date you recorded your voice memo, and buttons you can tap to do the following things with your selected voice memo:

✔ Tap the big wide button surrounding your voice memo's name to display a list of ready-made labels, and then tap the label that best describes your voice memo, as shown in Figure 4-13. To create a label of your own, tap Custom, type a descriptive name for your voice

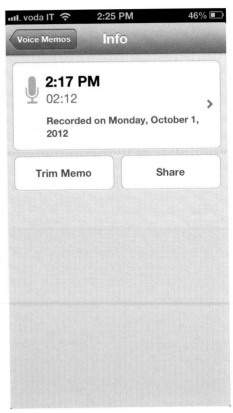

Figure 4-12: The Info screen lets you do more with your voice memos.

memo like "Lovely Linda Interview" or "Tweeting Sparrows," and then tap the Label button to save your custom label name. Tap Info to return to the Info screen.

✔ Tap Trim Memo to display the trim tool, and then drag the left or right edge of the guide toward the center to set the length you want to trim from either (or both) end, as shown in Figure 4-14. Tap the tiny play button to the left of the trim tool to hear a preview of your selection, and then make any necessary adjustments to your selection. When you're pleased with your cutting work, tap Trim Voice Memo button to save your edited selection (or tap Cancel if you change your mind and you don't want to trim your voice memo after all).

After you trim a voice memo, the part you deleted is gone forever, so be sure you want to trim before you save the trimmed memo; otherwise, tap Cancel to keep your entire voice memo.

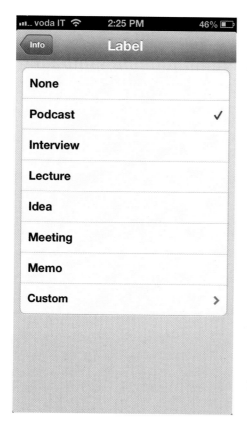

Figure 4-13: Assigning a descriptive label to a voice memo.

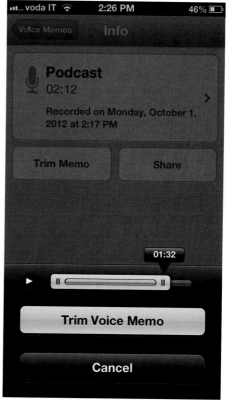

Figure 4-14: Trimming a voice memo down in size.

Book IV
Chapter 4

Creating and
Sharing Notes and
Voice Memos

✔ Tap Share, and then tap Email or Message to choose your preferred method of delivery. A new e-mail or MMS or iMessage containing an audio file icon of your voice message appears in the body of your new e-mail or message, as shown in Figure 4-15.

You can also e-mail the voice memo to yourself and avoid iTunes syncing.

If a message saying your voice memo file is too large to send appears, you need to trim your voice memo using the trim tool (see the previous bullet) before you can try sending your message again.

Fill in the To: field with the name of the person (or persons) you want to send your voice memo to. You can add a subject line, type a greeting or other text in the body of your message, and insert a photo or video as explained in Book III, Chapters 2 and 4, if you wish. Tap Send to send your voice memo message.

Figure 4-15: Send your voice memo in an e-mail or message.

Selecting a voice memo and then tapping the Share button on the voice memos list screen takes you to the same options we describe previously for sending your voice memo as an e-mail or MMS or iMessage.

Syncing voice memos with iTunes

Capturing voice memos on the fly is handy for remembering things you don't want to forget. After you've dealt with whatever your voice memos remind you to do, you can then delete those voice memos from your iPhone.

Other voice memos, like a gang of friends and family singing "Happy Birthday" at your mom's 80th, or an interview with a fast-talking politician you recorded for an article you're writing, may be ones you want to (or must) keep for personal or professional reasons.

But you probably don't need to keep those kinds of audio files on your iPhone, where they consume storage space you'd rather free up to store other stuff like every song ever sung by your favorite musical artist (or perhaps voice memos of *you* singing every song ever sung by said favorite artist).

The solution? Sync any voice memos you want to keep with iTunes on your computer, and those voice memos remain safe and sound, so to speak, until you want (or need) to hear them anew.

Because we give you the full lowdown on how to pick and choose the kinds of information and files (including voice memos) you want to sync between your iPhone and your computer using iTunes in Book II, Chapter I, we won't repeat ourselves here. Not completely, anyway. We would be remiss if we didn't take a moment to at least mention a few points worth knowing about when you're thinking about syncing your voice memos with iTunes, including

- ✓ iTunes automatically creates a playlist named (drum roll, please . . .) Voice Memos on your computer, and that's where you can track down new, not so new, and downright ancient voice memos you recorded and synced with iTunes syncs.

- ✓ Voice memos you delete from your iPhone remain safely backed up in your iTunes library.

- ✓ If you delete a voice memo from iTunes that you have saved on your iPhone that voice memo will be deleted from your iPhone the next time you sync with iTunes.

You can use a voice memo as a ringtone by trimming the file to shorter than 30 seconds, e-mail it to yourself then change the file extension to .m4r and open it. The file will import into iTunes as a ringtone, which you can then sync to your iPhone. If you use a Mac, you can trim and edit the file in GarageBand and save it as a ringtone.

Book V
Letting iPhone Entertain You: Photos, Video, Music, and More

The 5th Wave   By Rich Tennant

"You ever notice how much more streaming media there is than there used to be?"

today's announcement. The audience marveled at the device's accuracy. There wasn't a single interpretation error, no "there" for "their" nor "cat" for "cap."

Peter withdrew a small lid from his back pocket and turned it around to reveal a tiny keyboard. He snapped it onto the unit and finished his message by tapping out his thanks. "This is for all those holdouts who insist they want a keyboard," he said. "Or a wireless digital phone," he added, and the audience went nuts when he punched in the phone number of a local pizza shop. A moment later a voice came on the line and asked him what kind of pizza he wanted. "Sorry, wrong number," he said, and hung up.

When it comes to photos, music, videos, podcasts, and interactive learning your iPhone is a hands-down winner. This minibook is chock full of how-tos for capturing, viewing, listening, and sharing media. Chapter 1 focuses on using the front and back cameras for taking still photos and videos. We give you tips for using the flash and digital zoom and explain the iPhone's photo and video editing options. Chapters 2 and 3 are all about music and audio. Chapter 2 takes you through the iTunes Store, where you can shop for music, movies, and audiobooks. . In Chapter 3, we present your iPhone as an iPod — using your iPhone to listen to and manage your music and audio collection, including things you download and stream from the Podcasts catalog. We move through video and iTunes U in the last chapter, explaining how to watch videos from the iTunes Store and all about enrolling in the continuing education extravaganza of iTunes U.

Chapter 1: Capturing and Sharing Photos and Videos with Camera

In This Chapter

- ✏ Snapping a picture with Camera
- ✏ Taking in the panorama
- ✏ Focusing, flashing, and zooming
- ✏ Turning the lens on yourself
- ✏ Recording a video with Camera
- ✏ Editing photos and trimming videos
- ✏ Storing and sharing with Photo Stream

The Camera app on your iPhone takes advantage of two objective lenses on your iPhone. One is the 8-megapixel still and video camera (on iPhone 4S and 5; 5-megapixel on iPhone 4) on the back that takes regular photos and 240-degree panoramic photos plus high definition videos, both with LED flash. The other is the 1.2-megapixel still camera that also shoots 720 pixel HD video on the front of your iPhone so you can take self-portraits and use FaceTime, your iPhone's video chat app. All the functions work in portrait and landscape position.

In this chapter, we explain how to use the still and video cameras, front and back. We talk about focusing, flashing — er, using the flash — and zooming in on your subject. After you capture photos and videos in Camera, you probably want to edit them, so we show you how to use the Photos app to enhance the photo quality, crop photos, trim videos, and cure that terrible red-eye disease. At the end of the chapter, we give you all your options for sharing your photos and videos via iCloud's Photo Stream feature, e-mail, text messages, Twitter, YouTube, and good old-fashioned slideshows and printing.

Camera Features and Controls

The first time you open Camera, a message appears asking if Camera can use your location. Tapping OK lets Camera geotag your location. A geotag uses GPS (Global Positioning System), Wi-Fi, and cellular access to add the longitude and latitude of the location of the photos and videos you shoot. (In some situations, say, if you're standing in a lead-walled bunker, your iPhone may not be able to activate geotagging.) Like the date and time, a geotag is a piece of information about your photo that's kept in the metadata; that is, data you don't see that describes your data. You can then sort and search for photos based on the location — more about that later in this chapter.

If at some point you want to turn geotagging off, tap Home⮕Settings⮕Privacy⮕Location Services. You can turn Location Services off completely or turn Location Services off for specific apps, in this case, Camera.

Previewing through the viewfinder

We think the easiest way to learn about taking photos and videos with your iPhone is to snap a few shots or capture a few minutes of video. First, we show you the three simple steps for taking a photo, and then we explain the basics of capturing video. Because the tools are the same for both photos and videos, we go through the options that help perfect your photo and video skills.

The two basic "parts" of any camera that you need to know are the viewfinder and the shutter button. Unlike traditional cameras where you close one eye and put your open eye up to the viewfinder to see and frame your subject, your iPhone doesn't have a viewfinder. Instead, you point your iPhone at your subject and then look at the screen to see how it will be framed.

As for the shutter button, your iPhone actually has three:

- **Camera button:** Tap the button on the bottom of the screen in the center to snap a photo. The button is a red circle when you switch to video mode.

- **Volume buttons, either one:** Press one of the volume buttons on the left side of your iPhone to snap a photo or to start and stop video recording.

If your iPhone is locked, when you click the Home button or press the on/off sleep/wake button, a Camera button appears to the right of the Slide to Unlock slider bar, as shown in Figure 1-1. Touch and drag the Camera button up (as if you want to push the lock screen out of the way) to open the Camera app, and then take photos or video as explained next.

Taking photos with the back camera

Here's how to take a photo with the back camera:

1. **Tap Camera on the Home Screen or, if your iPhone is locked, unlock it by clicking the Home button and then drag the Camera button up.**

   A shutter opens, revealing a screen as shown in Figure 1-2.

2. **Point your iPhone at whatever you want to photograph.**

3. **Tap the Camera button or press one of the Volume buttons.**

   A clicking noise lets you know the photo was taken. You can mute the shutter sound by moving the ring/silent switch to silent.

   If you have a hard time holding the phone still, you can press on the shutter button, steady the camera, and then lift your finger.

4. **A thumbnail preview of the photo you took appears in the lower-left corner (in landscape mode, the lower-right or upper-left corner, depending on which direction you rotate your phone).**

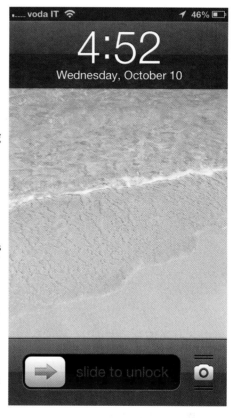

Figure 1-1: When your iPhone is locked, double-tapping the Home button brings up a Camera button by the unlock slider.

Shooting video with the back camera

iPhone 4S and later shoots video in high definition, up to 1920×1080 pixels and 30 frames-per-second. This means you can make smooth, clear full-motion videos. Each video can be up to an hour long, although one minute of video takes about 80MB of memory or close to 5GB for an hour of video.

To capture video:

1. **Tap Camera on the Home Screen or, if your iPhone is locked, click the Home button and then drag the Camera button up.**

2. **Tap the Camera/ Video Switch to move the button to Video.**

   The "shutter" has to open before you can flick the switch.

3. **Point your iPhone at the action you want to capture.**

4. **Tap the Video button, which is the red dot in place of the Camera button, or press one of the Volume buttons.**

   The button blinks while the video is recording.

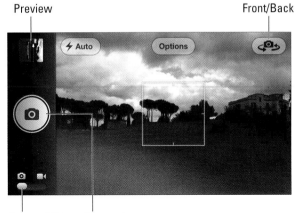

Figure 1-2: Your iPhone screen is your viewfinder. The buttons on the bottom shift to the side in landscape view.

5. **Tap the Video button or press one of the Volume buttons to stop recording.**

   You can also press the center button on iPhone's earphones to start or stop recording.

6. **A thumbnail of your video's keyframe appears in the lower-left corner in portrait orientation. In landscape, it will be at the upper-left if the volume buttons are on top, or the lower right if they're on the bottom.**

Turning the lens on yourself

The Switch Camera button in the upper-right corner of the screen switches the active objective from the back of your iPhone to the front so you see yourself on the screen. The front camera has lower resolution, no flash or zoom, but it can take advantage of the Backside Illumination Sensor and takes both still photos and video. It's handy for self-portraits (or if you find yourself without a mirror and some lettuce in your teeth) and FaceTime.

The Backside Illumination Sensor perceives low light conditions and makes adjustments to compensate. You can tap on areas that are too dark or too bright to adjust the lighting. The sensor corrects the contrast of the image as a whole. Figure 1-3 shows the difference between two photos.

Figure 1-3: The Backside Illumination Sensor perceives areas that are too dark or too light and corrects the contrast.

To use the front camera — that's the one above the screen:

1. **Tap Camera on the Home Screen.**

2. **Tap the Switch button in the upper-right corner.**

   You see yourself on the screen.

3. **Use the Camera or Video button to take a photo or shoot video of yourself, as explained in the two previous procedures.**

Setting the exposure and focus

The buttons, as shown in Figure 1-2, appear when you open Camera. The first thing you want to do is choose where you want Camera to focus its attention. Your iPhone's default autofocus is the center of the image on the screen, where you see the white box.

iPhone 4S and 5 use face detection and focus on the most prominent face. Face detection balances exposure across up to ten faces. If you want the Camera to focus on a subject that isn't in the center, tap that area on the screen. You see the focus and exposure change to put your chosen subject in the best light. (Unless you want the subject in the center, in which case you should move your iPhone until you see the subject in the center of the screen.)

You can change the exposure (that is, the amount of light that is allowed through the lens) and then focus on a different area. Tap and hold on the area on the screen that has the amount of light you want the photo to have. A blue box blinks to indicate that the exposure lock is on and the words "AE/

AF Lock" (Auto Exposure/Auto Focus) appear at the bottom of the screen. Move iPhone to the subject you want to photograph, and then tap the Camera button. Tap elsewhere on the screen to unlock the AE/AF Lock.

For example, if you point your iPhone out a sunny window and activate the AE/AF lock, the natural light needs less exposure. Then point your iPhone at a subject indoors, and take the photo. The exposure needed for the natural light is applied to the indoor setting and the photo comes out dark, even if the room seems well-lit.

Lighten up

Your iPhone has an LED light next to the objective lens on the back camera that functions as a flash. You see the flash button at the top left of the screen. Auto is the default position, meaning your iPhone turns the light on if it senses there's not enough light for the photo. Tap the flash button to turn the flash on or off manually, as shown in Figure 1-4.

Focus, flash, and the Backside Illumination Sensor work in both still photo and video mode.

To zoom or not to zoom

To zoom in on a portion of the subject you want to photograph, use the pinch and spread technique. iPhone's zoom is a digital zoom, which means it zooms by enlarging the image, not by getting closer to the subject. Digital zooming compromises the quality of the final image, so physically moving closer to your subject is by far the better choice. Try taking zoomed and normal photos to see if you can live with the compromise.

Figure 1-4: Tap the Flash button to show the options: Auto, On, or Off.

Macro mode kicks in automatically when you're about two inches away from the person or object you want to photograph. Tap the object you are focusing on to create a special effect where the main object is crisp and the background is blurry, as shown in Figure 1-5.

Using Grid

The Grid feature puts a three-by-three grid overlay on your screen, which divides the screen into nine sections. This helps you visualize the distribution of objects in your photo and is useful if you use the photographer's rule of thirds. To activate the grid:

1. **Tap the Options button at the top center of the screen.**

2. **Tap On next to Grid to turn the grid overlay on (you can see the grid in Figure 1-4).**

3. **Tap Done.**

Figure 1-5: Camera activates Macro mode when the subject is closer than two inches.

Other ways to obtain images

Taking photos with Camera isn't the only way to add images to your iPhone. We can think of at least five other ways:

✔ **Screenshot:** If you have an image on your screen — even during a FaceTime conversation — that you want to save or maybe send to a friend, tap the Home button while holding the On/Off button. You hear the shutter click and the image is saved to your Camera Roll in Photos.

✔ **Mail or Messages:** Tap the photo or video in the message that someone has sent to you. The photo opens in Photos. Tap the Action button and choose Save Image from the options.

✔ **Image Capture:** In Safari, tap and hold on an image on a web page. Tap Save Image from the options that appear. The image is automatically copied into the Camera Roll album in Photos.

✔ **Photo Stream:** If you activate Photo Stream, photos taken with other iOS devices or added to iPhoto or Aperture on a Mac connected to iCloud's Photo Stream will be in the Photo Stream album on your iPhone. See the section "Photo Stream" for more information.

✔ **From your computer:** Sync photos from iTunes (see Book II, Chapter 1).

Turning on iPhone's HDR

Digital photography is terrific in bright to shady situations, but in overly bright or very low light conditions, the quality can be poor and result in overexposed or underexposed photos. Using iPhone's High Dynamic Range option can help you get better shots when the conditions aren't perfect. Tap the Options button and then tap HDR on and off, and tap Done. HDR is off by default.

When High Dynamic Range is on, Camera takes three photos with different exposures and superimposes them to create a better image. Taking images with HDR takes a few seconds longer than shooting normal photos, so try to hold iPhone steady and ask the subject to remain still.

The LED flash doesn't work when HDR is on.

You can save both a normal version and an HDR version. In Settings⇨Photos, tap Keep Normal Photo on. If you turn this off, only the HDR version is saved.

Taking a panoramic view

One of the cool new features of Camera in iOS 6 is the possibility of taking 240 degree panoramic photos so you can capture the full width, or height, of your subject at hand. Here's how it works:

1. **Tap Camera on the Home screen.**

2. **Tap Options at the top.**

3. **Tap Panorama.**

4. **The arrow you see in the center, as shown in Figure 1-6, is a nifty tool that uses iPhone's built-in gyroscope to help you capture better images.**

5. **Tap the camera button and begin slowly but continuously moving your iPhone in one direction. Keep the arrow on the plumb line as you move in the direction of the arrow.**

    Left to right is the default but just tap the arrow, before beginning to take the photo, to go the other way.

Figure 1-6: Keep the arrow on the line to capture captivating panoramic photos.

6. **Tap Done when you finish capturing the panorama.**

   Your photo is saved in Camera Roll.

7. **Tap Done to return to normal Camera mode.**

Turn your iPhone to landscape view and take a vertical panoramic shot. This is great for capturing tall buildings in a single photo.

Browsing and Editing Photos and Videos

As soon as you tap the Camera or Video button in the Camera app, the photo or video is stored in the Photos app in the album called Camera Roll. After you've taken some photos and videos, you probably want to see them and you do that by simply tapping Photos on the Home screen, tap Camera Roll in the Albums list, and then in the thumbnail view, tap the photo or video you want to view. Flick left or right to move from one photo to the next and back again.

You can tap the Preview button in the Camera app to see Camera Roll but you can't view your other albums from Camera, only from the Photos app.

You can also create albums on your iPhone to make finding and viewing photos easier. You can place photos in an album from Camera Roll as well as from Photo Stream or from the Photo Library, which hold the photos you sync from your computer. You can sync albums from your computer to your iPhone, but albums you create on your iPhone don't sync to your computer.

Figure 1-7: The browse buttons at the bottom of the screen give you sorting and viewing options.

When you open Photos, you see a list of your Albums. At the bottom of the Albums screen, as shown in Figure 1-7, are browse buttons that give you options to view your photos in four ways:

✔ **Albums:** Shows Camera Roll, Photo Stream, Photo Library, and any albums that you create on your iPhone. Tap on an album to open a thumbnail view of the photos in the album, as shown in Figure 1-8.

✔ **Photo Stream:** Shows photos from all devices that are signed in to the same iCloud account with Photo Stream turned On. Photos taken with your iPhone or other iOS devices and those uploaded to your computer appear hear and can be saved to your iPhone if you want.

✔ **Events:** Shows collections of photos divided by event, as set up on your computer. Tap on an event to see thumbnails of those photos.

✔ **Faces:** Supported only by photos imported from iPhoto or Aperture on a Mac. Sorts photos by identifying people in the photo. Tap Faces and then tap a person in the list to see all the photos that person is in.

✔ **Places:** Takes advantage of geo-tagging. Tap Places and pins on a map indicate where photos were taken. Tapping a pin opens a thumbnail view of photos taken in that location.

Figure 1-8: Open an album, Photo Stream, Events, Faces, and Places to see thumbnails of all the photos stored there.

You see Events and Faces only if you imported photos to your iPhone from a Mac using iPhoto or Aperture, and Photo Stream only if you have the option turned on.

You can tell the difference between photos and videos in the thumbnail view because videos have a video icon and the playing time on the thumbnail (refer to Figure 1-8).

Creating albums

If you take a lot of photos, you can organize them in albums on your iPhone. The original photos remain in Camera Roll, Photo Library, or the existing album that you copy them from. Albums lets you put related photos together for easier viewing. To create a photo album, follow these steps:

1. **Tap the Photos icon on the Home screen to open Photos.**

   The Albums list appears. Tap Albums at the bottom of the screen if you don't see the Albums list.

2. **Tap the Edit button in the upper-right corner.**

3. **Tap the Add button that appears in the upper-left corner.**

   The New Album dialog opens.

4. **Type in a name for your new Album.**

5. **Tap Save.**

   The Add Photos screen opens.

6. **In the list of albums, tap Camera Roll, Photo Library, or an existing album, wherever the photos you want to place in the new album reside.**

7. **The thumbnail view of the photos in the album opens.**

8. **Tap all the photos you want to include in the new album, and then tap Done.**

9. **Your new album appears in the Album list.**

10. **(Optional.) To add more photos to the album, tap the album in the Album list to open the thumbnail view. Then tap the Edit button in the upper-right corner. Tap the Add button at the bottom and repeat Steps 6 through 8.**

11. **(Optional.) To delete an album, tap Albums at the bottom of the Photos screen. Tap the Edit button, and then tap the red and white minus sign to the left of the album name.**

12. **(Optional.) To change the order of albums on the Album list, tap the Edit button, and then touch and drag the Rearrange button to the right of the album name to move it to the position you want in the list.**

13. **Tap Done.**

Editing photos

If you use the iPhoto application on the Mac, the edit options in Photos will be familiar. Here's how to use them:

1. **Tap Photos on the Home screen.**

2. **Tap Camera Roll, an album, Photo Stream, Events, Faces, or Places —
   wherever the photo you want to edit resides.**

3. **Tap the photo you want to edit.**

4. **Tap the Edit button.**

   Four buttons appear at the bottom of the screen, refer to Figure 1-9:

   Rotate: Tap to rotate 90 degrees at a time. Tap Save when you like the orientation.

   Auto-Enhance: Tap to adjust the sharpness and contrast of the photo, and then tap Save. Auto-enhance also automatically looks for red-eyes and adjusts them.

   Red-Eye Removal: Tap the tool and then tap the red eye to correct the werewolf effect of your subject's eyes. If you like the result, tap Apply, and then tap Save. If not, tap on the eye-again to remove the black spot.

As handy as it can be, red-eye removal isn't perfect. If it doesn't recognize the red-eye, a message appears at the bottom which reads "Did not find red-eye to correct." Try zooming in and tapping again. Sometimes it finds more eye than you want and puts a black mark on the face of the person. Tap near the eye again to remove the extra black mark and try using Auto-Enhance or, better yet, another photo-retouching app such as iPhoto or Photoshop Express.

Crop/Constrain: Use your fingers to zoom, pan, and rotate the

Figure 1-9: You have four photo-editing options in Photos: Rotate, Auto-Enhance, Red-Eye Removal, and Crop/Constrain.

image until it appears as you wish. Drag the corners of the crop grid to set the area you want to crop or tap the Constrain button to choose one of the preset aspect ratios. Tap Crop to see the edits, and then tap Save. Your image is saved with the changes you made.

Tap Cancel if you don't want to Save your changes.

5. **Tap the previous button in the upper-left corner to return to the album where the photo resides.**

6. **Tap a button at the bottom of the screen to go to another album or press the Home button to leave Photos.**

Bonus Chapter 4 (online) suggests photo enhancement apps that you can download to your iPhone. For more on how to access the online bonus content, see this book's Introduction.

Viewing and trimming videos

Watching a video is as simple as browsing your photos. Open Photos, and then tap the album where your video is stored. The video icon and playing time stamped on the thumbnails distinguish videos from photos. Tap the video you want to watch, and then tap the Play button (the triangle in the middle of the screen and at the bottom center of the screen, where you see the playback controls). The Play button becomes a Pause button when the video is playing, but after a few seconds, the controls disappear to give you a cleaner viewing screen. Tap the screen to see the controls again.

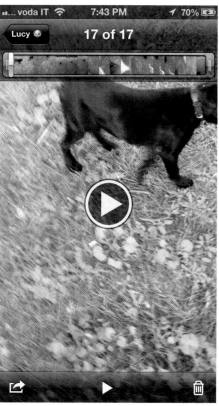

Photos gives you the possibility of trimming from the beginning or end of your video (but not in the middle):

1. **Tap the screen to make the controls visible, as shown in Figure 1-10.**

   A bar across the top of the screen displays the video frame by frame.

Figure 1-10: You can view and edit videos in Photos.

2. **Tap and hold an area of the frame bar.**

   The frames become shorter and you see more of them, so you can trim more precisely.

3. **Touch and drag the slider on the bar to move through the video in slow motion to identify where you want to trim.**

4. **Tap the left end of the bar to trim from the beginning of your video or tap the right end of the bar to trim from the end.**

   The yellow trim button appears in the upper-right corner and the bar is highlighted in yellow, as shown in Figure 1-11.

5. **Drag the end brackets toward the center to trim off the beginning and/or ending of the video.**

6. **Tap the Trim button when you have the bracket positioned where you want.**

   It's a good idea to stop a bit before the actual point where you want to trim.

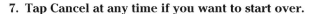
Figure 1-11: Trim removes frames from the beginning and end of your video.

You have the option to Trim Original, which overrides the original video, or Save as New Clip, which keeps the original and saves the trimmed video as an additional video in the Camera Roll album.

Video takes up storage space on your iPhone and saving as a new clip means you're storing not one but two videos. Consider moving your video to your computer only keeping the necessary copies on your iPhone.

7. **Tap Cancel at any time if you want to start over.**

If you want more editing options on your iPhone, you can purchase Apple's iMovie app at the App Store.

Ready, Action

After you're happy with your photos and videos, you might want to share one or more electronically or as an old-fashioned print. Photos lets you copy, print, and send photos and videos to others as e-mail attachments or multimedia messages (MMS or iMessage), or upload them to Twitter, Facebook, or YouTube. You can also delete photos and videos from Camera Roll or Photo Stream. First, we look at how to do things with a single photo or video, and then we explain managing batches of photos.

To take an action on a single photo or video:

1. **Tap Photos on the Home screen.**

2. **Tap the album where the photo or video you want to share, copy, or print resides.**

   The thumbnail view opens.

3. **Tap the photo or video you want to use.**

4. **Tap the screen to reveal the controls, as shown in Figure 1-12.**

   At the top of the screen, you see

   • **Camera Roll or "Album Name" button (Munich in the figure):** In the upper-left corner, this tells you where this photo resides. Tapping this button takes you back to the album where you began. From there, you can tap one of the buttons at the bottom of the screen.

   • **Photo number:** Indicates where in the lineup this photo or video falls (4 of 12 in our example).

Figure 1-12: The controls on the photo or video let you share images.

5. **Choose the action you want to take from the buttons at the bottom of the page:**

   ✔ **Action button:** Up to nine choices appear when you click it:

   - **Mail:** The photo is pasted into a new message. Type in the address and a message if you wish, and tap Send. (See Book III, Chapter 4.) You are asked to choose what size file you want to send: Small, Medium, Large, or Actual Size. The approximate megabyte size is indicated; if your e-mail service has size limits for attachments, choose an image that is about half the size of the limit.

   - **Message:** Pastes the photo in a New Message, which will be sent as an MMS or iMessage. Fill in the recipient and tap Send. (Refer to Book III, Chapter 2.)

   - **YouTube (video only):** Uploads video to your YouTube account. See Book V, Chapter 4 to learn how to do this.

   - **Photo Stream (photo only):** Sends the photo to someone else's Photo Stream account. You can choose whether to make the photo publicly viewable. See the upcoming section "Photo Stream."

   - **Twitter (photo only):** Sends your photo to your Twitter account. You must be signed in to Twitter to use this feature.

   - **Facebook (photo only):** Posts your photo to your Facebook profile. Add a comment and location if you like and tap Post. You must be signed in to Facebook to use this feature.

   - **Assign to Contact (photo only):** Assigns the photo to a person or entity in Contacts. See Book IV, Chapter 1 for complete details.

   - **Print (photo only):** Prints the photo to a printer on your wireless network. See Book I, Chapter 2 for details about wireless printing.

   - **Copy (photo only):** Puts a copy of the photo in the clipboard, which you can then paste in another app such as Notes or Pages.

   - **Use as Wallpaper (photo only):** Uses the photo as the background for your lock or Home screen. We explain how to do this in the section "Using a Photo as Wallpaper" later in this chapter.

   - **Cancel:** Tap to return to the thumbnail view.

   ✔ **Play Slideshow:** Opens a slideshow of the images in the album or begins playing the video. See the section "Viewing Slideshows" for the steps to take.

   ✔ **Trashcan (Camera Roll or Photo Stream only):** Tap to delete the photo or video. This option is available only for photos and videos shot directly on your iPhone (those in Camera Roll) or in Photo Stream. If you delete a photo from Photo Stream, it is deleted from the Photo Stream on all devices but remains on the device or computer itself (if it's still there). You can't delete photos or videos imported from your computer; you have to deselect those photos in iTunes and sync again.

You can upload photos to Flickr and other photo-sharing social networks directly on their web pages in Safari.

Batches

Sometimes you have more than one photo that you'd like to print or e-mail, or even delete. Photos lets you choose a group of photos and then take the same action for all of them at once. While in the thumbnail view of an album, do the following:

1. **Tap the Edit button in the upper-right corner.**

   In the Camera Roll album or albums you created on your iPhone, you see three buttons at the bottom on the screen: Share, Add To (Add in created albums), and Delete (Remove in created albums).

   In the Photo Library album, you see two buttons: Share and Add To. You can't delete photos imported from your computer from your iPhone, you have to re-sync the photo library with iTunes and not sync the photos you want to remove.

2. **Tap the photos you want to act on; they don't have to be consecutive.**

   A white checkmark in a red circle appears on the photo, as seen in Figure 1-13.

3. **The actions that can be taken have active buttons. Tap the button of the action you want to take:**

   • **Share:** Your choices depend on how many photos you select. If you select one photo, you have the same choices as outlined in the previous steps. The other limits are

     Mail: Up to five photos

     Message: Up to two photos

     Photo Stream, Facebook, Print, or Copy: unlimited.

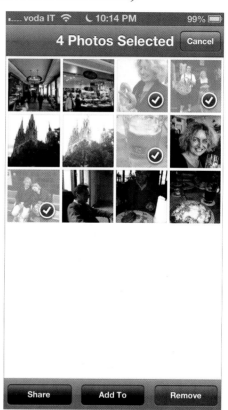

Figure 1-13: Batching lets you take an action on a group of photos.

Choose which action you want to take and then follow the same procedure as for a single photo, as explained previously.

- **Add To (Camera Roll):** Tapping this button gives you two options:

  Add to Existing Album: The album list opens and you tap the one you want to add the photos to.

  Add to New Album: The New Album dialog appears where you type in a name and tap Save.

- **Add (albums created on iPhone):** Lets you add photos from other albums to the open album. Tap Add and then tap another album (or Photo Stream, Events, or Faces) and select the photos you want to add to the album. Tap the plus sign to select all photos in an album. Tap Done when you complete your selection. The selected photos are added to the album you opened first (the one where you tapped Edit⟳Add).

- **Delete/Remove:** Deletes the batch of photos from the Camera Roll. Removes the batch of photos from a created album, but the original photos remain in Camera Roll.

Using a photo as wallpaper

You can customize the wallpaper, or background image, that appears on your lock screen and your Home screen. We explained how to do this from Settings in Book I, Chapter 4. Here we explain how to assign wallpaper directly from Photos:

1. **Select the photo you want to assign from any of the albums on Photos.**

2. **Tap the Action button in the bottom-left corner.**

3. **Tap Use as Wallpaper.**

   The Move and Scale screen opens.

4. **Pinch and spread the photo to zoom to the size you want and pan, or move, the photo around until the image is just how you want it on the screen.**

5. **Tap the Set button.**

6. **Choose one of the options that appear:**

   - **Set Lock Screen:** To use the image for the Lock screen.

   - **Set Home Screen:** To use the image for the Home screen.

   - **Set Both:** To use the image for both the Lock and Home screen.

   - **Cancel:** If you decide to leave things the way they are.

Viewing slideshows

Gone are the days of 35 mm slides and overstuffed guests falling asleep while you try to figure out which way to put the slide in the projector so it doesn't display upside-down and out of focus. With its larger Retina display, iPhone 5 shows off your photos beautifully, but earlier iPhones are nothing to sneeze at. You can also connect to a television or monitor to play your slideshow, which we explain in Book V, Chapter 4. To view a slideshow on your iPhone, follow these steps:

1. **Open the photo or album where you want the slideshow to begin.**

2. **Tap the slideshow button: It's the triangle between the Action and Delete buttons.**

   The Slideshow Options screen opens.

3. **Tap Transitions.**

   Choose the type of transition you want from the list. A transition is what happens on the screen between one photo and the next.

4. **Tap Play Music On or Off.**

   If you want music to accompany your slideshow, tap On. Start a song from the Music app and then return to Photos and begin a slideshow.

5. **Tap Start Slideshow.**

   The slideshow plays from the photo where you begin through to the end of the album.

The Slideshow settings give you a few viewing options. Tap Settings⇨Photos. In the Slideshow section, set the following:

- **Play Each Slide For:** Choose the duration of each image on the screen, from 2 to 20 seconds.

- **Repeat:** Plays the slideshow in a continuous loop.

- **Shuffle:** Plays the images in a random order.

Importing Photos and Videos to Your Computer

We talk about syncing in Book II, Chapter 1, where we mention that moving photos from your iPhone to your computer is handled by your photo management software. On a Mac, this might be Image Capture, iPhoto, Aperture, or another application that you prefer. On Windows, you may use Photoshop Elements (8 or later), Live Photo Gallery, or Pictures Library.

Essentially, when you connect your iPhone to your computer with the USB connector cable, the photo management application you use recognizes your iPhone as it would any other digital camera. If import photo choices don't appear automatically, you may have to go to a command such as File➪Import and choose to import all the photos or select only some of the photos you want to import.

Photo Stream

We saved the best for last in this chapter. Photo Stream is an incredible alternative to connecting your iPhone to your computer with the USB connector cable. As part of iCloud, Photo Stream both stores and lets you share your photos. Here we look at both functions.

Photo Stream storage

Photo Stream automatically uploads photos you take with your iPhone or other iOS devices to iCloud. Then, Photo Stream pushes, or downloads, them to the other devices and your computer. We've found this to be a priceless tool and timesaver in taking the screenshots for this book, seconds after capturing a screenshot on our iPhones, upon opening iPhoto they show up in the Photo Stream section under Recents on our Macs — no cable required.

Photo Stream also uploads photos from your computer. For example, if you take photos with a digital camera, and then move them to your computer, those photos are automatically uploaded to iCloud and pushed to your iOS devices, including your iPhone. You can view them on your iPhone for 30 days, giving you time to save a copy on your iPhone, too, if you like. Only photos uploaded after you turned Photo Stream on will be placed in Photo Stream.

The most recent 1,000 photos from all sources are stored in Photo Stream on iCloud for 30 days. As you add new photos beyond the 1,000 limit, the oldest ones are deleted.

Photos are downloaded and stored in full resolution on your Mac or Windows PC, but are optimized for download speed and storage for your iOS devices.

To start using Photo Stream, do the following:

- ✔ **On your iPhone**, go to Settings⊏⊃Photos & Camera and tap My Photo Stream On, as shown in Figure 1-14. You must be connected to Wi-Fi for Photo Stream to function.

- ✔ **On your Mac**, go to System Preferences⊏⊃iCloud and click the check box next to Photo Stream. Click Options and check both boxes in the dialog: My Photo Stream and Shared Photo Stream.

  In your Mac's photo management program, do the following:

  Go to Preferences and click the Photo Stream tab. Check the box next to My Photo Stream to turn it on, and while you're there, click the box next to Shared Photo Streams, which we cover in a few paragraphs. Then choose how you want Photo Stream to handle your photos:

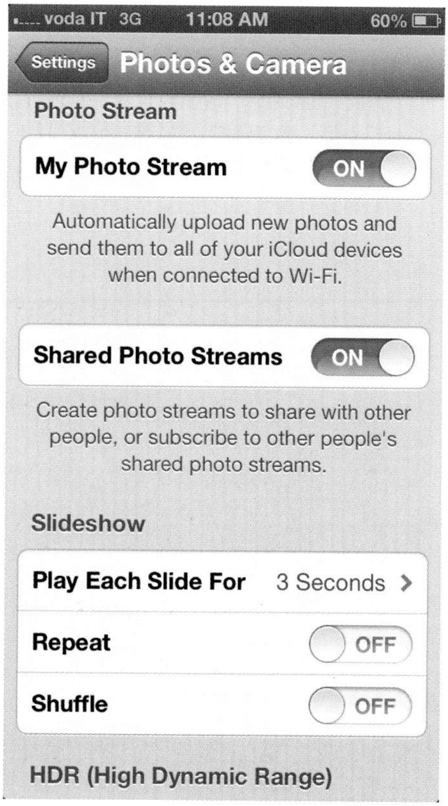

Figure 1-14: Activate Photo Stream on all your devices to share photos seamlessly.

Automatic Import Photos that are pushed to the Photo Stream library on your Mac are automatically imported to iPhoto or Aperture. With this box checked, your photos are permanently stored on your computer as an event named "*Month Year* Photo Stream" when they enter Photo Stream from another device.

Automatic Upload which sends all new photos from your computer to Photo Stream. Deselecting this box means you manually drag photos into the Photo Stream library or select the photos and then choose Photo Stream from the pop-up Share menu at the bottom of the window. Although Photo Share makes sure you don't exceed the storage space on your iPhone, manually managing photos that go from your computer to Photo Stream limits the number of photos pushed to the Photo Stream library on your other devices.

- ✔ **On a Windows PC**, download the iCloud Control Panel for Windows at `support.apple.com/kb/DL1455`. Open the iCloud Control Panel and click the check box next to Photo Stream.

On Windows, the process is manual: drag photos you want in Photo Stream from your photo management application to the designated Photo Stream folder. The default folder is: C:\Users\<user name>\ Pictures\Photo Stream\My Photo Stream, which you can change by clicking the Options button next to Photo Stream in the iCloud Control Panel.

Shared Photo Streams

Passing your iPhone around the table from friend to friend isn't the only way to share photos. Photo Stream lets you invite people to view specific photos or albums or open it up for the public to see. For example, if you're a realtor, you could take photos with your iPhone, create a Homes For Sale album, and then share that album by listing the Photo Stream URL for that album for people to view properties.

First, make sure Shared Photo Streams is On in Settings⇨Photos & Camera, and then do the following:

1. **Tap Photos on the Home screen.**

2. **Tap the tab for the album that has the photos you want to share.**

   To share just one photo, open the photo and then tap the Action button and go to Step 6.

3. **Tap the Edit button.**

4. **Tap the photos you want to share.**

5. **Tap the Share button.**

6. **Tap Photo Stream.**

   The dialog shown in Figure 1-15 appears, but with your name instead of Barbara's and the name you want to give the stream instead of Munich.

   You can have more than one shared Photo Stream album, and if you do, when you tap Share and then the Photo Stream button, you choose to add the photos to an existing Photo Stream album or create a new one.

Figure 1-15: Send an e-mail to the people you want to share photos with.

7. **Tap the To field and type the e-mail address of the person you want to invite to view your photos, or tap the Add button (it looks like a plus sign) to access your Contacts and choose recipients from there.**

8. **Repeat Step 6 to add more recipients.**

9. **Tap the Name field and type in a name for your Photo Stream.**

   Photo Stream is a bit of a misnomer because you aren't sharing every photo in your Photo Stream, unless you select them all. Think of it as creating an album on Photo Stream.

10. **Optional: Tap the switch by Public Website to the On position so people you invite who don't have an iCloud account can view the photos.**

11. **Tap Next.**

12. **Type a message to your recipients.**

13. **Tap Post.**

    Addressees receive an invitation to subscribe to your Photo Stream.

14. **After someone joins your shared Photo Stream, they'll be notified when new images are added.**

Book V
Chapter 1

Capturing and
Sharing Photos and
Videos with Camera

The people you invite to view your Photo Stream have to have an Apple ID which they use to sign in to your Photo Stream. Otherwise, turn Public Website On, and the e-mail they receive will contain a link to the Shared Photo Stream. Figure 1-16 shows an example of a Shared Photo Stream viewed in iCloud.com.

When you create a Public Photo Stream a URL is assigned to it. To view the URL, and then copy and paste it elsewhere, tap Photo Stream in the browse bar, and then tap the blue and white disclosure triangle to the right of the name of the public photo stream album. Tap Share Link, and then tap Copy. It's placed in the clipboard and you can paste it in another app such as Notes or Pages.

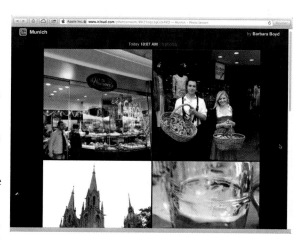

Figure 1-16: Shared Photo Streams are viewed on iCloud.com.

Another way to create Shared Photo Streams is to tap the Photo Stream button at the bottom of the screen to open the Photo Stream view. Tap the plus sign in the upper left, address and name the Photo Stream, and then tap Create. Tap the new Photo Stream from the list of Photo Streams and add photos the same way you add photos to an album.

You have some options for editing and managing shared Photo Streams. Follow these steps:

1. **Tap the Photo Stream button at the bottom of the Photos screen.**

   A list shows My Photo Stream, which contains all the photos you have on Photo Stream, followed by the Shared Photo Streams you created.

2. **To add photos, tap one of the Share Photo Streams, and then add photos as you would to an album: Tap Edit, tap Add, and then select the photos you want to add from Camera Roll or other albums in Photos. Tap Done.**

3. **To edit or delete a Shared Photo Stream, tap the blue and white triangle next to that Shared Photo Streams.**

   Refer to Figure 1-17, you can do the following:

   Tap the Name field to change the name of your Shared Photo Stream.

   Tap the disclosure triangle to the right of a name of a subscriber to resend the invitation or remove the subscriber.

   Tap Add People to invite others to see this Photo Stream.

   Tap Public Website On (or Off) to change the status of this Photo Stream.

   Tap Share Link, to share the link of a publicly Shared Photo Stream via Mail, Message, Twitter, or

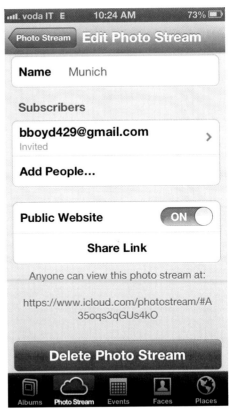

Figure 1-17: Edit and manage Shared Photo Streams.

Facebook or to copy the link so you can paste it elsewhere, such as a newsletter or website.

Tap Delete Photo Stream to delete this Shared Photo Stream.

Should you ever want to delete your entire Photo Stream from your iPhone, go to Settings⇨Photos & Camera and turn My Photo Stream Off. To completely empty Photo Stream, go to iCloud.com and sign in to your account. Click your Name in the upper right, click Advanced, and then click Reset Photo Stream. All photos are removed from iCloud but remain on the devices and computers they originated from.

Chapter 2: Acquiring and Browsing Music, Videos, Movies, and More

In This Chapter

✓ Copying media you already own to iTunes

✓ Changing import settings

✓ Browsing, sampling, and buying media with iTunes

✓ Managing and transferring purchases

✓ Tracking down free iTunes promotional music and other goodies

By now, you know that your iPhone isn't just a great phone: It's also a fabulous web browser, contact manager, calendar, alarm clock, and a terrific media player. Music, movies, TV shows, podcasts, and audiobooks sound and look crisp and clear on your iPhone. You can use HomeSharing to listen to and watch media stored on your Mac on your iPhone, or you can copy media onto your iPhone, which we explain in this chapter.

In this chapter, we first consider media you already own, which you copy to iTunes so that you can then sync it to your iPhone. We then take a closer look at the iTunes store, both on your iPhone and on your computer, and show you the ins and outs of browsing, sampling, and buying media. With the latest version of iTunes, there's little difference between the two. If you think iTunes is just for music, think again. We explore iTunes' other offerings, including movies, TV shows, audiobooks, and free promotional music. After you have media to enjoy on your iPhone, go to Chapter 3 to learn about using the Music and Podcasts app and Chapter 4 to get clued in on Videos and iTunes U.

	Songs	Albums	N.
Songs			S
	Grace Kate Havnevik		$0.99
	Grace Saving Jane		$0.99
	Grace Grey's Anatomy Cast		$0.99
	Hallelujah Buckley		$1.2

Moving Your Media to iTunes

Even if you only acquire music online, not all of your media is necessarily in iTunes. If you have a collection of CDs, you might not have copied them onto your computer because you didn't have any reason to. You may want to put some of that music onto your iPhone to listen to when you're away from your computer or stereo system, but first you have to move that music into iTunes on your computer. Here we explain the different ways to do that.

Media that's already on your computer

You may have media that you downloaded from another site like Amazon (www.amazon.com) or GoMusic (www.gomusic.com). You simply drag those files into your iTunes library. To make that task even easier, choose the Automatically Add to iTunes folder when selecting the destination for saving a downloaded file, and the file shows up in your iTunes library. If you subscribe to iTunes Match, those files go into iCloud even though they were purchased through another source.

For a yearly fee of $24.95, iTunes Match "matches" any song you have that's available from the iTunes Store and puts it in your iTunes in the Cloud library as an iTunes item. It also upgrades songs that are available in the iTunes Store to 256 Kbps (unavailable songs remain in the format you have them in). The upgrades alone could be good reason to purchase it, but since anything in your iTunes library is also in iTunes in the Cloud, with iTunes Match, even songs you didn't purchase through iTunes are available across all your devices. After the media is in iTunes, and you activate iCloud, you're just a syncing step away from having everything in your iTunes library accessible on your iPhone.

Media on a CD

To import media from a CD, follow these steps:

1. **Open iTunes.**

2. **Insert the CD you want to copy into the disc drive on your computer.**

   If the CD doesn't appear under the Library pop-up menu, go to iTunes⇨Preferences⇨General. Toward the bottom of the screen, you see the When You Insert a CD pull-down menu. Choose Show CD to see the CD under Devices. You can also change the default Settings here.

3. **Click on the CD in the pop-up menu on the top left of the window, as shown in Figure 2-1.**

   The songs are listed and selected by default. If you only want to import some of the songs, deselect those you don't want.

4. **(Optional) Click Import Settings to change the default settings for this import. (See the sidebar for details about import settings.)**

5. **Click Import CD.**

   The Import Settings window opens. Click the pop-up menu next to Import Using to change the default settings. (See the sidebar for details about import settings.)

**Book V
Chapter 2**

**Acquiring and
Browsing Music,
Videos, Movies
and More**

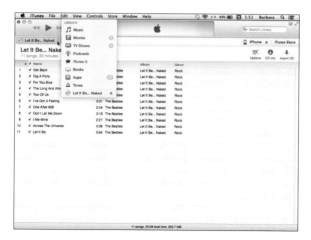

Figure 2-1: Select the CD from the source pop-up menu.

6. **Click OK.**

   The status display at the top of the screen displays the songs that are being copied and the time remaining.

   When finished, the songs are stored in the Music library.

7. **Click the Eject button to remove the CD from your drive.**

If you have an active Internet connection when you copy a CD to iTunes, click the Options button and choose Get Track Names. iTunes will automatically scan the Gracenote Internet music database for any information related to the CD and copy it into the Info about that CD. After copying a CD to iTunes, download any album artwork that's available in iTunes by clicking File⇨Library⇨Get Album Artwork. You have to have an Internet connection and sign in to your Apple ID account to use this feature.

iTunes encoding music settings

When iTunes imports music, it automatically compresses the file with the iTunes Plus encoder, which plays at 256 Kbps in stereo (128 Kbps in mono). However, iTunes also gives you the option of using a different encoder to compress music you import. Click Import Settings at the bottom right of the iTunes screen to change your settings for the active import (set your own default import settings by going to iTunes⇨Preferences⇨General and clicking the Import Settings button). You have five choices, each of which has an Auto setting, and four have custom settings.

Considering that CD quality audio is around 44,000 KHz per second with 16 bits of data over two channels for stereo listening, one minute of music requires 10MB of storage.

(continued)

(continued)

Compressing makes the file smaller so you can fit more songs on your personal listening device; that is, your iPhone. AAC and MP3 encoders compress the data by removing audio you wouldn't be able to hear unless you have bionic ears. AIFF, WAV, and Apple Lossless Encoders transform the data without removing any audio so it can be played on your computer or iPhone.

Here's a brief explanation of the settings to help you choose if you decide to change the encoder you use to import music:

- **AAC (Advanced Audio Coding) Encoder:** Offers better sound quality and more flexibility at the same bit rate as MP3. The Custom settings are iTunes Plus, High Quality (128 Kbps in stereo and 64 Kbps in mono), and Spoken Podcast (64 Kbps in stereo and 32 Kbps in mono). Files are compressed and tags identify information about the song, such as artist, CD, and title.

- **AIFF (Audio Interchange File Format) Encoder:** Custom settings let you choose a Sample Rate between 8,000 and 48,000 KHz; a Sample Size of 8 or 16 bit, and mono or stereo channels. AIFF and WAV offer the highest listening quality but don't copy tag information, such as the name of the artist, CD, or song (although iTunes does track that in its database, it won't show up if you burn to another CD), and the files are large because they aren't compressed. AIFF files can be read and created on iTunes on both the Mac and Windows, but they are more commonly used in the Mac environment.

- **Apple Lossless Encoder:** Offers only an automatic setting. Apple Lossless compresses files without removing (or losing)

any audio so you have audio quality similar to AIFF/WAV but with slightly smaller files. It also sets tags like AAC and MP3 encoders. The downside is that most non-Apple devices don't support Apple Lossless.

- **MP3 Encoder:** Choose Good Quality at 128 Kbps, High at 160, or Higher at 192. Custom settings offer Stereo Bit Rates between 16 and 320 Kbps; seven settings for Variable Bit Rate (VBR) encoding, ten choices for the Sample Rate between 8,000 and 48,000 kHz, mono or stereo channels, and normal or joint stereo mode. You also have an on/off option for Smart Encoding and Filter Frequencies Below 10 Hz. Files are compressed and tagged. This is the choice to make for non-iOS MP3 players or if you want to burn an MP3 CD to play in a portable CD player or car stereo.

- **WAV Encoder:** Offers the same custom settings as the AIFF encoder. iTunes on both Mac and Windows reads and creates WAV files. They are widely used with Windows and other operating systems.

To convert a song from one format to another, click on the song and then click Advanced⇨Create Version, where the version will be what you established in the Import Settings. Keep in mind there's no sense converting a lower quality file to a higher quality, for example, converting an MP3 file to AIFF. The encoder can't add in audio that was removed. You can go from one encoder to another of similar quality, such as AIFF to WAV or Apple Lossless to MP3 with good results, albeit slight additional detail loss.

You choice depends on how sensitive your ears are and what kind of output device you'll be using to listen to your music.

Browsing, Sampling, and Buying Music, Movies, and More at the iTunes Store

Have your Apple ID handy when you want to use iTunes because that's what you use to sign in. If you haven't yet created an Apple ID, see Book II, Chapter 1 for instructions.

When you first open the iTunes Store, it can seem overwhelming, and in a way it is: It offers more than 14 million songs. Besides all the music, iTunes also carries more than one million podcasts and thousands of movies and TV shows.

Luckily, the iTunes Store, on your computer and iPhone, is organized to help you narrow your choices. If you're familiar with the App Store, which we covered in Book II, Chapter 1, you'll recognize the iTunes Store setup.

On your computer

There's not much difference between the iTunes Store on your computer and on your iOS devices, including your iPhone. Tabs across the top of iTunes on your computer correspond to different types of media: Music, Movies, TV Shows, App Store (refer to Book II, Chapter 2), Books, Podcasts (Book V, Chapter 3), and iTunes U (Book V, Chapter 4). On the top left, you see your Apple ID, which is a tab, too. (The Apple ID in Figure 2-2 is barbaradepaula.) Tap a tab to see what's available in that media category. See Figure 2-2.

Figure 2-2: The iTunes Store lets you browse for music, movies, TV shows, and more.

At the top, you see rotating banner ads. Below the ads are sections along the lines of This Week or Hot Songs or New & Noteworthy as well as seasonal sections like Haunted House Sounds or Baseball Songs. You see both album and singles selections. You can scroll horizontally and vertically, and clicking any of the ads or icons in this smorgasbord of offers takes you to an information screen about that item.

When you click on a song or album icon or name from anywhere in the iTunes store, the album information window opens. Click on a TV show and the season information screen opens. Click on a movie and a movie information screen opens. Figure 2-3 shows an example. These are the parts of an information screen:

- **Name** (and artist if in the Music category): Click the arrow next to the artist's name to see more songs and albums by the same artist.

- **Release date**

- **Star Ratings:** The number of ratings appear in the parentheses.

- **Buy button:** Click to download the media. Each option, for example rent or buy, standard or high-definition, has its own button. Songs can be purchased singly by clicking the Buy button in the Price column or you can purchase the whole album by clicking the Buy button under the album; TV shows can be purchased singly or by season.

- **Share:** Click the triangle next to the Buy button to open a pop-up menu that has options to gift the item to a friend, add it to your own wish list, tell a friend about it, copy the link, or share the item info via Facebook or Twitter.

  You can't use a store credit to pay for a gift. You must pay with a credit card or PayPal account.

- **Ratings:** For movies only. The ratings are the usual G, PG, PG-13, R, and so on for US markets. Foreign films may have different ratings.

  Three tabs give you different information:

- **Songs** (Music), **Details** (all other categories): The first few lines of the description of the item are visible. If the description is longer, click More on the right to expose the complete description. This is where you find the song list if you're viewing an album, the episode list for TV Shows and Podcasts, Chapters for Books, and lessons or lectures for iTunes U.

- **Ratings and Reviews:** Users can give a simple star rating, from zero to five, or write a review. Reviews help your downloading or purchasing decisions.

- **Related:** Lists items by the same performers and other items purchased by people who bought that particular item. A fourth tab appears when bonus items such as iTunes Extras or LP are available.

Book V
Chapter 2

Acquiring and
Browsing Music,
Videos, Movies
and More

Figure 2-3: Information about the media item is displayed in iTunes.

Tap the History button next to the Library button at the top of the window to see a list of items you viewed recently in any category.

Finding music when you know what you're looking for

If you have a specific song or movie in mind, you can skip the rotating banner ads and lists of recommendations and search for the media you seek.

⌘+F takes the cursor to the Search field. Type the name or a couple key words in the Search field at the top right of the window, and then press return. A list of matching results appears. The results are culled from the entire iTunes Store but are divided by category. If you click Media Type in the list on the right, you'll only see that type of media.

You can also click one of the media type tabs at the top of the screen — Music, Movies, TV Shows — to see a greater selection in just one type of media. Click and hold to open the pull-down menu that displays genres or categories within a type of media.

Downloading media from iTunes

When you find something you like, click the Buy (or Rent) button and it's downloaded to iTunes. Either way, you have to sign in with your Apple ID account and pay the price. This happens two ways:

✔ **Credit Card:** Insert your credit card information into your Apple ID account. You did this either when you opened it, or you can do it by clicking Edit to the right of Payment Type. A window opens where you can choose the type of credit card you want to use (or PayPal) and type in the necessary information: account number, expiration date, billing address, and so on.

↙ **Redeem:** You can redeem Apple or iTunes gift cards, gift certificates, or allowances. (You can set up a monthly allowance for yourself or someone else. A set amount is charged to your credit card or PayPal account and credited to the designated iTunes account.) Click your Apple ID⇨ Redeem or click Redeem in the Quick Links section. Type in the code from the card or certificate or click Use Camera and hold the card up to your computer's camera. The amount of the card or certificate is added to your account and appears to the right of the Apple ID account tab.

After you download the item, close the iTunes store by clicking the Library button in the upper-right corner — it changes to iTunes Store when you're viewing your iTunes library. You return to iTunes library, which is non-store iTunes on your computer. Click the pop-up menu to choose the category for the type of media you downloaded (Music, Movies, and so on) to see your media. Click a tab at the top to choose the viewing style you want, and then click an item. Clicking an album shows you the album contents, as shown in Figure 2-4.

Figure 2-4: The Music section of the Library shows which songs, albums, and music videos you have in iTunes.

You can select Automatic Downloads so that whenever you download something on your computer or device, it's automatically downloaded to other computers or devices using the same Apple ID. On your computer, in iTunes, go to iTunes⇨Preferences and click the Store tab. Check the boxes next to the media you want automatically downloaded to other devices: Apps, Music, and/or Books. On your iPhone, tap Setting⇨Store and tap the switches next to Music Apps, or Books On. While you're there, you can choose to use the cellular network to download purchases by tapping the switch by Use Cellular Data On, although there are size limits for downloading on the cellular network. Use a Wi-Fi connection to download larger files.

Weighing renting versus buying options

Online rentals and purchases give you another option for watching movies and television shows.

Two things you have to consider when deciding whether to rent or buy a video or TV show from the iTunes Store:

✔ **How often do you want to watch the video:** If you think you'll only want to watch it once, renting is probably fine. At the time of publication, movie rentals cost between $3.99 and $4.99 and $.99 for TV shows. You have thirty days to begin watching the movie and 24 hours (48 hours for TV shows) to finish watching once you begin. If you think it's a classic or a keeper, you probably want to buy.

✔ **How much do you want to spend:** Rentals are $3.99 for a standard version and $4.99 for high definition. iTunes runs specials to purchase films for as low as $4.99 and new releases in high definition go for around $14.99.

With iCloud, you can access rented or purchased media from all your devices. When you start watching on one device, you can pause there, and begin playback on another device from where you paused on the first device. We explain viewing video on your iPhone in Book V, Chapter 4.

iTunes isn't just about music and movies: You can also find podcasts, audiobooks, and even university courses and K-12 lessons. While you browse, purchase or subscribe, and download those items from the iTunes Store on your computer, on your iPhone, you still find audiobooks in the iTunes app but after you download the associated apps podcasts are acquired through the Podcasts app and iTunes U courses have their own iTunes U app. (If you don't download the apps, you still find them in the iTunes app on your iPhone.) See Chapters 3 and 4 of this minibook to learn about each, respectively.

Authorizing iTunes to play your purchased music, videos, books, and apps

When you open an iTunes account or Apple ID, you automatically authorize that computer to open videos, books, and apps purchased from the iTunes Store with your account. The media and the computer have to have the same authorization. You can authorize up to five computers, which means you can access your iTunes account from each of those five computers. Follow these steps to authorization:

1. **From iTunes, click Store⊃Authorize This Computer.**

   A pane opens asking you to type in your Apple Account name and password. That's what you established when you set up your account on iTunes.

2. **Click Authorize.**

   A message appears telling you how many computers are authorized with this account.

At some point, you may want to deauthorize an account, say, if you buy a new computer and donate your old one to the local homeless shelter. Instead of clicking Authorize This Computer, click Store➪Deauthorize This Computer. Type in your Apple Account name and password, and then click Deauthorize. Any videos, books, or apps associated with that computer are no longer available.

If you turn on Home Sharing, the five computer limit is moot because you essentially put your iTunes collection on your home network and can access it from any number of computers on that network. iOS devices don't count.

On your iPhone

iTunes on your iPhone is a streamlined version of the iTunes Store. Banners run across the top of the screen and then sections such as New and Noteworthy or This Week appear along with seasonal and media-specific sections. The recommendations are all there, but because of the smaller screen space, you see less of it at once — which might be a good thing. You have to have a Wi-Fi or cellular data connection to use iTunes on your iPhone. When you tap the iTunes button on the Home screen, the screen shown in Figure 2-5 opens. The first time you open iTunes, the Music section appears, but if the last time you looked in iTunes you were browsing movies or audiobooks, when you re-open, that's what you'll see.

Tapping any of the buttons in the browse bar at the bottom of the screen takes you to the corresponding section of iTunes. Tap More to open a list of sections that aren't displayed in the browse bar. To search for media, do the following:

1. **Tap any of the media browse buttons: Music, Movies, TV Shows, or Audiobooks or Tones from the More menu to look for that type of media (as well as Podcasts and iTunes U if you didn't download the respective apps).**

2. **Tap Genres to see a list of genres for that media (called Categories in the Audiobooks section).**

   Tap a genre and you see specific selections in either the Featured or Charts view.

3. **Tap the Featured tab at the top center to see the banner ads and icon; tap Charts to see the most popular items in each media category.**

   If you want to see the Featured or Charts for all genres in a media category, tap All Genres at the top of the list.

Book V
Chapter 2

Acquiring and
Browsing Music,
Videos, Movies
and More

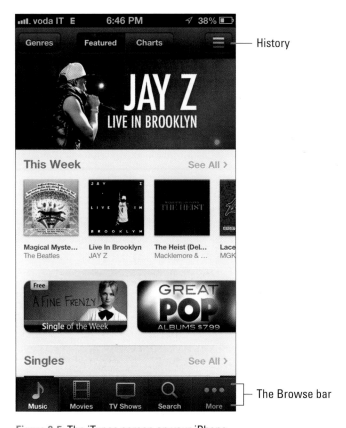

Figure 2-5: The iTunes screen on your iPhone.

Tap the History button in the upper-right corner to see your browsing history. This new feature is a great way to go back to something you had to think about before purchasing.

Scroll down to the bottom of any Featured screen to access the following:

> **Redeem:** Opens a screen where you enter the code from any gift card or iTunes codes you have; the amount is added to your Apple ID account.
>
> **Apple ID:** Click to sign in if you don't see your Apple ID there. If you have a store credit, the credit balance appears under your account name.

If you're looking for e-books, you find them as in-app purchases in the iBooks app.

Downloading to your iPhone

When you reach the center of the iTunes vortex and find the song, movie, or TV show you want to download, tapping the item opens an information screen. On items that have more than one component, such as an album that comprises songs, or a TV show that has multiple episodes, the information screen shows a list of each component, as shown in Figure 2-6. By the name and graphic of the item you see information such as the genre, release date and star ratings. Below there are three tabs that give you the following information:

- ✔ **Songs** (in Music) or **Details** (Movies and TV Shows) to see a description of the item and a list of songs or other details such as plot and actors for movies or a list of episodes for TV shows.

- ✔ **Reviews:** Shows star ratings, the total number of rankings, and written reviews. You can also write a review yourself by tapping Write a Review here.

- ✔ **Related:** Shows other items by the same artist or in the same genre and media, as well as other items people who bought this item bought.

To preview an item:

1. **Tap the item that interests you.**

2. **Tap the Preview button to the left of the name.**

   The Preview button transforms to a loading button and then a piece of the song or video plays.

You can preview video via Airplay on Apple TV by tapping the Airplay button.

To download an item:

1. **Tap on the price or Free button to the right of the item.**

   The price button transforms to read Buy Song/Album/Movie/Episode/ Season; Free becomes Download.

2. **Tap Buy Song/Album/Movie/Episode/Season or Download.**

   If you tap Buy by mistake, tap somewhere else on the screen, and it disappears.

   To purchase items, you must have credit or credit card information in your Apple ID account. Free items begin downloading immediately.

Go to Settings⊳iTunes & App Stores and turn on Use Cellular Data to process automatic downloads and iTunes Match through your cellular data service when Wi-Fi isn't available. Note that items larger than 50MB cannot be downloaded over the cellular network. For those you must connect to Wi-Fi to download large files or you can download them on your computer. Rented Movies or TV shows begin playing as soon as enough data has been downloaded to launch the video.

Bonus songs and video download to your iPhone; iTunes Extras, iTunes LP, and digital booklets can only be downloaded to your computer.
In iTunes, choose Store⇨Check for Available Downloads to retrieve these items.

3. **Downloaded items appear in the Purchased section of both the iTunes and Music apps on your iPhone and in the associated media library in Music.**

The last browse button

You'll see a few other options for iTunes on your iPhone. The default browse bar contains:

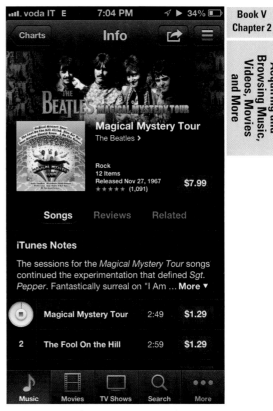

Figure 2-6: An iTunes information screen on your iPhone.

✓ **Search:** Tapping the Search button opens a search field. Tap in the field to open the keyboard. Tap type in the title or subject of the item you want to find, and then tap the Search button. iTunes lists potential matches to your search words, for example, if you type Grace, you can then tap All Results for Grace or tap Grace Potter, Grace Kelly, Amazing Grace, or another of the suggestions to see results for that narrower search. iTunes then searches its entire media database and displays matches by category, as shown in Figure 2-7.

The More screen

There are three more choices on the More screen that help you manage your iTunes experience. If you find you use one of them often, check out the Tip at the end for rearranging the buttons you find on the browse bar.

✓ **Purchased:** Choose the media type: Music, Movies, or TV Shows and then choose to displays by All, which is everything you've purchased on iTunes, or Not On This iPhone, where iTunes compares the media you've purchased and the media on your iPhone and shows you things that haven't been synced to your iPhone yet. Click the download button to download those items to your iPhone.

✔ **Genius:** Genius makes recommendations based on your iTunes purchasing history. To use Genius, tap iTunes⇨More⇨Genius. Tap the media you want recommendations for Music, Movies, or TV Shows. Genius gives you a list of results it thinks you'll like. Tap any of the results to go to the information screen. Purchase and download as instructed earlier in this section.

✔ **Downloads:** Shows a status list of pending and in-progress downloads. Tapping the Pause button pauses the download until you start it again. If you lose your Internet connection, iPhone starts the download when the connection re-opens, or iTunes on your computer completes the download the next time you sign-in to iTunes. Pre-ordered items remain in the list until they are available and you download them. Tap the item for release date information. When it's available, tap the item and then tap the Download button.

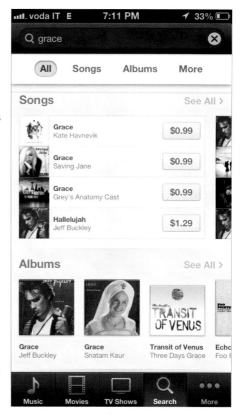

Figure 2-7: Search looks through iTunes' entire media database to find matches.

 From the More screen, tap the Edit button to rearrange the buttons you see at the bottom of the screen and those that appear in the secondary More screen. Just drag the icon of the button you want on the bar over the one you want to replace and they exchange places.

Managing and Transferring Purchases

Now that you've purchased and downloaded different types of media, you probably want to put them in a useable order. iTunes, on its own, puts the media into libraries so the songs and music videos are in the music library, movies are in the movie library, and so on.

One way you can organize your media is with playlists. Here, we explain how to create Playlists on your computer, which sync with your iPhone. You can also create playlists on your iPhone in the Music app, see Book V, Chapter 3.

Book V
Chapter 2

Acquiring and
Browsing Music,
Videos, Movies
and More

Change the media type of an item by clicking on the song or video and going to File⇨Get Info⇨Options. Choose a different media type from the Media Kind pop-up menu. This is handy, for example, if a podcast from another site ends up in your Music library.

Playlists

Playlists are groups of songs that you want played together in a certain order. Playlists are nice for listening to music on any device, but they're great for putting together a sequence of songs for your yoga practice or a dinner party — no more running to the stereo to change the CD or listening to the same CD repeat for an entire evening. Instead, just connect your iPhone to your stereo, plug it into the dock of your iPhone speakers, or connect to remote speakers with AirPlay. (We tell you about these kinds of accessories in Book II, Chapter 3.) To create a playlist,

1. **Open iTunes.**

2. **Click the Playlist tab at the top of the window.**

3. **Click the plus sign at the bottom of the window and choose New Playlist.**

   Or click File⇨New Playlist. Either way, the window is divided into two panes: Your music library is on the left and the empty playlist on the right.

4. **Type the name of your playlist.**

   Click the playlist to highlight it and type a new name.

5. **Drag songs you want in the playlist to your music library. Click a tab at the top of the window to change the view.**

6. **Click and drag the songs up and down to rearrange the order or click the sort menu and choose another way to sort, such as Name or Artist.**

Your playlists are copied to your iPhone when you sync.

You can also let iTunes do the work for you. There are two types of playlists that iTunes creates. Smart Playlists are based on criteria you set, whereas Genius playlists are created with songs iTunes thinks go well together. Genius also suggests new songs it thinks you'll like based on your purchase history and what you have in your library. Here's how to create these two types of playlists:

✐ **Smart Playlists:** Choose New Smart Playlist from the pop-up menu at the bottom of the window or click File⇨New Smart Playlist and set the criteria for the type of media, songs, videos, and podcasts you want put together in a playlist. iTunes creates a playlist based on that criteria. When you add a new song or video to iTunes, if it meets the criteria of an existing smart playlist, the new song or video is automatically added to the appropriate smart playlist. You can edit the criteria of an existing smart playlist by clicking the playlist, and then clicking File➪Edit Smart Playlist (or Control+playlist name).

✔ **Genius:** Click Store➪Turn On Genius. Sign in to your Apple account and agree to the Terms of Use. iTunes accesses the iTunes Store so it can review your interests in music, movies, and TV shows and make informed suggestions about media you might like. Click a song you like in any view and then click the action button, which is the arrow to the right of the song — not to be confused with the playback triangle. Choose Create a Genius Playlist from the menu that appears. A playlist is created from your music library with songs that iTunes thinks go well with the song you selected.

If you've created many playlists, you can organize them into folders. Click File➪New Playlist Folder. A folder appears in the Playlist library. Name that folder and then click and drag the playlists you want into the folder.

Tracking purchases

One of the nice things about iTunes is how it keeps a history of everything you ever downloaded, free or paid. This is really useful if your computer is stolen or irreparably damaged. You can transfer media directly from iTunes to a new computer, without having to re-purchase items you already bought.

Follow these steps to retrieve items you already downloaded:

1. **Open iTunes and click iTunes Store.**

   Sign in to your account if you aren't signed in.

2. **Click Purchased in the Quick Links list.**

3. **Click Not on This Computer in the upper-right section.**

   A list of the items that you purchased in the past but that aren't on your computer appears with a little cloud Download button next to them.

4. **Click the Download button for the item you want to retrieve or click Download All at the bottom of the screen.**

5. **The items are downloaded to the appropriate iTunes library.**

You can also view purchased and free items you've downloaded by clicking Purchase History on the Account Information screen of iTunes.

On your iPhone, tapping Purchased in the browse bar opens a list of the media you purchased. You can view all or only those that haven't yet been added to your iPhone.

Getting the Goods for Free

**Book V
Chapter 2**

**Acquiring and
Browsing Music,
Videos, Movies
and More**

You probably noticed the word "free" floating around on iTunes. Some things, like lectures from iTunes U and podcasts, are always free. Other things are iTunes promotions. You can find them in different places:

- ✔ **iTunes Store Home page:** Take a look around. There's usually at least one link to something free in the banner ads. Scroll through the other sections. Free and discounted items are marked with a yellow triangle on the upper right corner of the icon. At the very bottom of the page, there's a section called Free on iTunes. Tap See All to view the entire selection.

- ✔ **Music and TV Shows:** Click the Free link under Quick Links. Pilot episodes of new television series are often free.

- ✔ **Books:** Click the free button in the Top Charts section on the right side. Only electronic books are offered; audiobooks don't have a free section.

Chapter 3: Listening to Music and Audio

In This Chapter

- ✔ Meeting and mastering the Music App
- ✔ Searching Music for media
- ✔ Creating Playlists
- ✔ Controlling music and audiobook playback
- ✔ Customizing Music's settings
- ✔ Listening to podcasts

W e're not anthropologists, but even before humans began to speak, they probably made rhythmic sounds with sticks and rocks or hand clapping. Music seems to be part of our DNA and with your iPhone along, you never find yourself without something to listen to. Then language came along and we haven't stopped talking since.

In the previous chapter, we wrote about getting media onto your iPhone, either via your computer, from iCloud, or the iTunes Store. In this chapter, we talk about Music, the app you use to listen to music and audiobooks, and Podcasts, Apple's cool new app, which you use to listen to or watch — you guessed it — podcasts. In Book V, Chapter 4 we explore the Video and iTunes U apps, which are more about watching.

Meeting and Mastering the Music App

Now that you have media on your iPhone, you have the joy of listening to your favorite singers, bands, and audiobooks whenever you have your iPhone with you. First, we take you through the general layout of Music and then show you the basic commands for listening to music and creating playlists.

Tap Music on the Home screen and you see a screen as shown in Figure 3-1. You see five browse buttons across the bottom of the screen:

✏ **Playlists:** Displays a list of playlists you have either created on your iPhone or synced from iTunes, including Genius playlists. (You have to activate Genius on iTunes on your computer and then sync your iPhone with iTunes to see Genius on your iPhone.)

✏ **Artists:** Displays an alphabetical list of artists.

However, the first item in the list above the "A" section reads All Albums. Tapping All Albums opens a list of the albums on your iPhone. The first item in that list above the "A" section is All Songs, which takes you to the alphabetical list of songs.

✏ **Songs:** Shows a list of songs in alphabetical order by song title, as shown in Figure 3-2. Tapping the Shuffle button at the top of the screen begins playing all the songs on your iPhone in a random order.

Figure 3-1: The Music screen.

Figure 3-2: Tapping the Songs button in the browse bar opens an alphabetical list of songs.

- **Albums:** Shows a list of the albums the songs on Music come from. Even if you have only one song from an album, that album appears in the Albums list.

- **More:** Brings up a list of additional viewing options:

  - **Audiobooks:** Opens a list of audiobooks, if you have any on your iPhone.

  - **Compilations:** Shows a list of compilations, which are often songs from different albums or artists put together as one.

  - **Composers:** Displays an alphabetical list of composers. Tapping the name of the composer opens a list of songs written by that composer.

  - **Genres:** Shows a list of genres. Tapping the genre opens a list of media in that genre.

  - **Podcasts:** Displays a list of audio podcasts you have on your iPhone.

Tapping the Edit button in the top-left corner of the More screen opens a Configure screen. Tap and drag a button from the main part of the screen over one of the browse buttons. The two buttons exchange places. Tap Done when they're arranged as you like. This lets you put the buttons you use most in the browse bar.

Finding songs

Sometimes you want to hear a particular song; other times, a particular artist or album. You can play the song or album you want to hear from different views.

In Songs

Tap the Songs button in the browse bar; tap More if you don't see it there, and choose it from the list that appears. Now you have three choices:

- **Flick up to scroll through the list until you find the song you want to hear.**

- **Tap the letter of the first word of the song in the alphabet that runs down the right side of the screen.** "The," "A," and "An" don't count as first words.

- **Type the name of the song in the search field at the top of the screen.** If you don't see the search field, tap the status bar at the very, very top of the screen or the magnifying glass at the top of the alphabet that runs down the right side.

In Artists

Tapping Artists in the browse bar opens an alphabetical list of artists, sorted by first name. Find the name of the artist you want by using the search field, flicking through the list, or tapping the letter that corresponds to the artist's first name in the index that runs down the right side. Tap the name of the artist to see a list of songs by that artist.

In Albums

Tapping Albums in the browse bar opens a list of albums. Tap the album that has the song you want to hear and you see a list of the songs on that album, as shown in Figure 3-3. The name of the artist and the album name appear to the right of the album cover image. The number of songs and album playing time are shown as well. The playing time for each song appears to the right of the song name.

With Search

From a screen in Music in any category, you can open Search and look for a song. Tap the status bar at the very top of the screen and the Search field appears. Tapping in the Search field opens the keyboard. Begin typing the name of the artist, album, or song, and a list appears divided by category: artist, album, and song. The more letters you type, the narrower your search results. Search looks at all the words in a title, not just the first word and gives you results for songs that are part of an album name that matches your search criteria. For example, search for "blue" and you the results include all the songs on Joni Mitchell's album *Blue*, Diana Krall's version of the song "Almost Blue," as well as all the songs by the band Blue Sage, if you have those on your iPhone.

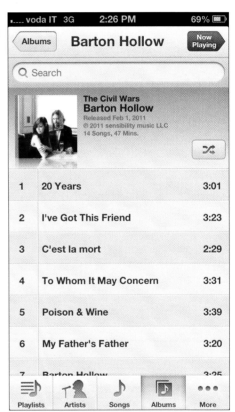

Figure 3-3: Tapping an album name in Albums view opens information and a song list for the album.

You can also search the iTunes Store: Scroll to the bottom of the result list to tap Continue Search in Store. The iTunes Store opens and displays songs, albums, and other media, such as audiobooks, ringtones, or movies, that matches your search words.

You can find media from outside Music, too. Open Spotlight Search, the farthest left screen of the Home screens, and type in a few letters or a word of the song or artist you seek. The results appear by App, so if a match is found in Music, it appears in the results list under the Music app.

Playing songs

When you find the song you want to hear, tap the song. The song begins playing and you see the Now Playing screen as shown in Figure 3-4. If you have any other songs in your library that are from the same album, those subsequent songs play until they're finished or you tap the pause button.

The main controls — Play/Pause, Previous/Rewind, Next/Fast Forward, and Volume — are at the bottom of the screen.

- **Play/pause:** Tap to begin playing the song or to pause. When the song is paused, it stays at that paused point even if you do other things on your iPhone. When you return to the song that was playing, it picks up where it left off.

- **Previous/rewind:** Tap to jump to the beginning of the playing song, unless you are in the first three seconds of the song, in which case you jump to the previous song. The numbers above the scrubber bar tell you which song in the lineup you're listening to. Tap and hold to rewind.

Figure 3-4: The Now Playing screen shows the album cover of the song that's playing along with the Music controls.

- **Next/fast forward:** Tap to jump to the next song. Tap and hold to fast-forward the song you are listening to.

You can also fast-forward or rewind in a song by dragging the playhead (the ball on the bar) along the scrubber bar. Slide your finger down to use half-speed scrubbing or keep your finger on the scrubber bar for high-speed scrubbing.

When you tap a song from the Songs list, the Now Playing screen opens. The Previous and Next buttons take you to the song before or after the playing song in your songs list. Shuffle randomly plays all the songs in your songs list.

If you only want to hear songs from a specific album or a particular artist, tap the Album or Artist browse button and choose your first song from there. The Previous and Next buttons function within the limits of the album. Shuffle randomly plays the songs in that album. You see three buttons under the scrubber bar, which are

- ✔ **Repeat:** Tap once to continuously repeat the album, playlist, or your entire song collection (whichever was your point of departure when you chose the song to play), the button turns orange, tap a second time to repeat only the song that's playing (a number one in a circle appears on the button), and tap a third time to stop repeating (the button turns white again).

- ✔ **Shuffle:** Tap once and music plays the songs of the album, playlist, or your entire song library in a random order (the button turns orange); tap again to turn off shuffle and hear the songs in the order they appear on the album or playlist (the button is white again). You can also shake your iPhone to Shuffle, unless you've deactivated that function in Music settings, which are explained a little later in this chapter.

- ✔ **Genius:** Tap once while you're listening to a song and Music creates a playlist that goes well with the song you're listening to. (If you don't see the Genius button, and you want to, go to iTunes on your computer and select Store⟳Turn Genius On and then sync your iPhone with iTunes.)

Tap Repeat album and Shuffle together (both will be orange) to hear the album, playlist, or your song library continuously in a random order.

The Back button at the top left of the screen returns you to the spot where you chose the song, which could be the album itself, the Songs list, the Artists list, and so on. You can also swipe to the right to go back.

The Track List button in the upper right switches between the Song Playing view, as shown in Figure 3-4, and the Album Playing view, as seen in Figure 3-5.

In the Album Playing view, you can assign a rating of one to five stars to each song. iTunes can then use your ratings to create a playlist based on your ratings; for example, a playlist of songs that have four or five stars. A blue triangle indicates the song that's playing and the controls at the bottom work the same way as in Song Playing view. Tap the Album/Song button again to return to the Song Playing view.

Playing albums

You can go directly to an album by tapping Albums in the browse bar (tap More in the browse bar if you don't see it) and then choosing the album you want to hear from the list. Tap the first song and the album begins playing. You can also start the album from another song or tap the shuffle button to let Music choose a random playing order.

Figure 3-5: The Album Playing view shows a list of the songs on the album and a rating for the song that's playing.

From the Now Playing screen, turning your iPhone to a horizontal position opens the Cover Flow view, as seen in Figure 3-6. Flick from left to right to scroll through your album collection. Tap on an album cover to open the track list. Tap a song to begin playing. You can tap the Play/Pause button in the lower-left corner to use those two controls; however, you have to turn your iPhone to the vertical position to use the other playback controls.

Figure 3-6: The Album view in Music.

Playlists

Playlists are sort of like creating your own personal radio station that plays songs you like all the time. You mix and match the songs you want to listen to together, in the order you want to hear them, and save it to listen to again and again.

Tap the Playlists button in the browse bar. The first two items in the list are Genius Playlist and Add Playlist. A playlist that iTunes creates for you using the music in your collection is a Genius playlist. A simple playlist is one you create yourself.

Creating Genius playlists

Make sure Genius is turned on in iTunes on your computer (select Store⇨Turn On Genius) and then sync your iPhone with iTunes as explained in Book II, Chapter 1. To create a Genius playlist, you select a song and iTunes creates a playlist of 25 songs it thinks go well with the song you selected. To create a Genius playlist, follow these steps:

1. **Tap Playlists from the browse bar.**

2. **Tap Genius Playlist.**

3. **Select the song you want iTunes to use as the basis for the playlist by tapping one of the browse buttons and scrolling through to find the song you want.**

4. **Tap the song you want to be the basis of the playlist.**

   The song begins playing.

   You may see a message that tells you don't have enough songs to make a playlist based on the song you chose.

5. Tap the Genius button.

If you have an iPhone 4S or earlier and don't see the Genius button, tap the album image on the screen to bring up additional controls.

6. Tap the Back button to see the Genius playlist iTunes created, as shown in Figure 3-7.

The playlist plays until you pause the song.

7. Tap Save to save the playlist; it's given the name of the song you based it on.

The name of the playlist is the name of the song you chose at the beginning. It appears at the bottom of the playlist list and the Genius icon is next to the name.

If you add more songs to your iTunes collection, you can update an existing Genius playlist. Tap the playlist to open it, and then tap the Refresh button. iTunes looks at your content and creates an updated playlist that may include songs you've added since the playlist was created, if any of those new songs meet the criteria of the old playlist.

Figure 3-7: iTunes creates a Genius playlist based on a song you select; the Genius Playlist screen shows the songs in the playlist.

To delete a Genius playlist, tap the playlist and then tap the Delete button.

You can create a Genius playlist directly from a song while you're listening to it — just tap the Genius button and iTunes creates a new playlist.

Creating your own playlist

If you already have a playlist in mind, you can create it yourself:

1. Tap Playlists in the browse bar.

2. Tap Add Playlist.

A New Playlist box appears as shown in Figure 3-8.

3. **Type a name for your playlist in the Title field.**

4. **Tap Save.**

   The Songs list opens.

5. **Tap the songs you want in your playlist.**

   You can also go to other views such as artist or album to choose songs.

6. **Tap Done when you're happy with your selections.**

   Your playlist appears on the screen.

7. **Tap the Edit button to do the following, as shown in Figure 3-9:**

Figure 3-8: Name your playlist when you tap Add Playlist.

Figure 3-9: You can edit playlists you create.

- Touch and drag the reorder buttons up and down to move the songs around in the order you want to play them. You can also let Music randomly reorder the sequence by playing the playlist with the Shuffle button.

- Tap the red and white minus sign next to a song you want to delete and then tap the delete button.

- Tap the plus sign to add more songs. The songs list opens and you select songs to add as in the initial steps.

Genius playlists may be edited the same way.

8. **Tap Done when you finish.**

9. **Tap the first song to begin playing your playlist or tap the Shuffle button to hear the playlist in a random order.**

If you want to change or delete your playlist at a later time, tap the playlist and follow Step 7 in the preceding list to add, delete, or reorder songs. Tap Clear to clear the songs on the playlist and start over with the same title. Tap Delete to eliminate the playlist entirely. You can also swipe across a playlist in the Playlists list and tap the Delete button that appears.

Playlists created on your computer, including Smart Playlists, on your iPhone are synced one to the other the next time you perform a sync.

Controlling Audio Playback

As with so many things iPhone, there are multiple ways and places to access the same information or controls. The playback controls are no exception. In addition to the playback controls in Music on the Now Playing screen, there are three other ways to control playback: from the multitasking bar, using the headset remote, and with Voice Control.

Using the playback controls in the Multitasking bar

Your iPhone is capable of multi-tasking, so you can listen to music and write an e-mail at the same time. Instead of opening Music and going back and forth to another app, try this:

1. **Double-click the Home button.**

   The Multitasking bar appears at the bottom of the screen, showing which apps are open.

2. **Flick from left to the right to open the playback controls, as shown in Figure 3-10.**

   The icon for the media app that was most recently open appears next to the playback controls for Rewind, Play/Pause, and Fast Forward, as well as the orientation lock button.

3. **Tap the button for the action you want to take.**

TIP

If you double-click the Home button when your iPhone is locked but you are listening to audio, the playback controls appear on the lock screen.

Using the headset remote to control playback

You likely listen to music or other media with the headset or EarPods that came with your iPhone. Both have a microphone and a center button that you press to answer incoming calls and up and down buttons to control the volume of the incoming call. These three buttons work when your iPhone is locked and, while listening to music, control playback. Here's how to use them:

Figure 3-10: The Playback Controls.

  ✓ **Volume:** Press the up or down buttons to increase or lower the volume.

  ✓ **Pause:** Press the center button; press again to resume playing.

  ✓ **Next song:** Press the center button twice quickly.

  ✓ **Fast forward:** Press the center button twice quickly and hold.

  ✓ **Previous song:** Press the center button three times quickly.

  ✓ **Rewind:** Press the center button three times quickly and hold.

If someone calls while you're listening to something, your iPhone rings both in the headset and from iPhone's speaker, unless you have the Silent/Ring button switched to Silent, in which case it just rings in the headset. You have these command options:

✓ **Answer the call:** Press the center button.

✓ **Decline the call:** Press and hold the center button for a couple seconds; two low beeps indicate you successfully declined the call.

✓ **Put a call on hold to answer another incoming call:** Press the center button; press again to return to the caller you left on hold.

✓ **Answer an incoming call but hang-up on the current call:** Press and hold the center button for a couple seconds; two low beeps let you know you ended the first call.

✓ **Hang up:** Press the center button. After you hang up, the music or audio you were listening to resumes playing where you were before the call came in.

If you want to listen to music through a headset that you've paired with your iPhone, you have to adjust the speaker settings in Music. While you're listening to a song, tap the Bluetooth button in the lower-right corner. Buttons appear giving you the option to choose which device you want iPod to play through. Tap the button for your headset.

Using Voice Control or Siri to control playback

We think Voice Control and Siri are great, especially when used along with the headset for an almost hands-free command center. Remember to speak slowly and clearly. If you find that Voice Control or Siri misunderstands you, try moving to an area with less ambient noise. If there are still problems, turn your iPhone off, wait a few seconds, and then turn it back on. To control playback with Voice Control or Siri:

1. **Press and hold the Home button until the Voice Control screen appears and you hear a beep or Siri asks how she can help you.**

   If you're wearing the headset, press and hold the center button until you hear the beep, and then speak the commands.

2. **Say one of the following commands:**

   • **"Play" or "Play Music"**

   • **"Pause" or "Pause Music"**

   • **"Next Song" or "Previous Song"**

- "Play album/artist/playlist," and then say the name of the album, artist, or playlist you want to hear

- "Shuffle" to shuffle the playlist or album that's playing

- "Genius" or "Play more like this" or "Play more songs like this" to create a Genius playlist

- Ask "What's playing?," "What song is this?," "Who sings this song?," or "Who is this song by?" to hear information about the song you're listening to

- "Cancel" or "Stop" to pause the song that's playing

Siri works when you have either a Wi-Fi or cellular data connection. When these are unavailable, you can turn Siri off in Settings and use Voice Control to command the Music app.

You can use Clock's Timer feature to set Music to play for a certain amount of time and you can choose a song as your alarm in Clock's Alarm feature. See Book IV, Chapter 2 to learn how to do both.

Listening to music with AirPlay

AirPlay is Apple's wireless technology that is also integrated into speakers and stereo systems from various companies that include Denon and JBL. You can choose to broadcast music from your iPhone to speakers in different rooms of your house. You can also use AirPlay to stream audio to an AppleTV or to speakers that are connected to an AirPort Express Wi-Fi router or an AirPlay-enabled stereo (such as the Denon AVR-991). Follow these steps to set up AirPlay:

1. **Tap Music on your Home screen.**

2. **Open the song, album, or podcast you want to hear.**

3. **Tap the AirPlay button.**

4. **Choose the speakers you want from the list.**

   If the speakers don't appear on the list of AirPlay devices, check that both your iPhone and speakers are on the same wireless network.

5. **Tap the Play button.**

   The music plays on the speakers you've chosen.

6. **To switch back to play on your iPhone, tap the AirPlay button again and then choose iPhone.**

Customizing Music's Settings

You control a few of your listening options in Settings. These options affect everything in Music, not just one individual song. Tap Settings on the Home screen and then scroll down to tap Music. Refer to Figure 3-11 and consider these options:

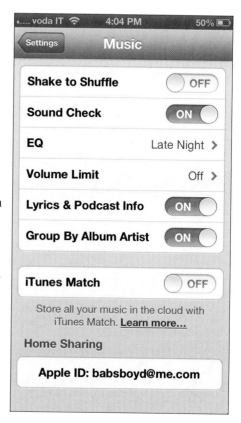

- ✓ **Shake to Shuffle:** Just shake your iPhone to immediately change the current song.

- ✓ **Sound Check:** Often media from different sources plays back at different volume levels. Sound Check corrects so that everything plays at the same volume, saving you from turning the volume up and down with each media change.

- ✓ **EQ:** Tap to open a list of equalizer settings. Choose one that is best associated with the type of media you listen to most. You may have to try a few different ones to see which you like best, but be warned that EQ drains the battery a bit faster than usual.

Figure 3-11: The Music settings give you options for your listening pleasure.

iOS 6 added the much talked-about Late Night EQ setting, which lowers the loudest parts of what you're listening to and amplifies the quieter parts so you can listen on speakers and create less disturbance. When you use the headset, this setting improves the sound in areas with a lot of ambient noise, such as an airplane.

- ✓ **Lyrics & Podcast Info:** If this setting is on, any lyrics or podcast information available from iTunes is displayed when you tap the album cover or image on the Now Playing screen.

✔ **Group by Album Artist:** By default, this option is on and it groups artists by the information listed under Album Artist instead of information in the Artist field.

✔ **iTunes Match:** A paid subscription ($24.95/year) where iCloud stores the music and playlists you have in iTunes on your computer. Even songs in your iTunes library that you didn't purchase through iTunes but that exist in the iTunes store are accessible through iCloud. Songs you have that aren't available in iTunes are uploaded. iCloud then pushes the songs to your iPhone if you turn on this feature. With iTunes Match, Genius Mixes and Genius Playlists on your iPhone are disabled.

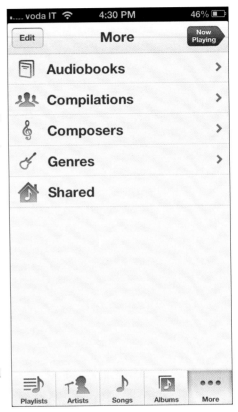

✔ **Home Sharing:** Listen to music from your computer on your iPhone. In iTunes, go to Advanced⇨Turn On Home Sharing and sign in with your Apple ID. On your iPhone, turn Home Sharing On. In Music, tap More in the browse buttons and then tap Shared, as shown in Figure 3-12, to see and listen to the music in iTunes on your computer. Use the Music controls as you would for music on your iPhone. Tap More⇨ Shared⇨My iPhone to return to your music collection there.

Figure 3-12: Home Sharing lets you listen to music from your computer on your iPhone.

Playing Audiobooks

Music isn't just for listening to music any more than iTunes is just for buying tunes. Audiobooks have been around for decades. When audiobooks came on the scene, giving commuters something to do with their commute time, it took a dozen cassette tapes (or, later, CDs) to listen to a whole book. Now, you can download an entire book on your iPhone and listen at your leisure without worrying about carrying around all those tapes or CDs.

> When a file is larger than 50MB, you have to connect to a Wi-Fi network or download the file to your computer and then sync.

To play an audiobook, the procedure is the same as for songs:

1. **Tap Music on the Home screen.**

2. **Tap More, and then tap Audiobooks (refer to Figure 3-12), which only appears if you have downloaded or synced audiobooks to your iPhone.**

3. **Tap the item you want to listen to.**

   A list of the audiobook chapters appears.

4. **Tap the chapter you want to hear.**

   The audiobook begins playing and you see the Now Playing screen.

5. **The playback controls — Previous/Rewind, Play/Pause, Next/Fast Forward, and the scrubber bar — are the same as for songs. The commands below the scrubber bar are slightly different:**

   • **Repeat:** Functions the same way as for music.

   • **15-second repeat/fast forward:** Tap to replay the last 15 seconds or move ahead 15 seconds.

   • **Playback Speed:** Tap to change the speed — 1X is normal (the button is white), 1/2X plays at half speed, and 2X plays at twice the speed (both are orange).

Listening to Podcasts

In earlier versions of Music (back when it was called iPod), podcasts were part of the scene. In iOS 6, podcasts have been removed from Music and promoted to having their own app. If, however, you choose not to install the Podcasts app, you can still download, manage, and listen to podcasts in Music. Nonetheless, we suggested you download it back in Book I, but if you didn't and podcasts interest you, go to the App Store and download the Podcasts app.

Finding podcasts

If you have podcasts in iTunes and synced them with your iPhone, you find them in the Podcasts app Library and can skip ahead to the next section to learn about the playback controls. If you don't have any podcasts, don't worry, just follow these steps:

1. **Tap Podcasts on the Home screen.**

   The Podcasts Catalog opens, as seen in Figure 3-13. If you've browsed or shopped at the App Store or iTunes Store, it will look familiar to you.

2. **Find a podcast that interests you by tapping one of the following:**

   - **Banners**: Tap an ad that interests you when it appears at the top of the screen.

   - **Buttons**: Scroll horizontally through a section, such as New & Noteworthy or tap See All to see a complete list for the section; scroll down to see more advertised podcasts and sections.

   - **Categories:** Tap to open a list of categories and then tap a category to see a list of podcasts in that category.

   - **Library:** Tap to view the list of podcasts you downloaded or synced to your iPhone.

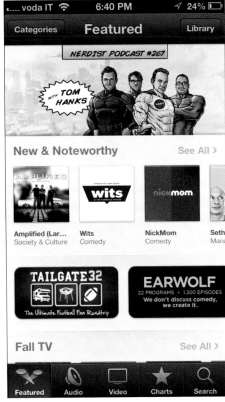

Figure 3-13: Search for podcasts in the Podcasts app.

   - **Browse buttons** across the bottom give you different ways to view your choices: Featured (what you see in Figure 3-13), Audio (see audio-only podcasts), Video (see video podcasts), Charts (see the top podcasts divided by audio and video), and Search (type a search word or two to find something you like).

3. **Tap a podcast that interests you, and the Info screen opens, as shown in Figure 3-14. You can do the following:**

   - **Tap Subscribe** to subscribe to the entire podcast series. As new episodes are added, they are downloaded to your iPhone.

- **Tap the download button** next to a single episode. Some podcasts download immediately so you can listen to it later; others launch the podcast player. You can immediately listen to it as it streams, but can't download it to your library until you subscribe.

  In that case, tap the Subscribe button. You can then download episodes to your library as explained in Step 5. Subscriptions are free, as are podcasts, and you can listen to down-loaded podcasts offline.

- **Tap Reviews** to read reviews and add your own. You can also Like the podcast on Facebook from the Reviews screen.

- **Tap Related** to see other podcasts that are similar.

- **Tap the Action button** (in the upper right) to share a link to the podcast via Mail, Messages, Twitter, or Facebook, or copy the link to another app of your choice.

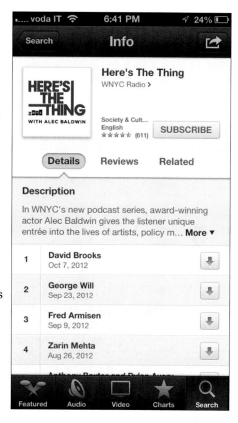

Figure 3-14: Subscribe to podcasts from the Info screen.

4. **Tap the back button in the upper left to return to the main Podcasts screen.**

Podcast playback

After you subscribe to one or more podcasts, they're stored in your podcast library, where you manage and listen to them. Follow these steps to play back a podcast:

1. **Tap the Library button in the upper right and tap Podcasts at the bottom.**

Your podcast library appears as in Figure 3-15. Tap the Grid or List button to change the view (tap the Status Bar if you don't see them). The number tells you how many unplayed episodes of that series you have.

2. **Tap a series on the grid or list to see a list of episodes, as shown in Figure 3-16. You can do the following:**

   • Tap the disclosure triangle to the right of the podcast name to view subscription and sorting settings for this podcast. You can customize the settings for each podcast subscription individually.

   • Tap the blue and white arrow to read a description of the episode.

   • Tap the download button to download the episode to your library, you won't see the download button if the episode is already downloaded.

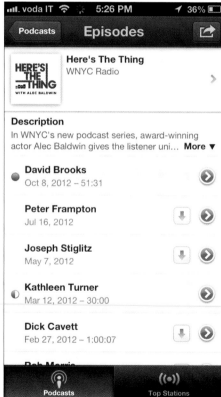

Figure 3-15: Manage podcast subscriptions in your Library.

Figure 3-16: See episodes in different states of listening.

- The blue dot indicates downloaded episodes that you haven't listened to yet. A half blue dot indicates you begin listening but didn't finish.

- Tap the Action button to share a link to the podcast via Mail, Messages, Facebook, or Twitter, or copy and paste the link in another app.

- Tap the episode to begin listening.

3. **Tap the cover of the podcast to reveal the playback controls in their entirety — we admit, it's one of our favorites. Here's the rundown on the controls as shown in Figure 3-17:**

   Play/pause button: Does just that.

   Previous/Rewind: Tap in the first few seconds of the podcast and you go to the previous episode. After that, tap once to return to the beginning; tap and hold to rewind.

   Rewind 10 seconds: Goes back 10 seconds.

   Go forward 30 seconds: Jumps ahead in the recording by 30 seconds.

   Next/Fast Forward: Tap to go to the next episode; tap and hold to fast forward.

   Volume slider: Drag left and right to lower or increase the volume.

   Scrubber bar: Touch and drag the red line to move to a specific place in the playback.

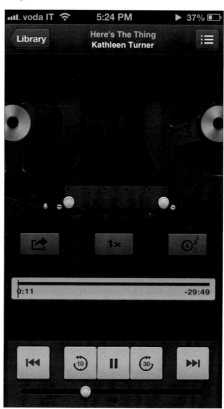

Figure 3-17: The playback controls are under the podcast cover.

Action button: Send a link to the episode via Mail, Messages, Twitter, or Facebook.

Playback Speed: Tap to change the speed from half through three times the normal speed.

Sleep Timer: Tap to see a list of choices for setting the podcast to stop playing after a certain time or when the episode ends.

Drag your finger down the screen to show the cover again.

Tap the episode list in the upper right to see a list of other episodes in the series.

4. **Tap Library to return to the episode list for this podcast on your iPhone.**

5. **Tap Catalog in the upper left to return to the Podcast Catalog search for more podcasts.**

If your iPhone is filling up with podcasts and you want to delete some, tap Edit on the opening screen of your Library and then tap the X in the upper-left corner to delete a podcast and the contained episodes. To delete episodes singly, open the podcast and swipe across the episode you want to eliminate, and then tap the Delete button.

Podcast streaming

When you're viewing your library, you might notice a Top Stations button at the bottom of the screen, on the right. Here you find streaming podcast programs. Think of it as a huge talk radio station where, instead of turning the dial to go from one station frequency to another, you go from one category frequency to another.

First, tap the toggle switch at the top to narrow your choices between audio and video, as shown in Figure 3-18. Then flick across the "dial" to move from one category to another. You see main categories at the top, such as Business or Health and subcategories underneath like Careers or Investing in the Business category.

After you settle on a category and subcategory, scroll up and down through podcast covers. Tap a cover to begin playing the current podcast, and then tap the Now Playing button to see the playback controls.

Figure 3-18: Top Stations offer a quick way to find podcasts by category.

Tap the "i" to the right of the cover to open an information screen that shows an episode list and the option to subscribe. You can also tap the plus sign at the top of the Now Playing screen to subscribe if you find you like the program after you begin listening to it.

Podcast Settings

In addition to the individual podcast settings that you find when you click the disclosure triangle next to the name of a podcast in your Library, here are two settings for the Podcast app that you find in Settings⇨Podcasts:

- ✔ **Sync Subscriptions:** You might want to turn this on if you listen to podcasts on different devices. That way, you'll find the same subscriptions and episodes on your iPhone, iPad, or iPod touch or Mac or Windows computer.

- ✔ **Use Cellular Data:** This setting uses your cellular data service to download episodes to which you have activated automatic download. If you have a limit to your cellular data usage, you might want to leave this in the Off position. In that case, your episodes are automatically downloaded only when you have a Wi-Fi connection.

Chapter 4: Watching Videos and iTunes U

In This Chapter

- Watching movies and videos
- Controlling playback
- Playing video on a bigger screen
- Enrolling in iTunes U

Your iPhone is not only great for listening to music and podcasts, but it's also great for watching music videos, video podcasts, movies, television shows, and lectures from iTunes U, not to mention for watching the home movies you make with the video recorder built in to your iPhone.

Apple developed pixels that are 78 micrometers wide and a pixel density of 326 pixels per inch. The Retina display uses in-plane switching (IPS) that offers a wider viewing angle and an 800 to 1 contrast ratio, which means brighter whites and darker blacks. LED backlighting and the ambient light sensor adjusts the image to let you see it best in the light available. If you're worried about scratches and fingerprints — don't be. The Retina display is made of super-durable, scratch-resistant, oleophobic (fingerprint-resistant) glass. To you, all this means crisp, clear images and type.

In this chapter, we concentrate on videos: specifically watching videos that you make or download. First, we go through getting video onto your iPhone, which could be in the form of home movies, rented or purchased movies, television shows, or music videos and how to convert the video if it's in a non-iPhone format. One by one, we give details of the video controls of the Video app, and how to hook up your iPhone to a television so you can watch your videos on a bigger screen. We also include a section on iTunes U, the online continuing education source for all learning levels and topics.

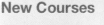

New Courses

HARVARD

Justice

PERSONAL FINANCE
Missouri State University
Personal Finance

Personal Finance
Finance

Getting and Watching Videos on Your iPhone

We use the term "video" as a generic term to mean a multimedia file, which combines audio with moving images. Video can be a music video, a movie, a television show, a podcast, a home movie, or pretty much anything that you watch, and you can watch most of them on your iPhone. The first thing you have to do is get the video to your iPhone. You have several ways to do that:

- **Camera app:** Make a video directly on your iPhone, as explained in Chapter 1 of this minibook. You watch these videos in the Photos app on your iPhone.

- **iTunes Store/Podcast Catalog/iTunes U:** Download a rented or purchased video from the iTunes Store, a video podcast, or an iTunes U lecture on your iPhone. See Chapter 2 of this minibook for the complete iTunes Store shopping guide. You watch video podcasts in the Podcasts app.

  You need a Wi-Fi connection to download movies, television shows, and videos.

- **Streaming:** Watch a video directly from the Internet using Safari or another video app, such as Netflix or Hulu.

- **Your computer:** Sync the videos on your computer to your iPhone via iTunes as explained in Book II, Chapter 1.

Your iPhone supports H.264 video up to 720 pixels and MPEG-4, part 10 video at 640 by 480 pixels, both at 30 frames per second with stereo audio in .m4v, .mp4, and .mov file formats. Motion JPEG (9M-JPEG) is supported at 1,280×720 pixels with stereo audio in .avi format. Although the popular Adobe Flash format is not supported directly, more website designers are offering Flash streaming for their online videos, so you can see videos that perhaps you couldn't see before.

If you copy a video to your iPhone and it doesn't open automatically, chances are it isn't in one of the supported formats. To see a video's format, open iTunes and click Movies, TV Shows, Podcasts, or iTunes U from the pop-up menu in the upper left, and then click the video you want information about. Click File ➪ Get Info. Click the Summary tab. Look next to Kind, as indicated by the arrow in Figure 4-1.

To save the video in an iPhone-readable format, click once on the video in the list in iTunes. Click Advanced ➪ Create iPod or iPhone Version. The file is saved in the MPEG-4 format with the same name as the original, so you'll want to rename it so that when you sync the file to your iPhone, you sync the one in the correct video format. (To rename the file, click on the name. When it's highlighted, type in a new name or add something like "iP" so you know it's iPhone's version.)

Figure 4-1: Determine the video format in Get Info on iTunes.

If you have a video that iTunes can't handle, you can try converting the file with a video transcoder utility on your computer such as Handbrake (`handbrake.fr/`).

Controlling playback

After you have a video on your iPhone or as soon as you begin downloading from the iTunes Store, tap Videos on the Home screen, and then tap the video you want to watch from the list, as shown in Figure 4-2. The list is divided by Rented Movies, Movies, TV Shows, and Music Videos, although you only see the categories in which you have media. If you have one or more television series, tap the series name to see a list of series' episodes opens, and then tap the episode you want to watch.

The video begins playing as soon as you open it. Ideally, you watch the video in landscape view. You can

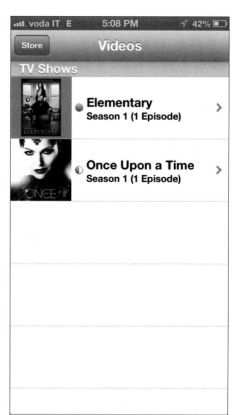

Figure 4-2: See a list of videos on your iPhone from the Videos app.

see the video in portrait view, but it is generally quite small, the exception being if video was recorded with the either camera on iPhone in portrait view.

Initially, you see the playback controls on the screen, which disappear after about six seconds. To open the playback controls, tap the screen. Refer to Figure 4-3 for the controls explained here:

Figure 4-3: The video playback controls.

- ✔ **Rewind:** Tap and hold to rewind; tap once to return to the beginning of the episode. If you're watching a movie that has chapters, tap twice to go back one chapter.

- ✔ **Fast forward:** Tap and hold to fast forward; tap twice to go to the next chapter.

- ✔ **Volume Scrubber Bar:** Drag the white ball on the volume scrubber bar to raise or lower the volume. You can also use the volume buttons on the side of your iPhone.

- ✔ **Playtime Scrubber Bar:** The time on the left is the time the video has played; the time on the right is the time remaining. Drag the white ball, known as the playhead, right and left on the scrubber bar to move forward and backward in the video. Slide your finger down as you drag the playhead to adjust the speed at which the video moves.

- ✔ **Done:** Press when you want to stop watching and return to the Videos list. If you stop watching before a video is finished, when you start again, it picks up where you left off. You can also press the Home button to stop watching and return to the Home screen.

You see a few control buttons only under certain circumstances:

- ✏ **Fill/Fit:** Tap the Fill/Fit button to toggle between two ways you can view video.

  - **Choose Fit** to see videos in their original ratios, although you will see black vertical bands on television shows and horizontal bands on movies, called *pillarboxing* and *letterboxing,* respectively.

  - **Choose Fill** to fill the whole iPhone screen but lose some of the edges of the original version.

- ✏ **Language:** Some movies have subtitle or language options. This button appears when they are available. Tap to see your options.

- ✏ **Audio Output:** Set the output device you want to use to view your video on another monitor.

If you're wearing the EarPods, you can use the volume buttons on the microphone. You can also click twice on the center part to skip to the next chapter, or three times to go back a chapter.

Video settings

You have control over a few Video settings. Tap Settings⇨Videos and the Video settings open, as shown in Figure 4-4. These are your options:

- ✏ **Start Playing:** Determines where your video picks up when you stop viewing midway through a video. Where Left Off is the default and it's what we refer to in this chapter — stop a video and when you restart, you pick up where you left off. The other choice is to start a video from the beginning when you restart. Tap Start Playing and check From Beginning if you prefer that choice.

Figure 4-4: Choose where you want to begin when you resume playing your video.

✔ **Closed Captioning:** When closed captioning is available, if this switch is on, you see captions. If the switch is off, even when captions are available, you won't see them.

✔ **Home Sharing:** Sign in with your Apple ID and password to stream video from your computer (in iTunes) to your iPhone. See the section "Streaming from Your Computer" to Your iPhone for more information about Home Sharing.

Exchanging Media

Technology is all about connections and sometimes you have media in one place but want to watch, or listen to it, from another. Here we explain two ways to connect your iPhone to a big — or at least bigger — screen television or monitor with and without cables to watch movies, television shows, and other videos stored on your iPhone. Then we show you how to stream media from your computer to your iPhone using the Home Sharing function.

Connecting to a monitor or TV

Your iPhone, especially if you have a version with 32 or 64 gigabytes of memory, is a portable video warehouse, and iPhone 5's larger screen and Retina display make watching a pleasure. Nonetheless, watching a documentary about the Himalayas on your iPhone really can't match the thrill of sweeping views that a large-screen monitor or television offers. You can watch the movies and television shows — slides shows of photos too — that are stored on your iPhone, on your iPhone, or you can connect your iPhone to a television or monitor and enjoy them on a bigger screen.

To attach your iPhone to a television, monitor, or projector, you need one of the following cables:

✔ **Lightning Digital AV Adapter (iPhone 5) or Apple 30-pin Digital AV Adapter (iPhone 4S):** Use this adapter to connect your iPhone to an HDMI cable (sold separately) connected to your HDTV, video projection screen, or other HDMI-compatible device.

✔ **Lightning to VGA Adapter (iPhone 5) or Apple 30-pin to VGA Adapter (iPhone 4S or 4)** This adapter, along with a VGA cable (sold separately) connects your iPhone to your VGA TV, projector, or monitor.

✔ **Apple Composite AV Cable: (iPhone 4S or earlier)** This connects to your iPhone dock at one end and your television's composite port on the other. Older televisions usually have composite connections.

To play your movie or television show:

1. **Connect the cable to both your iPhone and your television or monitor.**

2. **On your television, select the input device.**

   Refer to the instruction booklet for your television if you don't know how to do this.

3. **Play the video from Videos as you normally would on your iPhone.**

   You see the images on your television.

Playing video with AirPlay

You can stream video and images from the Internet across your iPhone and onto your television if you have an AppleTV or another AirPlay-enabled device. To play video wirelessly using AirPlay, follow these steps:

1. **Tap Videos on your Home screen.**

2. **Open the video you want to watch.**

3. **Tap the AirPlay button.**

4. **Choose Apple TV from the list.**

   If Apple TV doesn't appear on the list of AirPlay devices, check that both your iPhone and Apple TV are on the same wireless network.

5. **Tap the Play button.**

   The video plays on your television.

6. **To switch back to play on your iPhone, tap the AirPlay button again and then choose iPhone.**

You can connect to a monitor or use AirPlay to play slideshows and videos from the Photos app by following the same steps.

Streaming from your computer to your iPhone

If there's a video stored on iTunes on your computer that you would like to watch on your iPhone, you can access the video with Home Sharing. You have to have iTunes 10.2 or later and both the computer and your iPhone have to be on the same Wi-Fi network. You also need an Apple ID and password. Follow these instructions:

1. **On your computer, in iTunes, click Advanced⇨Turn On Home Sharing.**

2. **Enter your Apple ID and password, and then click Create Home Share.**

3. **On your iPhone, tap Settings⇨Video.**

4. **In the Home Sharing section, type in the same Apple ID and password (refer to Figure 4-4).**

   You see Home Sharing only if you have an active Wi-Fi connection.

5. **Open the Videos app from the Home screen or the multitasking bar.**

   The Shared screen opens with two choices: My iPhone and your user name.

6. **Tap your user name.**

7. **A list of the videos stored on your computer appears on your iPhone.**

8. **Tap the video you want to watch and follow the previous instructions for playback control.**

9. **To return to the content on your iPhone, tap Shared and then tap My iPhone.**

Streaming media is when whatever you're watching or listening to is stored somewhere else, as opposed to being stored on your iPhone. The media plays as it comes across the local network or from the Internet and isn't downloaded to your iPhone.

Enrolling in iTunes U

Although the iTunes U app doesn't come preinstalled on your iPhone, we highly recommend you download this free app and take advantage of all the interesting and informative media available in the iTunes U catalog.

Divided into 16 genres (think faculties), iTunes U features audio and video lectures from seminars and courses at universities around the world. iTunes U isn't limited to university, however. You find lectures and presentations from professional meetings and conferences, such as TED and the Prostate Health Conference, as well as K through 12 material. Aside from the vast selection of topics and the quality of the presentations, the best part is that the lectures are free!

Choosing courses

Here we briefly explain how the iTunes U course catalog is organized. As with the App and iTunes Stores and Podcasts catalog, iTunes U lets you look at its offerings overall, by genre, by most popular, and, of course, by searching.

You see "courses" and "collections." Courses have a syllabus, study materials, which might be e-books or worksheets, and the lectures themselves as either audio or video files to be followed in chronological order as you build upon gained knowledge from one lesson to the next. Collections are standalone lectures related to a similar topic; you don't need to listen or watch all of them to gain full knowledge. Here's how to find something that you want to learn more about:

1. **Tap iTunes U on the Home screen.**

   The iTunes U catalog opens. The opening screen is organized like the iTunes and App Stores and the Podcasts catalog. Banner ads scroll across the top, New Courses and other categorical sections follow, and all are tappable buttons that lead to more information about that course. The other buttons are

   • **Genres (Upper left):** Genres opens a list of the 16 "faculties" you can choose from. Tapping one of those then opens a selection of courses on that topic displayed like the opening screen — banners, buttons, and the like. Choose All Genres from the Genres list to return to the full catalog selection.

   • **Library (Upper right):** Library takes you to your collection of downloaded courses. We talk about that in the next section.

   The browse buttons at the bottom are

   • **Featured:** As seen in Figure 4-5, you see the latest course additions and then, scrolling down, find the most popular courses in the What's Hot section and the courses that Apple likes the most in Staff Favorites. This same type of selection appears when you select a specific Genre.

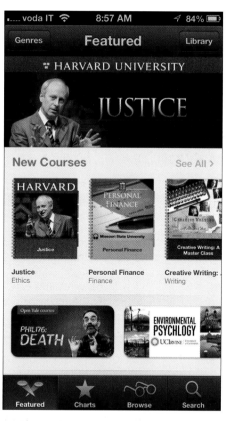

Figure 4-5: Search for courses in iTunes U.

- **Charts:** Divided into Courses and Collections, this view lists the courses and collections by the most popular on done.

- **Browse:** Choose the level you want: Higher Ed, K-12, or Other, and then scroll through the alphabetical list of institutions offering courses at that level.

- **Search:** Tap to open the search field. Type your criteria and then tap the Search button. You can then view the results by collections, courses, or all, which includes collections and courses as well as a list of episodes (lectures) and materials that meet your search criteria.

2. **Tap a course or collection that interests you, and the Info screen opens, as shown in Figure 4-6.**

   Tap Details to see descriptions, the course outline (if it's a course), and a list of lectures and materials. Tap More to see the complete information.

   Tap Reviews to see what others have to say about the course or collection.

   Tap Related to see other courses and collections on a similar topic that might interest you.

   Tap the Action button to share a link to the course via Mail, Messages, Twitter, or Facebook, or copy the link to another app.

3. **When you find a course or collection you want to watch or listen to, you have the following options:**

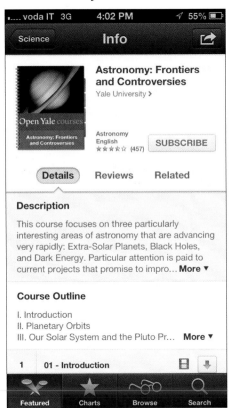

Figure 4-6: Subscribe to courses or single episodes from the Info screen.

- **Tap Subscribe** to subscribe to the entire course. Links to the materials are added to your Library and updates are added as they become available (this is the default setting that we show you how to change later).

- **Tap the download button** next to a single episode or material. The icon next to the download button indicates the type of file it is: a filmstrip icon means video; a speaker icon indicates audio; and a piece of paper icon means written materials, usually a PDF file.

4. **Tap the back button in the upper left to return to the iTunes U screen where you were before.**

If you scroll to the bottom of the screen, you see your Apple ID, a Redeem button for adding iTunes Store card credit, your credit balance, and a button that says Enrollment Code. Some courses have limited enrollment and you must request an enrollment code from the instructor to subscribe and attend. You can find more information about the instructor in the course description.

Attending class

After you subscribe to one or more iTunes U courses or collections, they're stored in your iTunes U library. Follow these steps to playback a podcast:

1. **Tap the Library button in the upper right.**

   The faux-wood grained bookshelf displays the courses and collections you subscribed to, as shown in Figure 4-7. The number tells you how many new episodes have been added since you first subscribed.

Figure 4-7: The iTunes U Library shelf displays courses you subscribe to.

2. **Tap a course or collection to open it and begin learning.**

   Collections display a simple list of the video or audio comprised, as in Figure 4-8. Tap the disclosure arrow next to the collection title to see more information, tap the "i" to see more information about a specific episode, or tap the download button to download an episode. Tap the Search button to search within the collection or a specific episode. Tap the Edit button to delete episodes you no longer want or remove the collection entirely.

   Courses are interactive and you can access several different types of material and views, as shown in Figure 4-9.

   The buttons at the top do the following:

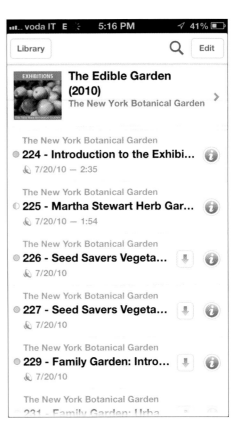

Figure 4-8: Collections display a list of episodes.

- Tap the Search button (the magnifying glass) to search throughout the course or within a specific episode.

- Tap the Action button to share a link to the course via Mail, Messages, Facebook, or Twitter, copy and paste the link in another app, or print what you see on the screen.

- Tap the Gear button to change the settings for that individual course: turn Subscription On to receive updated information automatically; turn Auto Download On to download new episodes and materials automatically.

- At any time, tap the button in the upper-left corner to return to the previous screen.

The browse buttons along the bottom contain the following:

- **Info:**
  - Tap Overview to read a description of the course, including the types of materials, what you can expect to learn, how long the course

usually takes, and what education level it's appropriate for. Tap the Info button in the upper left to return to the previous screen.

- Tap Instructor to read about the professor. You may find a link to send an e-mail as well.

- Tap Outline to see the syllabus for the course.

✓ **Posts:** These are the lessons and any supplementary material the instructor has provided.

✓ **Notes:** Notes you take are neatly organized here. You can view all your notes together or your course notes, audio/video notes, or book notes. Tap the Plus sign at the top if you want to add a note from this screen. You can also add notes while you are listening or watching an episode.

✓ **Materials:** Lists all the course materials (which sometimes must be purchased) and gives you the option to view by type: Audio, Video, and Books, as shown in Figure 4-10. Some books are readable only on an iPad.

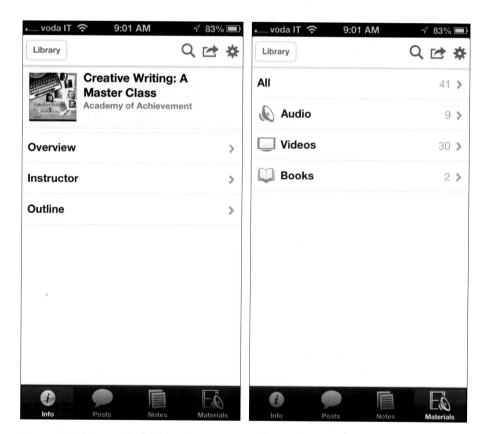

Figure 4-9: Courses offer diverse types of material and options.

Figure 4-10: Materials are divided by type.

Tap one of the choices to see the list of materials. See more information, download, and listen or watch the episodes the same way as you would for an episode of a collection. Tap Edit in the upper-right corner to remove downloaded episodes.

3. **Tap the episode to begin listening or watching, or tap a book if you want to begin reading course material. (Although, many of the interactive textbooks can be read only on an iPad.)**

The playback controls are similar to those you find for audio or video in other apps. You can go back 30 seconds, rewind, fast forward, jump back or forward an episode, and control the playback speed.

Course audio and video has the added feature of Notes. While you're listening or watching an episode, tap the Notes button in the upper-right corner and then tap the Plus sign. The keyboard opens (refer to Figure 4-11) so you can type a note related to the lecture, which continues to play while you take your note unless you tap Pause. The note shows the time during the lecture that the note was taken so you can easily return to the point related to your note. Tap Notes to see all your notes and then tap Done to return to the lecture. The red lines on the scrubber bar show where you took notes, as shown in Figure 4-12.

Figure 4-11: Take Notes while listening to or watching a lecture.

4. **Tap the back button to return to the episode list for this course, and then tap Materials to see the materials list.**

5. **Tap Library to return to your iTunes U library shelf; tap Catalog in the upper-right corner to browse more courses.**

To rearrange the icons on the iTunes U shelf, touch and hold an icon until it gets a bit bigger, and then drag it to a new position.

Figure 4-12: The Notes button appears on Course audios and videos.

iTunes U settings

In addition to the individual settings that you find when you click the disclosure triangle next to the name of a course or collection in your Library, there are two settings for the iTunes U app that you find in Settings⊏>iTunes U:

✔ **Sync Courses and Notes:** When it's on, you find the same subscriptions and episodes on your iPhone, iPad, or iPod touch.

✔ **Closed Captioning:** When closed captioning is available, if this switch is on, you see captions. If the switch is off, even when captions are available, you won't see them.

Index